CAMBRIDGE TEXTS IN THE
HISTORY OF POLITICAL THOUGHT

The British Idealists

CAMBRIDGE TEXTS IN THE
HISTORY OF POLITICAL THOUGHT

Series editors

RAYMOND GEUSS

Lecturer in Social and Political Sciences, University of Cambridge

QUENTIN SKINNER

Regius Professor of Modern History in the University of Cambridge

Cambridge Texts in the History of Political Thought is now firmly established as the major student textbook series in political theory. It aims to make available to students all the most important texts in the history of western political thought, from ancient Greece to the early twentieth century. All the familiar classic texts will be included but the series does at the same time seek to enlarge the conventional canon by incorporating an extensive range of less well-known works, many of them never before available in a modern English edition. Wherever possible, texts are published in complete and unabridged form, and translations are specially commissioned for the series. Each volume contains a critical introduction together with chronologies, biographical sketches, a guide to further reading and any necessary glossaries and textual apparatus. When completed, the series will aim to offer an outline of the entire evolution of western political thought.

For a list of titles published in the series, please see end of book.

The British Idealists

EDITED BY
DAVID BOUCHER
University of Wales, Swansea

CAMBRIDGE
UNIVERSITY PRESS

PUBLISHED BY THE PRESS SYNDICATE OF THE UNIVERSITY OF CAMBRIDGE
The Pitt Building, Trumpington Street, Cambridge CB2 1RP, United Kingdom

CAMBRIDGE UNIVERSITY PRESS
The Edinburgh Building, Cambridge, CB2 1RP United Kingdom
40 West 20th Street, New York, NY 10011–4211, USA
10 Stamford Road, Oakleigh, Melbourne 3166, Australia

First published 1997

Printed in Great Britain at the University Press, Cambridge

Typeset in Ehrhardt 9½ pt

A catalogue record for this book is available from the British Library

Library of Congress cataloguing in publication data

The British Idealists / edited by David Boucher.
p.   cm. – (Cambridge texts in the history of political thought)
Includes bibliographical references.
ISBN 0 521 45336 4 (hardback). – ISBN 0 521 45951 6 (pbk.)
1. Political science–Great Britain–History.   2. Sociology–Great
Britain–History.   3. Idealism–History. I. Boucher, David.   II. Series.
JA84.G7B675 1997
320′.092′241–dc21 96–36914 CIP

ISBN 0 521 45336 4 hardback
ISBN 0 521 45951 6 paperback

Contents

Contents

resulted in a communitarianism which posited the mutual interdependence of society and the individual.

For the most part the British Idealists were social reformers who believed that the work of the philosopher was to raise the consciousness of the working man to the level where he was capable of considering principles. They rejected the individualism of their age, which set man and the state in oppostion, and emphasised instead a relationship of mutual inclusion in which each is a reflection of the other. Society, or the state, was the sustainer of morality, rights and social values and the context in which the individual found expression. Far from the idea that extending the role of the state diminished individual responsibility, they argued that, properly conceived, the state enhanced the capacity of the individual for self-realisation. The enabling state could provide opportunities that were beyond the imagination of unregulated individual enterprise. It was a deeply spiritual philosophy which, in the hands of the likes of Green, Caird and Jones, viewed human progress in terms of the Divine Spirit, the source of all religion and morality, finding expression in human agency. Religion is an inextricable part of the process of self-realisation. For many of the Idealists, God is immanent in the world. The Divine and the human constitute the inseparable spiritual unity of the world. Christ is incarnate in the world reflecting the unity of God and man. God is not merely the Creator, but reveals Himself in man.[2] The test of a morally worthwhile existence is the extent to which the individual attempts to do God's work in the world by achieving his or her own potential and contributing to the common good. Social reform and moral development were closely linked with religious self-realisation in what was essentially a civic religion. The Absolute is realised in finite centres, and all the more so when they are spiritual. Man is what he is by virtue of God's presence in him. The religious convictions of the British Idealists were by no means orthodox, but at a time when religion was under attack from evolutionist scientific orthodoxy and materialist philosophies, Idealism was able to provide a rational basis for belief which, together with its emphasis on the unity and development of human potential, provided a philosophical basis for social legislation.

---

[2] D. G. Ritchie, *Philosophical Studies* (London, Macmillan, 1905), 241.

emanate from the community, and individuals are afforded the opportunity to achieve their maximum potential. It is a philosophy that emphasises the spiritual cohesiveness of the social organism. In this it is seen to be a forerunner of the communitarianism of Sandel, MacIntyre, Taylor and Walzer. Most recently David Miller echoes many of the Idealists' themes and conclusions in his defence of the ethics of nationality against ethical universalism. He argues that the obligations generated by communal relations diminish the opposition between self-interest and our obligations to others. Nationality, ideally when coupled with the state as the instrument of self-determination, is the sustainer of a moral life. This is not a position incompatible with universal ethics and human rights, but it does insist that it is through the ethical relations of co-nationals that they are sustained. This, as we will see, is the position of the British Idealists, and it is therefore somewhat ironic that in the area of modern international relations theory their writings should be invoked as the very antithesis of cosmopolitanism and international justice.[1] Their point was simply that it is through the state that ideals of humanitarian justice can be developed, promoted and sustained, not that such ideals could not be attained.

Philosophy, religion and politics

Although critics inveighed against Hegel for the practical implications of his political philosophy, he was clear in his own mind that philosophy had no such contribution to make to practical life. In *The Philosophy of Right* he maintained that philosophy always arrives too late on the scene to offer practical advice, the owl of Minerva taking flight only with the coming of dusk. For the British Idealists, with a few exceptions, notably Bradley and McTaggart, philosophy was integrally related to practical life and needed to be directed to improve the condition of society. They maintained that everything in experience is related to everything else. There could be no isolated individuals or facts. In the theory of knowledge, this led to the coherence theory of truth, and in social philosophy, it

---

[1] David Miller, *On Nationality* (Oxford, Clarendon Press, 1995), 79–80; Chris Brown, *International Relations Theory* (Hemel Hempstead, Harvester Wheatsheaf, 1992); and Janna Thompson, *Justice and World Order* (London, Routledge, 1992).

Introduction

The roots of British Idealism were established in Scotland and Oxford during the middle of the nineteenth century and rapidly became the dominant philosophy, through the writings and personal influence of such exponents as Fraser Campbell, Edward Caird, T. H. Green, F. H. Bradley, Bernard Bosanquet, Henry Jones, Andrew Seth, D. G. Ritchie, J. S. Mackenzie, William Wallace, W. R. Sorley, J. M. E. McTaggart and John Watson, until the turn of the century when its fundamental doctrines were challenged by John Cook Wilson, G. E. Moore and Bertrand Russell. From this time the march of Idealism was halted, and by the end of the First World War it was decidedly on the retreat. Through their teaching, personal influence and patronage, the British Idealists managed to permeate the whole English-speaking world with their doctrines. Even after the death of its leading surviving exponents, Bradley, Bosanquet, Jones and McTaggart, in the mid 1920s, it continued to dominate the professoriate and was able to count in its ranks able young converts such as R. G. Collingwood in Oxford, who published *Speculum Mentis* in 1925, and Michael Oakeshott in Cambridge, who published *Experience and its Modes* in 1933.

The social and political philosophy of British Idealism continues to resonate, and is invoked, often without discrimination, for both positive and negative reasons. On the one hand it provides a philosophical basis for opposing the extreme view that society is no more than the sum of its parts, while emphasising the socially constituted character of personality and morality. The state is viewed as the sustainer of a moral world within which rights and obligations

Acknowledgements

It gives me great pleasure to acknowledge my intellectual debt for my sustained interest in British Idealism to my teachers W. H. Greenleaf and Peter Nicholson, and to my friend and former colleague at Cardiff, Andrew Vincent. I would like to thank the Master and Fellows of Pembroke College, Oxford, for electing me to a Senior Associateship for the Hilary Term of 1996. I was able to bring this project to near completion in the friendly surroundings of that College. I am deeply indebted to William H. Rieckmann, President of Industrial Plastics, Inc., and fellow trustee of the R. G. Collingwood Society, for making it possible for me to take a leave of absence from the University of Wales Swansea, in order to work on this collection of writings by the British Idealists. I am very much indebted to Sue Irving for making my task much less arduous than it would otherwise have been. She scanned the original writings onto a computer disk and put them into a presentable format before I began my editorial work. For invaluable assistance in tracking down some of the references, I gratefully acknowledge the help of Clare Boucher, D. George Boyce, Knud Haakonssen, H. S. Harris, Neville and Brenda Masterman, Peter Nicholson, Francis O'Gorman, John Park, Howard Williams and particularly Marnie Hughes-Warrington, who tenaciously pursued some of the more obscure references. Finally, I would like to thank Michele Greenbank for her meticulous reading of the typescript, and Quentin Skinner for his helpful comments on the Introduction.

The religious backgrounds from which most of the Idealists came predisposed them towards the idea of doing 'good works' in society. Some of them, such as Caird, Green, Muirhead, Jones, Watson and Mackenzie, had aspirations to join the ministry before succumbing to the temptations of philosophy. British Idealists were almost evangelical in their reforming zeal and saw their position as professional philosophers carrying with it a social responsibility to identify and articulate the sources of injustice and depravity, and campaign for reform. To these ends they advocated for legislation, gave evidence to and served on government commissions, sat on school boards, were active in extending university education to women, and enthusiastically participated in university extramural schemes and the Workers' Educational Association. They were at the forefront in establishing and supporting university extension schemes to help the poor in the major cities of Britain. In the field of social work the British Idealists were the dominant group who, in demonstrating the relevance of philosophy to ordinary life, exercised a considerable influence in providing a frame of reference for social policy, public administration and education reform well into the twentieth century.[3]

British Idealism certainly imported the spirit of its philosophy from Germany, and in particular valued Hegel's forthright rejection of all dualisms, including Kant's distinction between things in themselves and things as they are experienced by the knowing mind. In particular they subscribed to his insistence on the unity of experience which raised the question of how this undifferentiated unity becomes differentiated into all its various modes. The British Idealists sought to demonstrate that there could be no absolute divisions, for example, between mind and nature, nature and environment, or the individual and the state. Each includes something of the other and their opposition is overcome in a unity, not one that obliterates differences, but one that is a genuine unity in diversity.[4] This is illustrated in Caird's insistence that true Socialists and true

---

[3] M. Richter, *The Politics of Conscience: T. H. Green and His Age* (London, Weidenfeld and Nicolson, 1964), 143; Andrew Vincent and Raymond Plant, *Philosophy, Politics and Citizenship* (Oxford, Blackwell, 1984), 116; and Jose Harris, 'Political Thought and the Welfare State 1870–1940', *Past and Present*, 135 (1992), 123.

[4] See Edward Caird, 'The Problem of Philosophy at the Present Time', *Essays on Literature and Philosophy* (Glasgow, Maclehose, 1892), vol. 1, 205–6.

Individualists have to acknowledge what is good in the point of view of the adversary (see p. 179). This emphasis upon the unity of experience as a whole is known as Absolute Idealism.

None of the major British Idealists accepted the stylised, dialectic method which Hegel used to address the process of differentiation. Green, for example, complained that the method actually hindered Hegel in reaching his conclusions, and accused Principal John Caird of too slavishly accepting it. It was the principle rather than the method of dialectic that attracted the British Idealists, a principle that was to be discerned in Plato.[5]

It is a misconception that the British Idealists made reality mind-dependent. They rejected Berkeley's psychological idealism because it made reality dependent upon the perceiving mind, whether the individual's or God's. With Hegel they contend 'that the known world is for us necessarily a world that exists only because we are thinking beings'.[6] This is not to deny the distinction between thought and reality, nor to assert that knowledge of a fact is that fact itself. The world didn't suddenly begin to go around the sun the minute that Copernicus had the idea that it did so. The idea that things exist only in being known is what J. S. Mackenzie calls 'False idealism'.[7] The point is not that every being knows reality, but that reality as the embodiment of thought is intelligible and capable of being known only by a being that thinks. Hastings Rashdall sums up the position when he says that Idealism assumes 'that there is no such thing as matter apart from mind, that what we commonly call *things* are not self-subsistent realities, but are only real when taken in their connection with mind – that they exist for mind, not for themselves'.[8] In other words, there is a unity between mind and matter, nature and spirit. This does not mean that nature is intelligent, merely that it is intelligible.

---

[5] T. H. Green, *Works*, ed. R. L. Nettleship (London, Longmans Green, 1888), vol. III, 146; and Andrew Seth, *Scottish Philosophy* (Edinburgh, Blackwood, 1890), 2nd ed., 198.

[6] John Watson, *The Interpretation of Religious Experience*m, the Gifford Lectures 1910–12, part I (Glasgow, Maclehose, 1912), 289.

[7] J. S. Mackenzie, 'Edward Caird as a Philosophical Teacher', *Mind*, n.s., 18 (1909), 519.

[8] Hastings Rashdall, 'Personality: Human and Divine', in ed. Henry Sturt, *Personal Idealism: Philosophical Essays* (London, Macmillan, 1902), 370.

There were internal divisions among the Absolute Idealists. Jones, for example, accused both Bosanquet and Bradley of failing to overcome the dualism between appearance and reality in positing an Absolute that was ultimately beyond experience. Nevertheless, appearance, for Bradley, in some way belongs to, or qualifies, reality. The principle of consistency and non-contradiction, the criterion of the coherence theory of truth, is a matter of degree; there are, therefore, degrees of reality, and not a yawning chasm between appearance and reality. Absolute Idealists, such as Caird and Jones, while agreeing with the monistic unity of the whole, give much more emphasis than Bradley or Bosanquet to the reality of the appearances. For Caird and Jones, the unity embodies the principle of rationality which is expressed in and through all the differentiations of the whole. Jones argued that while Idealism repudiates the psychological method of beginning a philosophical inquiry from the inner life of the subject it does not attempt to do without that inner life altogether.

Subjective, or Personal, Idealists objected to the propensity of Absolute Idealism to undervalue the individual, and of running the risk of allowing the individual to become absorbed into the Absolute.[9] Following Rudolph Eucken, Boyce Gibson contended that the central idea of Absolute Idealism – that the real is rational – is upheld by Personal Idealism, but 'from the point of view of the personal experient'.[10] Absolute and Personal Idealism had a common enemy in naturalism, but Absolute Idealism was deficient in two main respects. First, it criticised human experience, not from the vantage point of human experience itself, 'but from the visionary and impractical standpoint of human nature'.[11] Secondly, it refused to give adequate recognition to volition in human nature. In Seth's view, Absolute Idealism was in danger of consigning the individual to insignificance.[12]

Despite the internal differences of opinion, Idealism was a philosophy responsive to the crucial concerns of Victorian Britain, and

---

[9] Andrew Seth, *Hegelianism and Personality* (Edinburgh, Blackwood, 1888), 215.

[10] W. R. Boyce Gibson, 'A Peace Policy for Idealists', *The Hibbert Journal*, 5 (1906–7), 409.

[11] Henry Sturt, ed., *Personal Idealism*, x.

[12] A. Seth Pringle-Pattison, *The Idea of God in the Light of Recent Philosophy* (Oxford, Clarendon Press, 1920), 266.

opposed to excessive individualism. The extent to which British
Idealism rode the wave of enthusiasm for evolution has been little
noticed. It was able to adapt evolution to its own ends by eschewing
its naturalistic form and emphasising the developing spiritual unity
of existence and, for many of them, the centrality of God in this
process. In positing the unity of nature and spirit the British Idealists fully capitalised upon their superficial affinity with the
immensely popular naturalistic evolutionary theories.

Evolution and ethics

It is difficult to conceive the extent to which the idea of evolution
dominated intellectual life during the latter part of the nineteenth
century after Charles Darwin's and Alfred Russel Wallace's theories
were first revealed in 1858. Wallace's findings, as Darwin saw them
in 1858, proved to be the stimulus to the publication of *The Origin
of Species* in 1859, a rather hasty and much less detailed account of
evolution than Darwin had originally intended. Although the ideas
are presented in as mild and unprovocative a manner as he could
muster, taking care to avoid directly the subject of Genesis and the
origin of humanity, the implications of many statements were easily
drawn. He explicitly denied, for example, that each species was
'independently created'. Darwin argued that, on the contrary, each
species developed from a common ancestry, many had become
extinct, and few would transmit progeny unchanged to a distant
future.[13] The implications were immediately recognised. Darwin's
theory was a denial of the Creationist theory of the origin of species,
as exemplified, for example, in the natural theology of William
Paley.[14] A second implication, which caused a tremendous uproar,
was the view that man was descended from the apes. This was, in
fact, a perversion of Darwin's contention, which was that the apes
and man have a common ancestor. This constituted a denial of the
absolute distinction between Nature and Spirit, or animal and
human nature.

---

[13] Charles Darwin, *The Origin of Species by Means of Natural Selection: Or the Preservation of Favoured Races in the Struggle for Life*, ed. J. W. Burrow
(Harmondsworth, Penguin, 1985; first published by John Murray, 1859), 458–9.
[14] William Paley, *Natural Theology*, vol. IV, *Works* (London, George Cowie, 1837).

Evolutionary theory was much more accessible to the educated public than the physical and mathematical sciences. The unity of Nature and Spirit in the theory of evolution held out the possibility of a common form of explanation in the natural and social sciences. The allure of such an all-encompassing way of understanding the whole of existence was almost irresistible. It found expression not only in biology, geology, palaeontology and anthropology, but also in varying degrees of modification, in history, philosophy, poetry and even religion.

The extent to which Darwin influenced social evolutionists has been greatly exaggerated. Darwin and Spencer were frequently cited not as the originators of evolutionary theory, but as those most responsible for impressing it upon the popular consciousness. Spencer's populist biology, philosophically conceived, inadequately grounded in empirical research, and analogously applied to society, was received with immense enthusiasm by the reading public. Because Idealism in its British form was a practical philosophy aimed at transforming society, its exponents had little respect for Spencer's philosophical acumen, but nevertheless recognised the necessity of discrediting his ideas at the popular and philosophical levels.[15] Bosanquet, for example, accused Spencer of being mainly responsible for the tendency of importing conceptions, or 'new fangled analogies' fashionably drawn from anywhere, except experience of the phenomenon to be explained, resulting in crude distortions of fundamental truths which have been obvious for 2,000 years (see p. 57).

One of the crucial points of contention among evolutionists was the question of heredity. Did Darwinian natural selection eliminate those least adjusted to the environment, leaving those who survive to pass on their qualities through inheritance? Or could the environment modify organisms by Lamarck's idea of use or disuse, the modifications of which were then inheritable? Both forms of explanation are invoked, for example, in the political theories of Walter Bagehot and Herbert Spencer. Even though Spencer coined the term 'survival of the fittest', and Darwin began to favour it in

---

[15] Henry Jones, 'The Misuse of Metaphors in the Human Sciences', *Working Faith of the Social Reformer* (London, Macmillan, 1910), 44. Cf. A. S. Pringle-Pattison, 'Life and Philosophy of Herbert Spencer', *The Quarterly Review*, 200 (1904), 241–2.

preference to his own 'struggle for existence', Spencer was far less convinced by the explanatory force of Natural Selection than by Lamarck's theory of Use Inheritance, or inherited character.

August Weissman's Germ Plasm theory revolutionised genetics. By the latter part of the 1890s the overwhelming evidence of experimental cytology, the science of cells, was weighted against the theory of Inherited Characters. The British Idealists tended to reject the Lamarckian principle of inherited characters, or at least gave little significance to it, while at the same time stressing a strong environmental influence upon human personality. Natural Selection, Ritchie argues, is an 'indisputable fact', and in so far as use inheritance, or inherited character, is still in doubt we should not revert to dubious or unknown causes when there are known causes that are sufficient (see p. 73). Natural Selection was deemed to be at work in nature and society. Human beings inherit capacities which are capable of being developed or retarded by the social environment or civilisation which is inherited, but not biologically, by successive generations. Language, Ritchie argues, makes possible the transmission of experience which is not biologically inheritable. The possession of consciousness, the ability to reflect, and the use of language give human beings a tremendous advantage in the struggle for existence.[16]

It is possible to identify three types of evolutionary theory being deployed for political purposes at the end of the nineteenth century, each having different postulates, and each capable of generating a variety of political conclusions. The three types of evolutionary theory can broadly be designated Naturalistic, Ethical and Spiritual.

The first postulates a unity or continuity between Nature and Spirit, suggesting that the latter can be understood and explained with reference to the former. Nature was to be the guide to or standard for ethics. Seth argues, for instance, that the exponents of naturalistic evolution, which he terms ethical evolution, 'naturalise morality, to assimilate ethical experience to nature . . .' (see p. 38). In this respect they explain what comes later in terms of what came before. This is exemplified by Darwin and Spencer. Darwin, for instance, attempted to account for the development of moral and

---

[16] D. G. Ritchie, *Darwinism and Politics* (London, Swan Sonnenschein, 1901), 100–1. Cf. 131–2.

intellectual faculties in human beings by claiming that they are to be found in rudimentary form in lower animals. He argues that: 'the difference in mind between man and the higher animals, great as it is, certainly is one of degree and not of kind'.[17]

Ethical evolution opens up a division between Nature and Spirit, contending that organic evolution and moral evolution are the results of different causes. This position is argued in different ways by Wallace and Huxley. Alfred Russel Wallace, while not wanting to deny 'the law of continuity in physical or mental evolution', nevertheless attributes to Nature and Spirit different generative capacities. He rejects, for example, Natural Selection as the mechanism by which morality and the higher intellectual capacities develop. Organic evolution, including the development of the human organism, is subject to different laws from the development of the civilised mind. He argues that the spiritual world supervenes on the natural and generates in humans ethical, mathematical, metaphysical and aesthetic qualities. He also attributes to this 'unseen universe of Spirit' gravity, electricity, cohesion, chemical force and radiant force, without which the natural world is almost inconceivable.[18] By including such forces in the realm of Spirit, Wallace hardly left any grounds for the distinction between Nature and Spirit that he posited.

Huxley, a friend and admirer of Darwin, on the other hand, takes a much bolder step towards the divorce of Nature and Spirit. Huxley believed that zoological categories and explanations could not exhaust all that is to be comprehended in the human condition. Social existence required the amelioration of the struggle for survival, rather than its encouragement. The pursuit of natural rights, which he understood in naturalistic terms, benefited only the individual at the expense of society. Moral rights, on the other hand, have correlative obligations and are conducive to social progress.[19] The survival of the fittest could not in Huxley's view constitute an ethical standard because fitness is circumstantially related to the

---

[17] Darwin, *Descent of Man* (London, Murray, 1888), 126. Cf. *The Origin of Species*, 458.

[18] A. R. Wallace, *Darwinism: An Exposition of the Theory of Natural Selection With Some of its Applications* (London, Macmillan, 1889), 473–8.

[19] T. H. Huxley, 'Natural Rights and Political Rights', *The Nineteenth Century*, 25 (1890), 179–80.

variability of nature. Ethics are not 'applied Natural History'.[20] For him, the evolution of Nature and moral evolution are two different and discontinuous processes. The idea of the survival of the fittest belongs to the cosmic process which governs the evolution of nature and the human organism. But the capacities which lead to success in this process are a disaster for social existence. Morality emerges when the cosmic process is checked first by fear of the opinions of others, and then by shame and sympathy. Moral rules arise as a result of our feelings of approbation and disapprobation. These rules are acquired and we gradually become used to thinking about conduct in terms of them. This is what Huxley calls the artificial personality, or conscience, which counters the natural character of man. Huxley gave ammunition to his critics, however, by introducing an ambiguity. In a famous qualifying note in 'Evolution and Ethics' he says that, 'strictly speaking, social life, and the ethical process in virtue of which it advances towards perfection, are part and parcel of the general process of evolution'. Furthermore, Huxley contends, the 'general cosmic process begins to be checked by a rudimentary ethical process, which is strictly speaking, part of the former . . .'[21]

Spiritual evolution is the self-conscious synthesis of the naturalistic and ethical theories. The unity of Nature and Spirit is reasserted, but instead of the former accounting for the latter, the explanatory power is reversed. It is reference to the higher that accounts for the lower. Nature is infused with spirit and natural selection can just as easily account for both moral progress and organic development. The recognition of the spiritual principle at work in the universe is the condition of our understanding nature.[22]

Bernard Bosanquet, Henry Jones and Andrew Seth directly address Huxley's arguments. Whereas Bosanquet believes that Huxley's distinction is a 'fatal misconception' (see p. 57), Jones and Seth maintain that Huxley has provided an invaluable corrective to those

---

[20] T. H. Huxley, 'Evolution and Ethics', in ed. J. Paradis and G. C. Williams, *Evolution and Ethics: T. H. Huxley's Evolution and Ethics with New Essays on its Victorian Sociobiological Context* (Princeton, Princeton University Press, 1989), 132.

[21] Huxley, 'Evolution and Ethics', note 20. This was note 19 in the original version.

[22] Ritchie, *Darwinism and Politics*, 115.

theories which associate ethical life too closely with organic and physical processes. Jones argues that, however committed we may be to the unity of existence, it would be folly to ignore or understate the difference between naturalistic processes and rational moral activity. Nature, on Huxley's terms, can neither know nor think, and therefore it is not moral. On the other hand, Jones argues, knowing and thinking presupposes nature. Nature furnishes the data which intelligence interprets, an intelligence that nature herself has evolved. The product of intelligence, namely knowledge, belongs just as much to nature as to man. Intelligence is the instrument through which nature is expressed, and although not itself intelligent, it is intelligible only to mind. Mind and nature are interdependent, neither can exist without the other. Far from being opposed to morality, nature is a willing partner in its development. Seth argues that the strength of naturalistic theories of evolutionary ethics is their explicit recognition of the unity of the cosmos. Unity is not a proposition to be proved, but instead an inescapable assumption (see pp. 37–8) what Jones calls a colligating hypothesis or absolute assumption.[23]

The British Idealists look to Hegel, and not to the naturalistic theories of Spencer and Darwin, for their inspiration. Hegel himself lived during a time when biological theories of evolution were beginning to emerge. He favoured the idea of emanation over that of evolution. In Hegel's mind, we understand a part only by looking at it as part of a whole. The early stages of something are only properly understood when they are seen as the early stages of something more fully developed. This is the case in all specialist fields of knowledge, as well as in the attempt to conceive the universe as a whole. In Ritchie's view Spencer's evolutionary theory failed to acknowledge Aristotle's dictum that the true nature of a thing is to be found not in its origin but in its end.[24] Caird makes a similar point when he urges that, 'in the first instance at least, we must read development *backward* and not *forward*, we must find the key to the meaning of the first stage in the last'.[25] Seth, although critical

---

[23] Jones, *Faith That Enquires* (London, Macmillan, 1922), 95.
[24] D. G. Ritchie, *The Principles of State Interference*, 2nd ed. (London, Swan Sonnenschein, 1896), 44.
[25] Edward Caird, *The Evolution of Religion* (Glasgow, Maclehose, 1899), vol. I, 45.

of Hegel on many points, agrees with him that, 'Nothing can be more certain than that all philosophical explanation must be explanation of the lower by the higher.'[26]

The idea of evolution, far from being a denial of religious experience, in fact enables us to comprehend it all the better. Jones argues, for example, that evolution is nothing other than another name for the development of Spirit. Evolution is the hypothesis which provides 'the methodizing conception which we employ to render intelligible to ourselves the process which spirit follows in becoming free' and '. . . suggests a solution of the ultimate dualism of mind and its objects, and contains the promise of boundless help to religious faith'.[27]

Idealism and society

Nineteenth-century individualists tended to view society either as an aggregate or an organism. The communitarian theories of the Idealists therefore not only had to combat utilitarian individualism but also the organic individualism of Spencer and Stephen. Bradley and Green, for example, criticise utilitarianism because it fails to account for moral actions which cannot be reduced to the pursuit of pleasure. Morality is fundamentally social, and acting morally entails a reciprocal concern for others, and not merely a desire to achieve a private state of mind, namely happiness. They both associate morality with self-realisation, which unlike pleasure, is the object of moral action. Bradley, for example argues that self-realisation is a moral duty. We have a duty to realise our best self (see p. 101). They also associate self-realisation with the common good. The common good is inconceivable apart from membership in a society, and the self that is to be realised through moral activity is 'determined, characterised, made what it is by relation to others'.[28]

For the Idealists, society is a moral organism the cohesiveness of which is not mechanical or biological, as it was for Spencer and

---

[26] Andrew Seth, *Hegelianism and Personality* (Edinburgh, Blackwood, 1888), 89.

[27] Henry Jones, *Idealism as a Practical Creed* (Glasgow, Maclehose, 1909), 29; and Henry Jones, *A Faith that Enquires* (London, Macmillan, 1922), 98.

[28] F. H. Bradley, *Ethical Studies*, 2nd ed. (Oxford, Clarendon Press, 1927), 116. Cf. T. H. Green, *Prolegomena to Ethics*, 4th ed., sections 183 and 184 (Oxford, Clarendon Press, 1899).

Stephen, but instead depends upon the relation in which each person stands with every other. Its sinews and ligaments are the moral ideas and personal relations without which a society would be a mere aggregate of individuals. Bradley, for example, argues that society is an organism in which each individual is an organ working for the whole. The person is realised in the whole, and the whole realises itself through the person.[29] The individual and society are mutually inclusive; each is nothing without the other. Bradley is not suggesting that social institutions, or one's station and its duties, are the whole story. The outer side of morality to which the doctrine of my station and its duties refers has to be supplemented with personal morality, that is, ideals that are never fully realisable and which are the inner side of morality.[30] This provides a standard independent of my station by which to criticise and reform society.

When the Idealists refer to the State, we have to be careful to understand the sense in which they are using the concept. On the one hand, it is used to designate the totality of the common consciousness of a people or a nation and the purposes it embodies. Alternatively, the State is viewed as the instrument of government through which individuals act on behalf of the nation. Furthermore, it is important, as Bosanquet suggests, to distinguish the ideal character of the state and states as they exist empirically (see pp. 274–6). By associating sovereignty with the state they posit a general will which is the real will of the community and of which the real will of individuals is a reflection or manifestation. It is the idea that organised society embodies an idea of life, along with the will to pursue more elevated and spiritually rewarding ends than any single individual can attain.

Even critics sympathethic to collectivism were quick to point out the logical implications of positing a will higher than that of the individuals who comprised it. Joad contended that it is difficult to get away from the fact that the identification of the real will of the individual with the general will merely give the appearance of democracy and justice to what might otherwise be construed as the arbitrary and tyrannical acts of the state. Idealists were accused of

---

[29] Bradley, *Ethical Studies*, 176–7.
[30] Peter P. Nicholson, *The Political Philosophy of the British Idealists* (Cambridge, Cambridge University Press, 1990), 23.

subordinating the individual to the state, and of propagating a moral absolutism, the implications of which in international relations were imperialism and irresponsible militarism. Hobson, for example, complained that the Prussian theory of the state to which British Idealists subscribed, compelled the individual to regard himself, his will and activity as the instrument of the super-personality of the state.[31] Bosanquet argues that our external life is itself the product of dominant ideas in which we participate as persons living in communities. The general will is the system of dominant ideas which assigns a place and purpose to the individual members. It is the totality of minds in their relations with each other, conducive to a certain way of life which gives direction and expression to the readjustments in the social organisation (see p. 135).

The state for the Idealists was a moral agent with ideals and purposes which it formulated and pursued for the betterment of society as a whole. D. G. Ritchie, for example, saw the state as the most adequate representative of the general will in the community.[32] And for Bosanquet it was the sustainer of rights conducive to the good life (see pp. 276–7). Without the state the individual is nothing. This does not mean that the individual owed the state blind obedience. Contrary to the view of critics such as Laski, Joad, Hobhouse and Hobson, the state for the Idealists was only a moral absolute when acting in conformity with its purpose of promoting and sustaining the common good. They emphatically maintained that no individual can delegate responsibility for making judgements about what is right and wrong. States which contravene their purpose and promote factionalism must, on moral grounds, be resisted. Green, for example, imposed no unconditional duty on the citizen to obey the law at all costs, 'since those laws may be inconsistent with the true end of the state, as the sustainer and harmoniser of social relations'.[33] Similarly Ritchie argues that if a law is so at odds with a person's conscience, it must be disobeyed at any cost, otherwise one's self-respect and character are degraded (see pp. 153–4).

---

[31] For examples of such criticisms, see L. T. Hobhouse, *The Metaphysical Theory of the State* (London, Allen and Unwin, 1918); J. A. Hobson, *Democracy After the War* (London, 1915); and C. E. M. Joad, *Modern Political Theory* (Oxford, Clarendon Press, 1924).

[32] Ritchie, *The Principles of State Interference*, 138.

[33] T. H. Green, *Lectures on the Principles of Political Obligation* (London, Longmans Green, 1917), 148.

Even Bosanquet, the target of Hobhouse's criticism of the metaphysical theory of the state, is at pains to point out that the state is the sustainer of rights, and will not undermine them by force when adjustments can be made compatible with the common good (see p. 274). The state has no duty, however, to find in favour of the individual, and the individual's resistance may only be vindicated in the fullness of time.

Freedom and individuality were, for most of the Idealists, inextricably linked to citizenship, that is, to the idea of self-development within a civilised state. Freedom was not therefore associated with the absence of constraints, but with acting in accordance with the higher good, or general will of the community. Freedom is associated with choice, and to act rationally is to make the right choices in conformity with one's higher interests. The existence of poverty, social deprivation and appalling conditions of work were simply incompatible with these ideals. Economics had to be made subordinate to morality, and the state as the sustainer of the moral community had to take an active role in providing the conditions in which this transformation could take place. Rights belong to individuals as members of a community. They are justifiable claims recognised as rational and necessary for the common good of society.

In many respects, even though they were unduly suspicious of the Idealists' emphasis upon the moral character and higher personality of the state, such New Liberals as J. A. Hobson, L. T. Hobhouse, H. A. L. Fisher, C. F. G. Masterman, H. W. Massingham and to some extent A. A. Asquith, shared the aims of such Idealist New Liberals as Green, Caird, Ritchie, Bosanquet, Jones and Haldane. In their common view the role of Liberalism was to raise all members of society to a civilised condition, and this necessarily entailed positive state intervention, although they disagreed among themselves about the desirable level. Green and Bosanquet, for example, were much less convinced of the importance of State intervention than Ritchie, Jones or Haldane. Their disagreements on this issue really amount to a question of the right balance between individual and collective responsibility. Bosanquet, for example, endorses the desirability of a civilised society exercising its will through the state in order to encourage progress in the condition of its members, but not to the extent that it weakens the character of the individual by transferring responsibility to the state (see pp. 52–3). As Muirhead remarked: 'What the State could do was to remove hindrances to the free action of what for lack of a better name moralists call "conscience" – a faculty that might be deadened rather than quickened by a hasty ill-considered collectivism . . .'[34]

Herbert Spencer's Law of Equal Freedom was taken by most to be the defining criterion of Individualism. Spencer maintained that, 'every man may claim the fullest liberty to exercise his faculties compatible with the possession of the like liberty by everyone else'.[35] The Spencerian Individualists saw almost every act of legislation as a further encroachment upon liberty. For them the State and liberty were antithetical. Most of the Individualists took socialism in the broadest terms to be any attempt to extend the power of the state in social matters. The Idealists themselves accepted this broad definition of socialism, but at the same time differentiated between what they called the right and wrong types. For the Idealists morality presupposes freedom of choice. Necessity might produce results that could be condemned as wrong, but they could not be immoral if the actor is deprived of the element of choice. The State cannot make men moral, but it can remove the obstacles to self-realisation. Social improvement was dependent upon the individual's power of seizing and making the most of external conditions. State action could not be ruled out or ruled in *per se*, but instead had to be judged on its merits. The criterion of state action for Henry Jones, for example, was the contribution that legislation could make to moralising existing social relations. Caird argues it is the large cities, faced with the consequences of rapid industrial growth, that have had to confront the issue of the extent to which the community should 'interfere' in order to ameliorate the plight of the disadvantaged (see p. 180). The Idealists refuse to accept that there is an opposition between the individual and the state, and were unwilling to condone the rectification of the evils of class bias by shifting the emphasis of that bias to the working class. True individualism, that is the self-realisation of one's capacities in the context of society, is enhanced by the true or right kind of socialism, which uses the

---

[34] J. H. Muirhead, *Reflections by a Journeyman in Philosophy* (London, Allen and Unwin, 1942), 160.
[35] Cited in M. V. Taylor, *Men Versus the State: Herbert Spencer and Late Victorian Individualism* (Oxford, Clarendon Press, 1992), 3.

state to advance freedom of choice by removing the obstacles to the development of individual freedom. It is on the point at which individual responsibility might be undermined by too much interference over which they differ. Bosanquet and Green give a great deal of emphasis to self-reliance. Improved housing conditions in themselves do not improve moral character. People have to will self-improvement. Whereas Bosanquet took a hard line on Poor Relief, other Idealists such as Jones and Muirhead were much more sympathetic to its extension.

Democracy and education

With the 1832 Reform Bill which effectively enfranchised the upper middle class, the 1867 Act extending the franchise by about a million urban labourers at the upper end of their class, and Gladstone's third Reform Act of 1884 which enfranchised almost two million agricultural labourers, even the more Liberal-minded social reformers were becoming anxious about the potential social and political implications.

Carlyle, Arnold and Ruskin, for different reasons, but with similar fundamental predispositions towards a stable hierarchical social structure, at the top of which was a natural aristocracy of breeding and culture, were sceptical of democratic reform. Henry Maine and W. E. H. Lecky followed Tocqueville and J. S. Mill in believing that democracy and liberty were fundamentally at odds. They believed in their different ways that egalitarian pressures result in a uniformity of ideas and aspirations. Although Bentham was an advocate of democracy, John Stuart Mill's attitude was tempered by a vehement distrust of the power of public opinion consequent upon the rise of democracy. Mill perceived the individual as having become subdued under the weight of mass opinion. For Mill the individual, far from being the focus of democracy, is the elevated intellect standing against egalitarianism and acting as a counterpoise to government.

The New Radicals of the later nineteenth century, who mistakenly saw themselves as inheritors of Benthamite principles, and the Spencerian Individualists found it difficult to reconcile democracy with laissez-faire capitalism. They equated democracy with socialism and saw both as a threat to property rights. Ignorant voters pursuing their narrowly defined self-interests would detract from, rather than add to, the common good. The fear was that democracy would bring about class biased legislation detrimental to propertied interests. Liberals were not always the strongest advocates of democracy. Robert Lowe, James Fitzjames Stephen and Walter Bagehot, all committed Liberals, thought that the progressive reforming tendency might be severely jeopardised if the uneducated populace was enfranchised and gained influence over government. Bagehot believed that with the decline in reverence for their natural rulers and the realisation of their potential power, working men would become the target of the highest bidder, sacrificing national interest for narrow class bias.

The Idealists were also sensitive to the dangers of democracy and sought to emphasise that with the added responsibility of political participation came the obligation of society to eliminate gross inequalities which fuelled class antagonisms. This did not mean that they were committed to egalitarianism. Caird argues that it was not altogether a bad thing to have different class perspectives, as long as they did not develop into rigid dogmas (see p. 175). For Jones only a perspective that emphasised the unity of society could lead to social progress. The class politics of Labour amounted to eristic politics which were no match for the dialectic of liberalism. In Ritchie's view representative democracy was the greatest political invention the world had ever known because it gave rise to a form of government and constitution formerly unknown, and had considerably reduced the risks of democracy in its more traditional forms, particularly its inherent instability (see p. 85). Mackenzie argued that the fear that democracy leads to anarchy and the domination of politics by the uneducated majority had not been justified by modern representative democracy, which retains a commitment to qualitative differences in those chosen to be representatives. Ballot boxes and majorities are only the mechanism of democracy. It is in fact a mistake to think of self-government in terms of minorities and majorities. Instead the people should be conceived as a whole, a living, breathing, thinking unity, containing within itself the principle of self-rule, as opposed to the idea of a sovereign imposing its will from an external position. Conceived in such terms aristocracy and democracy are not incompatible. The democratic spirit acknowledges that to be governed by the best *is* self-government, and that the best may more adequately express the general will of the whole community. The spirit of democracy is to be found in the ideal that each person should be allowed to do, and trusted to do, that for which he or she is best equipped and suited (see p. 166).

Education and democratic reform had to go hand in hand. The Idealists, particularly Green, Caird, Haldane and Jones, like Matthew Arnold, explicitly and fervently linked democratic reforms with the need for reforms in education. Green, although a champion of the working class, was under no delusions about its depravity. The condition of the working class in Britain was, for Green, testimony to the failure of education. If the education of a gentleman was to be made available to promising working-class children, undiluted in its extension to a broader constituency, it would act as a great social leveller.[36] He proposed a system of scholarships that would progressively enable a boy of the working or middle class to take advantage of all levels of education, including university, if he had the ability. Knowledge for the Idealists is power – the capacity for self-realisation through personal development – and hence they put a high premium upon education, or freedom from ignorance.

Education, Green thought, would in time lead to the moral improvement of society, but in the meantime legislation could be used to reduce temptation, especially in relation to the sale of alcohol. Haldane had even greater faith in the efficacious powers of education to diminish social evils. As long as the state made provision for adequate housing, a living wage and education, most social problems would disappear. If the problems of poverty, housing and ignorance were properly addressed, Haldane optimistically predicted, 'Temperance will follow.' In Haldane's view the state should give every man and women the right to such education that would liberate them from circumstances that were not of their making and which prevent 'them individually from having a real chance in life'.[37]

Idealists pursued the goal of the institutional provision of education with missionary fervour, advocating that at all levels access to knowledge was a concomitant of the extension of democracy.

[36] T. H. Green, *Works*, III (London, Longmans Green, 1888), 460. Also see John MacCunn, *Six Radical Thinkers* (London, Arnold, 1910), 252.
[37] R. B. Haldane, *The Future of Democracy: An Address* (London, Headley, 1918), 11; and R. B. Haldane, *An Autobiography* (London, Hodder and Stoughton, 1929), 301.

Only an educated and enfranchised electorate could exercise the duties of citizenship responsibly. For many of the Idealists the practical work of social reform often took priority over their scholarly pursuits. On the broader front, education was conceived in the widest possible sense. Like Plato, Aristotle and Hegel, the British Idealists believed that the best education a person could have was to be a citizen in a good state. Men and women of integrity set the examples of conduct and virtuous living that were to be put before the ordinary person. In this respect, every place of work was to act as a school of virtue in which, as Henry Jones put it, relations would be moralised as they stood. The state itself was an educational institution charged with teaching only one thing, that is, 'the nature of the good'.[38]

International relations

In understanding the views of British Idealists about international relations, it is crucial to bear in mind what they conceived philosophy to be. The role of philosophy is to make intelligible what is here and now in terms of its rational development. The real is the rational. This does not mean that everything that exists is rational. What is real is that which is in conformity with the unfolding of reason in the world, that is the gradual development of freedom. In this respect international relations as they stood had to be accounted for, which was quite a different question from the view about how they might yet develop. Both imperialism and war were facts of life that had to be explained.

It was quite common among later nineteenth-century theorists influenced by evolutionary ideas to extend the struggle for existence beyond individual competition to groups or communities, particularly nations. Natural Selection was deemed to be a mechanism of evolution that operated not only at the individual level, that is, what Karl Pearson called intra-group competition, but also among groups ranging from small communities to nations which compete against each other in the struggle for survival. In Bosanquet's view, the division of labour and exchange of services mitigate nature's competition red in tooth and claw, and make the group itself 'the primary

---

[38] Henry Jones, *The Principles of Citizenship* (London, Macmillan, 1919), 117.

unit in the struggle for existence' (see p. 55). In Karl Pearson, the mathematician, and Benjamin Kidd, the civil servant (second only to Spencer in his popularisation of social evolution) and also to a lesser extent in David Ritchie, the idea of group selection led to a justification of imperialism in which the favoured races had a right to exploit the lower in the competition for existence. On the other hand Spencer rejected any such conclusion by suggesting that in the evolution from militant to industrial society, physical competition is replaced by commercial competition and co-operation.

Walter Bagehot saw national character as the primary form of social cohesion or group identity, and saw its transmission from one generation to another in Lamarckian terms. In the relations among nations he believed that it was a law of nature that the strongest prevail in the Darwinian struggle for survival. Leslie Stephen, while dubious about the methods of the English and Spanish in America, makes it clear that twenty million civilised whites are preferable to one million red savages populating the continent.[39] It was, as Leonard Hobhouse suggested, the Boer War that brought attitudes to imperialism to a head. Cecil Rhodes's justification of 'social imperialism' (the exploitation of savages in order to avert unrest among the British working class) and his methods in South Africa, especially his role in the Jameson Raid, were largely condemned by the Idealists and Liberals in general. Such Liberals as Campbell-Bannerman, Harcourt, Morley, Lloyd George, Hobhouse and Hobson, along with most of the leading Idealists, including Bosanquet and Caird, condemned the war wholeheartedly. Caird, for example, chaired a meeting in support of the campaign to highlight the plight of Boer women and children in the South African concentration camps, and strongly opposed Oxford University's conferment of an honorary degree upon Cecil Rhodes in 1899.[40] It was possible, however, to condemn the methods without necessarily opposing the war. There was a band of Liberal Imperialists, headed by Rosebery and supported by Asquith and Edward Grey, and

[39] Walter Bagehot, *Physics and Politics* in ed. Norman St. John Stevas, *The Collected Works of Walter Bagehot* (London, The Economist, 1974), 42–6; and Leslie Stephen, 'Ethics and the Struggle for Existence', *Contemporary Review*, 64 (1893), 166.

[40] Henry Jones and J. H. Muirhead, *The Life and Philosophy of Edward Caird* (Glasgow, Maclehose and Jackson, 1921), 153–4.

which counted among its adherents the Idealist philosophers Lord Haldane (a Liberal peer), David Ritchie and Henry Jones, who at once deplored the barbaric conduct of the war but at the same time supported the imperial principle at stake. Haldane, for example, thought the Jameson Raid a monumental blunder, and Britain's entry into the war avoidable, had negotiations been handled by someone with a more diplomatic temperament than Milner. The war itself, however, raised issues regarding Britain's credibility and vulnerability in future foreign relations. Haldane thought withdrawal would both undermine the troops already committed, and 'place ourselves in position of danger from the rest of the world'.[41]

The fact that imperialism existed, and would not simply go away, necessitated more than outright condemnation. In this respect even Hobhouse and Hobson, the most severe critics of Idealist politics, believed that there was a right kind of imperialism which entailed a responsible and sustained effort to prepare indigenous peoples for self-government. The Idealists agreed. Economic or social imperialism exhibited the most barbaric and reprehensible conduct against peoples ill-equipped to protect themselves (see pp. 245–6).[42] It was now up to the British Government, they argued, to ensure that a more humane and responsible attitude was maintained. The only justification for intervention in the affairs of the inferior races was to rule in their interests and, in so far as they have a capacity for participating in the good life, all forms of subjugation were prohibited. The only justification for imperialism, if indeed it could be justified at all, was the fundamental principle that the superior people saw it as its solemn duty to elevate the lower to its own level. Ritchie expressed a more extreme view when he argued that many of the lower races may never be fit to govern themselves, and for their own sakes we should rule over them in an imperial and despotic manner (see p. 92).

Contrary to the view that critics such as Hobhouse and Hobson had of the Idealist view of the relation of the state to other states,

---

[41] Lord Haldane, *An Autobiography* (London, Hodder and Stoughton, 1929), 135–9.
[42] For Hobhouse's and Hobson's endorsement of the right kind of imperialism see L. T. Hobhouse, *Democracy and Reaction*, edited with an introduction by Peter Clark (Brighton, Harvester, 1972: first published 1904 and revised 1909), 15, 45 and 47; L. T. Hobhouse, 'The Foreign Policy of Collectivism', *International Journal of Ethics*, viii (1899), 215; J. A. Hobson, 'Socialistic Imperialism', *International*

peace among nations was for them the natural condition of humanity. Bosanquet explicitly suggested that 'the normal relation of states is co-operative' (see p. 276). While some were less condemnatory than others, none saw war as a permanent condition. Ritchie, like Hegel, recognised the extent to which war contributes to the social unity of the nation. He argued that: 'So far as the history of the world has yet gone, war has been a more important factor than industrial competition in producing social *organisms* as distinct from mere social *aggregates*.'[43] On the other hand Green set the tone for the other Idealists in rejecting Hegel's international relations theory and contending that war is a consequence, not of healthy states, but of defective states failing to fulfil their purpose of promoting the common good, and no one side in such disputes can be totally absolved of blame (see pp. 227–9). Or, as Bosanquet puts it in this volume, war has to be understood, not as an absolute evil but as part of the moral life consequent upon man's fallible nature (see p. 294). We all have to take responsibility for the ultimate stupidity of war and work to eliminate it as we do with all other evils.[44]

The British Idealists all believed, in their different degrees, that there was the possibility of a general will developing out of the already existing attempts at international co-operation, such as the Empire, or in the relations which Canada, the United States of America and Great Britain enjoyed with each other. For these Idealists there is no opposition between the obligations of a citizen and the obligations of the person towards humanity, that is between political right and cosmopolitan right, because it is through the state that we most effectively contribute to the development of higher ideals and the establishment of a general will among nations. It is true that Bradley and Bosanquet were rather pessimistic about the extent to which international law could develop given the lack of an organised moral community in the international sphere, but they did not rule out states being superseded by a higher, organised and

Journal of Ethics, xii (1901–2), 47; and J. A. Hobson, *Imperialism: A Study*, ed. J. Townshend (London, Harvester, 1988), 246.

[43] D. G. Ritchie, 'Social Evolution', in *Studies in Political and Social Ethics* (London, Swan Sonnenschein, 1902), 167.

[44] Bernard Bosanquet, 'Function of the State in Promoting the Unity of Mankind', 301; Bernard Bosanquet, *Some Suggestions in Ethics* (London, Macmillan, 1918), 242.

more inclusive moral community. Other Idealists, such as Green, Caird, Jones, Sorley, Watson, MacCunn and Haldane were much more optimistic about the extent to which a moral community was developing beyond state borders. As Haldane insisted, morality consists of much more than formal laws and prescriptions, and resides in a common spirit which permeates a people and which imparts appropriate and inappropriate ways to behave. Acting in some ways, while not illegal, is simply bad form. It was this spirit that he saw gradually being extended among civilised nations. With the advent of the First World War, all of the Idealists, with differing degrees of optimism, put their faith in a League of Nations to develop, and to be the expression of, an international General Will sufficient to reduce conflict and promote peaceable relations, the natural condition of mankind.

While critics of British Idealism wished to attribute a good deal of blame to Hegel for German militarism, they did not bring into question the patriotism of his British admirers. The British Idealists were forced onto the offensive, however, not only by direct criticism of their philosophy in books like Hobhouse's *Metaphysical Theory of the State*, but also by the implied criticism contained in writings against German philosophy in books by such eminent philosophers as George Santayana and John Dewey.[45] The British Idealists all condemned German aggression, but differed considerably among themselves about the degree to which Hegel, and German philosophy in general, could be implicated. Most were concerned to suggest that Hegelianism, in the context of a more liberal atmosphere than prevailed in Germany, leads to a democratic rather than a militaristic society. In this volume John Watson argues that Hegel expressly denied that the cohesiveness of society rests upon force rather than will. Hegel's philosophy simply could not be taken as an endorsement of Treitschke's doctrine of power politics. Hegel and his generation of German philosophers sought to raise the consciousness of Germans above the level of mere parochialism and self-interest, and taught that such things must be renounced if it is possible to have a nation at all. They taught a form of patriotism,

---

[45] L. T. Hobhouse, *The Metaphysical Theory of the State* (London, Allen and Unwin, 1938: first published 1918); John Dewey, *German Philosophy and Politics* (New York, Books for Libraries: reprint of 2nd ed. of 1942: 1st ed. 1914); and George Santayana, *Egotism in German Philosophy* (London, Dent, 1914: second ed. 1940).

and not the militaristic expansionism of their modern-day compatriots.

Idealism, as portrayed in this introduction, fulfilled a number of purposes in a society experiencing the consequences of rapid industrialisation and the expansion of world trade. It acted as a counterbalance to the individualism of utilitarianism, offering a philosophy that gave a much needed emphasis to social cohesiveness and to the closeness of the relation between individual and collective responsibility. Idealism sought to heighten, rather than, as its critics contended, to diminish, individual responsibility by increased state intervention. It emphasised the development of moral character in the context of an enabling state. It was an intensely moralistic and judgemental philosophy, condemning all social evils. It emphasised both the responsibility of individuals to seize every opportunity to make themselves more virtuous, and of the owners of capital to transform their workshops into schools of virtue. The role of the State in all this was to ensure that any impediments to self-realisation were removed. In its international focus Idealism centred upon the responsibility of the State to broaden the moral community so that more and more people become our neighbours. As the embodiment of the General Will and as the representative and sustainer of the highest degrees of civilisation, the State had a duty to promote humanitarian ideals beyond its borders. In relations with 'lower races' the implication was a form of moral imperialism. In relations among civilised nations, Idealism advocated the injection of moral ideals and constraints in economic and political exchanges. While both a historicist and communitarian philosophy Idealism had no place within it for moral relativism. The reason for this was its emphasis upon rationality, the equation of freedom with choice in a social context, and spiritual self-realisation.

Idealist biographies

BERNARD BOSANQUET was born 14 June 1848, near Alnwick, Northumberland. He was educated at Harrow and Balliol College, Oxford. As an undergraduate he was greatly influenced by Jowett and Green. Green thought him one of the ablest men of his generation. From 1870 to 1881 he was a Fellow of University College, Oxford. He then went to live in London where he became a prominent figure in the activities of The London Ethical Society and the Charity Organisation Society, of which he became chairman of the Council in 1916. Bosanquet was president of the Aristotelian Society from 1894–8. In 1903 he succeeded D. G. Ritchie in the chair of moral philosophy, University of St Andrews, where he stayed until 1908. He delivered the Gifford Lectures at Edinburgh in 1911 and 1912. With Green and Bradley, Bosanquet was one of the three leading figures in the school of Idealism. He was, with Henry Jones, one of the most Hegelian thinkers among the British Idealists, and a prolific writer on all aspects of philosophy and politics. During and after the First World War he was unfairly criticised for advocating State absolutism. He died in 1923.

Biographical: A. D. Lindsay, *Dictionary of National Biography 1922–30*; A. C. Bradley and R. B. Haldane, 'Bernard Bosanquet' (1848–1923), *Proceedings of the British Academy*, x (1921–3); J. H. Muirhead, 'Bernard Bosanquet', *Mind*, xxxii (1923); Helen Bosanquet, *Bernard Bosanquet: A Short Account of His Life* (London, Macmillan, 1924); J. H. Muirhead ed., *Bernard Bosanquet and his Friends* (London, Allen and Unwin, 1935)

Principal works: *Aspects of the Social Problem* (1895); *The Philosophical Theory of the State* (1899); *The Principle of Individuality and Value* (1912); *The Value and Destiny of the Individual* (1913); *Social and International Ideals: Being Studies in Patriotism* (1917); *Some Suggestions in Ethics* (1918). All published by Macmillan, London.

FRANCIS HERBERT BRADLEY was born in Clapham, London on 30 January 1846. He was educated at Cheltenham College, Marlborough School and University College, Oxford. In 1870 he became a life Fellow of Merton College. He became more and more reclusive as he grew older, but he played his part in College administration. He was the recipient of many awards, including an honorary doctorate from Glasgow University in 1883, membership of the Royal Danish Academy in 1922, an honorary Fellowship of the British Academy in 1923, and the Order of Merit in 1924.

He was, like Green and Caird, greatly influenced by Hegel, but never regarded himself as an Hegelian because of the extent to which he disagreed with Hegel's fundamental ideas. He is widely regarded as the most intellectually rigorous of the British Idealists. Unlike most of his fellow Idealists, who had practical experience of the social evils of Victorian Britain, he wrote little about political issues, and is believed to have taken a conservative stance on the important social and political questions of the day. He died of blood poisoning in 1924.

Biographical: A. E. Taylor, 'Francis Herbert Bradley, 1846–1924', *Proceedings of the British Academy*, xi (1924–5); G. R. G. Mure, 'F. H. Bradley: Towards a Portrait', *Encounter*, xvi (1961); A. E. Taylor, 'Bradley, Francis Herbert', *Dictionary of National Biography 1922–1930*.

Principal works: *Ethical Studies* (London, Kegan Paul, 1876); *The Principles of Logic*, 2nd edn (London, Oxford University Press, 1922); *Appearance and Reality* (London, Oxford University Press, 1893: 2nd edn 1897); *Essays on Truth and Reality* (Oxford, Clarendon Press, 1914); *Collected Essays* (Oxford, Clarendon Press, 1935).

EDWARD CAIRD was born in Greenock on 23 March 1835. During his early years he lived with his aunt Jane Caird. He was educated at Greenock Academy until the age of fifteen when he entered Glasgow University in 1850. Ill health forced him to seek a change of air, first at St Andrews, and then at Errol in Perthshire where his

elder brother John, destined to become Principal of the University
of Glasgow, was the parish minister. In 1858 he resumed his studies
in Glasgow and took classes in Divinity, but then changed direction
and transferred to Oxford where he became re-acquainted with his
former class friend, John Nicol who founded the Old Mortality
Society whose members included A. V. Dicey and T. H. Green.
He was taught by Jowett at Oxford, and became extremely friendly
with T. H. Green, who he regarded as a kindred spirit in politics
and in his attitude towards education as well as in philosophy. Caird
graduated in 1863, and became a Fellow and tutor of Merton College until his elevation to the chair of moral philosophy at Glasgow
in 1866. After twenty-seven years he returned to Oxford as Jowett's
successor to the Mastership of Balliol College (1893).

He maintained an active interest in politics and social questions.
Throughout his career he was a strong advocate of university education for women and working men, giving his support to the establishment of Ruskin College, Oxford, and extending education to the
industrial areas by means of the University Extension Scheme. He
lectured in the East End of London, for example, on socialism.
In Glasgow he was the leading light in the establishment of 'The
University Settlement Association', modelled after Toynbee Hall in
London, and 'The Women's Protective and Provident League'
whose objective was to improve by protective legislation the
working conditions of women and children in industry. He was an
avid supporter of the Garibaldi rising in 1859 and of Abraham Lincoln in the American Civil War. He was an avowed opponent of
the Boer War and vehemently objected to Cecil Rhodes being hon-
oured by Oxford University in 1899. Caird was awarded honorary
doctorates from the universities of St Andrews (1883), Oxford
(1891), Cambridge (1898) and Wales (1902). He was an original
Fellow of the British Academy (1902) and a corresponding member
of the French Académie des Sciences morales et politiques. He
delivered the Gifford Lectures in St Andrews in 1891–2, and in
Glasgow in 1900. Caird died on 1 November 1908. He is buried
next to Green and Jowett in St Sepulchre's cemetery, Oxford.
Biographical: *The Times*, 3 Nov. 1908; *Glasgow Herald*, 6 Nov. 1908;
'Caird, Edward (1835–1908)', *Dictionary of National Biography*;
John Watson, 'Edward Caird as Teacher and Thinker', *Queen's
Quarterly*, xvi (1908); Bernard Bosanquet, 'Edward Caird 1835–

1908', *Proceedings of the British Academy*, 3 (1907–8); Sir Henry Jones and J. H. Muirhead, *The Life and Philosophy of Edward Caird* (Glasgow, Maclehose, 1921).
Principal works: *A Critical Account of the Philosophy of Kant* (Glasgow, Maclehose, 1877); *Hegel* (Edinburgh, Blackwood, 1883); *Essays in Literature and Philosophy*, 2 vols. (Glasgow, Maclehose, 1892); *The Evolution of Religion* (Glasgow, Maclehose, 1893).

T. H. GREEN was born at Birkin, the West Riding of Yorkshire on 7 April 1836. His father, Valentine Green, was an evangelical rector. Green was educated at Rugby and Balliol College, Oxford, where he was taught by Benjamin Jowett and Charles Parker. He became a Fellow of Balliol in 1860, and was re-elected in 1872. He received a LL.D. from Glasgow University in 1875, and was appointed Whyte's Professor of Moral Philosophy in 1878.

For parts of 1865 and 1866 Green was assistant commissioner for the Royal Commission of 1864 which inquired into educational provision for the middle class in England. Green was a radical on most of the important issues of his day. He was a champion of the North against slavery in the American Civil War and actively supported educational, parliamentary, and social reform (including liquor legislation) in Britain by speaking at public meetings and contributing to the practical success of schemes he helped to initiate. He was a personal inspiration to many leading reformers including Asquith, Alfred Milner, Charles Gore and Scott Holland. In 1876 he was elected to Oxford Town Council. He died on 15 March 1882.
Biographical: R. L. Nettleship, 'Memoir', in *Works of Thomas Hill Green* (London, Longmans Green, 1888); J. H. Muirhead, 'Thomas Hill Green 1832–1882', in *Great Democrats*, ed. A. Barrat Brown (London, Ivor Nicholson and Watson, 1934); Alan P. F. Sell, *Philosophical Idealism and Christian Belief* (Cardiff, University of Wales Press, 1995).
Principal works: *Prolegomena to Ethics* (Oxford, Clarendon Press, 1883); *Works of Thomas Hill Green*, ed. R. L. Nettleship, 3 vols. (London, Longmans Green, 1885–8).

HENRY JONES was born on 30 November 1852 at Llangernyw, Denbighshire, into a strong Calvinistic Methodist family. He left school at the age of twelve to follow his father's trade as a shoemaker. Shortly afterwards he continued his education while working. He won a scholarship to Bangor Normal teacher training college in 1870, and became the headmaster of the Ironworks School at Brynammam, South Wales, in 1873. He was a lay preacher and registered Calvinist minister. He won a scholarship to study at Glasgow University in 1875 where he came under the influence of Edward Caird and John Nicol. They persuaded him to give up his religious ambitions and make philosophy his vocation. On graduating Jones won the Clarke Fellowship. In 1882 he became a lecturer at University College, Aberystwyth, and then a professor at the University College of North Wales, Bangor (1884), St. Andrew's (1891) and Glasgow (1894).

In politics he was a Liberal and close friend of David Lloyd George. He believed passionately in the responsibility of university professors to give moral guidance to the general community. He took a lead in establishing and supporting the University Settlement in Glasgow and the Civic Society. He was committed to forging links between the University and business and getting businessmen to acknowledge their responsibilities to the broader community. He campaigned vigorously in Wales and Scotland for educational reform, including university education for women. He served on Haldane's Royal Commission of 1916–17 into the University of Wales. During the war he campaigned on behalf of the Parliamentary Recruitment Committee throughout Wales in an attempt to quell syndicalist opposition from miners in Merthyr and North Wales slate quarrymen.

He was awarded doctorates from the University of St Andrews and the University of Wales. In 1904 he was elected a Fellow of the British Academy. He was knighted in 1912 and became a Companion of Honour in 1922. He was the Gifford Lecturer at Glasgow University in 1920 and 1921. He died on 4 February, 1922.

Biographical: Henry Jones, *Old Memories*, ed. Thomas Jones (London, Hodder and Stoughton, 1922); J. H. Muirhead, 'Sir Henry Jones', *Proceeding of the British Academy*, x (1921–3); H. J. W. Hetherington, *The Life and Letters of Sir Henry Jones* (London, Hodder and Stoughton, 1924); H. J. W. Hetherington, 'Jones, Henry 1852–1922', *Dictionary of National Biography 1921– 1931*; *The Times*, 6 Feb. 1922; *John O'London's Weekly*, 11 March

1922; *Western Mail*, 6 Feb. 1922; Leonard Russell, 'Sir Henry Jones', *Mind*, XXXI (1922).
Principal works: *Browning as a Philosophical and Religions Teacher* (Glasgow, Maclehose, 1891); *The Philosophy of Lotze* (Glasgow, Maclehose, 1895); *Idealism as a Practical Creed* (Glasgow, Maclehose, 1909); *The Working Faith of the Social Reformer* (London, Macmillan, 1910); *The Principles of Citizenship* (London, Macmillan, 1919); *A Faith That Enquires* (London, Macmillan, 1922).

JOHN STUART MACKENZIE was born on 29 February 1860 at Springburn, near Hogganfield, Glasgow. He was orphaned in Buenos Aires and despatched back to Tollcross, Scotland, where he attended the local school, and then Annfield House Academy, Glasgow. He was taught by Caird and Jones at Glasgow University. On completing his degree, Mackenzie won the Clarke Fellowship and succeeded Jones as Caird's assistant. He then succeeded W. R. Sorley to the Shaw Fellowship at Edinburgh, and in 1886 followed the advice of his predecessor to study in Cambridge. There he became a close friend of J. M. E. McTaggart, whom he converted from his early enthusiasm for Spencer to an admiration for Hegel. His Shaw lectures were published as *Introduction to Social Philosophy* in 1890 and anticipated much of the social legislation that was to follow over the next twenty-five years, including the growth of adult education, unemployment insurance, and economic planning with respect to investments and labour. In 1895 he became professor of logic and philosophy at Cardiff. In 1911 he received the honorary degree of LL.D. from Glasgow and in 1934 was elected a Fellow of the British Academy. He retired in 1915 at the age of fifty-five. He unsuccessfully stood as a Labour candidate in 1918 for the University of Wales. He died on 6 December 1935.
Biographical: J. W. Scott, 'Mackenzie, John Stuart (1860–1935)', *Dictionary of National Biography 1931–41*; J. H. Muirhead, 'John Stuart Mackenzie', *Proceedings of the British Academy*, 21 (1935); J. H. Muirhead, 'J. S. Mackenzie (1860–1935)', *Mind*, n.s., 45 (1936); M. Mackenzie, ed., *John Stuart Mackenzie* (London, Williams and Norgate, 1936).
Principal works: *An Introduction to Social Philosophy* (Glasgow, Maclehose, 1895); *Outlines of Metaphysics* (London, Allen and

Unwin, 1902); *Manual of Ethic*, 5th edn (London, University
Tutorial Press, 1918); *Outlines of Social Philosophy* (London, Allen
and Unwin, 1918).

JOHN HENRY MUIRHEAD was born into an evangelical household
on 28 April 1855 in Glasgow. He was educated at Gilbertfield and
the Glasgow Academy. In 1870, at the age of fifteen, Muirhead
entered Glasgow University. At Glasgow he was greatly influenced
by the young Caird, at whose house Muirhead met T. H. Green in
1874. He graduated in 1875. Muirhead won a Snell Exhibition in
philosophy to study at Balliol, Oxford, under Green and R. L.
Nettleship. Muirhead graduated from Oxford in 1879 and accepted
the job of Junior Assistant in Latin at Glasgow University. In 1885
he briefly flirted with the idea of becoming a Unitarian minister and
studied at Manchester New College, London. During this time he
was an active member of the London Ethical Society, which led to
his involvement in the University Extension Scheme, which is how
he came to know J. A. Hobson. Although sympathetic to Fabianism,
even attending some of its meetings, Muirhead was distrustful of
its emphasis upon efficiency and its lack of sensitivity to how individuals reacted to collectivist reforms. In 1897 Muirhead went to
what was then Mason College in Birmingham, shortly to become
the University, to the chair of Philosophy and Political Economy.
He was anxious that the University become involved in alleviating
the social problems of Birmingham by means of co-operation with
industry and medicine. He visited factories to witness the conditions
for himself. He was also heavily involved in the University Extension scheme, Workers' Educational Association, and the work of
establishing secondary schools in the Midlands under the provisions
of the 1902 Education Act. He exemplified perfectly what Idealists
meant by active citizenship. He was opposed to the Boer War and
economic and social imperialism, and was an exponent of international co-operation along the lines presented by Kant in *Perpetual
Peace*. Muirhead retired in 1921 but nevertheless took up posts in
Edinburgh and California. He was the editor of the Library of Philosophy series, 1888–1940, and played a prominent role in The British Institute of Philosophy, and succeeded L. T. Hobhouse as
Chairman of the Council in 1930. He was elected a Fellow of the
British Academy in 1931. He died on 24 May 1940.

Biographical: *Glasgow Herald*, 30 May 1940; C. G. Robertson, 'Muirhead, John Henry (1855–1940)', *Dictionary of National Biography 1931–41*; J. W. Harvey, 'J. H. Muirhead 1855–1940', *Mind*, n.s., 50 (1941); C. G. Robertson and W. D. Ross, 'John Henry Muirhead 1855–1940', *Proceedings of the British Academy*, xxvi (1940); J. H. Muirhead, *Reflections by a Journeyman in Philosophy* (London, Allen and Unwin, 1942).

Principal works: *The Elements of Ethics* (London, Murray, 1892); *The Service of the State* (London, Murray, 1908); *By What Authority? Principles in the Reports of the Poor Law Commission* (London, Lodge and King, 1909); *German Philosophy in Relation to the War* (London, Murray, 1915); *The Platonic Tradition in Anglo-Saxon Philosophy* (London, Allen and Unwin, 1931).

ANDREW SETH PRINGLE-PATTISON was born Andrew Seth on 20 December 1856 in Edinburgh. Seth was educated at the Royal High School, Edinburgh before going on to the University in 1873. He was influenced by Campbell Fraser, and was a contemporary of D. G. Ritchie, W. R. Sorley, and R. B. Haldane, with whom he became a lifelong friend. He graduated in 1878, and was awarded a Hibbert travel scholarship to study for two years in Berlin, Jena and Göttingen. Among his teachers in Germany were R. H. Lotze, to whom he frequently refers in his writings. In 1880 Seth became class assistant to Campbell Fraser, succeeding W. R. Sorley, during which time he wrote for *The Scotsman*. In 1883 he was appointed professor of logic and philosophy at the University College of South Wales and Monmouthshire at Cardiff. From there he took up the chair of logic, rhetoric and metaphysics at St Andrews University and in 1891 he succeeded Campbell Fraser to the chair of logic and metaphysics at Edinburgh. He was awarded honorary degrees by St Andrews University (1892), Princeton (1898), Durham (1902) and Edinburgh (1919). He was elected a Fellow of the British Academy in 1904 and was invited to deliver the Gifford Lectures at Aberdeen (1912–13) and Edinburgh (1921–3). He retired in 1919.

In 1898, on the death of Mrs Pringle-Pattison, a distant relative, Seth inherited the family fortune and estate of The Haining, Selkirk in the Scottish Borders, on condition that he adopted her surname. Seth was not as actively involved in politics as many of the Idealists

and wrote little on social questions. He died at The Haining on 1
September 1931.

Biographical: *The Times*, 2 September 1931; *The Scotsman*, 2 September 1931; John Laird, 'Pattison, Andrew Seth Pringle- (1856–1931)', *Dictionary of National Biography 1931–41*; E. N. Merrington, 'A Scottish Thinker: Andrew Seth Pringle-Pattison', *The Australasian Journal of Psychology and Philosophy*, ix (1931); J. B. Baillie, 'Pringle-Pattison as Philosopher', *Proceedings of the British Academy* (1931); A. Seth Pringle-Pattison, *Balfour Lectures on Realism: With a Memoir by G. F. Barbour* (Edinburgh, Blackwood, 1933).

Principal works: *The Development from Kant to Hegel* (London, Williams and Norgate, 1882); *Hegelianism and Personality* (Edinburgh, Blackwood, 1887); *Man's Place in the Cosmos* (Edinburgh, Blackwood, 1897); *Studies in the Philosophy of Religion* (Oxford, Clarendon Press, 1930); *The Balfour Lectures on Realism* (Edinburgh, Blackwood, 1933).

DAVID GEORGE RITCHIE was born in Jedburgh, Scotland, on 26 October 1853, into a cultured family which included among its number academics and clergymen. His father was the parish minister, elected as moderator to the general assembly of the Church of Scotland in 1870. He was educated at Jedburgh Academy and entered Edinburgh University in 1869 where he was taught by Campbell Fraser and Henry Calderwood. He attended a botany class which stimulated a lifelong interest that would find expression in his ethical and political writings. He graduated in classics with first-class honours in 1875 and went on to Balliol College, Oxford. He was a tutor at Balliol from 1882–6. He was influenced by both T. H. Green and Arnold Toynbee. In 1894 Ritchie was appointed to the chair at St Andrew's. He was awarded an honorary LL.D. by Edinburgh University in 1898, and in 1898–9 he was president of the Aristotelian Society.

One of Ritchie's colleagues described him as a socialist and 'zealous' democrat whose way of thinking seemed to have little in common with ordinary people. He was an early member of the Fabian Society, but left in the mid-1890s. He was at the forefront in criticising the application of naturalistic theories of evolution to society. His *The Principles of State Interference* was one of the most widely read political tracts in the English-speaking world. Ritchie died on 3 February 1903 at St Andrews.

Biographical: E. S. Haldane, 'Ritchie, David George (1853–1903)', *Dictionary of National Biography 1901–1911*; Robert Latter, 'Memoir', in *Philosophical Studies by David D. Ritchie* (London, Macmillan, 1905).
Principal works: *Darwinism and Politics* (1889); *The Principles of State Interference* (1891); *Darwin and Hegel with other philosophical studies* (1893); *Natural Rights* (1894); *Studies in Political and Social Ethics* (1902). All published by Sonnenschein, London.

JOHN WATSON was born in the Gorbals, Glasgow, on 25 February 1847. After working as a clerk he entered Glasgow University in 1866 intending to become a minister, from which he was dissuaded by Edward Caird. Caird thought that Watson and Henry Jones were his best students, finding it difficult to decide between them when recommending a successor for his chair of Moral Philosophy at Glasgow in 1892. Jones, in the end, narrowly secured Caird's support. On the recommendation of Caird, Watson was appointed in 1872 to the chair of Logic, Metaphysics and Ethics at the traditionally Presbyterian University of Queen's in Kingston, Ontario, Canada. In 1889 he became Professor of Moral Philosophy, and was Vice-Principal from 1901–1924. He was awarded the degree of LL.D. by Glasgow University in 1880 and later by the University of Toronto. Michigan awarded him a Litt. D., and Knox College, Toronto, a D.D. Watson was a charter member of the Royal Society of Canada which was founded in 1882, and was the first Canadian to be invited to deliver the Gifford Lectures at Glasgow University (1910–12). He died in Kingston at the age of ninety-one. Watson was very influential in shaping university education in Canada.
Biographical: R. C. Wallace, *Some Great Men of Queen's* (Toronto, Ryerson, 1941); W. E. McNeill, 'John Watson', *Proceedings of the Royal Society of Canada*, 3rd series, xxxiii (1939); D. D. Calvin, *Queen's University at Kingston* (Kingston, Ontario, Queen's, 1941); *The Times*, 28 January and 3 February 1939; *Kingston Whig Standard* (Canada), 28 January 1939.
Principal works: *An Outline of Philosophy*, 4th ed. (1908); *The Interpretation of Religious Experience* (1912); *The State in War and Peace* (1919). All published by Maclehose, Glasgow.

Select bibliography of secondary sources

A. J. M. Milne, *The Social Philosophy of English Idealism* (London, Allen and Unwin, 1962); Melvin Richter, *The Politics of Conscience: T. H. Green and his Age* (London, Weidenfeld and Nicolson, 1964); Peter Gordon and John White, *Philosophers as Educational Reformers* (London, Routledge, 1979); I. M. Greengarten, *Thomas Hill Green and the Development of Liberal-Democratic Thought* (Toronto, University of Toronto Press, 1981); Andrew Vincent and Raymond Plant, *Philosophy, Politics and Citizenship* (Oxford, Blackwell, 1984); Geoffrey Thomas, *The Moral Philsophy of T. H. Green* (Oxford, Clarendon Press, 1987); Peter P. Nicholson, *The Political Philosophy of the British Idealists* (Cambridge, Cambridge University Press, 1990); David Boucher and Andrew Vincent, *A Radical Hegelian: The Social and Political Thought of Henry Jones* (Cardiff and New York, Wales University Press and St. Martin's Press, 1993); Alan P. F. Sell, *Philosophical Idealism and Christian Belief* (Cardiff, University of Wales Press, 1995). Sandra M. den Otter, *British Idealism and Social Explanation: A Study in Late Victorian Theory* (Oxford, Clarendon Press, 1996).

A note on the text

The selection of texts reprinted here is meant to be representative of the political writings of the British Idealists and the debates to which they contributed. T. H. Green's political writings are already available in a Cambridge University Press edition, *Lectures on the Principles of Political Obligation and Other Writings*, ed. P. Harris and John Morrow (1986). I have therefore included only one item from Green. I have chosen not to reprint F. H. Bradley's 'My Station and its Duties' because it has for too long mistakenly been identified as his own ethical position. Peter Nicholson has, however, convincingly shown that the theory of 'My Station and its Duties' is a partial and one-sided representation that gives a view of the external content of morality which, in the next chapter of *Ethical Studies*, Bradley then goes on to qualify by giving morality an internally generated source for its content, and point of reference for criticism of the external content. 'Ideal Morality' is, therefore, reprinted here as Bradley's ethical position. Had the collection been longer I would have included a section on punishment, an issue that exercised the mind of many a Victorian reformer.

The British Idealists had a habit of quoting from a variety of sources without giving references. Where I have had to add to their own footnotes, denoted by superscript letters of the alphabet, my additions appear in square parentheses. My own footnotes are denoted by Arabic numerals.

The sources for the items reprinted here are the following: 1, *Essays in Philosophical Criticism*, ed. Andrew Seth and R. B. Haldane (London, Longmans Green, 1883). 2, Andrew Seth, *Man's Place in the Cosmos* (Edinburgh and London, Blackwood, 1897). 3, *Aspects of the Social Problem*, ed. Bernard Bosanquet (London, Macmillan, 1895). 4, *Ethical Democracy: Essays in Social Dynamics*, ed. S. Coit (London, Swan Sonnenschein, 1900). 5, F. H. Bradley, *Ethical Studies*, 2nd edn (Oxford, Clarendon Press, 1927). 6, *Aspects of the Social Problem*, ed. Bernard Bosanquet (London, Macmillan, 1897). 7, D. G. Ritchie, *Darwin and Hegel with other philosophical studies* (London, Swan Sonnenschein, 1893). 8, *International Journal of Ethics*, 16 (1906). 9, Inaugural lecture to the Civic Society of Glasgow (Glasgow, Maclehose, 1897). 10, Henry Jones, *The Working Faith of the Social Reformer* (London, Macmillan, 1910). 11, T. H. Green, *Lectures on the Principles of Political Obligation*, ed. Bernard Bosanquet (London, Longmans Green, 1917). 12, *The Fortnightly Review*, 1 August 1900. 13, *Queen's Quarterly*, 23 (1916). 14, Bernard Bosanquet, *Social and International Ideals: Being Studies in Patriotism* (London, Macmillan, 1917).

Evolution and society

I
The Social Organism
HENRY JONES

English ethical philosophy is no longer purely individualistic. Hume pursued the principles of individualism to their logical conclusion, and refuted it as a theory of knowledge by revealing the absolute scepticism which it involves. The question which lies at the basis of the 'Critique of Pure Reason' shows that Kant considered Hume's work final, and individualism an exhausted vein of thought. History also corroborated the destructive teachings of Hume when individualism received its practical refutation in the French Revolution. Both theoretically and practically the disintegrating movement of thought completed its work and exhausted itself at the close of the last century. It isolated the individual from his physical and spiritual surroundings, and then found that he was only the shadow of a false philosophy. The present age is abandoning the philosophy which regarded mind as a thinking thing acting *in vacuo*, it has lost faith in moral Melchisedecs, and it demands from all the genealogy of their habits of thought and action.[1] The problems of individualism are losing their interest, and fresh problems, which lay beyond the horizon of the past age, have by the silent progress of thought come into the fore-front of our own. The educated attention of the present is directed to the relations of individuals rather than to individuals themselves: and these relations are regarded, in a more or less uncertain sense, as essential to, if not constitutive of, individuals. Modern speculation is, in a word, reconstructive in its tend-

[1] This appears to be a reference to Melchizedek, king of righteousness. He was priest of the 'supreme El' and king of Salem, to whom even Abraham had to pay tithes.

ency. It endeavours to free itself of its inherited atomism, and fit the individual into his surroundings. Theories of society are supplanting theories of the individual; and when the individual is made the subject of investigation he is found, at the worst, to be altruistic as well as egoistic.

But although English philosophy is moving away from the problems and practical issues of individualism, it is still, in a great degree, ruled by its presuppositions. Such writers as Mr. Spencer still speculate on its principles, although the thoughts which give them power are alien to it. Like the servants of the wounded Ahab, they stay their master in his chariot till the eve.[2] The interest and worth of the ethical speculations of Mr. Spencer arise from the use which he makes of the conceptions of evolution and organism; but no torture of individualism can cause it to yield these conceptions. They have been adopted out of the current thought of the age on scientific subjects, and then superimposed on an alien philosophy. Having proved themselves useful in the field of biology to a degree which it is difficult to over-estimate, they have been immediately applied to that of ethics. Nor do these ideas receive a new meaning from their new application, but they retain in the new context the significance that they had in the old. Now the ideas that are true and relevant in one sphere can be applied to another and different sphere only in the way of analogy and metaphor; and we believe that Mr. Spencer's ethical teachings as a whole consist on the one hand of an inherited Hedonism, and on the other of elaborate analogies drawn between the physical structures and habits of animals and the mental structure and ethical habits of men.

Such at all events is his doctrine of the organic structure of society. The living body is regarded as the type of an organic existence, and society is regarded as organic in so far, and in so far only, as it is like a living body. A quotation from his answer to the question, 'What is a society?' will establish our assertion. 'But now, regarding a society as a thing, what kind of thing must we call it? ... There are two great classes of aggregates with which the social aggregate may be compared – the inorganic and the organic. Are the attributes of a society, considered apart from its living units,

---

[2] Ahab was the king of Israel from around 871–852 BC. His wife Jezebel attempted to import foreign elements into religion and government, including the worship of Baal.

in any way like those of a not-living body? or are they in any way like those of a living body? or are they entirely unlike those of both?

'The first of these questions needs only to be asked to be answered in the negative. A whole of which the parts are alive, cannot, in its general characters, be like lifeless whole. The second question, not to be thus promptly answered, is to be answered in the affirmative. The reasons for asserting that the permanent relations among the parts of a society are analogous to the permanent relations among the parts of a living body, we have now to consider.'[a]

In his next chapter accordingly, Mr. Spencer finds these analogies in great abundance and displays them with great ingenuity. Society grows like a living body; it goes through processes of differentiation and integration like a living body; it adapts itself to its environment like a living body; it has alimentary, distributive, and regulative structures like a living body; it is now starved and now overfed like a living body; it has up-line and down-line railways like the double set of tubes in a living body. In this strain he has proceeded far, but there is no reason in the nature of *things* why he should not have proceeded further; for ingenuity has a greater hand than truth in the production of analogies, and there are no two objects in the universe absolutely different from each other.

'Do you see that cloud, that's almost in shape like a camel?' 'By the mass, and 'tis like a camel, indeed.' 'Methinks, it is like a weasel.' 'It is backed like a weasel.' 'Or, like a whale?' 'Very like a whale.'[3]

In his 'Qualifications and Summary' (Vol. 1. p. 614), however, Mr. Spencer says that he has 'used the analogies elaborated but as a scaffolding to help in building up a coherent body of sociological inductions.' 'Let us', he continues, 'take away the scaffolding; the inductions will standby themselves.' But an examination will show that the scaffolding has been built into his edifice, and that the structure tumbles down with its removal. Or, dropping metaphor, the moment that society ceases to be like a 'living body' it ceases to be organic. Abandoned by the 'living body' which guides him, Mr. Spencer stumbles into individualism. Failing to detect a social

---

[a] [Herbert Spencer, *Principles of] Sociology*, [London, Williams and Norgate, 1876] vol. 1, p. 466.

[3] Shakespeare, *Hamlet*, Act Three, Scene Two, Hamlet and Polonius.

sensorium by the method which revealed the social stomach and nervous system, Mr. Spencer acknowledges that there is an 'extreme unlikeness', a 'fundamental difference', between the social organism and the individual organism. 'The parts of an animal form a concrete whole; but the parts of a society form a whole that is discrete.'[b] Now, no one can deny the discrete character of society; and it will always remain true 'that the living units composing it are not in contact, but more or less widely dispersed.' But if society is an organic whole this discreteness must be overcome, and unity must assert itself through and amidst the differences. In other words, the notions that society is 'discrete' and that it is a 'whole' cannot be immediately combined in this way; and discreteness cannot be the permanent characteristic of that which is organic. But waiving this objection for the present, it is at least evident that the notion of discreteness is fatal to the organism of a living body. Hence society is inorganic because discrete; or, the living body is inorganic because concrete; or the living body is not the type and test of that which is organic.

Mr Spencer silently admits the first of these suppositions, and treats society in this particular as if it were inorganic. 'In the one' (the individual organism) he says, 'consciousness is concentrated in a small part of the aggregate. In the other it is diffused throughout the aggregate. . . . As, then, there is no social sensorium, it results that the welfare of the aggregate, considered apart from that of the units, is not an end to be sought. The society exists for the benefit of its members; not its members for the benefit of society.'[c]

Before attempting to show that Mr. Spencer in this passage treats society as if it were nothing more than an aggregate, and from an individualistic point of view, it will be well to note that 'the welfare of the aggregate considered apart from that of the units' is a welfare which no one can contend for or conceive. Verily, 'the claims of the body politic are nothing *in themselves*, and become something only in so far as they embody the claims of its component individuals. 'No one can deny that society apart from individuals is nothing; but this does not mean that the individual, as an individual, is everything. It is true that society is nothing apart from individuals; but,

[b] Spencer, *Sociology*, I, 475.
[c] Spencer, *Sociology*, I, 479.

if society is organic, it is equally true that *individuals apart from society* are nothing. Society must exist for the benefit of its component parts, and the component parts must also exist for-the benefit of society. Nay, more, if society is an organism, then it is impossible to separate the welfare of the whole from the welfare of the members, or the welfare of the members from the welfare of the whole. To separate the one from the other is to give independent existence to unreal abstractions and to empty the notion of organic unity of its distinctive content.

Mr. Spencer denies society as an end and makes it a means by which the welfare of individuals is secured; the last and the only end is the welfare of the individuals composing it. But means and end, first of all, exist apart from each other – the former has an existence and a meaning in itself, and the latter has also an existence and meaning in itself and for itself; and, secondly, the meaning of the former is cancelled in that of the latter. The means, say, of the ethical elevation of the life of the nineteenth century is the teaching of Mr. Spencer; that teaching then must first of all *be*, independently of the attainment of its end. If, on the other hand, it attains the end for which it exists, then it is dispensed with, lost in the end, and will be thrown aside as a husk when it has been absorbed into the characters of nineteenth-century Englishmen. Society, if it is a means for individuals, must in the first place exist outside and independently of its individuals, just as this pen exists apart from the ink which flows through it. But society, as Mr. Spencer admits, does not, and never has existed apart from the individuals composing it, and was, therefore, never mere means, but always means + something more. Again, if it is mere means, then, like all other means, it must perish in the attainment of its end; every society, therefore, that secures the welfare of its members perishes in the very act. But, as a matter of fact, it is the society which fails to secure the welfare of its members that is disintegrated, and not that which succeeds in doing so. The ideal of a progressive society which is mere means is the absolute disintegration of itself and the production of isolated, mutually independent individuals; and Mr. Spencer's chapter on 'Society is an Organism' should, consistently with this view, show how, as the world moves, the unity of society becomes more and more disintegrated and dissipated. Moreover, an individual who regards society as mere means, regards the individuals constituting society as mere means – unless society be something apart from them, which neither Mr. Spencer nor anyone else admits; and, if every individual regards his neighbours as means, then the rank and destructive individualism which, in the French Revolution, rent asunder every political and social bond, is the theoretic ideal; and the world is making for the state of nature in which its wise men will be running wild in the woods, and, as Voltaire suggests, 'running on all fours'.[4]

The conception of means and end is, however, not applicable to an organism. It is because that conception breaks down into difference, and, instead of expressing the intimacy and complexity of the relations of whole and members, holds them apart at arm's length, that the conception of organic unity becomes necessary. In the presence of even the lowest life, the scientific point of view must be abandoned for the philosophic.

The perfection of organic well-being is that the collective activities seem to be one. The physical organism into which no alien ingredient, material, chemical, electric, or nervous, has penetrated, 'has no system'; its life is 'a beam of perfect white light, itself unseen, because it is of that perfect whiteness, and no irregular obstruction has yet broken it into colours.' Its energy is one and indivisible; at no time can we say 'here is the activity of the member, there that of the whole'; for the activity of the member *is* that of the whole, and that of the whole is the activity of the members. The unity, because it is an organic unity, must not only persist under the differences, but it must differentiate itself, flow out into the parts, and again integrate the differences and flow back through the parts into unity. Here there is none of the self-seeking of means and end. No member secures its welfare at the expense of the whole: indeed it has no welfare except that which is also the welfare of the concrete organism.

If society therefore is an organism, it exists not only as end but also as means. The life that animates the individual is that of the social whole as much as it is his own. His purpose is not his own particular welfare, nor is it the particular welfare of his neighbours;

---

[4] In a letter from Voltaire to Rousseau, dated 31 August 1761, Voltaire says: 'One feels like crawling on all fours after reading your work.' *Correspondance complète de Jean-Jacques Rousseau*, édition critique établie et annotée par R. A. Leigh (Genève, Institut et Musée Voltaire, 1969).

but it is the welfare of the social whole to which they all belong and which lives in them. The notion of organic unity involves that the individual, cut away from society, becomes a severed limb, a lifeless, meaningless mass; that without the purposes of society he has no purposes at all, and cannot even be egoistic: and that the life which he perverts to selfish ends is not merely his own but that of the moral organism which lives in him.

> The light that led astray
> Was light from heaven,[5]

and heaven holds him responsible; for, although he went astray, 'twas light *from heaven*'.

The real meaning of the doctrine that society is an organism is, that an individual has no life except that which is social, and that he cannot realise his own purposes except in realising the larger purposes of society. No concatenation of parts, no contiguity in space, no joints and ligatures, can bind members into an organism. The bond must be inward, not outward; it must be essential, not accidental; it must be such, in a word, that the parts fall asunder into meaningless abstractions when the bond is broken. Whatever the difficulties may be in finding the unity of the social organism, if we hold by the doctrine and make it more than a metaphor, we must recognise that society and individuals actually form such a whole, and that apart from each other they are both nothing but names; and we must cease to speak of individuals as if they ever could exist apart from society, or could attain their purposes except by becoming its organs and carrying out its purposes. It seems to me that the first and last duty of man is to know and to do those things which the social community of which he is a member calls upon him to do. His mission is prescribed to him by the position

---

[5] Robert Burns,

> I saw thy pulse's maddening play,
> Wild send the Pleasure's devious way,
> Misled by Fancy's meteor ray,
> By passion driven;
> But yet the light that led astray
> Was light from heaven

The Works of Robert Burns (Edinburgh, James Thin, 1895), vol. i, xcii, 'The Vision', Stanza XVIII, lines 103–8, p. 239.

in society into which he is born and educated, and his welfare depends upon its performance. Hamlet did not create his duties: the time was already out of joint, and he was born to set it right. The demand was not made by himself nor by any other individual, but by the ethical organism of which he was a member, by the spirit of the age whose instrument he was. Nor is this the case with princes alone. Everyone, however humble, finds his duties in the social organism. Let society be dumb, let it cease to prescribe duties and have purposes of its own, and every individual component must hold his hands idle. The interests which men have differ widely in extent, but the interests of all are the interests of the station or circle which constitutes their society, and all do their duties to themselves if they give themselves up to these interests and constitute themselves consciously into organs of their 'universal'. We have very different views about the extent of the ethical horizon, and our sky is often so low that we strike it with our sublime heads, but still the large heavens shelter us all. The humblest breast rises and falls with the breath of the universal, and our ethical salvation consists in being its willing organs. The heart beats, the brain operates, the hand works, through the power and for the sake of the whole; and the highest moral ambition consists in sacrificing particular ends and realising those of the social organism. The social ends comprise the highest ends of all men, for the ends of all are but the product of the organic life which differentiates itself in the individuals and returns through them enriched. But Mr. Spencer's social organism is not this; it is rather a resultant, a mechanical and temporal equipoise produced by the opposition and collision of individuals, each of whom seeks his own welfare and not that of society. If society has no purposes, if there are nothing but ends of individuals, it is difficult to see how the organism is, after all, anything better than an aggregate. The social whole is unable to gather itself back out of its discreteness, and it is inorganic because it is 'fundamentally' unlike a 'living body'.

Must we then give up the doctrine of the organic nature of society? Does the organic idea as well as the organic metaphor break down before the discreteness of society? Or may it not be proved that society is more concrete as well as more discrete than any physical type of organism; that it is more concrete *because* it is more discrete; and that its self-integration is more intense because its

self-differentiation is more complete? In a word, may not society be
unlike a living body because it is *more* organic, and not because it
is less so? I think it may, and must endeavour to prove it. We cannot
here attempt to trace the organic idea in its successive manifes-
tations from the vegetable and animal organism up to humanity. It
may be at present sufficient to *assert* that it is first manifested in a
living body, and not in a dead body: and that it is the life – whether
that be, as Mr. Spencer teaches, a power to adapt itself to its
environment or not – and not the tissues and nervous currents,
which bind the parts into a unity. Tissues and currents can only
consist of contiguous atoms: their parts, however thinned and eth-
erealised, lie outside of each other. Tissues and currents are only
parts of an organism, but by means of sensation they are retracted
out of their outwardness and become organs. I know that my hand
is a part of my physical organism, not primarily because I know
that it is connected to it by nervous currents, but because it is a
source of pain or pleasure to *me*. Sensation abolishes difference. As
long as it lasts organ and organism are not distinguishable, but the
whole organism in its concrete existence is present in all its sensations. It is not the palate that feels pleasure or the ear that feels
pain, but it is the organism as a unit that feels the pleasure and the
pain. Although sensation, however, gathers up the parts into an
intense unity, it does not gather them into *permanent* unity. Sensation is itself fleeting; and when it vanishes, the organism falls back
into difference and its parts are indifferent to it. Sensations may
appear in quick succession, like the atoms of a fluid, but nevertheless they can but repeat the same tale, assert the unity of the organism and then deny it in disappearing. Sensations overcome the outwardness of space, and are themselves overcome by the discreteness
of time. But when sensations are related to the ego, when they are
known as *in me*, or as *mine*, then they attain fixity and permanence.
They are no longer a mere manifold *capable* of being arranged by
the intelligence; they are not merely expressed by inarticulate cries;
but can be spoken of and described as pleasant or painful, sweet or
bitter. In a word, they are thoughts, integral parts of my intellectual
possessions that will to some degree modify my future. The unity
of the organism, which was not present in the physical structure,
and which was only temporarily manifest in sensation, becomes in
consciousness a permanent fact. In a more accurate way, and by

entirely repudiating this dualism of sense and thought, it might be said that the thought which exists as sensation does not come to itself in sensation, does not overcome its own difference by knowing itself, as it does in self-conscious existence. The life of an animal is not a complete unity because it is not a unity for the animal itself. The animal, or at any rate the being which is only sensitive, is not a permanent object to itself; it cannot return upon its sensations and weld them into a single, united experience. It cannot overcome the difference of time. It lives in the moment, and it cannot constitute the past into the possibility of its future, or the future into the motive of the present. In truth it has no past, present, or future, but an undistinguished, ever-recurring *now*. To an observer the life of an animal may present a rude outline of the complex organism of his own life, for consistent processes are carried on through long periods of time by the animal. Means are subordinated to ends, proximate ends to further ends, and the whole to an ultimate and all-embracing end. Nor are such concatenations as we find in the actions of a bird in building its nest and in producing and protecting its young accidental or meaningless. They suggest a life ruled by an end. But it is difficult to believe that the animal itself grasps this end. The unerring and direct character of its actions precludes such a notion. The end is nature's and not the animal's. The animal's function is to obey laws which it cannot disobey, to realise purposes which it has not understood, to be an instrument in the hand of a power which *has* purposes and which attains these purposes through the actions of the animal. It is, however, a matter for science, and not for philosophy, to determine what animal first realises the meaning of its own life; where the line between consciousness and self-consciousness is drawn is perfectly indifferent, at least to idealism; and all that we need insist upon here is that the animal which is incapable of grasping its own end is an instrument, and not an organism in the true sense of the word. The necessity of the actions of such a living body lies outside of itself. But the necessity of a thing is its deepest meaning, and the instrument can only be adequately explained in the end for which it exists. Hence the significance, the meaning, of the animal's life not only lies beyond its own grasp, but can only be found in the whole of which the animal is a part. The naturalist knows the animal when he recognises it as a manifestation of some of the laws of nature, and looks at it from the point of view of the species. In other words, it is the wisdom of *nature* that he detects maintaining itself as an unbroken unity amidst all the differences of the sensitive and atomic life of the animal; and it is by no means the wisdom of the animal itself. The meaning of the life of the animal, the thought, which it is, and on account of which it is intelligible, does not come back to itself; and hence it is not completely organic.

But in the intellectual and practical life of man thought is at home with itself. The meaning of a man's life is within his own grasp. He can stand above his environment, look before and after, recognise the forces which play around him, and by recognising them overcome them. Like every other animal, he has to assert himself against the complex powers of his environment, which tend to dissipate his life into the self-external atomism of inorganic exist-ence. But, unlike other animals, he can detach himself from his environment – i.e. know himself as existing apart from it. He can *understand* his environment, and by understanding it he can take its necessity into himself; or, in other words, he can impress the environment with the stamp of his own intelligence and elevate the natural into the spiritual. The struggle between man and his surroundings is unequal, and must end in the victory of spirit. For the conditions imposed upon a man by his environment are nothing to him until they have penetrated into his consciousness, and when they have done that they have subjected themselves to a power which has transmuted them. They are no longer mere conditions but *thoughts* – parts of the possession of the power which under-stands them. Into the 'crystal sphere' of the intelligence nothing can enter except by giving up its opposition and submitting to become a part of that sphere. In fact, the struggle between the-self-conscious being and his environment must not be compared to the collision of two balls, or the clash of two forces in the same plane. Man is not a particular amongst particulars. Thought does not cease to be where the physical world begins, but it overlaps it and brings it back interpreted into itself. Man, as a rational being, is his own limit. Whatever the necessity may be which encircles his life, it cannot affect his character until he has put his signature to it, adopted it, and made it his motive. But if it is his motive it is *in* him, not around him or above: it is his own necessity and not an alien one. It is not our intention to minimise the significance of that necessity the voice of which we hear, if we are considerate, long before time has furrowed our faces, saying with omnipotent authority, 'This way shalt thou go, not that.' But yet the necessity has no ethical character until I have given it meaning. The humblest can use the words of Caesar and say-

> We were two lions litter'd in one day,
> And I the elder and more terrible.[6]

My poverty, my wealth, my health, my sickness, seem almost everything to me; but they are not everything; that which is greatest, after all, is that power which I have of constituting my poverty, my wealth, my health, and my sickness, into my bane or my blessing, my good or my evil. It is I, in the end, who give my surroundings significance.

This doctrine, old as the record of the choice of the forbidden fruit, is the Alpha and Omega of ethics. Man is self-conscious, man is free, man is his own limit, his own necessity, his own fate; this is the last foundation of every theory of ethics which has any meaning. For if this is not true, if man serves purposes which he can neither reject nor accept, if he is the slave of his conditions, then ethics will be a science which treats of the conditions of actions and not the science of human life. Ethics should then be laid aside with astrology, as a science of that which is not; a plaything of the world's infancy, unworthy of the attention of a scientific age. Science should turn away from man, and endeavour only to understand the huge mechanism with which the human cog or crank moves, it should reveal the absurdity of practical hortative ethics, and teach that good and evil are but names of phenomena that appear in man, and emanate out of his conditions. Freedom, self-consciousness, the organic completeness of man, is the fact with which ethics begins and ends; and we cannot begin lower, as Mr. Spencer does, unless we believe that animals, too, are moral and immoral, are ends in themselves,

[6] Shakespeare,

> danger knows full well
> That Caesar is more dangerous than he:
> We are two lions litter'd in one day,
> And I the elder and more terrible:
> And Caesar shall go forth.

Julius Caesar, Act Two, Scene Two.

and therefore not to be used as instruments by man. But the necessity to live will be a sufficient practical defence against this side of Mr. Spencer's 'data of ethics'; for we cannot afford to recognise the life of every creeping thing as of infinite value in itself. In the sphere of nature we shall still seek for utility; we shall still recognise that the end for which the life that is not self-conscious exists lies beyond that life, and protect the life by using it with reference to its end.

But on the other hand freedom cannot be disproved, because it is impossible for intelligence to disprove itself by making itself a mere instrument. It is intelligence that guides the disproof as well as the proof; the disproof is only a new manifestation of the existence and energy of intelligence. Reason cannot commit suicide although man can, and absolute scepticism is impossible. 'It is a medicine which removes itself as well as the disease.'[7] Every effort made by theoretical and practical reason is but a reassertion of its own infinitude; it is not the establishment, but the removal, of a limit; it is a process by which something which *was* not for the individual is brought within and made a part of his intellectual or moral being.

In this sense Mr. Spencer's view of society as a 'discrete' whole is true; for every individual is his own limit, a complete organism, with his meaning in himself. The discreteness, however, is far deeper than anything which finds expression in Mr. Spencer's writings. For the social organism is not only 'sensitive' in every part, but it is self-conscious in every part. Individuals are not merely 'not in contact', but they are ethically isolated in so far as everyone is always his own end. Good and evil are farther from each other than the east and west; and a ruptured society is not so easily put together as a broken pot. The forces that hold men asunder have a stronger repellent power than anything material. Hence, if society is organic, it must conquer difference in its strongest citadel, and conquer it too by ethical means. No theory of the organism of society can avail, if in its ardour to reconstruct society it does violence to the individual's independence and compromises his right to seek his own welfare. Man must be fitted into his surroundings, and made the means of the good of society without compromising

---

[7] I have been unable to find the source of this quotation.

his right to realise his own purposes. It is not enough to emphasise his environment, and make him, as Mr. Spencer does, a mere vane which turns round when the wind shifts; for, unless freedom is a myth and ethics a scientific superstition, life is more than a process of self-adaptation. It adapts the environment to itself as well as itself to its environment, and this is a side which Darwinian development, in all its applications, tends to minimise. For the environment which this age is never weary of emphasising, and which individualism of necessity neglects, is after all but the raw material of the life, and only *capable* of being converted into physical or intellectual wealth by the energy of that life. Whatever be the influence of an individual's surroundings, however deeply he is indebted to the past for what he is at present, true as it must be that he is in some sense the heir of the experience of the ages, it is also true that the experience of the ages must receive the stamp of the individual's own character, and thereby assume a meaning and form which could not be inherited.

The doctrine that society is an organism must take up the good that was in individualism into itself. No theory of ethics can afford to cast away the absolute liberty and infinite worth of the individual. Freedom has been bought at too great a price to be bartered away. It is the product of the toil of modern history from the time when Christ taught the equality and brotherhood of mankind, to the time when liberty, equality, and fraternity were abstractly realised in the French Revolution. Before the individual's growing consciousness of freedom, the Roman Empire, the Roman Church, and the terrors of a monotheistic God had to retire. The world at length has been educated into an uncompromising consciousness of its right to freedom, and the individual is now bidden see to himself. This freedom manifested itself in France as a freedom from restraint. It assumed a hostile attitude to the institutions of the time, swept away the accumulated wisdom of the past, and reduced the State into a *carte blanche*. Freedom has the same power in it still; it is omnipotent when opposed to restraint, simply because spirit is stronger than nature. But yet this freedom is itself the only permanent bond of society. In the right of the individual to seek his own welfare lies the possibility of his seeking the welfare of the social organism. Or, to speak from the social point of view, society not only goes out into difference, and invests its component individuals with absolute rights, but gathers itself into a unity through that freedom which is at first repellent, and converts the rights of the individual into duties, and his self-seeking into a means of realising the general good. Out of the dust and powder of individuality it creates a nation which is one because its members are free, and whose members are free because they live its life in their own. The organism of society is only possible because its components are themselves organic. The bond of the social organism, that which is its self-differentiating, self-integrating life, is freedom.

How then is the freedom of the individual consistent with and *constitutive* of the organism of society is the question that now remains. At first there seems to be a contradiction between the individual's right to realise himself, and his duty to realise the purposes of society. When the individual first becomes conscious of his freedom, and recognises that he is to walk in the light of his own spirit, he assumes a negative attitude towards all that seems to limit this freedom. The State with its laws, Society with its habits, the Church with its dogmas, present themselves to him as restraints. It is therefore his highest duty to himself to oppose them; for neither Church, nor Society, nor State can dictate to a free man, and the only categorical imperative to him is that of freedom. Every action is dead unless it is born of freedom, the rights of subjectivity are the highest, and man cannot be compelled to contradict that which is his spiritual life. This, the inviolable character of a free man, was the good which worked amidst the ruins of the French Revolution.

But a deeper consciousness of freedom reveals the abstractness and unreality of subjective liberty. The freedom of indifference has received its quietus from Kant, and it is on all sides theoretically recognised that freedom from limit is freedom *in vacuo*, incapable of movement from the sheer absence of resistance. An individual who is free in this sense repudiates all that comes from without to determine his actions. He can act just as he chooses. He may go here, or there, or nowhere; he may do this, or that, or nothing. He recognises no demands that arise from his environment; they are not *duties*; and the '*ought*' is nothing more than inherited habit clad in the terrors of inherited superstition. His actions must flow from the abundance of his own heart, and not be wrung out of him by the pressure of law and duty. His freedom has superannuated him. He finds all his motives in himself. But then comes the question,

what motives *can* he find in himself? Is the demand that he find his
motives in himself not equivalent to a demand that he should lift
himself up by his own waistband? A motive is a reason for action
of some sort. This reason or motive is *there*, independent of and
outside the individual. It is that which he reaches after, and seeks
to bring into himself through his action. Were the end or motive
already in him there would be no action. An action arises from a
consciousness of limit, and a consciousness of something beyond
the limit. Every action seeks after some ideal which is in the future,
and the ideal, whether it be true or false, a self or a state of self, is
ever outside the present self. Man cannot then find a motive *in
himself*. Subjective freedom, freedom from all limit, is therefore
nothing more than absolute incapacity to act at all.

Both philosophy and history indicate that the first escape from
this bare and motionless freedom is into caprice. As a matter of fact,
the individual who repudiates all outward restraint gives himself up
to the satisfaction of his own desires, and Hedonism in some of its
forms has ever been the prevalent theory of ethics to a people freed
from external limit. Hedonism flourished when the paternal Greek
States ceased to engross the citizen, when the Roman Empire
became indifferent to the individuals that lived within it, and when
the terrors of a monarchical God and the restraints of Puritanism
lost their hold on English minds. But the escape into the pursuit of
pleasure is only an escape into the tyranny and monotony of passion
and caprice. To pursue pleasure is to pursue pleasant sensations;
and sensations are particular not only in the sense that they are the
individual's own, but in the sense that they are fleeting, and have a
semblance of permanence only when they are repeated. This pure
Hedonism we cannot here criticise, further than to endeavour in a
few words to show that because its ideal is particular it has no
ethical character. In the first place, the individual is the sole judge
of that which gives him pleasure, for his sensations are his own and
incommunicable. He can induce his neighbour to read a book or
taste a wine which gives pleasure to himself, he can lay before him
the conditions of his own pleasure; but he cannot communicate the
pleasure to his neighbour, for the pleasure involves the relation of
the conditions to the neighbour's feelings. His neighbour can turn
upon him and say, 'This wine, or this book, gives me no pleasure';
and there is no room for argument. Each individual is the measure

of all things, and he is the measure of all things because he is a sensitive being. Hence Hedonism can afford no universal law. The well-worn 'profligate' has every right, on this view, to prefer the future pain and discontent of self-indulgence and self-degradation to the present pain of self-restraint. He may be pitied in his disappointment, but he has not acted immorally, for he sought his pleasure and endeavoured to realise the ethical ideal.

In the second place, Hedonism can afford no imperative; there is no '*must*' or '*ought*' in the system. This follows immediately from the fact that Hedonism has no universal. The only apparent imperative is, that the individual ought to seek his own pleasure. But this 'ought' is not objective simply because a state of the individual's own feelings is the ideal, and 'state of feelings' is entirely within. The imperative springs from the particular self, and the particular self may at any moment turn round upon the ought, and say, 'I ought not.' But if there is no imperative binding on the individual, then ethics is a mere matter of choice; and no free action is *not* a matter of choice. The drunkard chooses to be drunk rather than sober, the suicide chooses strangling rather than life, and Hedonism turns round and says, 'You are both right, for you choose.'

In the third place, Hedonism can, strictly speaking, afford no ideal. It levels all actions, as already suggested. And, moreover, that which is sought after is a state of feelings, and not a self. The same self is projected into a different and future state; and this state cannot penetrate into the self without escaping out of the sphere of feeling into that of consciousness. Feeling, in other words, cannot attain any fixity; and perhaps the best refutation of Hedonism is the fact that in order to attain this ideal feeling we must forget it, as Mr. Mill admits. But if this be true, if the ideal must not be my conscious ideal, it cannot be an ideal at all. In order to live a life of pleasure, it is better to confine one's self to the moment and forget the future. Pleasure must not be the ideal because we cannot attain it by seeking it; and Hedonism admits of no other ideal. The truth of this contention is attested by the repeated attempts of a 'man of pleasure' to find his ideal in that which has disappointed him. After the satisfaction of that false appetite which comes from the projection of the infinitude of thought into a finite and particular object, comes the consciousness of failure. The ideal was false; he is where he was before. He has not accomplished that progress which an ideal involves. Hence comes the monotonous repetition of the same act and enslavement to a single passion. Life of pleasure is mere tautology; and the ideal is the 'bad infinite' which is both attained and missed in every pleasure-seeking action. The ideal is the-same self, and is therefore necessarily attained, but it is a different state of the self, and therefore passes away in the act of attainment. Hence, if Hedonism affords no ideal, the individual must confine himself to the present, and this is what practice teaches as well as theory. But life on these conditions would be disintegrated into a sensitive existence, where everything is well in so far as there is neither past nor future. Well might one say to the Hedonist,–

> 'Still thou art blest, compared wi' me,
> The present only toucheth thee,
> But, oh! I backward cast my ee
>   On prospects drear,
> And forward though I canna see,
> I guess and fear.[8]

Hedonism is an attempt to find the individual's motives in the individual's particular self. Its instruments are external, for pleasure is sought in a relation to objects, but its ideal, if we still call it so, is subjective. Hedonism seeks after no higher and larger self, but for a new state of the present self; whereas the very nisus of ethical action comes from the fact that morality is a sphere of comparison, and that the individual, holding his present self in the face of the self that he wishes to be, seeks to be another. Every effort of ethical life is an effort after regeneration. The ideal which the good man seeks to attain is one in which he would merge and forget the present self; and, compared with that, the 'state of feelings' is insignificant.

If, then, the individual cannot find the good in himself, where is he to seek it? The very assertion of the right of subjectivity has given rise to the need of escaping from it. Freedom from the restraint of duty has proved to be self-destructive. He who severs himself from his surroundings and lives entirely in and for himself, contradicts his freedom. As a matter of fact man cannot absolutely do so. We have never known an intelligent being who has lived

---

[8] Robert Burns, 'To a Mouse', *Works*, vol. 1, lxxvi, p. 160.

entirely apart from society; for an absolutely bad individual is an ethical impossibility. We can no more imagine an individual 'who has not suckled at the breast of the universal ethos',[9] who has not lived in a spiritual environment and converted (or perverted) that environment into his own nature, than we can conceive an oak tree which has grown where there is neither earth nor water nor air, without light and without darkness. In the environment he finds the raw material of his character; and there, too, he must find the standard of his action.

But what is that standard? Where can he find a *good* that is universal and imperative, and lifts him above the slavery of capricious subjectivity? Are we to find the law of conduct in a universal will which is opposed to the wills of all individuals as such?

In the first place, it is to be noticed that the good cannot, as Mr. Spencer contends, be evolved out of the struggles of individuals against their natural environment. The only motive that can come into play in such a struggle is that of the preservation of self as a particular existence. It is only in the presence of another self-conscious being, recognised as such and not reduced into a thing, that the individual finds it necessary to regulate his conduct according to a law other than his own caprice. It is in the collision of wills, as Rousseau teaches, that evil arises; and, we may add, there too does good. It is the collision of wills that first reveals the need and existence of a Universal will; a Universal will which stands equally above all individuals, and is, so far, the escape of all out of the caprice of subjectivity. But the Good will must be a universal in another sense also. It must be a permanent ideal, one that can always be realised by all without contradiction.

Nor has the individual the choice of obeying or not obeying it. The Good will confronts him with an imperative; it is armed with an ought from which there is no appeal. For if he is allowed a choice, morality is again subjected to caprice, and the individual lapses into that subjectivity from which he seeks to be free.

Lastly, the Good will is to be realised for its own sake. Obedience to it from desire to attain such a further good as that of the pleasure of virtuous conduct is obedience to pleasure and not to the will: the Universal will is but means that *happen* to be necessary. But the law

---

[9] These appear to be Jones's own words placed in quotation marks.

must be obeyed for its own sake, not from the contemplation of further good, nor from particular impulse, habit, or sentiment. The Good will must alone fill the mind, and the maxim of action will be to obey the law for the sake of the law. Thus escape from subjectivity is apparently found in a Universal, Objective, Imperative will. But is it an escape?

Our criticism of this law must be shorter even than our statement. This universal law is formal in the sense that it has no content and can suggest none, and yet is indifferent to any content. Nothing can be got out of it, and everything can be put under it. It demands that man should act from contemplation of duty; but its duty is duty in general, and man must act in *particular* ways and perform particular definite duties.

It is objective; but it is objective only because it is not *sub*jective. It is an eternal *not-self*, and as a pure *not-self* it is nothing to the individual. It so immediately suggests despair that it crushes effort. It is a universal which cannot be either realised in a particular action or by a particular being. It is universal and objective, but it is also alien. It is the demand of an alien law, and springs from an alien authority. But the true ethical ideal is a self as well as a not-self. It is the individual's future self, it is that which he conceives himself able to work into his own character, and what he wishes to be. By attaining it he attains his true self; apart from the attainment he *ought to be*, but is not. And here is the source of the categorical imperative. The good is my true self; and it is imperative because I must be real. It is an ethical necessity, deeper than the physical necessity, which compels me to maintain my existence. Lastly, the universal *is* not, until it is realised in the individual's life. Prior to that it is only an 'ought', a mere conception, a picture flung out by a well-intentioned individual on the canvas of the future. And unless the 'ought' *is*, it has no power over and no claim on the individual. The ethical ideal must not only be itself real, but it must be that which makes the individual real.

Thus the categorical imperative corrects the errors of subjectivity, but it falls itself into the opposite errors. The one ideal is a mere *seyn*, the other is a mere *sollen*; the one is subjective only, the other is objective only; the one is a mere particular, the other is a bare universal. Both are abstract, they each stand in need of the other. The ideal for the individual must be also real; the objective not-self must also be the individual's self, realisable though not realised; the universal must be also particular, and live in its own details. In a word, the good must be an organism really existing in the world and yet an ideal for every individual.

Such an ideal is found in the social organism, or rather in the moral organism which is embodied in the various forms of society. In it all the demands of what we may call subjectivity and objectivity are met. It is on the one hand not a mere 'ought', but really exists in the world. It is that to which the family, the social communities, and the State owe their strength and their stability. They *are*, because their laws are; and their laws are ethical facts. A family that departs from the ethical law of love, a commercial community which violates its law of measured rectitude, and a State which seeks no longer to advance the complex rights of the freedom of its components, already totter to their ruin. They cease to be, when that which 'ought' to be no longer is. But, on the other hand, the ideal is not a mere *seyn*, like, subjectivity. It is a law, an ideal, a *sollen* for the individual. The task of his life is to answer the demands of his station and to perform duties which he has not chosen, but finds imposed upon him by his social environment.

Moreover, the moral organism is not a formal universal without content, but is differentiated into laws and institutions which direct the conduct of individuals in the details of daily life. Nor is this ideal indifferent and alien to the individual. He himself gives voice to and interprets his social environment, and in that sense *creates* his ideal. He recognises the tasks which he finds in the sphere into which he has been educated as his duties, and therefore as the law of his action and his ideal self. And by this means he gives force to the social imperative. He knows himself to be moral only when he finds that he has duties, and he knows his duties and has duties only when he knows himself to be free; and he is free because there is a social imperative.

Thus subjective and objective, the self and the not-self, the particular and the universal, the individual and society, interpenetrate and become an organic whole. Society exists only in the individual, and the individual exists only in society. Apart from society the individual cannot realise his freedom; neither his own particular self nor the Universal will could afford him a single motive. The individual is free only because he finds his duties in society, and his duties are his ethical life. And, on the other hand, it is the freedom of the components of a society that gives the society real and permanent existence. It is because the State is a higher realisation of freedom that it has greater permanence than the family. The unity of the family, which is thought in the latent state of feeling, i.e. love, is broken against the growth of its components into maturity and independence, and is always in danger from its property; but the unity of the State, which is self-conscious, where every individual is his own master and carries his own responsibilities within him, this unity, like self-consciousness itself, is a unity that has overcome its differences and cannot be broken by them.The freedom of its components is the force of attraction that binds its members together. A State of slaves, for instance, is impossible. A slave has no rights, and therefore has no duties. In the eye of his master he is a *thing*, and a thing is not consulted and persuaded, but *forced*. The claims that are made on the slave are such that he will contend against, and if possible repudiate. And a State of slaves would be nothing but a sphere where force holds force in check. But such a State never existed; for no State can be alien to the individuals that compose it. A constitution which is either too good or too bad for a people cannot be held together. A people must feel *itself* in the constitution, find it to be *its* law of social life; that is, its necessity, its law of conduct must not be an alien necessity, but a necessity which the people has taken into itself and which therefore constitutes its freedom. The individual then finds his freedom in society, and society is possible only because its members are free.

It is on these accounts that society is an organism. Not because it is like an animal, and because the individual components are like joints and limbs; but because the individual realises himself as an ethical being in society, and society-realises itself in the individual. The individual is free because he is a member of society, and society realises its aims in the freedom of the individuals. Freedom is the *life* which forms the unity of the moral organism. The State, for instance, endows its individuals with freedom, and thereby creates an ethical claim on their services. It points out *duties* by means of its laws, and the duties have moral force because the laws are recognised by the individuals as their *own* laws, their own guide of conduct, their own ideal self, and not a foreign necessity. Freedom, the unity, the life, differentiates itself; it flows out into the individual in the form of rights, and returns to itself through its members in the form of services and duties.

The social organism is thus a concrete, living, self-integrating, self-differentiating whole, apart from which neither the universal – the abstract society, nor the particular – the abstract individual, can be. Isolated from each other they are but names; sunder their relations and they cease to exist. They exist in and through each other, and are constituted by their relation.

If this be true, then we can no longer speak of individual aims and individual welfare, apart from social aims and social welfare, any more than we can speak of social aims that are not also aims of individuals. The welfare of the individual is in the performance of his duty (whatever that be) and his duty is nothing other than the demand of his environment, the welfare of his sphere. From this point of view it becomes unnecessary to effect a 'compromise' or to 'conciliate' egoism and altruism – the last effort of inconsistent Hedonism to extend its narrow teachings so as to correspond with the facts of ethical life.[d] We have already endeavoured to show that egoism – pure subjectivity – is an impossible and self-contradictory aim. It remains to show that altruism is as one-sided as egoism; and that a man who, if he could, lived for the sake of others only, is as immoral as he who, if he could, lived solely for himself and in himself. Altruism is in fact the opposite abstraction to egoism. It is its logical other, just as the 'enthusiasm of humanity' of the Comtist, which tends to extinguish the individual for the sake of the general good,[e] is the logical counterpart of the teachings of Rousseau, which abolished the general good for the sake of the individual. The latter neglects the fact that the individual's life is universal, the former that the universal is particular, and that the purposes of humanity are those of the individuals composing it. Rousseau would not wash the feet of his neighbour. Comte would wash 'not his feet only but his hands and his head', and drown himself in addition.[10] Altruism

---

[d] Spencer's *Data of Ethics* [London, Williams and Norgate, 1879] chapters 13 and 14. [This book later became part I of *The Principles of Ethics*, published in 1892–3, republished by Liberty Classics, Indianapolis, 1978 from the 1897 edition.]

[e] See Comte's *Doctrine of Immortality*.

[10] *Bible*, John, 13:9.

as opposed to egoism is the realisation of the aims of another as opposed to the realisation of one's own aims. But morality from beginning to end is *self*-realisation. He who has made the welfare of the race his aim, has done so, not from a generous choice, but because he regards the pursuit of this welfare as his imperative duty. The welfare of the race is his own ideal; what he must realise in order to be what he *ought* to be. The welfare of the race is his own welfare, which he must seek because he must be *himself.* Cromwell, Luther, Mohammed, were heroes,[11] not because they did something over and above what they *ought* to have done, but because their *ideal self* was co-extensive with the larger self of their world. 'Ich kann nichts anders', was the voice of each.[12] A necessity had been laid on them as on Paul to 'preach their gospel'.[13] They were compelled by their conception of their duty to rise above the pursuits of mere individual or family welfare – to transcend the ordinary limits of the ethical efforts of ordinary individuals. Their large purposes were what they owed to themselves just as much as to their world. They were instruments in the hand of a divine power; for the good that is in the world called upon them with the stern imperative of duty. This imperative duty had become so truly their *own*, that they were its conscious willing instruments. It was their *enthusiasm*, it had penetrated their whole being, it *was* their whole being for it had absorbed them. The conflict between the particular and the universal self had ended in the victory of the latter, not by crushing the former but by penetrating it, and elevating even feeling into a power which worked for the good that had become their ideal.

Thus the largest altruism is after all but an earnest struggle for one's own ethical life. Altruism and egoism are but abstract theories that can attain meaning only when they are taken up into an organism in which altruism exists through egoism, and egoism through altruism. They are not 'compromised' or 'reconciled', but lost in that which takes both into itself. The progress of humanity is not from egoism to altruism, but from an egoism which is from the first

---

[11] This is an allusion to Thomas Carlylse, *Hero Worship* (London, Chapman, 1872). Mahomet is the hero as prophet, Luther as Priest, and Cromwell as king.

[12] 'I can do no other.' These are Martin Luther's words spoken at the Diet of Worms, 18 April 1521, and inscribed on his monument.

[13] *Bible*, St Paul, 69:2.

altruistic to an altruism which must ever remain egoistic. The growth of character is intensive as well as extensive, and intensive because extensive. If I have larger interests, I have a larger and deeper self. The life which seeks the welfare of the community as well as that of the family, of the State as well as of the community, and of humanity as well as the State, is a life that has brought their interests within itself and cannot realise itself except in them. Morality is not a generous knight-errantry which has to seek for wrongs to rectify. It ever finds the wrongs within itself; its earnest and engrossing business is to perform the duties that are its own and obey its own imperative. Morality is not a mere flow from the superabundance of a generous heart. 'It is a necessity which is not chosen but chooses.' It is not an ill-regulated generosity which is weakness rather than strength, which ruins its agent and pauperises its object; but it is a universal imperative, immovable and stern and eternal.

There is still one point which our limits will allow us to touch upon. The great difficulty of recognising the organic character of society, according to Mr. Spencer, comes from the fact that it has no individual consciousness. Its life, which, if it is an organism, ought to be *one* in the deepest sense, seems to be broken up amongst the individuals which compose it. 'Consciousness is diffused throughout the aggregate . . . There is no social sensorium.'[f] 'The parts of a society form a whole that is discrete . . . the living units composing it are free, not in contact, and more or less widely dispersed.'[g] We think Mr. Spencer's attempt to re-create the social unity by means of 'emotional language, and by the language, oral and written, of the intellect', inadequate and superficial, though we cannot here fully discuss it. For what is community of language apart from the deeper community of thought which it expresses? Is there such power in words, and will the universal brotherhood come by the adoption of one language? Even 'patriotic feeling' often asserts itself against a common language, and patriotic feeling roused into national excitement such as broke the strength of Napoleon in Spain is not an adequate bond of society. Language is a bond only where there is a deeper bond of common interests, and

<hr>

[f] Spencer's *Sociology*, I, p. 479.
[g] Spencer's *Sociology*, I, p. 475.

these interests are ultimately ethical, if they are permanent. Language is often one of the evidences of the unity of a social life, but it is not the unity itself.

Where, then, is the unity, the individual self-consciousness of the social organism? The directest answer is to say that there exists no such thing as individual self-consciousness. To seek it is to lapse back into that view which regards the individual as existing apart from the universal, and the universal apart from the individual. It is to neglect the fact that the individual is conscious of himself only because he has distinguished himself from his environment. But this distinction is impossible except in so far as he knows both in some degree. The division of the self and *not*-self is one of the facts I am certain of; the distinction is one of *my* ideas and is within me. Consciousness reaches under both factors; the individual overlaps his other; the notself is *his* not-self.

It is true that we cannot find a social sensorium or social pineal gland, and say of its self-consciousness, Lo here! or Lo there! But still the social organism is self-conscious, for it is conscious of itself in every self-conscious being. To say that I know myself in society is exactly equivalent to saying that society knows itself in me. In knowledge the universal and particular come together. But to illustrate. We have seen that the individual finds his duties confronting him in the social community of which he is a member. He finds them because they are *there*, ready to hand, awaiting his performance. But on the other hand they became duties only through his interpretation of them. They are duties only because he first recognises them and then adopts them. Or, to take another example, an artist finds an idea in a picture because it is *there*: and his neighbour, if he has a cultivated taste, will also find it there. The idea is in the picture for everyone. But, on the other hand, the idea comes into actual existence only when it is interpreted. The picture becomes something more than a mass of colours only when the idea is lifted out of the dead material by the power of an artistic intelligence. We can either say that the artist finds meaning in the picture, or that the picture reveals itself to the artist. We can either say that the scientific man discovers the thoughts of nature, or that the thoughts of nature reveal themselves to the scientific man. The idea of the transmutation of forces is that of the scientific man, but it is his only because it is nature's also. The true attitude of science is to abandon preconceived opinions, submit itself to nature, put itself in its path and on its lines, and wait for the interpretation which it gives of itself. The continued effort of experiment is an effort of the individual to place himself in such an attitude that he can hear nature speak. Experiment, in a word, is the abstraction of foreign elements, the help which the scientific man gives to nature, that its many sounds may be disentangled, and that its voice may be articulate. In science, in art, in ethics and theology, the individual must stoop to conquer; make himself the vehicle of the universal, and thereby both understand the universal and make it articulate.

As a literary half-poetic, half-mystic truth, it has long been recognised that a great man is the voice of his age, the articulate expression of its otherwise inarticulate forces. This we would prove as a hard fact; that every individual, however humble, is, in his own little way, the exponent as well as the product of his time. Apart from the individual the social forces and duties are not actually there: it is he that gives them voice and utterance; it is in him that they attain external and definite existence. The necessity of a time that fails to find voice in the life of an individual or people that understand it is a blind and monstrous force, and not an ethical necessity. As in the French Revolution, it works fortuitously, confounding and crushing together the good and the evil. But the individual who recognises the necessity labouring beneath the contingencies of his time lifts it from a natural into an ethical existence, makes it first an object of thought and then an ideal of conduct. Society, in a word, finds its meaning, comes to self-consciousness in him. It is thus in some degree that society comes to self-consciousness and attains its purposes in the self-consciousness and purposes of *every* individual. The social organism is an organism of organisms. The life of the whole is the life of every part. Nor is it torn amongst them into shreds and patches. The reason that is in the world in all its wealth and greatness is the legitimate inheritance of everyone, and this inheritance is an *ethical* inheritance, where there is no mutual exclusion. It is the kingdom of heaven upon earth where all are kings because all are subjects.

2

Man's Place in the Cosmos

Professor Huxley on Nature and Man

ANDREW SETH (PRINGLE-PATTISON)

PROFESSOR HUXLEY'S Romanes Lecture on 'Evolution and Ethics' deservedly attracted a large amount of attention on its appearance. That attention was due not only to the importance of the subject handled and the reputation of the lecturer, but quite as much to the breadth and scope of the treatment, to the nobility of tone and the deep human feeling which characterised a singularly impressive utterance. Popular interest was also excited by the nature of the conclusion reached, which, in the mouth of the pioneer and prophet of evolution, had the air of being something like a palinode. Criticisms of the lecture appeared at the time by Mr Leslie Stephen in the *Contemporary Review*, and by Mr Herbert Spencer[1] in a letter to the *Athenaeum*;[a] and many discussions appeared in theological quarters.[2] But the subject as a whole was perhaps dismissed from public attention before its significance had been exhausted, or indeed properly grasped. Professor Huxley's argument and the criticisms it called forth illuminate most instructively some deep-seated ambiguities of philosophical terminology, and at the same

---

[a] The Romanes Lecture was delivered on the 18 May 1893, and published shortly thereafter. Mr Spencer's letter appeared in the *Athenaeum* of August 5, and Mr Leslie Stephen's article in the *Contemporary Review* of August 1893. The present paper was published in *Blackwood's Magazine*, December 1893.

[1] Leslie Stephen, 'Ethics and the Struggle for Existence', *The Contemporary Review*, 64 (1893), pp. 155–70; Herbert Spencer, 'Evolutionary Ethics', *Athenaeum*, 3432, 5 August 1893, pp. 193–4. Seth's references to Huxley are to the edition published by Macmillan, London, 1893. The qualification made by Huxley in footnote 19 becomes footnote 20 in later editions.

[2] For a theological perspective see St. G. Mivart, 'Evolution in Professor Huxley', *The Nineteenth Century*, 198 (1893).

time bring into sharp relief the fundamental difference of standpoint which divides philosophical thinkers. The questions at issue, moreover, are not merely speculative; already they cast their shadow upon literature and life. The opportunity of elucidation is therefore in the best sense timely, and no apology seems needed for an attempt to recall attention to the points in dispute and to accentuate their significance.

The outstanding feature of Professor Huxley's argument is the sharp contrast drawn between nature and ethical man, and the sweeping indictment of 'the cosmic process' at the bar of morality. The problem of suffering and the almost complete absence of any relation between suffering and moral desert is the theme from which he starts, and to which he continually returns. 'The dread problem of evil', 'the moral indifference of nature', 'the unfathomable injustice of the nature of things' – this is the aspect of the world which has burned itself deeply into the writer's soul, and which speaks in moving eloquence from his pages. The Buddhistic and the Stoic attempts to grapple with the problem are considered, and are found to end alike in absolute renunciation. 'By the Tiber, as by the Ganges, ethical man admits that the cosmos is too strong for him; and, destroying every bond which ties him to it by ascetic discipline, he seeks salvation in absolute renunciation' (p. 29). Is the antagonism, then, final and hopeless, or can modern science and philosophy offer any better reconciliation of ethical man with the nature to which as an animal he belongs, and to whose vast unconscious forces he lies open on every side? As Professor Huxley puts the question himself in his opening pages – Is there or is there not 'a sanction for morality in the ways of the cosmos'? Man has built up 'an artificial world within the cosmos': has human society its roots and its justification in the underlying nature of the cosmos, or is it in very truth an 'artificial' world, which is at odds with that nature and must be in perpetual conflict with it? The Stoic rule which places virtue in 'following, nature' is easily shown to be a phrase of many meanings, and to demand qualification by reference, first, to the specific nature of man, and then to a higher nature or guiding faculty within the mind of man himself. But the modern ethics of evolution apparently claim to have bridged the gulf and to have made the ethical process continuous with the cosmic process of organic nature, – they claim, in short, to exhibit the ethical life as only a continuation, on another plane, of the struggle for existence.

If this claim is well founded, and the two worlds are really continuous, then the maxim, 'Follow nature', will have been proved to be, after all, the sum and substance of virtue.

It is against this naturalisation of ethics that Professor Huxley protests in the strongest terms. He readily allows that the ethical evolutionists may be right in their natural history of the moral sentiments. But 'as the immoral sentiments have no less been evolved, there is, so far, as much natural sanction for the one as the other . . . Cosmic evolution may teach us how the good and the evil tendencies of man may have come about; but, in itself, it is incompetent to furnish any better reason why what we call good is preferable to what we call evil, than we had before' (p. 31). That is to say, the origin of a belief and the validity of a belief, or the origin of a tendency and the ethical quality of that tendency, are logically two distinct questions. But the evolutionist is apt to make the answer to the first do duty as an answer to the second also, because he has in reality no standard of appreciation to apply to any phenomenon except that of mere existence. 'Whatever is, is right',[3] or at all events, 'Whatever is predominant, is right', is the only motto of the consistent evolutionist. This is embodied in the phrase 'survival of the fittest', which is used – illegitimately, as we shall see – to effect the transition from the merely natural to the ethical world.

In opposition to such theories, Professor Huxley contends that the analogies of the struggle for existence throw no light on the ethical nature of man.

> Cosmic nature is no school of virtue, but the headquarters of the enemy of ethical nature (p. 27). Self-assertion, the unscrupulous seizing upon all that can be grasped, the tenacious holding of all that can be kept . . . constitute the essence of the struggle for exist-

---

[3] Alexander Pope,

> All Nature is but Art, unknown to thee;
> All Chance, Direction, which thou canst not see;
> All Discord, Harmony, not understood;
> All partial Evil, universal Good:
> And spite Pride, in erring Reason's Spite,
> One truth is clear, 'Whatever is, is RIGHT'.

An Essay on Man, ed. Maynard Mack (London, Methuen, 1950), pp. 50–1. Epistle I, lines 289–94.

ence . . . For his successful progress as far as the savage state, man
has been largely indebted to those qualities which he shares with
the ape and the tiger (p. 6).

So far is this struggle from explaining morality that

> the practice of what is ethically best – what we call goodness or
> virtue – involves a course of conduct which, in all respects, is
> opposed to that which leads to success in the cosmic struggle for
> existence. In place of ruthless self-assertion, it demands self-
> restraint; in place of thrusting aside, or treading down, all competi-
> tors, it requires that the individual shall not merely respect, but
> shall help, his fellows . . . It repudiates the gladiatorial theory of
> existence . . . Laws and moral precepts are directed to the end of
> curbing the cosmic process and reminding the individual of his
> duty to the community, to the protection and influence of which
> he owes, if not existence itself, at least the life of something better
> than a brutal savage.

In short, 'social progress means a checking of the cosmic process at
every step, and the substitution for it of another which may be
called the ethical process'. This leads up to the characteristic call to
arms with which the address concludes: 'Let us understand, once
for all, that the ethical progress of society depends, not on imitating
the cosmic process, still less in running away from it, but in combat-
ing it' (pp. 33, 34).

Such is the logical framework of the lecture. It is obvious that
the important points of the treatment are: (1) The emphasis laid
upon the division between man and nature, which a reviewer in the
Athenaeum[b] called 'an approximation to the Pauline dogma of nature
and grace;[4] and (2) the mood of militant heroism, not untouched,
however, by stoical resignation, which naturally results from contemplation of the unequal struggle between the microcosm and the
macrocosm.

Before proceeding to consider the consistency of Professor Huxley's argument and the ultimate tenability of his position, I wish to
say, in regard to the first point, how timely, it seems to me, is his

[b] July 22, 1893.

[4] The review is anonomous and appeared in No. 3430, pp. 119–20 of the *Athenaeum
Journal*.

insistence on the gulf between man and non-human nature; how sound is the stand he takes upon the ethical nature of man as that which is alone of significance and worth in the 'transitory adjustment of contending forces', which otherwise constitutes the cosmos. Whether the breach is to be taken as absolute or not, it is at least apparent that if man with his virtues and vices be included *simpliciter* and without more ado in a merely natural order of facts, we inevitably tend to lose sight of that nature within nature which makes man what he is. The tendency so to include man has become a settled habit in much of our current literature. I need not speak of the documents of so-called Naturalism, with their never-ending analysis of *la bête humaine* [the human beast] – analysis from which one would be slow to gather that any such qualities as justice, purity, or disinterested affection had ever disturbed the brutish annals of force and lust. But in other quarters, even where the picture is not so dark, the fashion still is to treat man *as a natural product*, – not as the responsible shaper of his destiny, but, void of spiritual struggles and ideal hopes, as the unresisting channel of the impulses which sway him hither and thither, and issue now in one course of action, now in another. This literature is inartistic, even on its own terms, for, blinded by its materialistic fatalism, it does not even give us things as they are. The higher literature never forgets that man, as Pascal put it, is nobler than the universe;[5] and freedom (in some sense of that ambiguous term) must be held to be a postulate of true art no less than of morality. But besides being bad art, literature of this sort has a subtly corrosive influence upon the ethical temper. For the power of will, as Lamennais said, is that in us which is most quickly used up: 'Ce qui s'use le plus vite en nous, c'est la volonte.'[6] Hence the insidious force of the suggestion that we do not will at all, but are merely the instruments of our desires. For this is to justify, or at least to excuse, every passion on

---

[5] Pascal,

But, if the universe were to crush him, man would still be more noble than that which killed him, because he knows that he dies and the advantage which the universe has over him; the universe knows nothing of this.

Pensées (London, Dent, 1947), section VI, 347.

[6] Félicité Robert de Lamennais, or La Mennais (1782–1854) was a French religious writer and Christian democrat. He said, 'what is most quickly used up in us is the will'.

the ground of its 'natural' origin. This temper of mind is found invading even more serious writers, and it is traceable ultimately to the same confusion between the laws of human conduct and the workings of nature in the irresponsible creatures of the field. M. Renan, it will be remembered, delicately excuses himself in his *Souvenirs* – rallies himself, as we may say – on his continued practice of chastity: –

> I continued to live in Paris as I had lived in the seminary. Later, I saw very well the vanity of that virtue as of all the rest. I recognised in particular that nature cares not at all whether man is chaste or not. I cannot rid myself [he says elsewhere in the same volume] of the idea that after all it is perhaps the libertine who is right, and who practises the true philosophy of life.[7]

Many will remember, too, how Matthew Arnold took up this parable when he discoursed in America on the cult of the great goddess Lubricity, to which, as he said, contemporary France seemed more and more to be devoting herself. After much delicate banter and much direct plain-speaking, Mr Arnold turns upon M. Renan and cuts to the root of the fallacy in a single sentence. 'Instead of saying that nature cares nothing about chastity, let us say that human nature, *our* nature, cares about it a great deal.'[8] And when we meet the same fallacy invading our own literature, the same answer will suffice. I think it may be worth pointing out a notable instance in a novel widely read and highly praised within the last few years. Mr Hardy's *Tess of the D'Urbervilles* is unquestionably a powerful work, but it suffers, in my opinion, both artistically and ethically, from this tendency to assimilate the moral and the natural. To smack of the soil is in many senses a term of praise; but even rustic men and women are not altogether products of the soil, and Mr Hardy is in danger of so regarding them. What I wish, however, to point out here is the pernicious fallacy which underlies

---

[7] Seth appears to have made his own translation of Ernest Renan, *Souvenirs d'Enfance et de Jeunesse* (Paris, Calmann Lévy, 1883), 359. For the English version see Joseph Ernest Renan, *Recollections of My Youth*, translated from the French by C. B. Pitman and revised by Madam Renan (London, Chapman Hall, 1883; 2nd edn 1 1892), 'First Steps Outside St. Sulpice', Part IV, section iv, 315.

[8] Matthew Arnold, 'Numbers or the Majority and the Remnant', *The Complete Prose Works*, vol. X, *Philistinism in England and America* (Ann Arbor, University of Michigan Press, 1974), 160, lines 35–7.

a statement like the following. Tess, after she has fallen from her innocence, is wont to wander alone in the woods, a prey to her own reflections, 'terrified without reason', says the author, by 'a cloud of moral hobgoblins'.

> It was they [he continues] that were out of harmony with the actual world, not she. Walking among the sleeping birds in the hedges, watching the skipping rabbits on a moonlit warren, or standing under a pheasant-laden bough, she looked upon herself as a figure of guilt intruding into the haunts of innocence. But all the while she was making a distinction where there was no difference. Feeling herself in antagonism, she was quite in accord. She had been made to break an accepted social law, but no law known to the environment in which she fancied herself such an anomaly.[9]

The implication of such a passage is that the 'accepted social law' is a mere convention, and that the deeper truth, 'the actual world', is to be found in the hedgerows and the warrens. To satisfy an animal prompting without scruple or hesitation, and without the qualms of a fantastical remorse, is only to fulfil the law of nature, and to put one's self in harmony with one's surroundings. The shallowness of such revolt against 'accepted social laws' is too apparent to need further exposure. A convention truly, in one sense, the moral law in question is; but upon this convention the fabric of human society and all the sanctities of the family rest. He must be strangely blinded by a word who deems this sanction insufficient, or who would pit in such a case a 'natural' impulse against a 'social' law.

In view of pervasive misconceptions and fallacies like these, it is eminently salutary, I repeat, to have our attention so impressively recalled by Professor Huxley to the idea of human life as an *imperium in imperio* – a realm which, though it rises out of nature, and remains exposed to the shock of natural forces, requires for its laws no foreign sanction, but bases them solely on the perfection of human nature itself. For, even though Professor Huxley's way of stating the opposition should prove ultimately untenable, the breach between ethical man and pre-human nature constitutes without exception the most important fact which the universe has to show;

[9] Thomas Hardy, *Tess of the D'Urbervilles* (Harmondsworth, Penguin, 1994: first published 1891), 108.

and for a true understanding of the world it is far more vital to grasp the significance of this breach than to be misled by a cheap desire for unity and system into minimising, or even denying, the fact.

It is time, however, to examine Professor Huxley's position and arguments more closely. His critics have not been slow to remark upon the ambiguity lurking in the phrase 'cosmic process', which occurs so often throughout the lecture, in antithesis to the ethical process – to the moral and social life of man. And they point with one accord to Note 19 [note 20 in the reprint] as containing, in effect, a retractation of his own doctrine by Professor Huxley himself. 'Of course, strictly speaking', we read in the note, 'social life and the ethical process, in virtue of which it advances towards perfection, are part and parcel of the general process of evolution.' As Mr Spencer pointedly asks, 'If the ethical man is not a product of the cosmic process, what is he a product of?'[10] Or as Shakespeare expressed it in the often quoted lines –

> Nature is made better by no means
> But nature makes that means: so, o'er that art,
> Which you say adds to nature, is an art
> That nature makes.[11]

If the cosmic process be understood in the full latitude of the phrase, this is, indeed, so obvious, and the critic's victory so easy, that it is hard to believe Professor Huxley's position rests altogether on a foundation so weak. The term 'nature', and still more an expression like 'the cosmic process', may be taken in an all inclusive sense as equivalent to the universe as a whole or the nature of things; and if so, it is obvious that human nature with its ethical characteristics is embraced within the larger whole. The unity of the cosmos – in some sense – is not so much a conclusion to be proved as an inevitable assumption. Professor Huxley apparently denies this unity in the text of his lecture, and is naturally obliged to reassert it in his note. This constitutes the weakness of his position. The part must be somehow included in the process of the whole; there is no extra-cosmic source from which a revolt against the principles of the cosmos could draw inspiration or support.

[10] Spencer, 'Evolutionary Ethics', 193.
[11] *The Winter's Tale*, Polixenes, King of Bohemia, to Perdita, Act IV, Scene iv.

Now the strength of the evolutionary theory of ethics lies in its frank recognition of the unity of the cosmos; and in this it is, so far, at one with the philosophical doctrine of Idealism to which it is otherwise so much opposed – the doctrine which finds the ultimate reality of the universe in mind or spirit, and its End in the perfecting of spiritual life. But each of these theories exhibits the unity of the world in its own way. The way taken by the ethical evolutionists is to naturalise morality, to assimilate ethical experience to nature, in the lower or narrower sense in which it is used to denote all that happens in the known world *except* the responsible activities of human beings. And it is against this removing of landmarks that Professor Huxley, rightly, as it seems to me, protests. For though Mr Spencer and Mr Leslie Stephen may be technically in the right, inasmuch as human nature is unquestionably part of the nature of things, it is the inherent tendency of their theories to substitute for this wider nature the laws and processes of that narrower, non-human world, to which the term nature is on the whole restricted by current usage.

This tendency is inherent in every system which takes as its sole principle of explanation the carrying back of facts or events to their antecedent conditions. And, as it happens, this is explicitly formulated by Mr Stephen, in his article in the *Contemporary Review*, as the only permissible meaning of explanation: 'To "explain" a fact is to assign its causes – that is, give the preceding set of facts out of which it arose.' [pp. 157–8]. But surely, I may be asked, you do not intend to challenge a principle which underlies all scientific procedure, and which may even claim to be self-evident? I certainly do not propose to deny the formal correctness of the principle, but I maintain most strongly that the current application of it covers a subtle and very serious fallacy, for *the true nature of the cause only becomes apparent in the effect.* Now, if we explain a fact by giving 'the preceding set of facts out of which it arose', we practically resolve the fact into these antecedents – that is to say, we identify it with them. When we are dealing with some limited sphere of phenomena, within which the facts are all of one order – say, the laws of moving bodies as treated in mechanics – there may be no practical disadvantage from this limited interpretation of causation. But when we pass from one order of facts to another – say, from the inorganic to the organic, or, still more, from animal life to the self-conscious life of man – the inadequacy of such explanation stares us in the face. For 'the preceding set of facts', which we treat as the cause or sufficient explanation of the phenomenon in question, is *ex hypothesi* different from the phenomenon it is said to explain; and the difference is, that it consists of simpler elements. To explain, according to this view, is to reduce to simpler conditions. But if the elements are really simpler, there is the fact of their combination into a more complex product to be explained, and the fact of their combination in such a way as to produce precisely the result in question. And if we choose to take the antecedent conditions, as they appear in themselves, apart from the all-important circumstance of the production of this effect, we have, no doubt, a 'preceding set of facts', but we certainly have not, in any true sense, the *cause* of the phenomenon. We have eliminated the very characteristic we set out to explain – namely, the difference of the new phenomenon from the antecedents out of which it appears to have been evolved. Hence it is that, in the sense indicated, all explanation of the higher by the lower is philosophically a hysteron proteron. The antecedents assigned are not the causes of the consequents; for by antecedents the naturalistic theories mean the *antecedents in abstraction from their consequents* – the antecedents taken as they appear in themselves, or as we might suppose them to be if no such consequents had ever issued from them. So conceived, however, the antecedents (matter and energy, for example) have no real existence – they are mere *entia rationis* [creatures of reason], abstract aspects of the one concrete fact which we call the universe. The true nature of the antecedents is only learned by reference to the consequents which follow; or, as I put it before, the true nature of the cause only becomes apparent in the effect. All ultimate or philosophical explanation must look to the end. Hence the futility of all attempts to explain human life in terms of the merely animal, to explain life in terms of the inorganic, and ultimately to find a sufficient formula for the cosmic process in terms of the redistribution of matter and motion. If we are in earnest with the doctrine that the universe is one, we have to read back the nature of the latest consequent into the remotest antecedent. Only then is the one, in any true sense, the cause of the other.

Applying this to the present question, we may say that, just as within the limits of the organic world there may be exhibited an intelligible evolution of living forms, so within the moral world we may certainly have an evolution of the moral sentiments and of the institutions which subserve ethical conduct. But as, in the one case, we must start with the fact of life – that is to say, with the character-istic ways of behaving which are found in living matter and which are not found in dead matter – so, in the other case, we must carry with us from the outset the characteristics or postulates of moral experience – namely, self-consciousness, with the sense of responsi-bility, and the capacity for sympathy which is based on the ability to represent to one's self the life and feelings of another. Such an evolution within the moral sphere does not justify us in presenting morality as an 'evolution' from non-moral conditions – that is, in resolving morality into non-moral elements. And this Mr Leslie Stephen seems to admit in an important passage of the article already referred to. 'Morality proper', he says, 'begins when sym-pathy begins; when we really desire the happiness of others, or, as Kant says, when we treat other men as an end, and not simply as a means. Undoubtedly this involves a new principle no less than the essential principle of all true morality.' I cannot but regard this as an important admission, but at the same time I am bound to say that, till I met this unexpected sentence of Mr Stephen's, I had supposed that the admission of 'a new principle' was precisely what the evolutionists were, of all things, most anxious to avoid.

It seems to me, therefore, that though Professor Huxley may have put himself technically in the wrong by speaking of 'the cosmical process', his contention is far from being so inept as a verbal criti-cism would make it appear. It is really directed against the submerg-ence of ethical man in the processes of non-ethical and non-human nature; and if any justification is to be sought for the use of the phrase, we may find it in the tendency inherent in the evolutionary method of explanation – the tendency already explained to substan-tiate antecedents in abstraction from their consequents, and thus practically to identify the cosmos with its lowest aspects. If the evolutionists do not make this identification in their own minds, they are at least singularly successful in producing that impression upon their readers.

On another important point connected with, and indeed involved in, the foregoing, Professor Huxley, by an unguarded statement, laid himself open to a pretty obvious and apparently conclusive rejoinder. 'The cosmic process', he says in one place, 'has no sort of relation to moral ends.' But 'the moral indifference of nature', even in the restricted sense of the term, cannot be maintained so absolutely. Nature undoubtedly puts a premium upon certain virtues, and punishes certain modes of excess and defect by decrease of vitality and positive pain. As Mr Stephen says: 'That chastity, temperance, truthfulness, and energy are on the whole advantages both to the individual and the race does not, I fancy, require elaborate proof, nor need I argue at length that the races in which they are common will therefore have inevitable advantages in the struggle for existence.' But if so, then it would seem that cosmic nature is not, as it was represented, 'the headquarters of the enemy of ethical nature'; to a certain extent it may even be regarded as a 'school of virtue'. The sphere, however, in which this holds true is a comparatively limited one, being substantially restricted to temperance, in the Greek sense of the word – that is to say, moderation in the indulgence of the animal appetites, to which may, no doubt, be added, with Mr Stephen, energy. But nature, as distinct from that human nature which organises itself into societies and adds its own sanctions to the moral ideal which it is continually widening and deepening – non-human nature seems to have no sanctions even for such fundamental virtues as truthfulness, justice, and beneficence, still less for the finer shades and higher nobilities of character in which human nature flowers. And even in regard to the list of virtues cited, it might be argued that cosmic nature sanctions and furthers them only when we deliberately restrict our survey to the present stage of the evolutionary process – the stage during which man has grown to be what he is on this planet. Within this limited period nature, through the struggle for existence, may be said to have favoured the evolution of the morally best. But it is no intrinsic quality of the struggle to produce this result. Here, it appears to me, we strike upon the deeper truth which prompted Professor Huxley's somewhat unguarded statement, and we are under an important obligation to him for the exposure of what he appropriately calls 'the fallacy of the fittest'.

Fittest [he writes] has a connotation of 'best'; and about best there hangs a moral flavour. In cosmic nature, however, what is 'fittest' depends upon the conditions. Long since, I ventured to point out that if our hemisphere were to cool again, the survival of the fittest might bring about, in the vegetable kingdom, a population of more and more stunted and humbler and humbler organisms, until the 'fittest' that survived might be nothing but lichens, diatoms, and such microscopic organisms as those which give red snow its colour; while, if it became hotter, the pleasant valleys of the Thames and Isis might be uninhabitable by any animated beings save those that flourish in a tropical jungle. They, as the fittest, the best adapted to the changed conditions, would survive (p. 32).

Mr Spencer has been forward to emphasise his agreement with this position, and has recalled attention to an essay of his own, twenty years old, in which he makes the same distinction:

> The law is not the survival of the 'better' or the 'stronger', if we give to these words anything like their ordinary meanings. It is the survival of those which are constitutionally fittest to thrive under the conditions in which they are placed; and very often that which, humanly speaking, is inferiority, causes the survival. Superiority, whether in size, strength, activity, or sagacity, is, other things equal, at the cost of diminished fertility; and where the life led by a species does not demand these higher attributes, the species profits by decrease of them, and accompanying increase of fertility. This is the reason why there occur so many cases of retrograde metamorphosis ... When it is remembered that these cases outnumber all others, it will be seen that the expression 'survivorship of the better' is wholly inappropriate.[c]

Out of the mouth of two such witnesses this point may be taken as established. But if so, I entirely fail to see where, on naturalistic principles, we get our standard of higher and lower, of better and worse. If changed conditions of life were to lead to the dehumanising of the race, to the dropping one by one of the ethical qualities which we are accustomed to commend, whence the justification for pronouncing this process a 'retrograde metamorphosis'? There can be no other sense of better or worse, on the theory, than more or less successful adaptation to the conditions of the environment, and what survives is best just because it survives. The latest stage of the process must necessarily, therefore, be better than all that went before, from the mere fact that it has maintained itself. Mere existence is the only test we have to apply, and at every stage it would

[c] *Essays*, vol. I. p. 379, 'Mr Martineau on Evolution'.

seem that we are bound to say, Whatever is, is right. But this is tantamount to saying that, when the theory of evolution is taken in its widest scope, it is not really legitimate to say that nature abets or sanctions morality; since the result of further evolution – or, to speak more properly, of further cosmical changes – might be to dethrone our present ethical conduct from its temporary position as the fittest, and to leave no scope for what we now regard as virtue. The type of conduct which would then succeed, and which would so far have the sanction of nature on its side, we should be constrained, it seems to me, to pronounce superior to the conduct which, from our present point of view, seems to us better; because the latter, if adopted, would in the altered circumstances set us at variance with our surroundings, and so fail. Failure or success in the struggle for existence must, on the theory, be the sole moral standard. Good is what survives; evil is what once was fittest, but is so no longer. Thus, our present good may become – nay, is inevitably becoming – evil, and that not, as might be contended, in the sense of merging in a higher good. We have no guarantee that the movement of change, miscalled evolution, must continue in the line of past progress: it may gradually, and as it were imperceptibly, assume another direction – a direction which our present moral ideas would condemn as retrograde. Yet, none the less, the mere fact of change would be sufficient to convert our present good into evil.

Such, I must insist, is the only logical position of a naturalistic ethics. But an important outcome of the recent discussion has been to show that the most prominent upholders of the theory do not hold it in its logical form. Mr Spencer, as we have seen, has strongly insisted that survival of the fittest does not mean survival of the better, or even of the stronger; and Mr Stephen tells us that the struggle for existence, instead of being the explanation of morality, 'belongs to an underlying order of facts to which moral epithets cannot properly be applied. It denotes a condition of which the moralist has to take account, and to which morality has to be adapted, but which, just because it is a "cosmic process", cannot be altered, however much we may alter the conduct which it dictates.' Surely this comes very near to admitting Professor Huxley's contention, that our moral standard is not derived from the struggle for existence, but rather implies its reversal, substituting for selfishness sympathy for others, and, in Mr Stephen's own words, 'the sense of duty which each man owes to society at large', Mr Spencer speaks of an 'ethical check' upon the struggle for existence: it is our duty, he says, 'to mitigate the evils' which it entails in the social state. 'The use of morality', says Mr Stephen, 'is to humanise the struggle, to minimise the sufferings of those who lose the game, and to offer the prizes to the qualities which are advantageous to all, rather than to those which serve to intensify the bitterness of the conflict.' But this is neither more nor less than to say that, as soon as man becomes social and moral, he has to act counter to the leading characteristics of the struggle for existence. He becomes animated by other ideals, or, to speak more strictly, he then first becomes capable of an ideal, of a sense of duty, instead of obeying without question the routine of animal impulse.

But if this is so, I still ask the evolutionist who has no other basis than the struggle for existence, how he accounts for the intrusion of these moral ideas and standards which presume to interfere with the cosmic process, and sit in judgment upon its results? This question cannot be answered so long as we regard morality merely as an incidental result, a by-product, as it were, of the cosmical system. It is impossible on such a hypothesis to understand the magisterial assertion by itself of the part against the whole, its demands upon the universe, its unwavering condemnation of the universe, if these demands are not met by the nature of things. All this would be an incongruous, and even a ludicrous, spectacle if we had here to do with a natural phenomenon like any other. The moral and spiritual life remains, in short, unintelligible, unless on the supposition that it is in reality the key to the world's meaning, the fact in the light of which all other phenomena must be read. We must be in earnest, I have already said, with the unity of the world, but we must not forget that, if regarded merely as a system of forces, the world possesses no such unity. It acquires it only when regarded in the light of an End of absolute worth or value which is realised or attained in it. Such an End-in-itself, as Kant called it, we find only in the self-conscious life of man, in the world of Truth, Beauty, and Goodness which he builds up for himself, and of which he constitutes himself a citizen. If it were possible to consider the system of physical nature apart from the intelligent activities and emotions of rational beings, those worlds on worlds,

> Rolling ever
> From creation to decay[12]

would possess in themselves no spark of the value, the intrinsic worth, which we unhesitatingly assert to belong, at least in possibility, to the meanest human life. The endless redistribution of matter and motion in stupendous cycles of evolution and dissolution would be a world without any justification to offer for its existence – a world which might just as well not have been.[d] But if we are honest with ourselves, I do not think we can embrace the conclusion that the cosmos is a mere brute fact of this description. The demand for an End-in-itself – that is, for a fact of such a nature that its existence justifies itself – is as much a necessity of reason as the necessity which impels us to refund any phenomenon into its antecedent conditions. And further, unless we sophisticate ourselves, we cannot doubt that we possess within ourselves – in our moral experience most conspicuously – an instance and a standard of what we mean by such intrinsic value. As Carlyle has put it in one of his finest passages, –

> What, then, is man! What, then, is man! He endures but for an hour, and is crushed before the moth. Yet in the being and in the

---

[d] Without encumbering the main argument by inopportune discussion, one may perhaps ask in a note in what sense even existence could be attributed to a system of unconscious forces – a material world *per se*. We cannot perform the abstraction required of us in conceiving such a system. Nature refuses to be divorced from the thoughts and feelings of her children and her lords, and we need not be subjective idealists to hold the literal truth of the poet's words that 'in our life alone does Nature live'.[13]

[12] Percy Bysshe Shelley,

> Worlds are rolling ever
> From creation to decay,
> Like the bubbles on a river
> Sparkling, bursting, borne away.

The Complete Poetical Works of Shelly Including Material Never Before Printed In Any Edition Of The Poems, ed. Thomas Hutchinson (Oxford, Clarendon Press, 1904), 1023.

[13] Coleridge,

> O Lady! we receive but what we give,
> And in our life alone does Nature Live:

'Dejection: an Ode', *Poetical Works*, ed., E. H. Coleridge (Oxford, Oxford University Press, 1967), 365, verse iv, lines 1–2.

45

working of a faithful man is there already (as all faith, from the beginning, gives assurance) a something that pertains not to this wild death-element of Time; that triumphs over Time, and *is*, and will be, when Time shall be no more.[14]

This conviction of the infinite significance and value of the ethical life is the only view-point from which, in Professor Huxley's words, we can 'make existence intelligible and bring the order of things into harmony with the moral sense of man'. And it is impossible to do the one of these things without the other. To understand the world is not merely to unravel the sequence of an intricate set of facts. So long as we cannot 'bring the order of things into harmony with the moral sense of man', we cannot truly be said to have made existence intelligible: the world still remains for us, in Hume's words, 'a riddle, an enigma, an inexplicable mystery'.[15]

What, then, is Professor Huxley's final attitude? The lecture breathes throughout the loftiest temper of ethical idealism. It is the writer's keen sense of the superiority of ethical man to non-ethical nature that prompts him to pit Pascal's 'thinking reed'[16] in unequal struggle against the cosmic forces that envelop him; and the noble words at the close stir the spirit by their impressive insistence on the imperishable worth of human effort inspired by duty. Yet this unflinching conviction does not lead Professor Huxley to what seems the legitimate conclusion from it – namely, that here only, in the life of ethical endeavour, is the end and secret of the universe to be found. It serves but to accentuate the stern pathos of his view of human fate. His ultimate attitude is, theoretically, one of Agnosticism; personally and practically, one of Stoical heroism. Substantially the same attitude, it appears to me, is exemplified in the Religion of Humanity – the same despair, I mean, of harmonising human ideals with the course of the universe. The Religion of Humanity rightly finds in man alone any qualities which call for adoration or worship; but it inconsistently supposes man to develop these qualities in a fundamentally non-ethical cosmos, and so fails

---

[14] Despite sustained searches by numerous scholars, including Carlyle specialists, the source of this quotation has not been found.

[15] David Hume, *Natural History of Religion*, ed. A. Wayne Clover (Oxford, Clarendon Press, 1976), 95, line 10.

[16] Pascal, *Pensées*, vi, 347. 'Man is but a reed, the most feeble thing in nature; but he is a thinking reed.'

to furnish a solution that can be accounted either metaphysically satisfying or ethically supporting. But we must bear in mind, I repeat, the principle of the unity of the world. The attitude of the Agnostic and the Positivist is due to the separation which they unconsciously insist on keeping up between nature and man. The temptation to do so is intelligible, for we have found that nature, taken in philosophical language as a thing in itself – nature conceived as an independent system of causes – cannot explain the ethical life of man, and we rightly refuse to blur and distort the characteristic features of moral experience by submerging it in the merely natural. We easily, therefore, continue to think of the system of natural causes as a world going its own way, existing quite independently of the ethical beings who draw their breath within it. Man with his ideal standards and his infinite aspirations appears consequently upon the scene as an alien without rights in a world that knows him not. His life is an unexplained intrusion in a world organised on other principles, and no way adapted as a habitation for so disturbing and pretentious a guest. And the consequence is that he dashes his spirit against the steep crags of necessity, finds his ideals thwarted, his aspirations mocked, his tenderest affections turned to instruments of agony, and is driven, if not into passionate revolt or nerveless despair, then at best into stoical resolve. Some such mood as this appears also in much of Matthew Arnold's poetry, and is to my mind the explanation of its insistent note of sadness.

> No, we are strangers here, the world is from of old . . .
> To tunes we did not call, our being must keep chime.[17]

It is powerfully expressed in the famous monologue or chant in 'Empedocles on Etna', with its deliberate renunciation of what the poet deems man's 'boundless hopes' and 'intemperate prayers'.[18] It

---

[17] *The Poems of Mathew Arnold*, ed. Kenneth Allot, 2nd edn, Miriam Allot (London, Longman, 1979), 'Empedocles on Etna', Act I, Scene ii, ll, 181 and 196.

[18] *Poems of Mathew Arnold*, 22 Resignation, lines 271–4:

> And even could the intemperate prayer
> Man iterates, while these forebear,
> For movement, for an ample sphere,
> Pierce Fate's impenetrable ear.

'boundles hopes' is to be found in *Poems of Mathew Arnold*, 101 'The Better Part':

inspires the fine lines to Fausta on 'Resignation',[19] and reappears more incidentally in all his verse. But calm, as he himself reminds us, is not life's crown, though calm is well; and the poet's 'calm lucidity of soul'[20] covers in this case the baffled retreat of the thinker. We have, in truth, no right to suppose an independent non-spiritual world on which human experience is incongruously superinduced. If we are really in earnest, at once with the unity of the world and with the necessity of an intrinsically worthy end by reference to which existence may be explained, we must take our courage in both hands and carry our convictions to their legitimate conclusion. We must conclude that the end which we recognise as alone worthy of attainment is also the end of existence as such – the open secret of the universe. No man writes more pessimistically than Kant of man's relation to the course of nature, so long as man is regarded merely as a sentient creature, susceptible to pleasure and pain. But man, as the subject of duty, and the heir of immortal hopes, is restored by Kant to that central position in the universe from which, as a merely physical being, Copernicus had degraded him.

To a certain extent this conclusion must remain a conviction rather than a demonstration, for we cannot emerge altogether from the obscurities of our middle state, and there is much that may rightly disquiet and perplex our minds. But if it is in the needs of

'Long fed on boundless hopes, O race of man', line 1.

    And, 2 'Cromwell':

> 'That day of boundless hope and promise high
> That day that hailed his triumphs, saw him die.' lines 211–12.

[19] 'To Fausta' is the sub-title of 'Resignation'.

[20] Arnold, 'Youth and Calm' in *Poems By Mathew Arnold* (London, Macmillan, 1885).

> 'Tis death! and peace, indeed, is here,
> And ease from shame, and rest from fear.
> There's nothing can dismarble now
> The smoothness of the brow.
> But is acalm like this, in truth,
> The crowning end of life and youth,
> And when this boon rewards the dead,
> Are all debts paid, has all been said?

The reference to 'calm lucidity of soul' appears to be from 'Resignation'. 'Fate Gave, what Chance shall not control, His sad lucidity of soul.'

the moral life that we find our deepest principle of explanation, then it may be argued with some reason that this belongs to the nature of the case; for a scientific demonstration would not serve the purposes of that life. The truly good man must choose goodness on its own account; he must be ready to serve God for naught, without being invaded by M. Renan's doubts. As it has been finely put, he must possess 'that rude old Norse nobility of soul, which saw virtue and vice alike go unrewarded, and was yet not shaken in its faith'.^e This old Norse nobility speaks to us again, in accents of the nineteenth century, in Professor Huxley's lecture. But because such is the temper of true virtue, it by no means follows that such virtue will not be rewarded with 'the wages of going on, and not to die'.[21]

^e R. L. Stevenson, Preface [by way of Criticism] to *Familiar Studies of Men and Books* [London, Chatto and Windus, 1920, xiii].

[21] Alfred Lord Tennyson,

> To rest in a golden grove, or to bask in a summer sky:
> Give her the wages of going on, and not to die.

'Wages' in *Works* (Ware, Hertfordshire, Wordsworth, 1994), 617.

3
Socialism and Natural Selection[a]

B. BOSANQUET

My reason for attempting a treatment of this difficult subject is twofold. First, I am greatly impressed by what seems like a lack of thorough patience and goodwill in the controversy on both sides. A student of philosophy has not the special knowledge possessed either by Mr. Huxley or Professor Haeckel in biology, or by Mr. Karl Pearson in mathematics,[1] not to speak of other writers who

[a] A lecture given before the London Ethical Society.

[1] Ernst Haeckel was a German biologist who formulated a deterministic theory of the ontogenetic development of the individual. Haeckel believed in the truth of spontaneous generation, not because it could be proved in the laboratory, but because a denial of it led to belief in a Creator. He was known as the 'German Darwin' because of the enthusiasm with which he introduced Darwin's ideas into Germany. His *Generelle Morphology* is a thoroughly and consciously Darwinian book. He is frequently cited in Charles Darwin, *The Descent of Man: Selection in Relation to Sex* (London, Murray, second edition, 1888). Darwin says, for example, that 'Professor Haeckel was the only author who, at the time when this work first appeared, had discussed the subject of sexual selection, and had seen its full importance . . .' p. 3. It was Haeckel who extended the debate about natural selection into the social sphere, and who expressed astonishment at the possibility of natural selection being compatible with socialism. He maintained that it was natural selection which drove people to attain higher levels of culture. He had a firm belief in the natural law of progress which he thought that neither tyrant nor priest could resist.

T. H. Huxley (1825–95) was a distinguished biologist and social commentator. He popularised many of Darwin's ideas, but did much valuable work of his own. In terms of ethics he made the famous distinction between cosmic evolution and ethical evolution. His ideas are discussed in the introduction to this volume, and in Andrew Seth's contribution.

Karl Pearson (1857–1936) was a biologist and mathematician with a keen interest in statistically proving Darwin's theory of natural selection. He was critical of have entered upon this debatable land perhaps too light-heartedly; but he ought to possess above all things the goodwill and habit of patience which enable him to track out common elements in different phases and processes, and to hold together ideas which the noticeably impatient mind of exact science or semi-political publicism pronounces to be *ab initio* incompatible. I cannot help it if this implication is considered insolent; in the *popular* utterances of natural and exact science nothing strikes one so forcibly as their impatience. And secondly, it appears to me that certain classes of facts known to those closely occupied with administration of charity or of Poor Law relief form at least an important contribution to the problem in question, and that, though touched upon from time to time, they have not been treated with adequate knowledge, and their rather ambiguous import has therefore not been rightly read.

I will begin by referring to an observation of Lotze which applies very widely to the attitude of our time.

> Our own generation, maintaining its opposition to philosophy, endeavours to console itself for its want of clearness in respect to general principles by a vivid exercise of the sensuous imagination. If we come upon pile-dwellings in some forgotten swamp, we piously gather together the insignificant remains of a dreary past, supposing that by contemplating them we shall grow wiser, and learn that which a glance into the affairs of everyday life would teach us with less trouble.[b]

Something of this kind is forcibly suggested by the necessity which modern culture appears to be under of attempting to designate well-recognised phenomena of civilised society by names drawn from the evolution of the plant and the lower animal world.

[b] Lotze, *Metaphysics*, English tr., p. 417.

Spencer, Haeckel and Huxley for portraying natural selection as the competition among individuals. Like Benjamin Kidd, he applied the theory of natural selection to international relations and to justify imperialism. Pearson agreed with Carlyle and Ruskin that England must hold its place in the world and protect the welfare of her own people at the expense of other peoples of a lower order, if necessary. He was also a socialist who lectured on the ideas of Marx and Lassalle. He was not, however, a Marxist. He espoused the idea of class unity, rejected working-class internationalism and embraced, instead, an ardent patriotism.

We have the struggle for existence, natural selection, and panmixia,[2] asserted and denied to be conditions of human progress, and the absurdity culminates when Mr. Herbert Spencer, in an ethical treatise,[c] speaks of a human society as 'a local variety of the species'. But where a continuous evolution is concerned, mere difference and mere sameness are more than usually inadequate instruments to express the relation between its stages; what is really needed is very patient and very careful interpretation and analysis directed to tracking the true strand of continuity.

For the sake of clearness, I will at once briefly indicate my conclusion. I believe in the reality of the general will, and in the consequent right and duty of civilised society to exercise initiative through the State with a view to the fullest development of the life of its members. But I am also absolutely convinced that the application of this initiative to guarantee without protest the existence of all individuals brought into being, instead of leaving the responsibility to the uttermost possible extent on the parents and the individuals themselves, is an abuse fatal to character and ultimately destructive of social life. The abolition of the struggle for existence, in the sense in which alone that term applies to human societies, means, so far as I can see, the divorce of existence from human qualities; and to favour the existence of human beings without human qualities is the ultimate inferno to which any society can descend. This view, it will be seen, is practically that of Mr. Kidd in his work on *Social Evolution*.[3] In no critical question has patience been more necessary and more wanting than in forming an estimate of that remarkable popular treatise. It is easy to show that Mr. Kidd is neither a scholar nor a philosopher; his estimate of social conditions is, in my judgment, misleading, and it does not appear probable that he is a master of natural science. But all this is no proof that on a particular issue he has failed to hit the nail on the head,

---

[c] *Principle of Ethics*, vol. II, p. 329.

[2] In Weismann's theory, *Panmixia* relates to what is called 'Germinal Selection'. Degeneration is explained in terms of genetic selection and was deemed one of the more important ideas supplementing Darwin's idea of natural selection without having to resort to Lamarck's ideas of use and dis-use inheritance. Spencer focuses on this aspect of Weissmann's theory.

[3] First edition, London, Macmillan, 1894: 2nd edn 1895: 3rd edn 1898.

and mere candour compels me to say that, in the essential distinction on which his attitude to Socialism is founded, I am fully in agreement with him. I refer to the distinction which he chooses to call that between true Socialism, which aims at arresting competition and guarantees existence without protest to all individuals, and State Socialism, which regulates the competitive struggle while enhancing the efficiency of competition.[4]

Now let us remind ourselves what is the fundamental meaning of the Struggle for Existence as conditioning natural selection in the world of plants, and of animals below man. 'I should premise', Mr. Darwin writes, 'that I use this term (Struggle for Existence) in a large and metaphorical sense, including dependence of one being on another, and including what is more important, not only the life of the individual, but success in leaving progeny'.[d] The examples which follow explain that not only may two dogs, when food is scarce, be said to struggle for food; but a plant on the edge of a desert struggles against drought – that is, is dependent upon moisture, though there is in this case no competition with other plants at all; a plant may again be said to struggle with other plants for the means of disseminating its seed, or, I may venture to add, for the chance of fertilisation by insects, in which two cases its individual life is in no way or degree necessarily risked in the struggle. That is to say, the organism which wins in the struggle for existence, from the very beginning, is that so adapted to surrounding influences and objects that it not only arrives at maturity, but leaves offspring, to a relatively large extent, under such conditions that they also are likely to arrive at maturity. The 'existence' depends upon definite qualities which may no doubt be noxious, or, again, may be beneficial to the objects and creatures in contact with them.

---

[d] *Origin of Species*, ed. 6, p. 50. [See Charles Darwin, *The Origin of Species*, ed. J. W. Burrow (Harmondsworth, Penguin, 116).]

[4] Kidd defines true socialism as: 'the final suspension of that personal struggle for existence which has been waged, not only from the beginning of society, but, in one form or another, from the beginning of life' (3rd ed., 208–9). Idealists such as Caird, Jones and the Australian Idealist Francis Anderson use the distinction differently. For them true socialism is that kind of socialism which uses the State to enhance the individual's capacities. It does not suppress individualism, but, on the contrary, empowers individuals to act in spheres that were previously not possible. False socialism is that which suppresses individuality and legislates in the interest of one class.

When the struggle for existence is regarded with reference to selection, then in the plants and lower animals a further consideration enters in. The natural resources on which they depend cannot by their action be artificially supplemented, and prudential restraints from leaving progeny cannot exist. This being so, more individuals are produced than can possibly be maintained, and those of the surplus which are not destroyed by other agencies must perish of starvation. Natural selection determines according to their qualities which individuals shall survive and which shall not, and also which individuals shall leave progeny and which shall not. It is thus untrue even of plants and the lower animals to say that natural selection operates *exclusively* through destruction of individuals. In the main, moreover, artificial selection, of which sexual selection is the elementary form, and which need not act at all through extermination of individuals, does not differ in principle from natural selection, so long as it proceeds with a view to qualities which have power to set in motion the selecting agency by means which may be called natural – that is, otherwise than through a sheer conscious desire on its part to guarantee support to all existent individuals as such. For this reason, I suppose, the term natural selection is, and fairly may be, used to cover the processes of competition in society (although in them selection is conscious), so long as in these processes existence, except under protest, is determined by definite qualities which naturally set in motion the selective agency. The true line of demarcation at which the whole principle underlying natural selection is abandoned, must be where selection ceases to be selective – that is, where any agency guarantees to individuals existence without protest,[e] irrespective of human qualities. Natural selection in the wider sense suggested by this contrast plainly does not operate by starvation, but by varied forms of acceptance, rejection, and discouragement; and, at least, by abstinence from anti-selective action, i.e. from retrogressive or negative selection.

Natural selection, then, is the process by which the struggle for existence determines the perpetuation of those stocks or family

---

[e] I use the term 'existence under' or 'without protest', because in human society it is impossible forcibly to prevent the production of individuals destitute of co-operative qualities, or to starve them when produced. All that can be done is to express a protest by want of encouragement, or by penalty directed against any visibly in fault, whether parents or individuals themselves.

strains which have qualities most enabling them to conquer or to use their surroundings, especially so as to obtain success in the rearing of offspring. Now, further, the absence of what has been called 'selective value' in any quality – that is, its inability to exercise determining influence on the success or non-success of its possessor – withdraws it from the influence of selection, and there is no reason to expect that such a quality will be maintained in efficiency. 'Variations' which have no selective value 'must disappear again'.[f] This result, which Spencer finds in Darwin and himself fully accepts (*loc. cit.*), appears to me – speaking with great diffidence – to contain all that is really important in the disputed principle of 'Panmixia', which he rejects. But for our purpose, the transmission of qualities as modified by use and disuse would serve the same purpose. Qualities which are not imperatively demanded by society will not be maintained either by natural selection or by exercise.

We are now prepared to consider the case of social animals and of human communities. In proportion as exchange of services by division of labour within a group takes the place of competition of all against all, the group itself becomes the primary unit in the struggle for existence. Now, selection as between competing groups can only make adaptations in them by transforming the individuals of which they are composed, and this it is found to do with astounding thoroughness and variety. According to Weismann's recent contention, which seems likely to be justified, selection as between groups has power in the case of social insects to modify even the sterile members of the community by selecting the stocks or families from which sterile members with socially useful qualities are destined to proceed. How then does group selection affect the relations of the members of the community to each other? Plainly, I think, in this way, that the competition of communities without operates by means of the competition of individuals within. By the necessi-

---

[f] Herbert Spencer, *Inadequacy of Natural Selection*, pp. 11, 12. Herbert Spencer speaks of 'a variation' and of 'a faculty'. The same rule must surely apply to an organ (cf. *Principle of Ethics*, vol. II, p. 429). Spencer does not seem to contend that his principle of the transmission of acquired qualities would prevent the destruction of social characteristics by retrogressive selection, and, in fact, the same conditions of environment which would destroy the selective value of these qualities must also ensure their disuse. [The articles that comprise *Inadequacy of Natural Selection* first appeared in *The Contemporary Review*. The book was published in London by Williams and Norgate, 1893.]

ties of the community certain conditions are imposed on life within the community, and the 'existence' struggled for, which even at first, as we saw, included the successful rearing of progeny, now includes the conditions, be they less or more, which attach to one or another form of co-operative living.[g] The struggle for existence has, in short, become a struggle for a place in the community; and these places are reserved for the individuals which in the highest degree possess the co-operative qualities demanded by circumstances. The bee or ant has been precisely moulded to every detail of its work by this form of natural selection; and I take it that that community has always been victorious in which a place has been denied to those individuals in whom the co-operative qualities were absent. Where, however, as in the case of the bee, there are no competing stocks within the community, the absence or destruction of useless individuals is a consequence of group-modification and essential to its full effect, but is hardly in its turn a perpetuating cause of such modification.

If we now turn to human society, we find that the so-called 'existence', which is the aim of the so-called 'struggle', has received a yet further accretion of qualities. Although it would be obviously a blunder to say that every human individual aims at the common good – for if so, every one would be moral – yet it is true that the existence which any human beings regard as tolerable is made what it is by ideas which depend on a social conception – in short, by a standard of life. Further, it is very noticeable and very natural that, owing to the freedom allowed by an aim presented to intelligence the conflict of stocks within the group revives in human society as not only an effect but a cause of group modification, seeing that some stocks perish and others survive within the group, by reason of their respective qualities.

Now, at this point, I must recur to the subject of my opening remarks. We have gained but little by applying inadequate conceptions, drawn from the life of plants and of lower animals, to the life of man. The struggle for existence, and the process of natural selection, especially when understood by popular science and publicism in a way far more crude and less pregnant than that indicated by Darwin himself, are terms which do not adequately designate the

---

[g] Frequently, of course, in the social insects, involving sterility.

phenomena of human adaptation. But the worst evil which has come from applying these, as Lotze says of other conceptions, without so much as a glance at the affairs of everyday life, has not been of the most obvious kind. It is bad enough that a fundamental truth should be crudely and rudely formulated and misapplied, because people think it modern and up to date to use conceptions drawn from anything else rather than from our experience of the matter in hand. For this evil we have largely to thank Mr. Herbert Spencer, and in spite of his great abilities and untiring industry, or rather because of them and their abuse, I think that a Dante of philosophers ought to grant him the distinction of the lowest circle in the inferno.[5] But the more terrible evil, a natural consequence of the former, is that the fundamental truth, having got into low company, is repudiated as a disreputable acquaintance by the impatient purist among social reformers, and things which were known 2000 years ago, and which are obvious, as I am forced to believe, to those who look straight at the facts in question, are disputed because of the new-fangled analogies which are meant to support, but which really disguise, them.

Unquestionably, in human society, instincts and tendencies are modified by ideas. A human community does not aim at mere survival, but at a certain kind of survival; and rather than survive on certain terms, a decent society would choose destruction. A human individual, again, does not aim at mere survival, but at a certain kind of survival; and although, in the general interests of humanity, it is considered right to cling even to bare existence, yet in spite of this scruple, a being with full human qualities will readily forfeit such existence in preference to endangering these qualities in itself or in others. This we see in the phrase, 'All that makes life worth living.' It is, therefore, I submit, a fatal misconception by which Mr. Huxley tells us[h] that in human society the struggle is not for

---

[h] *Evolution and Ethics*, p. 40. [T. H. Huxley, *Evolution and Ethics and Other Essays*, vol. XI, *Collected Essays* (London, Macmillan, 1894).]

[5] Dante's *Divine Comedy* gives us a vision of hell, purgatory and heaven. *The Inferno* is divided into circles. One to five comprise upper hell, and six to nine lower hell. The ninth circle is the habitat of the treacherous who fall into four zones, or categories: those who are treacherous to family and friends; traitors to their country and causes; those who are treacherous to guests; and those who are treacherous to superiors. *The Divine Comedy*, trans. C. H. Sisson (London, Pan, 1981).

existence but for enjoyment; rather, the struggle is for a certain kind of existence, and failure to secure this entails, on the whole, immediate or rapid extinction of the particular stock which fails. Under a similar misconception, it is alleged that survival of the fittest is nothing more than survival of the fittest to survive. No one can deny that there are eddies and back currents in the river of life; but a complete discontinuity between the principles of nature and of humanity is extremely improbable, especially if we consider that the latter has come into being by the processes of the former. And this improbability is intensified to impossibility when we examine from the logical side the nature of those victorious ideas which have imposed themselves as moral upon the human race, for they are seen to be marked throughout by organic quality – by the power of arranging life and dealing with circumstance; and it is precisely this quality, however caricatured in some phases of its growth, which forms the essential strand in the development of living things. Those may sneer at strength who do not believe that reason is the ultimate power, but those who hold a different conviction cannot but judge that the survival of the most vigorous in the struggle for the existence which is aimed at, is, on the whole, the survival of the most reasonable. I repeat emphatically, 'in the struggle for the existence which is aimed at', for vigour is a term relative to circum-stances; and the most vigorous in a struggle determined by one standard of life is the weaker in that determined by another. We have to consider, then, not only the bare fact of survival, but the nature of the struggle in which survival has to be sought. 'It is for us to struggle', said Aristeides to Themistocles, 'both now and ever, which of us shall perform the greatest services to his country.'[6] But, emphatically, the development is continuous; the struggle of Aristeides is an arduous struggle still, and competition is not less but more strenuous in proportion as its purpose is more complexly determined. Does any one seriously doubt that there are in every society worse and better varieties, always remembering that the

---

[6] Herodotus, *Histories*, book eight, 79. The Penguin translation of 1972 reads: 'At this moment, more than ever before, you and I should be rivals, to see which of us can do most good to our country' (550). In Plutarch, Aristeides again makes reference to his rivalry with Themistocles: 'We two, Themistocles, if we have any sense, will have to stop this vain and childish feud of ours. From now on we ought to begin a more honourable kind of contest to save our country. . . .' Plutarch, *Rise and Fall of Athens: Nine Greek Lives* (Harmondsworth, Penguin, 1960), 118.

minimum test of excellence, by success in the struggle for existence, involves *from the first* capacity to give the progeny a good chance of maturity – in short, to furnish what we call good birth and breeding?

And, once more, the conception of panmixia in the general import, in which, as I think, Spencer himself affirms it, applies by analogy to human society. If selection for certain qualities ceases, the qualities in respect of which it ceases cannot maintain themselves; and if worse varieties – those of bad birth and breeding – are encouraged to perpetuate themselves, does any one doubt (what Plato already knew) that society must deteriorate?

But, it is asked of us, can there be the same cosmic process in society as in lower nature, when in society you can in some degree restrict the reproduction of individuals so as not to exceed the food-supply, and in nature there is perpetual excess of multiplication over the means of subsistence? Does the pressure on which the struggle depends exist at all in society? Mr. Huxley is inclined to say that this is so to a very small extent,[i] and that therefore the processes are not the same in kind. But first, as the supply of necessaries for civilised life is wholly produced by labour, every individual born is *prima facie* in excess until he justifies his existence by definite qualities. For if not, why should some one else work that he may eat? This is at once a powerful pressure in the way of producing selection, and a source of resistance to all multiplication. Secondly, if multiplication is restricted, the restriction must be either selective or non-selective. If non-selective, it is *not restriction* for our purpose, for it may well chance to diminish the supply of necessaries, which is wholly artificial, more than it diminishes the population. If selective, it is *not opposed to the cosmic process*, but itself effects the same end in a presumably less painful though analogous way. This argument from the apparent absence of severe pressure in civilised communities really shows that if society is to prosper, the cosmic process of selection by definite qualities is, and must be, continued in them perhaps *under the name of restriction*. And this Mr. Huxley recognises by his simile of the garden, the difference between which and wild nature depends chiefly on the despotic selection of the horticulturist. The requirements of despotic selection, which Plato too made an absolute condition of his artificial

[i] *Loc. cit.*

society,[7] Mr. Huxley sees to be impracticable because of the incapacity of man,[i] to which I will add the deeper reason that no despotic selection can exercise the causal action which belongs to the human analogue of natural selection. It is a question throughout not merely of birth but of breeding – 'success in leaving offspring' in the widest sense – and in human society the breeding or training is almost the more important condition for preservation of offspring. But quality of breeding material and moral upbringing for a human being, operating mainly through ideas and expectations, cannot be secured without definite conditions which mere despotic selection within a wholly uncompetitive society would absolutely exclude. No social selection – I do not shun the paradox – no social selection can be moral except natural selection in the large sense explained below; for it alone operates through character and through ideas.

I will now indicate what I conceive to be the true analogue of natural selection in human society, and I will name it at once as comprising two elements: first, the moral and material responsibility of the family; and secondly, the direct interference of society and the State, considered more especially as abstaining or not abstaining from retrogressive selection. It is not the action of the spur of hunger nor the greed of gain; these are not human motives, and each of them is operative, as Huxley rightly implies of the former, throughout only a small section of society, strictly perhaps not at all. If you reply that the spur of hunger is a phrase for the desire to live, and to live a human life, then I say that it is an ill-chosen phrase, used on both sides, we must remember, in this controversy, and that we can never obtain a correct analysis of anything till we are careful to say what we mean. That existence even on the lowest plane of our society involves a standard of life and not mere animal

---

[i] A probable instance of this struck me in relation to the modification of sterile individuals; probably Plato's government would try to breed from geniuses, but it may be that geniuses are fitted to be the last offshoots of vigorous races, and that to get them you must breed not from them but from such stocks as produce them, which is more difficult.

[7] 'We must, if we are to be consistent, and if we're to have a real pedigree herd, mate the best of our men with the best of our women as often as possible, and the inferior men with the inferior women as seldom as possible, and bring up only the offspring of the best. And no one but the Rulers must know what is happening, if we are to avoid dissension in our Guardian herd.' Plato, *Republic* (Harmondsworth, Penguin, 1987), 459d–e.

needs, is shown by the fact that to many aliens English slum or workhouse life appears a paradise.

First, then, of the family. The Western monogamic family as we know it is neither opposed to the State nor independent of it; it is largely the creation of Roman law, is supported by the law in all civilised countries, and could be destroyed or disfigured beyond recognition by indifferent or hostile State action. Now, broadly speaking, the co-operative individual, as demanded by civilised life, can only be produced in the family, and therefore by a stock capable of forming a true family; and the test and engine of his production is the peculiar form of moral responsibility, supported by law and covering both material and moral incidents, which the family implies. Its unique importance as an agent of selection arises, of course, from the fact that to the family is entrusted the multiplication of the species, and its automatic action as a selective agency depends on the recognition of the principle that this union should only be entered on where the conditions of success in the struggle for a distinctively human existence, including as throughout a proper rearing of offspring, may be reasonably anticipated. The question of population is not a mere numerical question; of some qualities of population it is impossible to have too much, for they are self-limiting, of others every individual is in excess. The main difference between these kinds of population depends on the material and moral responsibility for the family being left with those who have voluntarily formed it, and on every possible discouragement being thrown in the way of unions taking place where the true conditions of family life do not exist. I say, then, that the struggle to realise the conditions of true family life in its moral and material senses is the human 'struggle for existence' within the group, and that defeat in this struggle does largely entail, and ought as far as possible to entail, the extinction of the stock so failing. The moral responsibility on its material side is one which, above all, needs care and patience in analysing. Even if it includes, by misfortune, the need of meeting the pressure of hunger, it is not the mere appetite so described; the need of providing necessaries and decencies for wife and child is not mere greed or hunger in the man. But although I repudiate such phrases as 'the necessity of the spur of hunger', I fully recognise the fact that an absolutely secured material position, such as that of the wealthy class, is not favourable, on the whole, to productivity in the interests of society; and I desiderate for every one, for their own sake, some possibility of falling into distress by lack of wisdom and exertion. It is not the same thing, however, to hold a position which, with all its possibilities as a human life, may easily be forfeited through indolence or folly, and to be urged on by the mere animal terror of starvation. The former is that scaffolding or support afforded to the internal by the external conscience (to use George Eliot's phrase) which no one need be ashamed of requiring. We are all of us at times poor creatures; and the most high-minded is none the worse for being kept up to his work. But the latter is an animal motive; and I doubt whether, in a technical sense, it can ever be rightly identified with the mainspring of a true human life. Yet none the less, the large fact is that natural selection by the struggle for existence is, in the sense I have indicated, essential to the prosperity of human society, and the means of this selection is the fullest recognition both by law and by public opinion of the responsibility attaching to the author of a family, both for its material and for its moral requirements.

Time does not permit me to analyse fully the drift and import of modern sentiment and legislation regarding the family. My point is sufficiently clear if I explain that such analysis should be directed to distinguishing between two movements which have much in common – which, in fact progress in curves perhaps even coincident for a portion of their arcs. The free school, the improved and co-operative dwelling and factory, the library, the club, and the permanent organisation of labour, may all of them be agencies for ennobling and enlarging the family life and making its basis more solid. It is also possible that they, or extensions of them, may be made agencies for destroying it. And here we come face to face with the direct selective or anti-selective action of the State, or of wholesale philanthropy.

I wish very distinctly to insist that this is also capable of two directions, and that the problems arising are not to be solved by administrative nihilism, but by care and analytic experience and patient continuance in well-doing. But subject to this reservation, I desire to call attention to the frightful dangers that attend any over-riding of what is relatively natural selection through family responsibility, by the direct interference of administrative or other philanthropy. I do not at all deny that sometimes the evils caused by partial interference may demand completer interference. Time only permits me to indicate a few typical points.

I begin by a general statement applying to our whole social life which very clearly emphasises the difference between the improvement of surrounding conditions of life, and the operation of natural selection in the extinction of the worst varieties. It is alleged[k] that the Registrar-General's analysis of the death-rate for the period from 1858 to 1890, distinguishing the causes of death preventible by improved surroundings from those dependent on hereditary constitution, shows the former to be diminishing, but the latter to be increasing in their operation. This would mean that the weakly, who are saved from neglect and from acute disease, live past the time of child-bearing, only to fall victims to constitutional ailments which, meantime, they have transmitted to descendants. Life is longer, but death from old age is rarer than thirty years ago.[l] If this is true, and I give it with some reserve, the inference is plain. The severer selective agencies have been arrested by improved surroundings; but family responsibility, the only practical substitute, has not yet operated in their place, and the race is less robust.

Passing from this general tendency to the direct action of the State, we find, of course, that, to some extent inevitably, the *Poor Law* encourages an element of the population for whom the family does not exist, or who are preserved only to hand on to others the defects which, but for our elaborate hospitals and infirmaries, would have perished with them. Particularly frightful in this connection is the case of those known as feeble-minded pauper girls, who become recurrent inmates of the workhouses, where the best medical attendance is furnished to them, and of whose children the kindest-hearted woman will often say, '*fortunately* the child died'. Here it may be that a further interference may help. These girls are not fit to protect themselves in the world, and though they cannot be certified as proper inmates for a lunatic asylum, it seems possible to prevent the evils that attach to their life and its perpetuation by some form of attractive custodial home.

---

[k] [John Berry] Haycraft, in *British Medical Journal*, 24th February 1894. See *Darwinism and Race Progress*, by this author, about to be published by Sonnenschein and Co. [The article referred to is an abstract of lecture II in the series 'The Milroy Lectures on Darwinism and Race Progress'. The book was published in 1895.]

[l] The appearance of this is partly owing to increased accuracy of diagnosis.

And apart from the question of medical care as such, there is no doubt that the public provision for the destitute must to some extent, and may to a terrible extent, be the cause of early and reckless marriages which fulfil no moral nor material conditions of the union, of desertion of wife and children, and of irregular unions. In all these cases, besides the direct evil of ill-nurture, a bad variety is almost certainly perpetuated.[m] I forbear at this late hour to introduce the whole miserable story of the old Poor Law, with its payment per head for children born out of wedlock, by which it was rightly said that the English law had abolished chastity. If any one thinks that wholly and in principle these evils have now been annihilated, he is unacquainted with the subject, and with the difficulties inherent in a system which is bound to deal humanely with all comers of every kind, and therefore cannot but be in some degree a refuge in which the wreckage of society refits, only to be wrecked again to the lasting injury of the community. The typical case of the American Jukes family, 1200 descendants of which, in seven generations, were estimated to have cost £260,000 in prison expenses and public relief, is an example of the worst varieties, which, with the best administration, are not easily extinguished, and with every laxity multiply like a bacillus.[8]

Now the general conclusion which I desire to draw is not in the direction of recurring to severity against the helpless, but it urges the absolute necessity of regarding all these interferences as unavoidable evils and not as precedents for more general action. We should make them thorough and effective where they are essential, and convert, where possible, the very treatment which might otherwise encourage a bad variety into a hindrance to its perpetuation, as by the seclusion of the hopeless inebriate and the feeble-minded girl-pauper, or by the best possible nurture of the pauper child, the almost insuperable difficulty of which shows the hazard of the whole system. We should avoid in every way the protrusion of analogous

[m] At present, in a case of which I have information, five illegitimate children of a single pair are being maintained by the ratepayers. Being unmarried, the father cannot be compelled to maintain them except by procedure initiated by the mother. She will take no action, and he can laugh at the public. See also IV.

[8] This was a widely cited example. Herbert Spencer uses it in *The Man Versus the State* (Indianapolis, Liberty, 1982), 110. Also see R. L. Dugdale, *The Jukes: A Study in Crime, Pauperism, Disease and Heredity* (North Stratford, New Hampshire, Ayer, 1973).

interference into the healthy life of the industrial class. We should never forget that the system is a necessary evil, nor ever handle our public initiative, whether through the Poor Law or through more general legislation, so as to relieve the father of the support of the wife and children, or the grown-up child of the support of his parents. We should raise no expectation of help, or of employment invented *ad hoc*, which may derange the man's organisation of life in view of the whole normal responsibilities which, as a father, he has accepted. Whether by any particular measure we are destroying a man's responsibilities or helping him to face them is in each case, so to speak, a question for the jury. The distinction of principle is all that I plead for in this page.

The same points are illustrated by the results observed from the action of vast voluntary agencies whose operations approach in magnitude those of the State. I read a couple of extracts from a trustworthy Report from East London. This is a Report from experienced people, who, having been asked to help cases of the kind referred to, have gone into them carefully in detail. The question is the old one of the effect of Shelters and Refuges.

> Such shelters[n] confer no real or permanent benefit on those who use them; they are not centres of reform, and they do not restore their inmates to independence or self-support. They are merely places of temporary lodging, from which their inmates go away in the same condition as that in which they arrived, if not in a worse one. So far from lessening the number of destitute people without regular means or employment, they tend to increase it, because they make the life of the shiftless and the idle more easy, and so offer a new temptation to those who are too willing to live, as far as possible, at the expense of others.
>
> Beyond this, these refuges appear to us to make it easy for husbands and wives to evade their mutual responsibilities, and to neglect the education and proper bringing up of their children. We have met with instances of the husband being in one shelter, the wife and children in another; or of the husband altogether deserting his family and living away from them, apparently doing little for his own support, and nothing for theirs; whilst they, in the refuges, are supported by the charitable. In regard to the children of those who frequent these institutions, it is almost inevitable

---

[n] This letter has since been published as a letter from the Whitechapel Committee of the C.O.S. in C.O. [Charity Organisation] *Review*, November 1894.

that they should suffer morally and physically from the nature of their surroundings. There is no discrimination in regard to the admission of inmates, many of whom are of the most degraded character, and the least fitted to associate with the young or respectable.

As a rule, children from the refuges do not attend school, and it is very difficult for the School Board, in their case, to exercise their legitimate authority. We know, as a fact, that parents and children are turned into the streets from morning till evening to pass the day as best they can, sitting or standing about in public places, and often, no doubt, employed in begging. This must be bad alike for mind and body.

We believe that in this district, at any rate, the evil is on the increase, *and is having an appreciable effect upon the population of the district.*° I may mention as an instance of this, that the superintendent of one of the shelters said, that the average number of those who passed through it is 1500 per month. They are not allowed to remain more than three days at a time in the shelter, but may return after a short interval, which is usually spent in other institutions of the same kind.

I quite understand that to many hearers this will appear an isolated piece of grumbling, and in no way typical of rocks ahead in social interference by retrogressive selection. But I venture to think that to those who have attended both in detail and in principle to the history and symptoms of the social problem, it is merely a rather striking example of what everyday and universal experience both of State and of wholesale private action has long made familiar.

I am therefore convinced that the general distinction on which Mr. Kidd has lighted in his treatment of modern Socialism is sound in principle. If Socialism means the improvement of society by society, we are going on that track more or less today, as civilised society has always gone, and the collective organisation of certain branches of production is a matter open to discussion with a view to its consequences. But if Socialism means the total suppression of the personal struggle for existence, as above described, and the collective guarantee of support to all children, or still worse to all adults, without enforcing the responsibilities of parents or of sons and daughters, then I think that it really is in hopeless conflict with

---

° The italics are mine [B.B.].

the universal postulates of the struggle for existence and natural selection, as justly interpreted of human society. Experience has amply shown that such conditions operate on man as panmixia operates among lower organisms. The worst varieties throughout the whole community are perpetuated equally with the best, and if we believe in inherited degeneration by disuse, then for this reason too social qualities must in such conditions degenerate. The best are indeed heavily handicapped by having to support the others, and the tendency is for the whole community to lose the efficiency of its human qualities. An aim of the kind has quite certainly been suggested by some Socialist writers[p] – I mention Mr. Bellamy, and, so far as concerns the children, explicitly, Mr. Blatchford[q] see also Mr. Shaw[r] and Mr Wallas,[s] – but I attach less importance to the avowed aim than to the intellectual drifting which makes leeway towards a result of this kind, under the influence of precedents such as the Poor Law or Free Education, first theoretically misunderstood and then practically distorted step by step. I have attempted this evening to indicate the confusion and its source.

---

[p] And see generally the manifesto of English Socialists signed, among others by the Fabian Society, urging 'the free maintenance of all necessitous children', not, it will be observed, suggesting any restriction to the children of necessitous parents, nor any attempt to remove, in each case, the evil of which the children's need is a symptom.

[q] *Merrie England*, p. 19: 'I say there is no need for any struggle for existence', p. 44; 'I would have all our children fed and clothed and educated at the cost of the State.' [London, Clarion/Walter Scott, 1894].

[r] *Fabian Essays*, 'Transition', p.[199–] 200, first edition: 'One can see that [. . .] the economic independence of woman [women], and the supplementing [supplanting] of the head of the household by the individual as the recognised unit of the State, will materially alter the status of children and the utility of the institution of the family.' [Published by Scott in London, 1899 and edited by George Bernard Shaw.]

[s] *Fabian Essays*, p. 146: 'If we wish to wean the children from the selfish isolation of the English family.' The passage from Morris and Bax, quoted by Professor Flint in *Socialism*, p. 284, throws a painful light on the attitude of some Socialists to the family. [Published in London by Ibister, 1894.]

4
Ethical Democracy: Evolution and Democracy

D. G. RITCHIE

'Evolution' is very generally looked upon as the central idea of modern scientific and philosophical thought. 'Democracy' is for many the final goal, or at least it is the inevitable path, of our political and social progress. It is reasonable to connect the two terms and to ask ourselves what light can be thrown by biological conceptions upon the theoretical and practical problems of society. But we must guard carefully against the rhetorical and un-critical use of phrases which have a scientific sound, or which have served as the watchwords of eager struggles. Those who believe themselves advanced thinkers are sometimes apt to treat everything that takes place through evolution as if it were identical with progress, and to take it for granted that the democratic movements of our age must, simply because they *are* the movements of our age, be all of them of a progressive kind. More cautious thinking suggests many difficulties; and it is sometimes even argued that biology throws no light whatever upon sociology, theoretical or practical. In the enthusiasm caused by the theories of Mr Herbert Spencer and the discoveries of Darwin it was often too lightly assumed that society could be explained by the direct application of the formulae which had proved so successful in the biological sphere. 'The social organism' seemed to be a key to unlock political and social mysteries. The structure and the functions of society were thought to be fully intelligible only if approached from the biological side. Social evolution has been supposed to need the law of natural selection and that alone to make its tendencies scientifically interpretable. These exaggerations have naturally provoked reaction: and we now find some thoughtful writers refusing to allow any value whatever to the conception of the 'social organism': it is only a metaphor, and a very misleading metaphor. The science of sociology must be kept clear of biological influence.[a] Now this is an exaggeration on the other side. Human beings, whatever else they may be, are animals, and, as such, are subject to biological laws; and no careful study of social conditions, with a view to their understanding or their amelioration, can afford to neglect the biological facts of heredity and sex and the primitive, but ever present, struggle for food and for the means of rearing off-spring. Though the attempts to carry out into detail the image of the social organism have often led to absurdity, and though practical deductions from it of a perfectly contradictory kind can easily be made, the metaphor has at least helped to free discussion of political problems from artificial assumptions, such as those of the social contract theory; and the word 'evolution' may at least serve to remind the impatient reformer of institutions that he is dealing with what cannot be suddenly changed, nor in any arbitrary direction. The idea of social evolution goes along with less revolutionary methods than the older doctrines of social contract and natural rights.

In the wide philosophical sense of the term, the conception of evolution does not perhaps give much help towards understanding or forecasting or judging the movements of society, except in so far as it may suggest some general considerations for estimating progress. If evolution be the transition from incoherent homogeneity to definite heterogeneity, this would seem to show that the more highly developed society must be that in which there is at once greater social order and greater diversity in the type of individual development. The formula of evolution does not indeed give us any standard by which we can balance 'order' and 'liberty', unity and diversity, against one another: and it must be remembered that the

---

[a] I may refer to the writings of M. Tarde and M. Coste, who take very different views of sociology, but are agreed on this matter. Mr R. Mackintosh holds the same view in his book, 'From Comte to Benjamin Kidd'.[1]

[1] Jean Gabrikel Tarde, *Social Laws: An Outline of Sociology*, trans. H. C. Warren (New York, Macmillan, 1899); Adolphe Coste, *L'Expérience des peuples et les prévisions qu'elle autorise* (Paris, 1900); and R. Mackintosh, *From Comte to Benjamin Kidd: the Appeal of Biology or Evolution for Human Guidance* (London, Macmillan, 1899).

process of evolution may include degeneration as well as what we call progress, greater adaptation on the whole being secured by the sacrifice of individual completeness or independence. Still, this general conception of evolution may prevent us from accepting an ideal of society which underestimates the value and the need of cohesion and discipline – an ideal of *laissez faire* such as Mr Herbert Spencer retains from the individualistic Radicalism of his youthful days in spite of all his biological formulae. On the other hand, the significance of differentiation in development may guard us against the monotonous rigidity of some collectivistic ideals, which provide no sufficient scope for individual initiative and no sufficient security against the crystallisation that means decay and death to societies. From the general formula of evolution – a formula such as most philosophers from the time of the Ionian Greeks downwards might accept – we are at least warned that the only safe movement of social change is one which shall avoid anarchy on the one side and over- regulation on the other. The golden mean is a vague ideal and standard of conduct; and yet it is a more useful principle than many that seem more definite by being more abstract.

When, however, the conception of evolution is applied to politics, people are generally, and rightly, thinking of specially biological conceptions: and of these the most prominent is that of Natural Selection. If progress depends upon a perpetual struggle for existence, there seems indeed a *prima facie* argument for liberty in the negative sense of *laissez faire*; but everything else that may be included in democratic ideals appears to be condemned as hopeless or mischievous in its consequences. Nature produces not equality but inequality; nay, inequality is even requisite for natural selection to work upon. Fraternity, again, seems clearly impossible when ceaseless struggle and ruthless elimination of the unfit are the very means of progress. The argument from biology to politics would appear to support, not democracy, but aristocracy, and to enforce the enduring necessity of war and of unchecked industrial competition. If democracy can be defended on the basis of scientific thinking about society, it seems to be only in so far as democracy means the opening of careers to those who have the talents for them, and the abolition of institutions and sentiments that hamper the struggle for life and interfere with 'that beneficent private war' which leads to the survival of the fittest.

Some such inferences are, indeed, what are commonly drawn by literary opponents of radical and socialistic ideals. The 'aristocratic preferences' of nature and the ceaseless competition by which alone fitness for existence is produced and maintained, supply excellent rhetorical common-places, when the advocate of things as they are wishes to confute advanced politicians in the name of advanced science. There is an important element of truth in such arguments; but the practical inferences are very crudely and carelessly drawn from their supposed biological premises. We must seek to realise much more precisely what is the exact meaning of natural selection, and how far, or with what modifications, it can be applied to the interpretation of social evolution. Then only are we entitled to find any guidance in our criticism of political aspirations or in our search for safe methods of reform.

There has recently been a disposition among certain biologists to minimise the significance of Darwin's great discovery of natural selection. It is said, for instance, that natural selection only means elimination of the less fit: it is a merely negative process. The important factor in development would thus seem to be the positive element – whatever that may be – which determines the variations upon which natural selection works. Now, it is perfectly true that the theory of natural selection presupposes variations. But the fact of a tendency to variation (in different degrees) in vegetable and animal organisms admits of no doubt. Examine the flowers that spring from the same root, the plants grown from seeds taken from the same seed-vessel, the puppies of the same litter, the children of the same parents, – variation will always be found, sometimes slight, sometimes startling in amount. This indefiniteness or instability of nature is the material for natural selection. How to explain it is certainly a task for the biologist; but so also is the fact of hereditary likeness. That the offspring resembles the parent on the whole, and that the offspring differs more or less from the parent – these are undoubted facts, and each of them looked at by itself constitutes a difficult problem, when attention is directed to it. Heredity and variation – i.e, identity or continuity and diversity or change – are presupposed as facts by the theory of natural selection, which is not meant to explain *them* but to account historically for the existence of species – i.e. to explain why certain variations become the permanent and inherited characteristics of whole groups of organisms.

Those variations which prove advantageous to the organism in its particular environment are selected, because those organisms with unfavourable variations are less successful in finding nourishment and in leaving a numerous or vigorous offspring behind them. In this sense natural selection is certainly a negative process; but to call it 'merely negative', as if it were therefore unimportant, is just as if we were to call the work of the sculptor merely negative, because the marble block must be there and he only chips away what he does not want for his purpose. When variations are described as 'accidental' or 'spontaneous' it must of course be understood that these terms mean only 'not as yet fully accounted for'. One can indeed understand how variation in the protozoa is caused simply by the action of the environment on the organism. Again, one can easily see how the existence of sex produces variations which do not arise in asexual reproduction: and this explains why the appearance of sex in the world should immensely accelerate the process of evolution by giving natural selection a greater number of variations to work upon. A tendency to vary greatly within certain more or less definite limits is itself an inherited and inheritable tendency: and such a tendency would clearly be advantageous to a species which had to meet diverse or fluctuating conditions, and this tendency to variation might therefore be itself preserved and increased by natural selection. Other explanations of variation may be requisite; but it is certainly no scientific explanation to say that a variation is due to some definite choice or purpose in nature. Such phrases are scientifically on a level with 'occult qualities', or 'the soporific virtues' of opium. To suppose that a Divine Artificer gives organisms a tendency to vary in certain definite useful directions and then looks on while they fight for survival with one another is an inconsistent mixture of mythology and natural science: it is lame science and it is very unphilosophical theology. The difficulty before us is not merely this and that puzzling knot requiring a *Deus ex machina*. The whole process of things, the existence of nature and man, is a problem for thought, whether man be made straight away from inorganic dust or slowly evolved out of lower animal forms by the working of natural selection. The philosophical problem arises equally out of either belief; but scientifically the two explanations stand on very different levels. The process of natural selection leads to the survival of the fittest; and so, looking back on the whole process, we may say that nature 'intends' the fittest. But we must not introduce this intention or purpose here and there to fill up gaps in the chain of material and efficient causes, 'Final cause' or purpose may be the only point of view from which we can understand the meaning of the whole; but the episodic introduction of final causes here and there is rightly repudiated by science and by all careful philosophy.

Natural selection, as a theory, has the enormous advantage of being an indisputable fact. Anyone who watches a piece of neglected garden ground, or a collection of fish and other animals in an aquarium, can see the process going on. Those kinds and those individuals alone survive which are best fitted to survive in the particular environment. They are not necessarily the kinds and individuals we like best or wish to keep alive. Those that are less able to obtain the nourishment they need are perpetually eliminated. Natural selection is thus a *vera causa*; it is a fact, not in itself an hypothesis. The question that has to be solved is simply, How far does it serve as a sufficient explanation of the differences between species and of the relative stability of types? Darwin's and Russel Wallace's theory of natural selection has thus an immense logical advantage, as an hypothesis, over the Lamarckian theory of use-inheritance or its modern revivals; because the mere fact of the inheritance of acquired characteristics, however convenient and plausible as an explanation, is open to doubt, and, on 'the principle of parsimony', we should not resort to a doubtful or unknown cause if a known cause is sufficient. The theory of natural selection is, moreover, only the form under which the movement of bodies in the line of least resistance appears in the more complex biological sphere. Why has a stream taken this direction rather than that? It is because in one direction its course is impeded by very hard rock, in another it can work its way through softer materials. The environment 'selects' the channel of the stream by hindering it from moving in other ways. If we like, we may call the onward rush of the water under the law of gravitation a positive cause, and the selection due to the environment a merely negative process. But if anyone were asked why the river flowed in a particular direction, and answered, 'Because by nature it had a tendency to go in that direction', he would not be thought to throw much light on the problem; whereas he who points out the influence of the environment does give a causal explanation.

At the other end of the scale it seems to me that the process of thought, the process by which the mind, having before it various hypotheses or possibilities, rejects those which it regards as unsuitable and accepts that which presents fewest difficulties and gives most satisfaction – this process of thought is not, in any sincere person, a process of arbitrary choice or deliberate 'will to believe' or to disbelieve, but a process of natural selection in the mental sphere. What seems to A certain or probable may seem to B absurd; the theory which best fits in with the existing system of knowledge and belief in one mind may be unfitted to thrive in a different mind, and the orthodoxy of one intellectual environment may be incapable of growth or survival in a different spiritual soil. The process by which we accept and reject opinion is not merely *analogous to* natural selection. It is that same process in a higher sphere, though we may prefer to call it 'the dialectic movement of thought' or by some other term which is free from biological associations. The element of consciousness differentiates intellectual selection from biological natural selection, just as life differentiates biological natural selection from what takes place in the merely physical realm. But the obvious difference should not blind us to the underlying identity. Nature in the widest sense includes the mind of man as well as his bodily organism; it includes the facts dealt with by psychology as well as those dealt with by physics and biology. And I can see no absolute objection to applying Darwin's term 'natural selection', or Mr H. Spencer's term 'survival of the fittest', outside the purely biological sphere in order to express this identity of principle. Of course, if by conscious selection be meant the deliberate choice of this idea rather than that, because of some extraneous authority to which the mind submits without real inner conviction, the process is then analogous to artificial selection. If I deliberately keep and sow, year by year, all the seeds of red sweet peas and destroy all the pods of the purple flowers, that is not natural selection; and, similarly, if I deliberately read only one kind of book, and associate only with one type of person, I am artificially shaping the contents of my mind, and consequently determining what I shall have a chance of assimilating and to what I shall refuse the opportunity of finding a place in my thoughts. But the process of mental selection is seldom purely artificial; the greater part of what honest persons call their conscious thinking goes on in them and determines their beliefs often in spite of their personal inclinations. Not 'I will to believe', but 'Ich kann nicht anders' is the utterance of the man who has earnestly grappled with a theoretical or a practical problem. He may or may not be deluded in the eyes of those who consider themselves competent judges, but a mind and character of a certain type and training can only assimilate certain ideas, and must reject all others, *while it remains what it is*.[b] The scholar interpreting an ancient classic, the honest juryman deliberating on his verdict with the evidence before him and his own prejudices unconsciously in the background, or any conscientious person who has to adopt a line of conduct, may often be in great doubt as to what is right, but if he comes to a decided conviction, he does so, not because of an arbitrary resolution adopted beforehand, but because he feels that the truth must be so and not otherwise. His mind can only harbour certain ideas or principles, and must reject what is inconsistent with the system of his knowledge and beliefs as that exists at the time.

If, then, the principle of natural selection applies even in the sphere of intellectual processes, there need be little doubt that it is applicable to the less conscious processes which make up the most of our social life. There may be some inconvenience in extending a biological term to the sociological sphere, but, as already said, it is important to recognise an identity of principle amid different modes of application. There seems a gap between the evolution of animal organisms and the evolution of customs and institutions and all that constitutes the materials of civilisation; but the transition from the one kind of evolution to the other is gradual. The use of tools and the use of vocal language make a vast gap between man and the lower animals: they certainly lead to the gap becoming greater and greater in the later stages, but in their beginnings they are only the extension of what the higher animals below man have already in faint germ. The first brute ancestor of man that used a stone to break a hard nut made it possible for his human descendants to do many things for which their mere bodily frame is unfitted. This

---

[b] This last clause recognises the psychological facts misinterpreted in the ordinary free-will doctrine. I purposely do not touch on the metaphysical aspects of the problem here.

was a variation which may have originated by 'chance' – i.e. without any deliberate adaptation of means to end; but, once there, natural selection could work upon it, and we have the beginning of a new epoch in which changes in the bodily organism might cease, in which the bodily organism might even deteriorate in efficiency, and yet in which social progress could go on with a rapidity impossible in the merely biological stage of natural selection. Even on the Lamarckian theory of use-inheritance there can be only a very slight increase of power to each generation through the transmission of acquired characteristics. Thus the experience acquired by the individual perishes with him, either altogether or almost entirely, unless he is able to store up the results of such experience in a form independent of his own life and even of the life of his descendants.

Tools – and from the crudest type of implement the most elaborate kinds of machinery and the most complicated and enduring structures differ only in degree of development – tools and language, when language rises beyond the emotional stage and becomes capable of describing and so of preserving the traditions of past experience, can be handed on not merely to offspring, but to others of different race, if only they have reached a sufficient stage to use such alien inventions. Here at once we have an important difference between biological and social evolution, and yet the principle of natural selection is operating in both of them. Tools, language, institutions, ideas, are varied from time to time by accident, by attempts at imitation which turn out to be inexact copies, by the combination of several different models. Variations which suit this or that set of circumstances are selected and transmitted by social inheritance. Others die out or survive only if harmless or not very hurtful. But this process of selection and transmission can go on to a great extent independently of the survival of races. It is the characteristic advantage, and at the same time the characteristic danger, of all the appliances which make up civilisation that they can be transmitted and inherited independently of biological heredity. A race may be decaying in vigour while nevertheless continuing for a long time to have an advantage in the competition with other races; but, on the other hand, the vigorous, less-civilised race may make an immense step forwards by adopting an equipment which others have perfected and, when the advantage in respect of equipment is nearly equalised, the more physically vigorous may

easily overthrow an exhausted, though long-civilised, stock. Civilisation – or, to take a wider term, inheritable equipment (equipment,
I mean, in respect of stored-up experience, science, mechanical
appliances, institutions, etc.) – produces a relative cessation of natural selection in its biological sense. There is never any cessation of
natural selection in that wider sense in which it includes the competition between languages, institutions, customs, and all the other
kinds of social equipment. But, though biological natural selection
may be relatively and temporarily in abeyance, it is working to some
extent all the time. The race may not be to the swift nor the battle
to the strong so far as individuals, so far even as existing social
groups, are concerned: the less swift may travel by steam, and the
less strong may be armed with machine-guns, may be better disciplined, or more skilfully led. But after several generations the cessation of biological natural selection must tell against the energy and
capacity of a people, though they inherit the equipment of more
vigorous ancestors. Wherever natural selection is in abeyance there
will be racial degeneration, owing to the survival in relatively
increasing numbers of the physically less fit, unless the 'natural'
process of weeding-out can be replaced by judicious artificial selection. This seems to me the briefest statement that can be given of
the main problem that confronts all who value harmony, peace,
culture, and who dread the cruelty of nature's mode of selection
when it takes place among conscious and thinking human beings,
whose souls suffer from the struggle that keeps in health and vigour
the wild beasts who are not plagued by a reflective conscience or
too keen a sense of pity. Wherever there are institutions and traditions, there artificial selection of a kind is going on – e.g. if certain
customs about marriage have grown up which interfere with the
primitive struggle for mates,[c] or if prudence or ascetic religion lead

[c] Sexual selection, in Darwin's sense, means a certain interference with strict natural
selection, and is an aesthetic luxury in which animals can only indulge where
natural selection is not very severe. Thus very gorgeous colouring, like that of the
male bird of Paradise, would be a disadvantage and a danger, except in a locality
where the birds had not many enemies, till Europeans came to obtain adornments
for their own unfeathered females.[2]

[2] See Charles Darwin, *The Origin of Species By Means of Natural Selection: Or the
Preservation of Favoured Races in the Struggle for Life* (Harmondsworth, Penguin,
1985), 136–38; and *Descent of Man. and Selection in Relation to Sex*, 2nd edn.
(London, Murray, 1888).

to the continuance of the species being left mainly to the most reckless. No human race, however rudimentary its language, however rude its institutions, however meagre the range of its ideas, is subject to mere biological natural selection. To get the advantage which natural selection gives to plants and animals in the wild state we should have to cease to be human. Our only resource is, therefore, to make our institutions and ideas as useful and as reasonable as possible in order to prevent the inevitable artificial selection of civilisation being injurious to the race.

While, then, biological natural selection must apply to human beings as to all other animals, its effects are complicated and in many ways counteracted by the artificial selection which is due to man's external equipment (I borrow this Aristotelian phrase to express the equipment which is not part of his bodily structure). These external equipments are themselves subject to a natural selection, identical in principle with biological natural selection, but producing very different results. Moreover, among human beings we have a very great extension of a type of struggle and selection of which the beginnings are to be found among the gregarious animals. There is a struggle between one social group and another: and this struggle between groups at once mitigates and complicates the struggle between individual and individual within each group. But, whereas an animal who belongs to a social group belongs only to one group (herd, hive, flock, etc.), human beings, as they rise in the scale of civilisation, belong each to a greater variety of social groups. This seems curiously forgotten by many who have made much use of the conception of the social organism. The social organism is often taken as if it could only be identical with the nation. Again, by others it is made to mean human beings as grouped by their economic wants – the political structure being strangely regarded as something extraneous and inorganic. Sometimes the social organism is spoken of as if it included the whole of mankind. Now, one thing that makes a social organism so very different from an animal organism is just this, that every human being, except those belonging to the most primitive types of society, which are nearest to the mere animal herd, belongs to many social organisms. Family, nation, parish, church, profession, trade-union, club, political party, social set – all these are social organisms, more or less definite in structure, more or less centralised; and many of them overlap. A man's kindred may belong to several different nationalities; his religion may make him the member of an international society or may cut him off from the ties of kindred. Each of these social organisms has its own life and is subject to natural selection. Many of them conflict with one another, compete for members, and flourish only by the decay of the others. The individual's allegiance is often divided, and he has to face painful conflicts of duties because of the non-coincidence of the organisms to which he belongs.

It is thus sufficiently obvious that the interpretation of social phenomena in the light of the theory of natural selection is no easy matter. In fact, it might almost seem as if whilst natural selection must apply in social evolution, it were impossible for any finite intelligence to say how in any given case it will apply. The light which evolutionary conceptions seemed to promise turns out to be a bewildering series of cross-lights and interlacing shadows. In any case the greatest caution must be exercised, and we must guard against the uncritical use of biological analogies. The phrase 'struggle for existence' leads many people to think of war as its typical exemplification in human society. Struggle suggests fighting; and, on that ground, indeed, the Darwinian idea has sometimes been resented as unjust to nature, which, it is urged, is not all 'red in tooth and claw', not a mere 'squabble around the platter', but contains elements as well of peace and love and mutual help. But, though the phrase 'struggle for existence' suggests a battle, the phrase, as used technically by Darwin, is taken by him 'in a large and metaphorical sense, including dependence of one being on another, and including (what is more important) not only the life of the individual, but success in leaving progeny'.[d] On the theory of natural selection, the helplessness of infancy is a main factor in producing stable institutions and moral ideas. But war, also, in spite of much prevalent rhetorical metaphor, is something very different from the act of the lion or the vulture seizing its prey. It is something more than the hunting of a pack of wolves; for an army, at least any army that is likely to be formidable or successful against another army, involves not mere instinctive common action of predaceous individuals, but a highly-developed system of conscious co-operation. Thus war comes to be an important factor in the

---

[d] 'Origin of Species', 6th edn p. 50. [Penguin edition, p. 116.]

making of nations, in the production of united social organisms, within which the animal struggle for existence is therefore mitigated. If we look among human beings for the strict continuance of the biological struggle, we find it rather in industrial and commercial competition. Shopkeepers in the same line of business, lawyers, doctors, schoolmasters, clerks, labourers who are 'free' – i.e. who are neither slaves nor members of trade-unions – are struggling for existence in the Darwinian sense, though the poor-law, 'charity', family ties, and the inheritance of property may introduce artificial interference with natural selection. Even between nations the Darwinian struggle is illustrated more completely in the continuous competition for markets, than in an occasional war, which is usually only a symptom of a wider and more persistent rivalry. A war between civilised powers is the primitive form of a lawsuit; it is a lawsuit between parties who do not acknowledge a common sovereign. War between a civilised power and barbarians or savages may be often simply a matter of police: and the conquest of barbarians by a civilised power will result in the cessation of war among the barbarians, the diminution of famines and pestilences, the rapid increase of population, and, consequently, in the long run, the intensification of the 'peaceful' animal struggle for existence.

So complicated, then, is the operation of natural selection in human society, so varied and entangled are the organisms affected by it, that we might despair of finding any help from the idea of evolution. The chief lesson would seem to be extreme caution in accepting any biological metaphors or phrases as arguments and a sense of the necessity of going behind the more obvious applications of them. In one respect, however, the conceptions of organism and natural selection are of immense service to our ethical and political thinking. They put the utilitarian theory upon a scientific basis, they free it from the objections which intuitionists could so easily make to it, and they rescue ethics and politics from the arbitrary and subjective standards of intuitionism. I do not think that the theory of natural selection can give a complete explanation of the meaning of right and wrong; it can only attempt to explain the matter or content of our ethical judgments. The ultimate question of the relation of the ideal to the actual, of 'ought' to 'is', of the sense in which man is more than a mere part of nature – this ultimate question (whether soluble or not) belongs to the metaphysic of ethics. But for the practical discussion of what is better or worse in social conduct and institutions we gain greatly by having the questions removed from the region of prejudice, superstition, and sentiment. In all democratic communities (unless they are ancient and extremely conservative democracies like some of the small Swiss cantons), rhetoric has an importance which it could not possibly obtain in very oligarchical states. The orators and 'sophists' of ancient Athens, the popular leaders and journalists of England, France and America, help to mould the opinions of today and the action of tomorrow; and democracies are therefore peculiarly apt to suffer from unreasoning sentiment and from bad metaphysics. Appeals to traditional prejudice, appeals to the Law of Nature and natural rights, may contain in them much that is noble and inspiring, but they require to be criticised 'in a calm hour'. And we must find some standard that does not depend entirely on an individual conscience which regards its oracular utterances as infallible. 'The Greatest Happiness of the Greatest Number' was supposed to be such a standard – scientific because it introduced a quantitative principle, and democratic because it consulted the interests of the majority. The appearance of precision in this standard, however vanishes after examination. The calculus of pleasures gives rise to endless difficulties when any attempt is made to work it out. How is intensity to be measured against duration? How are one person's pleasures to be compared with another's? How is the inferior or more transitory pleasure of the many to be balanced against the intenser or more lasting pleasures of a few? The real historical significance of the Benthamist formula is to be found, not in its attempt to introduce quantitative precision in a region that does not admit of it – that fatal fascination of misplaced mathematics – but in the democratic appeal to the interests of the majority. Historically and practically the utilitarian principle meant that the good of the whole community was to be the standard by which political institutions were to be judged, and not any merely traditional maxims nor any arbitrary theories of a Law of Nature which everyone might interpret in his own way. The difficulties of the utilitarian theory arise from its individualistic basis, from its assumption that a society is only an aggregate of individuals – a survival from that very doctrine of natural rights which the theory was intended to overthrow. The practical value of the theory remains if we interpret the common good as the well-being of the social organism of which the individual is a member.

The theory of natural selection fits in with utilitarianism as thus modified; for, according to that theory, the customs and ideas of the more successful society must be such as are advantageous to it – i.e. such as tend to its stability and endurance. Natural selection makes the fittest society or race survive, but the process is slow and costly in suffering to individuals. If in any case we can forecast what customs and institutions will promote social well-being, we may by adopting them obtain such stability and endurance without the same sacrifice of individual life and happiness. An intelligent and far-sighted utilitarian policy is a system of rational artificial selection. The standard of social well-being is not free from difficulties of its own; but every ethical principle formulated in general terms may give rise to some casuistical problems. How are we to balance the mere continuance of a society against the advantages of a less stable system which may open the way to greater progress and be the transition to a better type of society? Or, again (it is really the same problem in other words), which organism is to be preferred, when there is a conflict between the interests of two or more? These are difficulties; but they are far less than those arising out of the old utilitarian formula. It is only in quite exceptional cases that the individual needs to consider the extinction of his nation's independence or the abolition of the privileges of his social caste and the merging of it in some possibly higher organism: and it is well that, in moments of reflection, he should consider whether *esprit de corps* may not lead him to ascribe an excessive value to some society that may have served its purpose in the past and may be standing between him and a higher type of patriotism. He must make very sure, however, that his judgment is based on the principle of the well-being of some social organism, actual or possible, and not upon irresponsible individual sentiment. In the moment of action most persons are not likely to ponder such questions, and it would generally be unwise to do so. Casuistry cannot be altogether escaped, but it will be of a less dangerous kind, if it only turns on such rare conflicts of allegiance than if it be required and promoted by the assumption of an infallible and absolute Law of Nature or by the theory that a sum or quantity of pleasures has to be sought after and portioned out to individuals. On the principles of evolutionary ethics, the discovery of the likings of a majority, the counting of heads, is not an essential part of the moral standard, but at most a convenient escape from dangerous disputes. The habit of yielding to a majority, till we can alter that majority by persuasion, is a security for stability and peace, and does not concede that majorities are always, or generally, in the right. Evolutionary ethics certainly do not entitle us to say that democracy is the best form of government, but they lift the controversy out of the region of prejudice and sentiment and compel us to ask what institutions in any given case best further social cohesion and harmony without hindering the possibility of reform, if change should become necessary.

Democracy, it has been said, is only a form of government. In the strict and original sense of the term that is certainly true: and it is important to be reminded that democratic institutions are not an end in themselves for the attainment of which everything else ought to be sacrificed. They are merely a means, a piece of machinery, a contrivance by which their advocates suppose that certain good results may be obtained and certain bad results avoided. In many respects democratic institutions may be accepted not as good in themselves, but as less mischievous or dangerous than anything that could in the circumstances be got instead of them. Democracy was defined by a great man on a memorable occasion as 'government of the people by the people for the people'. Abraham Lincoln knew well the advantage to his country, in a crisis, of great political power being left in the hands of one strong man: and I do not suppose that, with his remarkable freedom from abstract prejudices, he valued popular government save as usually the best means for securing the common welfare among a fairly intelligent people of strongly conservative instincts. '*For* the people' is the end of government, the professed end of all governments, if we take 'the people' to mean the whole community; and this end may be missed through the stupidity or indifference or short-sighted passion of a majority under democratic institutions as well as by the prejudices or selfishness of a despot or a ruling caste.

Democracy as the name of a form of government includes many different types: and all generalisations about it are therefore risky as are also all inferences drawn from the character and history of the democracies of the past to those of the present, or from what happens in one country to what is likely to happen in another.

Democracy, in any careful use of the term, could certainly not be a primitive type of government, as the practice and the idea of rule, of superiority and inferiority, which government involves, could not begin with an equality between the members of a society. Equality is not suggested by the habits of gregarious lower animals, nor by what we can learn of the most primitive types of society among mankind. The State is an outgrowth from the clan or from the family – though we must give 'family' a much wider and vaguer meaning than that of the patriarchal family of Semitic tradition or of Hindoo and early Roman law. The primitive chief is the head of his clan, leader in battle, judge in disputes, and usually priest as well. The tribe may have a more definite or a less definite organisation, according to circumstances; but it is a mistake to suppose that very backward races, who manage to live on with very little organisation because they are few and scattered, or because they inhabit mountains or forests or marshes or deserts or remote islands which secure them against most attacks from without, are a type of a happy society which nearly approaches an ideal anarchy, and to which government-tormented mankind may some day return. The necessities of defence or of expansion to meet the needs of a growing population make the real beginning of the State in its distinctive sense as something more than the family, the horde or the clan. And the first great type of State is either monarchical or an aristocracy which is in reality a league of small monarchies. Herodotus assures his somewhat incredulous readers that one of the Persian nobles who overthrew the Magian usurper really argued in favour of democracy as the best government for the Persians; but, in spite of his assurance, we are more likely to believe that, in this interesting passage about the respective merits of democracy, aristocracy and monarchy, we have simply the earliest piece of Greek political philosophy.[e] The Oriental may recognise the miseries of being under an absolute king; but for him the alternative to monarchy is the rule of a priestly caste or of a band of nobles, each being sovereign in his own district. Yet in such undemocratic institutions we may see the germs out of which the idea of democracy develops. The equality of noble with noble – the idea of a 'peerage' – is an idea which, beginning in the ruling caste, may filter downwards. All

---

[e] Herodotus iii. 80–82. [*The Histories*, Harmondsworth, Penguin, 1972.]

the world over, people imitate and adopt the fashions and the notions of those whom they look upon as their social superiors: like sheep, they follow the leader. In this way it may be truly said that an aristocracy of equals is the parent of the idea of democracy. But the actual realisation of democracy has generally been due to the work of absolute monarchy crushing before it the privileges and pretensions of noble and priest and reducing its subjects to a common level. It was so in ancient Greece, where the tyrants destroyed the old aristocracies; and it was so in modern Europe, where the absolutism and centralised power of kings weakened the feudal aristocracies, so that they ceased to stand as a breakwater between the extreme types of monarchy and democracy.

The idea of democracy, like the name, comes to us from the Greeks; but Greek democracies were everywhere, according to modern terminology, slave-holding 'aristocracies', and it was indeed only the institution of slavery which made direct democracy possible as a form of government in ancient city states. The labour of slaves secured for the mass of free citizens such leisure for war and politics and such sentiment of being a ruling class as was elsewhere only known to a caste of nobles. The idea of equal right to share in government could, so far as we can see, only originate by contrast with some class of persons regarded as inferior. We never perceive anything distinctly except by contrast. The mere fact of not being a slave, the mere fact of being civilised among barbarians, the mere fact of being a white man among black or brown or red men, gives a feeling of superiority (often, in large part, illusory) which makes every member of this superior caste more ready to acknowledge every other member of it as, in some sense, a peer.

We have taken the term 'democracy' from the Greeks, and adapted it to mean a form of government in which political power belongs to a majority of all the permanent inhabitants, at least of all the adult males. So far, democracy is more extreme in character in the modern than in the ancient sense. In other respects we have made it less extreme: for we are content to call a constitution democratic if it gives the suffrage to every full citizen, although only a few may ever have any practical opportunity of exercising deliberative or executive functions, even in local matters. Representative government is the greatest political invention (if we may use such a term) which the world has yet known; it is the most valuable 'variation', and has brought about a species of constitution which did not exist in antiquity. It has removed a great part of the danger and instability of democracy, and it alone has made it possible for vast nations to enjoy internal peace without submitting to that absolutism of one man, which, however beneficial at times and for a time, is certain to produce torpor and decay. The citizen of a modern nation does not, indeed, lead so exciting a political existence as he would have done had he belonged to ancient Athens, where every citizen, one might say, was a member of parliament and had his chance of being in the ministry. The daily paper, the public meeting, and a rare visit to the polling-booth, are dull substitutes. Modern patriotism is not so immediately stimulated by sight and sound: it needs more reflection and more imagination, if it is to be kept alert and active. The Swiss 'Referendum' and 'Initiative' are sometimes advocated on the ground that they bring back direct democracy in the only manner in which this can be adapted to large political communities. Now, personally, I think the 'Referendum' (not the 'Initiative', to which there are many special objections) may, under certain conditions, be a useful supplement to (not a substitute for) parliamentary legislation; though we must not expect that an institution which has grown up under the special conditions and traditions of Switzerland would prove equally well adapted to other soils and climates. But I certainly think that no argument for it whatever is to be found in the fact that it means 'pure and direct democracy'.[f] If history can teach us anything – and it is from the details of history, and not from the wide formulae of biological sociology that we can safely learn – it teaches that 'pure' democracy may be very corrupt, and that it is an unstable form of government unless under the simple conditions of some small thinly-populated country, with a stationary population, not altered by immigration, and therefore tenacious of old habits. At its very best, pure and direct democracy is open to the objection that in many matters it is likely to be excessively conservative and adverse to progress. At its worst, there seems hardly a limit to the folly, corruption, and tyranny to which it may give rise.

All government must be government by the few over the many. The only question is, how are the most suitable few to be found? The

[f] This argument is used e.g. by Mr M'Crackan in his 'Rise of the Swiss Republic', p. 353.

ideal government must always be 'aristocracy', in the literal sense of the term – i.e. government by the best – 'the best' meaning not the best scientific investigators, nor the best artists and poets, nor the best generals, nor the best and most pious divines, nor the most eloquent orators, nor (though they may think it) the best and most successful journalists, but the best for the special work of making and administering laws. This ideal of aristocracy, however, gives no necessary sanction to the privileged rule of an hereditary caste. An hereditary caste decays and degenerates, under the artificial conditions of civilisation, if not constantly recruited from without: that is the lesson both of biology and of history. And the methods by which hereditary castes have generally been recruited, through new 'creations' or marriages outside the caste, have not been regulated by the scientific care or skill of the gardener or the breeder of animals. A class of persons with a traditional interest in the business of government is, however, a very great advantage to a country; but the influence of such a class is greatest and is least apt to provoke suspicion or dislike when its members depend, in some degree at least, upon popular election for their tenure of political power. A small number of persons elected by the many, and in their turn directly or indirectly determining the very few to whom administrative functions are to be delegated – this is not perhaps an ideal state, nor is it the most strictly democratic form of realising the sovereignty of the people; but this representative democracy, which may include in it monarchical and aristocratic elements, is the best average constitution for civilised human beings, if they have got accustomed to its working and are sufficiently united by a general patriotic sentiment to have among them only constitutional parties and not anti-constitutional factions. Representative democracy is undoubtedly not suited to the lower races of mankind at present, and some of them may never be fit for it at all; for though all mankind are social animals, they are not all in the fullest sense 'political animals'. Even where experience of self-government might seem to make it a perfectly safe form, we sometimes see a tendency in the 'government of the people by the people for the people' to degenerate into a government of the people by the 'boss' for the speculator. When, however, the corruptions and the scandals of a democracy are branded, it must always be remembered that under popular government, with keen rivalries and unmuzzled journalists competing in sensational noise, much more will be heard about corruptions and scandals than under other more apparently decorous forms of government, and sometimes a little more than the bare truth.

'The great tide of democracy is rolling on, and no hand can stay its majestic course.' This sort of thing has been said by many people besides the rhetorician whose words I quote. Democracy is regarded, by many who dread it, as well as by its enthusiasts, as 'inevitable'. The inference, if based upon historical reflection, is based only upon the history of the last hundred years. What does seem true is that the elements for a revival of anything like feudal aristocracy or feudal monarchy have disappeared; and thus natural selection may seem to have decided for democracy by the extinction of these rival types. But the experience of the past and certain tendencies observable in the present make it quite possible that there may be a considerable future for monarchy based upon democracy – monarchy of a more or less constitutional type. The mass of mankind crave visible symbols of authority, and they are more given to worship a hero, or what they take for one, than the members of a privileged governing class (for the most enduring republics have been aristocracies) : and the failures of democratic institutions to satisfy the cravings of distress and discontent, may in many cases lead to the old story of 'the people's friend' becoming the despot. 'Pure democracy' especially may mean only the right of the most easily deceived to elect a tyrant or to sanction a usurper. Impatience under the slowness of reform in constitutionally governed countries is always a source of danger to free institutions. The benevolent despot may do more for the people, and may do it more rapidly and in a more enlightened way, than the people can for themselves; but there is always the risk that his successor may not be as benevolent, or that he may be a weak man holding the sceptre of the strong – and that is about the worst thing that can happen. The slowness of constitutional government is safer in the long run than the quick changes wrought by a tyrant, one or many. We do not expect to find our ideal state in a philosopher-king in any literal sense. The permanent truth in Plato's dream is this, that good government can only be found when the laws and administration are based upon sound knowledge. No business can prosper, and certainly not the business of government, unless the expert is trusted, and scientific knowledge is allowed to direct practical policy. The mass of mankind feel wants and cravings, but have very vague or crude notions of how these are to be satisfied. That a people with some education and some traditional habits of self-government in local matters should have a voice in determining who are to be their legislators and administrators is reasonable, and is often necessary as a check upon tyranny and selfishness. But that the mass of the people should dictate the details of policy or administration is unreasonable; and the attempt to make the people self-governing in this sense can only injure a nation's prosperity in the long run, and therefore on the principles of evolutionary ethics must be wrong.

Every one at all acquainted with history or comparative politics will admit the enormous gain to Great Britain in its permanent non-party civil service. The parliamentary head of the department brings the changing currents of public opinion through safe and regulated channels to freshen administration and to prevent the stagnation of a bureaucracy; so that the country has the advantage of the experienced official without being completely at his mercy. It has been pointed out that the experience of trade-unions has led them away from the abstract principle that one man is as good as another (the principle on which extreme Greek democracies elected officials by lot) to the practical conclusion that business can only be managed well by a special class of professional experts.[g] It may be found impracticable to introduce the expert directly into the work of legislation – the electorate being apt to suspect the self-interest of a professional class, and a professional class having often a narrow outlook beyond their own subject. The lawyer and the engineer have the advantage of dealing with highly technical matters, and are more easily left alone by popular agitation. The physician, the educationalist, the economist, are more exposed to the risk of having their advice disregarded because of some widespread sentiment, prejudice, or superstition. The only remedy under democracy for distrust in the expert is the diffusion of scientific knowledge. The more soundly educated a man is, the more likely is he to be aware of his own ignorance outside his special studies, and the more ready to accept the authority of the special students in other departments. The most difficult class of persons to deal with are those who are

---

[g] Cf. Sidney and Beatrice Webb, 'Industrial Democracy' [London, Longmans Green, 1897] ii. pp. 843, 844.

just sufficiently roused from the apathy of complete ignorance to be keenly critical and suspicious of authority: and this class of the slightly educated (it would be exaggeration to call them 'half-educated') possesses great influence in democracy. But there is no reason for the despair which arises from the disappointed hopes of the enthusiasts for democracy or from the regrets of those who look back on the aristocracies and old *régimes* of the past, when distance has softened their outlines. Any education, however elementary and imperfect, any interest in religion, or in anything beyond the mere animal struggle to live, any capacity for grasping the common weal as an end to be looked to, is a soil in which ideas may be sown and in which they may grow up. The thinker, the 'philosopher' in Plato's sense, who feels the mission to serve his nation, but who finds that the multitude will only listen to leaders who use the phrases that are familiar to it, need not wait for the unlikely chance of an absolute king who will call him to office: he may even now 'descend into the cave', and by educational work or popular writing help the growth of a sounder and healthier public opinion. I do not mean that every chemist should leave his laboratory, and every scholar neglect his historical researches, in order to give magic-lantern lectures in village school-rooms. It is not every one who has the gift of missionary work, and the 'call' to it. What I mean is that the original researcher should never under-value the social utility of the populariser. It is a very bad thing in any country if there is a complete gap between an educated few, wrapped up entirely in their own self-culture, and a multitude, many of whom are eager for light, but who are left to the heated harangues of the narrow enthusiast, or to the speeches of the party politician, who needs to be a very strong man indeed, in order to be a teacher and not a flatterer.

Admitting that there is an inevitable tendency towards democracy, we must avoid the fatalism which sometimes results from the first crude application of scientific conceptions to human society. The spectacle of the onward rush of forces that seem independent of the individual is apt to paralyse initiative, and to make us forget that variations due to conscious thought and deliberate purpose are among the materials for sociological natural selection. In human, as distinct from animal, evolution, ideas and ideals become factors in the process. Free discussion is the struggle for existence on the intellectual plane. Ideas can, however, only influence conduct and mould institutions, when they gather round them feelings and impulses. 'Intellect alone moves nothing', said Aristotle: an idea by itself is never an efficient cause. Ideas must be gradually worked into people's minds, and must grow a part of the permanent self in order to become significant factors in the habitual standards of judgement and the habitual motives of conduct. Education is this process of working ideas into the mind. 'We must educate our masters', was said somewhat cynically perhaps; but it remains the truest precept for those who are apt to turn away in disgust from the politics of a democratic state. There is an ethical danger in the merely materialistic view of history which ignores the distinction between the blind processes of mere nature and the partly conscious process of human evolution. There is a danger also in the false idealism which either shrinks from contact with the rude and unpleasant facts of life or does not recognise the material conditions under which the realisation of ideals is made possible but by which it is at the same time restricted.

'Democracy means properly a form of government.' It is well to be reminded of this, to be reminded that parliaments, and county-councils, and parish-councils, and the right to vote, are only machinery, means to an end, not things to be prized or feared on their own account. But it is not quite true that democracy is *only* a form of government. There is a democratic spirit that may prevail where the form of government contains many undemocratic elements, and may be absent where the machinery is professedly democratic. This democratic spirit may be supposed to be expressed in the three famous, but ambiguous, words, 'Liberty, Equality, Fraternity.' Liberty has, indeed, been too often taken in the merely negative sense of absence of State-action – a principle which, if worked out consistently, would mean anarchy, and a return to savage life, but which, when applied to a modern society established on the basis of existing economic and legal institutions, and under democratic government, means the unfettered industrial and commercial struggle for existence, leading to the social and political preponderance of wealth. Democracy in this sense means plutocracy. Liberty, however, admits of a positive ethical meaning – the fullest possible development of the individual's physical, intellectual, and moral potentialities. In this sense the slave is not free, but neither is the 'free' labourer, if he has no training for healthy self-culture and insufficient opportunities even for quiet home life. In this sense of liberty, the state has very extensive functions, and extremely democratic constitutions do not necessarily fulfil these functions better than less democratic constitutions, if the latter are permeated by this ideal of freedom.

Equality, again, may be used for claims of exact equality in every respect, claims which are incompatible with social stability and progress; but equality may simply mean that the ethical ideal, just now expressed by liberty or freedom, should be open to every one – not that every one is, as a matter of fact, fit to attain to it. As already pointed out, this ideal of equality arose among the members of a privileged class. This is a necessity in the case of such ideals. The isolated prophet must arise, marked out from his fellows, before anyone can wish that all the Lord's people should be prophets; there must be separate kings and priests before there can be a vision of redeemed humanity as kings and priests unto God; there must be the few who are noblemen or gentlemen, in order to suggest the desire for the education of a gentleman open to all who prove themselves fit for it, or the poet's dream of the nobility of all mankind.

Of these democratic ideals the greatest is Fraternity. The narrow exclusiveness of families or clans, for whom the stranger was the enemy, produced in time the ideal of a brotherhood of mankind – an ideal that may indeed be used in anarchical fashion to break up the ethical bonds of smaller social groups which alone can discipline human beings for the membership of wider circles. But the ideal of fraternity may also serve to correct a great deal of the bad metaphysics and unpractical politics due to abstract or rhetorical applications of the ideals of liberty and equality; 'fraternity', 'brotherhood', may serve to recall the needs of mankind as a family. In the family it would be cruelty to give the children equal rights and responsibilities with their elders, or to leave them to their own devices; and the family ideal of the state may save us from the cruelty that results from non-interference with the more helpless of our own people or the non-intervention which would leave the lower races to the native despot, the slave-raider, or the European adventurer, unchecked by the control of civilised government. These lower races are our younger brothers, they are like children, as their best friends tell us, and they require paternal government in spite of all democratic theories.

We cannot predict the political map of future centuries. Many unexpected things are sure to happen. But, so far as can at present be foreseen by us, there is (as Kant saw a hundred years ago) no hope for durable peace, except through a federation of the civilised nations of the world, each nation being itself a 'republic' – i.e. constitutionally governed. The alternative of a universal Empire would, as in the case of the Roman Empire, mean degeneration, and disarmed civilisation might again fall before militant barbarians. But outside our league or federation of civilised peoples, with more or less democratic constitutions, there will probably always be large regions of the world occupied chiefly by races unfit for full self-government; and these must for their own sakes be governed in some more or less imperial and despotic fashion. To leave the lower races to themselves is impossible, now at all events when our earth has been nearly all explored. The growth of population in temperate climates is alone sufficient to produce a demand for the food supplies of the tropics. In tropical climates labour must be done by the coloured man, but it has to be supervised and directed by the white man. A tropical country left to independence is a white tyranny or a black anarchy. Some control from constitutionally governed countries, some system like that of our Crown Colonies, is the best solution yet reached.[h] Under good paternal government the main difficulty, indeed, is the rapid increase of protected lower races.

Will democracies prove themselves capable of taking up 'the white man's burden' in the highest sense? This is one of the serious questions that confront us. It will not be settled by appeals to sentiment or the rights of man. The ideas of evolutionary ethics help us only in so far as they tend to 'clear our minds of cant', and lead us to abandon some of the traditional phrases of the democratic creed, to accept the lessons of experience, and to face the problems of human society without exaggerated expectations, but without selfishness and without despair.

---

[h] It is satisfactory to find that thoughtful citizens of the United States of America, under the new responsibilities which the occupation of the Philippines are forcing on them, have come, in spite of traditional dogmas about natural rights, to recognise that some such treatment of barbarous races is alone wise and just. See the discussion on the government of dependencies in 'The Foreign Policy of the United States: Addresses and Discussions at the Annual Meeting of the American Academy of Political and Social Science', April 7–8, 1899.

Individualism, Collectivism and the General Will

5
Ideal Morality

F. H. BRADLEY

In our criticism of the view developed in Essay V [of *Ethical Studies*] we saw that, however true the main doctrine of that Essay may be, it is no sufficient answer to the question, What is morality? and, guided by its partial failure, we must try to find a less one-sided solution.

We saw (in Essay II [of *Ethical Studies*]) that the end was the realizing of the self; and the problem which in passing suggested itself was, Are morality and self-realization the same thing,[a] or, if not altogether the same, in what respect are they different?

That in some way they do differ is clear from the popular views on the subject. Every one would agree that by his artistic or scientific production an artist or a man of science does realize himself, but no one, not blinded by a theory, would say that he was moral just so far as, and because, what he produced was good of its sort and desirable in itself. A man may be good at this or that thing, and may have done good work in the world; and yet when asked, 'But was he a good man?' we may find ourselves, although we wish to say Yes, unable to do more than hesitate. A man need not be a good man just so far as he is a good artist; and the doctrine which unreservedly identifies moral goodness with any desirable realization of the self can not be maintained.

Can we then accept the other view, which, as it were, separates morality into a sphere of its own; which calls a man moral according

---

[a] Cf. p. 228, and note, pp. 244, 218–19 [F. H. Bradley, *Ethical Studies*, second edition (Oxford, Clarendon Press, 1927)].

97

as he abstains from direct breaches of social rules, and immoral if he commits them; while it forgets that the one man may be lazy, selfish, and without a wish to improve himself, while the other, with all his faults, at least loves what is beautiful and good, and has striven towards it? We can not do that unless, while we recognize the truth of the doctrine, we shut our eyes to its accompanying falsity.

And, finding in neither the expression of our moral consciousness, we thankfully accept the correction which sees in 'conduct' nine-tenths of life, though we can not expect the main question to be answered by a coarse and popular method, which divides into parts instead of distinguishing aspects; and though, in the saving one-tenth and the sweeping nine-tenths alike, we can see little more than the faltering assertion of one mistake, or the confident aggravation of another.

A man's life, we take it, can not thus be cut in pieces. You can not say, 'In this part the man is a moral being, and in that part he is not'. We have not yet found that fraction of his existence in which the moral goodness of the good man is no more realized, and where 'the lusts of the flesh'[1] cease to wage their warfare. We have heard in the sphere of religion, 'Do *all* to the glory of God',[2] and here too we recognize no smaller claim. To be a good man in all things and everywhere, to try to do always the best, and to do one's best in it, whether in lonely work or in social relaxation to suppress the worse self and realize the good self, this and nothing short of this is the dictate of morality. This, it seems to us, is a deliverance of the moral consciousness too clear for misunderstanding, were it not for two fixed habits of thought. One of these lies in the confining of a man's morality to the sphere of his social relations; the other is the

---

[1] St. Paul, Second Epistle to the Corinthians 3: 17. Authorised King James translation. 'For the flesh lusteth against the Spirit, and the Spirit against the flesh . . . so that ye cannot do the things that ye would.'

[2] St. Paul, First Epistle to the Corinthians 10:31. Authorised King James translation. 'So whether you eat or whatever you do, do it all for the glory of God.' The Authorised Version has been criticised for being too literal and almost unintelligible in parts. Arthur S. Way translates this passage thus: 'If I partake of my food with thanksgiving, I am not to be calumniated for eating that for which I give God thanks. So then, whether you are eating, or drinking, or whatever you are doing, do all things to the Glory of God.' *Letters of St Paul to Seven Churches and Three Friends with the Letter to the Hebrew*, sixth edition (London, Macmillan, 1926).

notion that morality is a life harassed and persecuted everywhere by 'imperatives' and disagreeable duties, and that without these you have not got morality. We have seen, and have yet to see, that the first has grasped only part of the truth; and on the second it is sufficient to remark that it stands and falls with the identification of morality with unwilling obedience to law, and that, according to the common view, a man does not cease to be good so far as goodness becomes natural and pleasant to him.

But we shall be met at this point with an absurdity supposed to follow. Work of any sort, it will be said, is, we grant you, a field for morality, and so is most of life in relation to others; but there must be a sphere where morality ceases, or else it will follow that a man is moral in all the trifling details of his own life which concern him alone, and no less again in his amusements. If morality does not stop somewhere, you must take it to be a moral question not only whether a man amuses himself, but also how he amuses himself. There will be no region of things indifferent, and this leads to consequences equally absurd and immoral.[b] We answer without hesitation that in human life there is, in one sense, no sphere of things indifferent, and yet that no absurd consequences follow. If it is my moral duty to go from one town to another, and there are two roads which are equally good, it is indifferent to the proposed moral duty *which* road I take; it is not indifferent *that* I do take one or the other; and whichever road I do take, I am doing my duty on it, and hence it is far from indifferent: my walking on road A is a matter of duty in reference to the end, though not a matter of duty if you consider it against walking on road B; and so with B – but I can escape the sphere of duty neither on A nor on B. In order to realize the good will in a finite corporeal being it is necessary that certain spheres should exist, and should have a general character; this is a moral question, and not indifferent. The detail of those spheres within certain limits does not matter; not that it is immaterial that there *is* a detail of trifles, and hence not that this and that

---

[b] Expressed in other language the objection is, 'There is a sphere of rights which falls outside the sphere of duty, or else it will follow that all my rights are my duties, which is absurd.' For the answer, see p. 210 [Note to Essay V, *Ethical Studies*]. Here we may say, it is right and a duty that the sphere of indifferent detail should exist. It is a duty that I should develop my nature by private choice therein. Therefore, *because* that is a duty, it is a duty *not* to make a duty of every detail; and thus in every detail I have done my duty.

trifle has no moral importance, but that this trifle has no importance *against that trifle*. Qualify a trifle by subordinating it to a good will, and it has moral significance; qualify it by contrast with another trifle, and morally it signifies nothing. This is plain enough, and, so far as it goes, will I hope be sufficient. The reader no doubt will see that, if a class of acts is morally desirable, then whatever falls within that class is also morally desirable, so far as falling therein; though in its other relations it may be indifferent.

But the difficulty which remains will be something of this sort. The reader will feel that, to a certain extent, the regulation of the times and fields of amusements, &c., and, to a still larger extent, the choice of trifling details therein, involves no reflection, no deliberate choice, is not made a matter of conscience, is in a word done naturally; and he may find a difficulty in seeing how, if this is so, it can be said to fall within the moral sphere. Morality, he may feel, does tell me it is good to amuse myself, and more decidedly that I may *not* amuse myself beyond certain limits; but within those limits it leaves me to my natural self. In this, it seems to us, there is a twofold misapprehension, a mistake as to the limits, and a mistake as to the character of the moralized self. It is, first, an error to suppose that in what is called human life there remains any region which has not been moralized. Whatever has been brought under the control of the will, it is not too much to say, has been brought into the sphere of morality; in our eating, our drinking, our sleeping, we from childhood have not been left to ourselves; and the habits, formed in us by the morality outside of us, now hold of the moral will which in a manner has been their issue. And so in our lightest moments the element of control and regulation is not wanting; it is part of the business of education to see that it is there, and its absence, wherever it is seen to be absent, pains us. The character shows itself in every trifling detail of life; we can not go in to amuse ourselves while we leave it outside the door with our dog; it is ourself, and our moral self, being not mere temper or inborn disposition, but the outcome of a series of acts of will. Natural it is indeed well to be; but that is because by this time morality should be our nature, and good behaviour its unreflecting issue; and to be natural in any sense which excludes moral habituation is never, so far as I know the world, thought desirable. In a good and amiable man the good and amiable self is present throughout, and that self is for us a moral self. This brings us to the second mistake, which also rests on the same misapprehension of the cardinal truth that what is natural can not be moral, nor what is moral natural. 'What is natural does not reflect, and without reflection there is no morality. Hence, where we are natural *because* we do not reflect, there we can not be moral.' So runs the perversion. But here it is forgotten that we *have* reflected; that acts which issue from moral reflection have qualified our will; that our character thus, not only in its content, but also in the form of its acquisition, is within the moral sphere; and that a character, whether good or bad, is a second nature. The man to whom it 'comes natural' to be good is commonly thought a good man, and the good self of the good man is present in and determines the detail of his life not less effectually because unconsciously. So far facts speak loudly, and the only path which remains open to the objector is to deny that the good self is necessarily a moral self, on the ground not that its content is non-moral, but that its genesis is so; in other words, because, though moral in itself, it is not so for the agent. We may be told, the genesis of the good self generally is not a moral genesis, or in this and that sphere or relation it is not so, and hence, though good, it need not, so far as good, be moral. To the consideration of this question we shall have to come later, and at present can only observe that we refuse to separate goodness conscious or unconscious from the will to be good, or the will to be good from morality; and we assert that, because the good self shows itself everywhere, therefore there is no part of life at which morality stops and goes no further. Thus much against the notion that in our amusements, &c., we cease to be moral beings, that there is a tenth part of life where conduct is not required. But as to the remaining nine-tenths we need surely say no more: wherever there is anything to be done not in play but in earnest, there the moral consciousness tells us it is right to do our best, and, if this is so, there can be no question but that here is a field for morality.[c]

It is a moral duty to realize everywhere the best self, which for us in this sphere is an ideal self; and, asking what morality is, we so far must answer, it is coextensive with self-realization in the sense

---

[c] It may even be my moral duty to be religious in the sense of acting with a view to the support and maintenance of the religious consciousness, the faith which is to reissue in religious-moral practice. Hence though morality, as we shall see, does not include everything, yet nothing in another sense falls outside of it.

of the realization of the ideal self in and by us. And thus we are led to the inquiry, what is the *content* of this ideal self.[d]

From our criticism on the foregoing Essay we can at once gather that the good self is the self which realizes (1) a social, (2) a non-social ideal; the self, first, which does, and, second, which does not directly and immediately involve relation to others. Or from another point of view, what is aimed at is the realization in me (1) of the ideal which is realized in society, of my station and its duties, or (2) of the ideal which is not there fully realized; and this is (a) the perfection of a social and (b) of a non-social self. Or again (it is all the same thing) we may divide into (1) duties to oneself which are not regarded as social duties, (2) duties to oneself[e] which are so regarded, these latter being (a) the duties of the station which I happen to be in, (b) duties beyond that station. Let us further explain.

The content of the good self, we see, has a threefold origin; and (1) the first and most important contribution comes from what we have called my station and its duties, and of this we have spoken already at some length. We saw that the notion of an individual man existing in his own right independent of society was an idle fancy, that a human being is human because he has drawn his being from human society, because he is the individual embodiment of a larger life; and we saw that this larger life, of the family, society, or the nation, was a moral will, a universal the realization of which in his personal will made a man's morality. We have nothing to add here except in passing to call attention to what we lately advanced, viz. that the good man is good throughout all his life and not merely in parts; and further to request the reader to turn to himself and ask himself in what his better self consists. He will find, if we do not mistake, that the greater part of it consists in his loyally, and

---

[d] On the genesis of the ideal self and of the good self, or the self whose will is identified with its ideal, we shall say what seems necessary in other connexions.

[e] I may remark that a duty which is *not* a duty to myself can not possibly be a moral duty. When we hear of self-regarding duties we should ask what is meant. (*[Bradley's addition], This *might* mean a duty towards myself as this or that member of society.) A '*self*-regarding duty' in one sense of the word says no more than 'a duty'; in another sense it says 'a duty which is the direct opposite of what a duty is', i.e. a *selfish* duty: or again, it means a non-social duty. Confusion on this head leads to serious mistakes.

according to the spirit, performing his duties and filling his place as the member of a family, society, and the state. He will find that, when he has satisfied the demands of these spheres upon him, he will in the main have covered the claims of what he calls his good self. The basis and foundation of the ideal self is the self which is true to my station and its duties.

But (2) we saw also that, if we investigate our good self, we find something besides, claims beyond what the world expects of us, a will for good beyond what we see to be realized anywhere. The good in my station and its duties was visibly realized in the world, and it was mostly possible to act up to that real ideal; but this good beyond is only an ideal; for it is not wholly realized in the world we see, and, do what we may, we can not find it realized in ourselves. It is what we strive for and in a manner do gain, but never attain to and never possess. And this ideal self (so far as we are concerned with it here) is a social self. The perfect types of zeal and purity, honour and love, which, figured and presented in our own situation and circumstances, and thereby unconsciously specialized, become the guides of our conduct and law of our being, are social ideals. They directly involve relation to other men, and, if you remove others, you immediately make the practice of these virtues imposs-ible.[f]

This then is the ideal self which in its essence is social; and concerning this many difficulties arise which we can not discuss. Among these would be the two inquiries, What is the origin, and what the content of this ideal self ? In passing we may remark that the first contains two questions which are often confused, viz. (a) How is it possible for the mind to frame an ideal; or, given as a fact a mind which idealizes, what must be concluded as to its nature? Can anything idealize unless itself in some way *be* an ideal? This, we need not say, suggests serious problems which we can not even touch upon here. Then (b) it contains also the questions, What was the historical genesis of the ideal; by what steps did it come into the world? And again, What is its genesis in us? And these can scarcely be separated from one another, or from the further inquiry, What is its content?

---

[f] Virtues such as chastity, which might be practised in solitude, are either negative of the bad self, or conditions of the good will. If you wrongly consider them by

The historical genesis we shall not enter on; and as to the genesis in the individual, we will merely remark that we seem first to see in some person or persons the type of what is excellent; then by the teaching, tradition, and imagination of our own and other countries and times, we receive a content which we *find* existing realized in present or past individuals, and finally detach from all as that which is realized wholly in none, but is an ideal type of human perfection. At this point we encounter a question of fact, namely, how far the ideal which serves as a guide to conduct is presented in an individual form. No doubt two extremes exist. A large number of men have, I think, no moral ideal beyond the station they live in, and of these some are even satisfied with the presentation of this or that known person as a type; while again in the highest form of morality the ideal is not figured in the shape of an individual.[g] But between the extremes must be endless gradations.

We have previously said something as to the way in which the ideal is made use of in moral judgements, and what remains is to call attention to the content of this social ideal. It is obvious at once that it is a will which practises no other kind of virtues than those which we find in the world; and we can see no reason for supposing this presented ideal self to be anything beyond the idealization of what exists in human nature, the material idealized being more or less cosmopolitan, and the abstraction employed being more or less one-sided.

And with these cursory and insufficient remarks we must dismiss the ideal of a perfect social being.

But (3) there remains in the good self a further region we have not yet entered on; an ideal, the realization of which is recognized as a moral duty, but which yet in its essence does not involve direct relation to other men.[h] The realization for myself of truth and

themselves, they are not positively desirable. We may call them, if we will, the 'ascetic virtues'.

[g] The difficulty everywhere is, Is the embodiment used to fire the imagination, while the type is not that of this or that individual; or is it otherwise? The solution is to be found in the answer to the question, Is the impersonation modified; and if modified, how, and by what, and to suit what is it modified?

[h] Morality, on its own ground at least, knows nothing of a universal and invisible self, in which all members are real, which they realize in their own gifts and graces, and in realizing which they realize the other members. Humanity as an organic whole, if a possible point of view, is not strictly speaking a moral point of view. See more below.

beauty, the living for the self which in the apprehension, the knowledge, the sight, and the love of them finds its true being, is (all those who know the meaning of the words will bear me out) a moral obligation, which is not felt as such only so far as it is too pleasant.

It is a moral duty for the artist or the inquirer to lead the life of one, and a moral offence when he fails to do so. But on the other hand it is impossible, without violent straining of the facts, to turn these virtues into social virtues or duties to my neighbour. No doubt such virtues do as a rule lead indirectly to the welfare of others, but this is not enough to make them social; their social bearing is indirect, and does not lie in their very essence. The end they aim at is a single end of their own, the content of which does not necessarily involve the good of other men. This we can see from supposing the opposite. If that were true, then it would not be the duty of the inquirer, as such, simply to inquire, or of the artist, as such, simply to produce the best work of art; but each would have to consider ends falling outside his science or art, and would have no right to treat these latter as ends in themselves. 'Nor has he', may be the confident answer. I reply that to me this is a question of fact, and to me it is a fact that the moral consciousness recognizes the perfecting of my intellectual or artistic nature by the production of the proper results, as an end in itself and not merely as a means. The pursuit of these ends, apart from what they lead to, is approved as morally desirable, not perhaps by the theory, but, I think, by the instinctive judgement of all persons worth considering; and if, and while, this fact stands, for me at least it is not affected by doctrines which require that it should be otherwise. To say, without society science and art could not have arisen, is true. To say, apart from society the life of an artist or man of science can not be carried on, is also true; but neither truth goes to show that society is the ultimate end, unless by an argument which takes the basis of a result as its final cause, and which would prove the physical and physiological conditions of society to be the end for which it existed. Man is not man at all unless social, but man is not much above the beasts unless more than social.

If it be said that, morally considered, the realization of the social self is an end, and that of the non-social nothing but an outward means, and that hence science and art are not to be pursued independently, no doubt it would be possible to meet such an assertion

by argument from and upon its own ground. We might urge that
science is most useful, when treated as more than useful. But we
decline by doing this to degrade and obscure the question. We
repeat that the assertion is both unproven and false, and the decision
is left to the moral consciousness of the reader.

And if again it be said that the social self is the one end, but yet
none the less science and art are ends in themselves, and to be
pursued independently; they are included in the social self, and
therefore, as elements in the end, are themselves ends and not mere
means – then, in answer, I will not reply that this is false (for indeed
I hope it may be true), but only that it is utterly unproven. It is on
the assertor that the burden of proof must lie. To us it seems plain
that the content of the theoretical self does not in its essence involve
relation to others: nothing is easier than to suppose a life of art or
speculation which, as far as we can see, though true to itself, has,
so far as others are concerned, been sheer waste or even loss, and
which knew that it was so. This is a fairly supposable case, and no
one, I think, can refuse to enter on it. Was the life immoral? I say,
No, it was not *therefore* immoral, but may have been *therefore* moral
past ordinary morality. And if I am told Yes, it was moral, but it
was social: it did in its essence involve relation to others, because
there is a *necessary* connexion (nothing short of this proves the
conclusion) between theoretic realization in this and that man, and
the realization of him there in and thereby in relation to others, and
perhaps also of society as a whole – then I answer, You are asserting
in the teeth of appearances; you must prove this necessary connexion, and, I think I may add, you can not do it. What you say
may be true, but science, or at all events your science, can not
guarantee it; and it is not a truth for the moral consciousness, but
leads us further into another region.

Our result at present is as follows. Morality is co-extensive with
self-realization, as the affirmation of the self which is one with the
ideal; and the content of this self is furnished (1) by the objective
world of my station and its duties, (2) by the ideal of social, and (3)
of non-social perfection. And now we have to do with the question,
How do these spheres stand to one another? And this is in some
ways an awkward question, because it brings up practical everyday
difficulties. They are something of this sort. May a man, for the

sake of science or art, venture on acts of commission or omission which in any one else would be immoral; or, to put it coarsely, may he be what is generally called a bad man, may he trample on ordinary morality, in order that he may be a good artist? Or again, if the perhaps less familiar question of the relation of (1) to (2) comes up, the doubt is, Must I do the work that lies next me in the world, and so serve society, even, as it seems, to the detriment of my own moral being? May I adopt a profession considered moral by the world, but which, judged by my ideal, can not be called moral?

The first point to which we must call attention is that all these are cases of colliding duties. In none of them is there a contest between the claims of morality and of something else not morality. In the moral sphere such a contest is impossible and meaningless. We have in all of them a conflict between moral duties which are taken to exclude one another, e.g. my moral duty as artist on the one hand and as father of a family on the other, and so on: we have nothing to do with examples where morality is neglected or opposed in the name of anything else than an other and higher morality.

And the second point, which has engaged us before (*Ethical Studies*, pp. 156–9, 193 foll.), and on which we desire to insist with emphasis, is, that cases of collision of duties are not scientific but practical questions. Moral science has nothing whatever to do with the settlement of them; that would belong, did such a thing exist, to the moral art. The difficulties of collisions are not scientific problems; they arise from the complexity of individual cases, and this can be dealt with solely by practical insight, not by abstract conceptions and discursive reasoning. It is no use knowing that one class of duties is in the abstract higher than another: moral practice is not *in abstracto*, and the highest moral duty for *me* is *my* duty; *my* duty being the one which lies next me, and perhaps not the one which would be the highest, supposing it were mine. The man who can give moral advice is the man of experience, who, from his own knowledge and by sympathy, can transport himself into another's case; who knows the heart and sees through moral illusion and the man of mere theory is in the practical sphere a use-less and dangerous pedant.

And now in particular the relation of the two ideal spheres to the real sphere is precisely what subsists inside the real sphere between its own elements. We saw (pp. 156–7 [of *Ethical Studies*]) that, as in no one action can all duties be fulfilled, in every action some duties must be neglected. The question is what duty is to be done and left undone *here*; and so in the world of my station neglect of duties is allowed. And, apart from the difficulty (often the impossibility) of distinguishing omission and commission from a moral point of view, we saw (*ibid.*) that positive breaches of moral law were occasionally moral. And hence if an artist or man of science considers himself called upon, by his duty to art or science, to neglect, or to commit a breach of, ordinary morality, we must say that, in the abstract and by itself, that is not to be condemned. It is a case of colliding duties, such as happens every day in other fields, and its character is not different because extraordinary.

And further, if a claim be set up, on the ground of devotion to no common end, to be judged in one's life by no common standard, we must admit that already within the sphere of my station that claim is usually allowed. We excuse in a soldier or sailor what we do not excuse in others, from whom the same duties are not expected. The morality of the pushing man of business, and still more of the lawyer and the diplomatist in the exercise of their calling, is not measured by the standard of common life; and so, when the service of the ideal is appealed to in justification of neglect and breaches of law, we say that the claim is valid in itself, the abstract right is undeniable, the case is a case of collision, and the question of moral justification is a question of particular fact.

Collision of duties carries all this with it on the one side, but we must not forget what it carries on the other. In raising that excuse we are saying, 'I neglect duty because of duty'; and this means we recognize two duties, one higher than the other. And first it implies that we are acting, not to please ourselves, but because we are bound by what we consider moral duty. It implies again that we consider what we break through or pass by, not as a trifle, but as a serious moral claim, which we disregard solely because, if we do not do so, it prevents us from performing our superior service.

Common social morality is the basis of human life. It is specialized in particular functions of society, and upon its foundation are erected the ideals of a higher social perfection and of the theoretic life; but common morality remains both the cradle and protecting nurse of its aspiring offspring, and, if we ever forget that, we lie open to the charge of ingratitude and baseness. Some neglect is unavoidable; but open and direct outrage on the standing moral institutions which make society and human life what it is, can be justified (I do not say condoned) only on the plea of overpowering moral necessity. And the individual should remember that the will for good, if weakened in one place, runs the greatest risk of being weakened in all.

Our result then is that ideal morality stands on the basis of social, that its relation thereto is the same relation that subsists within the social sphere, and that everywhere, since duty has to give way to duty, neglect and breaches of ordinary in the name of higher morality are justifiable in the abstract (and that is all we are concerned with); but if the claim be set up, on account of devotion to the ideal, for liberty to act thus not in the name of moral necessity, or to forget that what we breakthrough or disregard is in itself to be respected, such a claim is without the smallest moral justification.[i]

The highest type we can imagine is the man who, on the basis of everyday morality, aims at the ideal perfection of it, and on this double basis strives to realize a non-social ideal. But where collisions arise, there, we must repeat, it is impossible for mere theory to offer a solution, not only because the perception which decides is not a mere intellectual perception, but because no general solution of individual difficulties is possible.

To return to our main discussion – the field of morality we find is the whole field of life; its claim is as wide as self-realization, and the question raised before (p. 64 [of *Ethical Studies*]) now presents itself, Are morality and self-realization the same and not different? This appears at first sight to be the case. The moral end is to realize the self, and all forms of the realizing of the self are seen to fall within the sphere of morality; and so it seems natural to say that morality is the process of self-realization, and the most moral man is the man who most fully and energetically realizes human nature. Virtue is excellence, and the most excellent is the most virtuous.

---

[i] I have not entered on the questions whether as a fact breaches of common morality are demanded by the service of the ideal, and, if so, when they are to be committed. The first is a matter of fact it would not profit us to discuss in connexion with the abstract question; and the second in our opinion can not be theoretically determined. Which duty or duties weigh heaviest in this or that case is an affair for perception, not reasoning. We may remark, however, that the doctrine of the text will not be found to err on the side of laxity.

If we say this, however, we come into direct collision with the moral consciousness, which clearly distinguishes moral from other excellence, and asserts that the latter is not in itself moral at all; and, referring back (p. 143 [of *Ethical Studies*]), we find the deliverance of that consciousness in the emphatic maxim that nothing is morally good save a good will. This maxim we shall forthwith take to be true, and so proceed.

Morality then will be the realization of the self as the good will.[j] It is not self-realization from all points of view, though all self-realization can be looked at from this one point of view; for all of it involves will, and, so far as the will is good, so far is the realization moral. Strictly speaking and in the proper sense, morality is self-realization within the sphere of the personal will. We see this plainly in art and science, for there we have moral excellence, and that excellence does not lie in mere skill or mere success, but in single-mindedness and devotion to what seems best as against what we merely happen to like. Θεωρία [contemplation] is at the same time πρᾶξις [an action], and so far as it is πρᾶξις, so far is it moral or immoral.[k] And even in the sphere of my station and its duties, when in the stricter sense you consider it morally, you find that the same thing holds. From the highest point of view you judge a man moral not so far as he has succeeded outwardly, but so far as he has identified his will with the universal, whether that will has properly

---

[j] Morality and Self-realization, how different? See, pp. 309–10 [of *Ethical Studies*], 214 [p. 97], 232–7 [pp. 113–17], 244 [p. 124] [of this volume and *Ethical Studies*]. 'Morality' is Self-realization, or the production (and existence) of excellences, so far as they can be taken as the expression (if not the result) of the will for good.
There is a difficulty as to how far the merely 'natural' still comes in here really. Clearly not all the 'admirable' is moral. There is a difficulty, again, as to what is 'the will for good'. Is it *any* willing so far as good? Or is it only what can be taken as the willing *against* the bad? And in what sense *bad*? Cf. p. 237 [p. 117], second paragraph.

[k] Cf. Aristotle, Pol. vii. 1325, b. 14–23. [*Politics*, translated by Benjamin Jowett (Oxford, Clarendon Press, 1921) 'If we are right in our view, and happiness is assumed to be virtuous activity, the active life will be the best, both for every city collectively, and for individuals. Not that a life of action must necessarily have relation to others, as some persons think, nor are those ideas only to be regarded as practical which are pursued for the sake of practical results, but much more the thoughts and contemplations which are pursued for the sake of practical results, but much more the thoughts and contemplations which are independent and complete in themselves; since virtuous activity, and therefore a certain kind of action, is an end, and even in the case of external actions the directing mind is most truly said to act.']

externalized itself or not. Morality has not to do immediately with the outer results of the will: the results it looks at are the habits and general temper produced by acts, and, strictly speaking, it does not fall beyond the subjective side, the personal will and the heart. Clearly a will which does not utter itself is no will,[1] but you can not measure a will morally by external results: they are an index, but an index that must be used with caution. We shall return to the question, What is the measure of a man's morality?

The general end is self-realization, the making real of the ideal self; and for morality, in particular, the ideal self is the good will, the identification of my will with the ideal as a universal will. The end for morals is a will, and my will, and a universal will, and one will. Let us briefly refer on these heads to the moral consciousness.

Nothing, we have seen, is good but a good will. The end for morals is not the mere existence of any sort of ideal indifferently, but it is the realization of an ideal will in my will. The end is the ideal willed by me, the willing of the ideal in and by my will, and hence an ideal will. And my will as realizing the ideal is the good will. A will which obeys no law is not moral, a law which is not willed is nothing for morality. Acts, so far as they spring from the good will, are good, and a temper and habits and character are good so far as they are a present good will, result from it and embody it; and what issues from a good character must thus likewise be morally good.

That the good will for morality is my will is obvious enough, and it is no less plain (pp. 144, 162 [of *Ethical Studies*]) that it is presented as universal. That does not mean that everybody does or has to do what I do, but it means that, if they were I, they must do as I have to do, or else be immoral; it means that my moral will is *not* the mere will of myself as this or that man, but something above it and beyond it. And further, again, the good will is presented as one

[1]
> Thyself and thy belongings
> Are not thine own so proper, as to waste
> Thyself upon thy virtues, them on thee.
> Heaven doth with us, as we with torches do,
> Not light them for themselves: for if our virtues
> Did not go forth of us, 'twere all alike
> As if we had them not. Spirits are not finely touch'd
> But to fine issues.

[William Shakespeare, *Measure for Measure*, Act One, Scene One, lines 31–3]

will; in collisions, going to our moral consciousness, we are told that, if we knew it, there is a right, that the collision is for us, and is not for the good will. We can not bring before us two diverse good wills, or one good will at cross purposes and not in harmony with itself; and we feel sure that, if our will were but one with the universal, then we too should be one with ourselves, with no conflict of desires, but a harmony and system.

Such is the will presented to itself by the moral consciousness, but for the moral consciousness that is ideal and not real. Within the sphere of morality the universal remains but partially realized: it is something that for ever wants to be, and yet is not.

We saw that the will of the social organism might be called a universal will, and a will which was visibly real, as well as ideal; but we saw too that the sphere of my station and its duties did not cover the whole good self; and further, even within that sphere, and apart from difficulties of progress, for morality in the strict sense ideal and real remain apart. The bad self is not extinguished, and in myself I see an element of will wherein the universal is unrealized, and against which it therefore remains (so far as my morality is concerned) a mere idea; for, even if we assume that society gets no hurt, yet I do not come up to my special type.

For morals then the universal is not realized within my station, and furthermore the moral consciousness does not say that it is realized anywhere at all. The claim of the ideal is to cover the whole field of reality, but our conscience tells us that we will it here, and that there again we do not will it, here it is realized, and there it is not realized, and we can not point to it in ourselves or others and say, Here is the universal incarnate, and fully actual by and as the will of this or that man; and indeed we see that for the ideal self to be in the world as the expressed will of this or that spiritualized animal is quite out of the question.

Of course if religion, and more particularly if Christianity be brought in, the answer must be different. The ideal here is a universal, because it is God's will, and because it therefore is the will of an organic unity, present though unseen, which is the one life of its many members, which is real in them, and in which they are real; and in which, through faith for them, and for God we do not know how, the bad self is unreal. But all this lies beyond morality: my mere moral consciousness knows nothing whatever about it. And we must give the same answer, if we are told on other grounds that humanity is an actually existing organic community, in which we are members, and whose will is present in us.[m] For supposing that the identity (not mere likeness) of the best self in all men is proved, and further the right established to use the word 'humanity', not as an abstract term for an abstract idea, nor as a name for an imaginary collection of all past, present, and future individuals, but for a real corporate unity, yet still we must say, My conscience tells me that my bad self is real; and whether on speculative grounds you try to show that it is unreal, or bring in faith, yet in either case you have gone beyond morality; for morality the good is still only realized in part, and there is something against which it still remains a mere idea.

The ideal self then for morals is not visibly universal nor fully actual. It is not visibly and in the world seen to be an harmonious system, but in the world and in us realizes, it would seem, itself against itself. And in us it is not a system; our self is not a harmony, our desires are not fully identified with the ideal, and the ideal does not always bring peace in its train. In our heart it clashes with itself, and desires we can not exterminate clash with our good will, and, however much we improve (if we do improve), we never are perfect, we never are a harmony, a system, as our true idea is, and as it calls upon us to be.

Thus morality, because its end is not completely realized, is after all ideal; and what we have next to see is that it is not simply positive; it is also negative. The self, which, as the good will, is identified with our type, has to work against the crude material of the natural wants, affections, and impulses, which, though not evil in themselves, stand in the way of good, and must be disciplined, repressed, and encouraged. It is negative again of what is positively evil, the false self, the desires and habits which embody a will directly contrary to the good will. And further it belongs to its essence that it should be so negative of both, because a being not limited, and limited by evil in himself, is not what we call moral. (Cf. pp. 145–6 [of *Ethical Studies.*]) A moral will must be finite, and hence have a natural basis; and it must to a certain extent (how far is another matter) be evil, because a being which does not know

---

[m] Humanity as invisible organism: see p. 205 [of *Ethical Studies*].

good and evil is not moral, and because (as we shall see more fully hereafter) the specific characters of good and evil can be known only one against the other, and furthermore can not be apprehended by the mere intellect, but only by inner experience. Morality, in short, implies a knowledge of what the 'ought' means, and the 'ought' implies contradiction and moral contradiction.

So we see morality is negative; the non-moral and the immoral must exist as a condition of it, since the moral is what it is only in asserting itself against its opposite. But morality is not merely negative; it is a great mistake to suppose that the immoral is there already,[n] and that morality consists simply in making it not to be. The good will is not that which merely destroys the natural or the immoral; it does indeed destroy them as such, but this by itself is not morality. It is when it destroys them by its own assertion, and destroys them by transmuting the energy contained in them, that the will is moral.[o]

The good self is not real as the mere abolition of reality. On its affirmative side (and it is moral only when it is affirmative) it is the position of the universal will, as the true infinite, in the personal will of this or that man; and here it has reality, not complete, not adequate, but still certain. You can not separate negation and affirmation without destroying the moral world. The abstract non-existence of the non-moral is nothing; and the existence of nothing (if that were possible) is not a moral end. The assertion of the moral, the positive realization of the good will to the negation of the natural and bad will, is morality, and no one element of this whole is so; for in the destruction of the bad it is only the affirmation of the good which is desirable (cf. p. 27 [of *Ethical Studies*]).

The realization of the good in personal morality is the habituated will, the moral character of individuals. It is actual in the virtues of the heart, and those virtues are the habits which, embodying good

---

[n] By its very essence immorality can not exist except as against morality: a purely immoral being is a downright impossibility. The man who has become entirely immoral has ceased to know good and evil, has ceased to belong to the moral sphere, is morally speaking dead.

[o] This in general is wholly true. There are, however, cases of repression of bad impulses where it is true perhaps only *generally*. The positive assertion, that is, is always there, but can it always be said to use up the *particular* impulse, and transmute *that*? It asserts the good will in *that general sphere – yes! but more*, perhaps not.

acts of will, have become part of the man's self, and which answer to the various sides of his station, or more generally to his various relations to the ideal.

Morality then is a process of realization, and it has two sides or elements which can not be separated; (1) the position of an ideal self, and the making of that actual in the will; (2) the negation, which is inherent in this, the making unreal (not by annihilation but transformation) of the for ever unsystematized natural material, and the bad self. And this account removes many of the difficulties we encountered in Essay IV [of *Ethical Studies*].

It does not remove them all. Morality does involve a contradiction; it does tell you to realize that which never can be realized, and which, if realized, does efface itself as such. No one ever was or could be perfectly moral; and, if he were, he would be moral no longer. Where there is no imperfection there is no ought, where there is no ought there is no morality, where there is no self-contradiction there is no ought. The ought is a self-contradiction. Are we to say then that that disposes of it? Surely not, unless it also disposes of ourselves; and that can not be. At least from this point of view, we are a self-contradiction: we never are what we feel we really are; we really are what we know we are not; and if we became what we are, we should scarcely be ourselves. Morality aims at the cessation of that which makes it possible; it is the effort after non-morality, and it presses forward beyond itself to a super-moral sphere where it ceases as such to exist.[p,q]

It is at this point we find problems too great for us, and, if we follow any further, it will be only in our Concluding Remarks, and merely with a view to clear up what has gone before. But at our present point of view we must remain, till we have answered some objections and attempted to remove some difficulties. The rest of this Essay will have to do with ἀπορίαι [difficulties or puzzles]

---

[p] It does not concern me to go out of my way to say more on endless moral progress. I have already (p. 155 [*Ethical Studies*]) referred to Hegel's annihilating criticism. Progress to an end which is completeness and the end of progress and morality, is one thing. Endless progress is progress without an end, is endless incompleteness, endless immorality, and is quite another thing.

[q] To some extent this is even realized in and through morality. We can and do admire, in some cases, the goodness which is, or has (in part) become, 'natural instinct', and admire it *more* than the moral (strictly). Of course this, however, is only partial, and is based on, and ready to return to, what *is* moral (strictly).

which arise in respect of morality, and the next one will try to make more clear what we mean by the bad self which opposes the good.

The first one-sided view of morality which must engage us may be put as follows: 'Morality is not the realization of a content, but the identification of the will with the universal. The moral end is consequently the production of a system, a harmony in the desires, the heart and will; and therefore we may and must suppress aspiration in order to get moral harmony.' We answer – It is true morality is not the mere realization of a content, since in itself that content is not, strictly speaking, moral. The performance is not moral apart from the will. That is one side. But on the other side the will which is not the will to perform is not moral at all. To try to be good not in science, art, or any other ideal pursuit, nor to be good socially, but to be virtuous simply in oneself, or to realize the good will with no content to it, is not to be moral in any way. A mere formal harmony is not a moral end: the end is not system, but the systematic realization of the self whose will is in harmony with the ideal. For example, if the question arises, Am I to advance as a good man or a good artist? morality says, 'Of course as a good man'; but then the whole matter turns on this, What line of action, the doing of what, does make me the best man? In collision of morality with morality it does not hold that the higher the morality the more harmonious the self. You may have harmony of a sort (*not perfect* harmony) without any morality, and you may have morality with but little harmony.

There are other one-sided views, from which consequences follow opposed to the moral consciousness. We may state them so; 'The most systematic man is not the most moral, since he need not have done what he could and therefore should have done; is then the most energetic realization of the good self the most moral man? Suppose we say Yes. Then (1) the difference of capacity and circumstances is left out of the account, and the stronger and more successful nature will be the more moral; and again (2) the different amount of drawbacks is not considered: no credit is given to a man for moral struggles however severe; and in both cases we are in collision with the moral consciousness.

'Or if we say, No, you must look not to the positive realization but to the negative, to the victory over the bad self; – that, again, is against morality, because it unjustly favours the weaker nature; the more energetic may, because he is more energetic, have therefore more bad self to conquer.

'Again if we say, Neither negative nor positive realization is to be looked to, for morality is a struggle and it is the struggle which is of importance – then it will follow that, to increase the struggle and with it morality, the bad self must not be allowed to decrease beyond a certain point; and, further, it will follow that either all men are morally equal, since all struggle, and no one can do more than struggle; or else, if the most moral man is the man who struggles most, the quantity (intensive and extensive) of the struggle, and not the degree in the scale of qualitative advance, will count for morality. And of these, as of the other conclusions, every one is immoral.'

It would not repay us to investigate these difficulties in detail; they arise from doctrines which are not false in themselves, but each of which is false if taken as the expression of the whole truth, and their solution will come readily from the answer to the question, Who for the moral consciousness is the most moral man?[r]

Who is the most moral man? 'Moral' with an emphasis. We do not ask who is the most perfect man. We do not say, Whose will is most identified with *the* ideal human type? but, Whose will is most identified with *his* ideal?

For the moral consciousness tells us that a man is not good morally according as he stands in the scale of human progress; that a man's morality may in one sense be higher than another man's, yet he himself may be, strictly speaking, morally lower. It tells us that, if we judge by a purely moral standard, the low savage may be, not a higher, but a better man than the civilized European; and, we see, (1) the most moral man is the man who tries most to act up to what his light tells him is best. But in that we must remember is included the getting the best light which, up to his light, he can.

(2) Suppose now that the lights of two men are equal, can we then look to the greater or lesser realization of their ideal, and judge them accordingly? Morality says, No. It says the formal energy in all men is not the same; and, unless selves are equal to start with,

---

[r] Degrees of morality. Here we see again that the Good is wider than the *moral* Good. It is not true that nothing is good but a good will. (Cf. p. 228 [of *Ethical Studies*].)

they can not be morally compared simply with an eye to their respective realization.

(3) And again men vary, not only in light and in formal energy, but also in disposition. Disposition no doubt is not moral character; that does not begin until a man is self-conscious, and by volition the good and bad selves get their specific character one against the other;⁵ but none the less is natural disposition the material from which the moral self is built up. And dispositions or natures vary indefinitely: some are more harmonious than others, and some again are more chaotic and lead inevitably to jars and painful contradictions. The material of some men offers more resistance to the systematizing good will, and gives more openings for the increase and strengthening of the bad self, than does that of others. And, unless in this too individuals are equal, you can not simply compare them by the result.

(4) And further we have to consider external circumstances in relation to disposition, as bearing on the facility of appropriating the good, and again on the difficulty of controlling the bad self; and our conclusion at present is this. Men equal in light, formal energy, natural disposition, and circumstances, and equal also in present extent and intent of their good and bad selves, are morally equal.

Even here we are not at the end:ᵗ but this is enough to show that for us to make an accurate comparison is scarcely possible, and fully to justify the saying that 'only God sees the heart',³ if we mean by that not that morality is a matter of the heart in the sense of staying there, but that the data for solving the psychological problem are not accessible to us. This is not to be regretted: in morality we have nothing to do with others and what they do or neglect; we have nothing to do with what we ourselves may in past time have succeeded with or failed in, except so far as it is present in our will; what is before us is the relation of our private will to the good will, what we are and do and have still to do.

To resume, after making these four qualifications we may say men are equal morally, whose good and bad selves are equal in extent and intent; but here we have two sides to consider and not

⁵ See more in following Essay [Essay VII of *Ethical Studies*].
ᵗ See what follows in the next paragraph.

³ 1 Samuel 16:7, '. . . the Lord looks at the heart'; 1 Chronicles, 28:9, '. . . the Lord searches every heart . . .'; Acts 15, 8, 'God who knows the heart . . .'

one, and it does not appear how these stand to one another, and how the problem is to be worked.

You can not measure by comparative lessness of bad self, because morality is not merely negative; nor again by moreness of good self, because it is not merely affirmative. You can not go by severity of struggle between bad and good, because, other things being equal, the more of good against less of bad, and hence lessness of struggle, is the better. Greater or less struggle is a test only when it points to greater or less affirmation, when, being a negative condition,[u] the moreness of it points to the moreness of the positive, the condition of which it is. It is a serious mistake to argue, 'because more *sin qua non*, therefore more'. Nor again can you go by relative absence of struggle, because that may mean relative absence of the good will, and moral deadness.

To measure morality you must take the two sides, good and bad together, and then comes up the question of their relation. May we (1) say the bad self is in itself indifferent, and so measure simply by the good; or must we (2) treat it as a minus quantity and subtract it from the good?

(1) In 'in itself indifferent' the *in itself* is the important point. So far as the bad self thwarts the good by direct opposition, no one would call it indifferent. And then, beside its open hostility, it creates consequences which thwart the good, and in addition appropriates to itself a share of the general energy which should have gone to the good, and so weakens it. And all this no one would call indifferent.

But 'in itself indifferent' does not mean this.[v] It means, the bad self matters so far as it lessens the good, but by itself it is only a negation; and, after you have allowed for its negative properties, you need not consider it at all. The more or less of position of the good self in relation to light, energy, disposition, and circumstances, constitutes the more or less of morality. The bad self only takes

---

[u] A condition is negative when, not its existence as such, but the negation of its existence is necessary to that of which it is the condition.

[v] The reader no doubt is aware that there is a view which reduces the distinction of good and bad to a mere *quantitative* difference; virtue and vice differ only in being a little more or a little less of the same thing. This view makes great play with its 'all is relative', 'it all depends on which way you look at it', and the rest of the phrases behind which shallowness tries to look like wisdom. But we shall not stop to discuss it.

from that position; so that you need only find out what position after all you have, and then there is no occasion to consider the bad self. If in two men with equal light, energy, &c., the good selves are equal, it does not matter whether one has more bad self than the other, and we can strike that out of the account. This is the first proposal. Is it satisfactory?

I think we must say it is not. Practically it might never mislead us, because the consequences of the affirmation of the bad self in immoral acts result in a weakening of the good will far more extensive than might seem at first sight. The doctrine might not take us wrong, but we are asking, Is it theoretically accurate as an exposition of the moral consciousness? And this we must deny, since for that consciousness the bad self is not in itself indifferent.

(2) Considered otherwise, and not in relation to morality, the bad self may be *only* the negative condition of the affirmation of the good; the presence of which is necessary for morality, but of which anything more than the mere presence is the decrease of the affirmation. It may be something to work against, a resistance which is good for the reaction of energy, but the greater resistance of which does not carry more reaction with it. But this, if a possible point of view, is not a (mere) moral point of view, and as such is here untenable. The bad self for morality is not simply a negation, but the positive assertion of self. The self-conscious self which is positive, which is the very affirmation we know, is in the bad self, feels and knows itself therein as really as it does in the good self. Evil deeds are not mere comings-short, but, apart from their consequences, they are (I do not say sins, for they are that only in and for religion, but) offences, over-steppings, crimes. The bad self is the positive assertion of evil by and in the self; and the will, so far as bad, is not a defect of will, nor a non-moral natural will, but it is an immoral will, and for the moral consciousness it is as real[w] as the good will.

Hence I am moral not only according to the relative extensive and intensive affirmation of the good will in me, but from that result must be further deducted the relative assertion of the bad will in me, as something which not only takes up space, uses energy, and so

---

[w] Yes, I think so, *for the moral consciousness.* On the bad self see Essay VII [in *Ethical Studies*].

starves the good will, besides thwarting it and creating consequences (psychical and physical) which thwart it, but which also, as a positive minus, must be deducted from the plus of the good self, in order to arrive at the final result.

That result can not be worked out with accuracy. On the side of the good you can not reduce intent to extent, so as to count the plus quantity; and on the side of the bad for the same reason you can not count the minus quantity; and even if you could, yet you could not reduce the minus units and the plus units to a common denomination, so as to get by subtraction a quantitative result. But, though practically useless, our answer so far will I hope be found to be the solution of the foregoing ἀπορίαι [difficulties or puzzles].

It is perhaps necessary to say something on another point, viz. as to whether a man is moral because of his present or also because of his past state. When we put it in this way the question seems to admit of but one answer; for clearly I am moral because I *am*, and not because I have been, good. But in a different form it may occasion difficulty. Suppose we have three men equal at the start, and one of them has been good and now has fallen away, another has before fallen away and now is trying to be good, and a third has never been far either one way or the other; how do we judge these morally? Is it fair not to count the past?

The answer is that a man's morality, on the one hand, is not the summing up of a past result; and we can consider only the present state, can look only at the will as it is now. This is one side. But on the other hand the will is what it has done; and the present is thus also the past. Evil deeds must survive in a present evil will which is a positive evil, just as good deeds are not lost, but live in a present good will. No one becomes bad or good all at once, however much men may sometimes seem to do so. And we believe that at the last the existing positive bad and positive good available energy of will (after making all the proper qualifications and allowances, which include, of course, bodily changes) is the true representative of the good and evil the man has done.[x] If in the sphere of morality we are to measure men's lives morally as wholes, this perhaps is how we are to do it, if we do it at all; though from another point of view, and not by us, it may perhaps be done differently.

---

[x] This perhaps cannot be shown.

In conclusion, we must warn the reader against supposing that morality is to be estimated by the intensity of the moral consciousness. It is true that a man who has never known himself to be good or bad is as yet not strictly either, is not yet within the moral sphere. Knowledge of good and evil is necessary for morality, and that (see Essay VII [of *Ethical Studies*]) depends on a self-conscious volition with which responsibility begins, and after which we are answerable for acts of will not self-conscious, because now we know their character, and ought to have them under our control. Self-consciousness is necessary for a moral being, but it is a dangerous mistake to think that all morality must therefore be self-conscious. To be moral, a man need not know that he is acting rightly; still less need he know that he is acting rightly for the sake of morality, and for no other sake. It does not follow, because self-consciousness is the condition of imputation, that therefore everything which is imputed must be done with self-consciousness. The will both for good and evil need not be deliberate volition, still less the deliberate volition of the good simply because it is good, or the evil because it is evil. To will the evil because it is evil is, we think, impossible; to will the moral because it is moral, and for the sake of morality, demands a certain pitch of culture, and then is not common. To will the right as the right, though not for the sake of rightness, is common enough; but, in most of our moral actions, we do not do so much as this, because we act from habit and without reflection. Habits are all-important, and habits need not be self-conscious; and yet habits are imputable, because what makes the habit is within the region of conscious volition, and can not be disowned by it. The habits we encourage or suffer, we are aware of or might be aware of; we know their moral quality, and hence are responsible for them. Our character formed by habit is the present state of our will, and, though we may not be fully aware of its nature, yet morally it makes us what we are.[y] Our will is not this, that, or the other conscious volition, nor does it exist just so far as we reflect upon it. It is a formed habit of willing, such a potential will as, apart from counteracting causes, and given the external conditions which we have a right to expect, must issue in acts of a certain sort. It is such a will

[y] We have consciously, and with knowledge of their moral character, committed ourselves to volitions with which our habits are essentially connected, or have failed to do so when we might have done so; and hence those habits are ours, and constitute our standing will.

as this which makes a man moral, and it need not everywhere and in all its acts be aware of what it is doing.

To sum up, in estimating morality you take the amount of the present extent and intent (conscious or unconscious) of the will for good, less the present extent and intent of will (conscious or unconscious) for bad, and all in relation to what may be called chance, i.e. the amount of obtainable light, formal energy, natural disposition, and external circumstances of every kind, under which head must come that increase or decrease of general energy for which we are not accountable. Morality, in the sense of personal morality, may either be self-conscious or not so. It wills the end explicitly and directly as a moral end, as one not outside the heart and inner will, and, so far, it is self-conscious. Or again, it wills the end for its own sake, simply and directly, and, so far, not as an end within the heart and will; and further, it need not always even be aware that it is acting rightly: in these cases it is not self-conscious. But *morally* considered one morality is not higher than the other.

Personal morality, then, is the process of the assertion of the ideal self, considered not directly as the position of its content, but with respect to the intensity of the process as will. And it must be taken in relation to natural energy, disposition, and all circumstances; and again with respect to the intensity of the negation of the false self, since this negation is an inseparable element. It further includes the willing of psychical changes in the self, in the way of systematization, since these are means to the assertion of the ideal, and the negation of the bad self. And the ground and result of morality is habit or state, which answers to process as its psychical embodiment and basis, and which, as standing will in a man for good, is virtue, just as the habitual will for bad is vice.

Or otherwise, morality is the systematization of the self by the realization therein of the ideal self as will; such ideal taking its content from (1) the objective realized will, (2) the not yet realized objective will, (3) an ideal, the content of which can not (without going beyond morality) be realized as objective will.

It is the process of self-realization from one point of view, i.e. as the negation of the will which has a content other than the true content of the self, and the affirmation of the will whose content is that ideal in which alone the self can look for true realization.

And being a process, involving a contradiction as the *sine qua non* of its existence, it tries to realize the for ever un-real, and it does desire its own extinction, as mere morality, in desiring the suppression of its finitude.[z]

Morality is approximative; and, before we proceed, we must learn more accurately how this is to be understood. The reader, recalling our criticism of the Hedonistic chief good (pp. 97–8 [of *Ethical Studies*]), may now object that the contradiction we discovered there is inherent in all morality: that in all we aim at a mark we do not hit, and endeavour to get nearer to an impossibility. We must try to clear up this matter.

(1) That in morality we fail *altogether* to realize the end is not true. If it were so we should not be moral. In our hearts and lives the ideal self is actually carried out, our will is made one with it and does realize it, although the bad self never disappears and the good self is incoherent and partial. 'Well but', comes the objection, 'Hedonism can say this too. There too the end is partially realized.' Not so, we reply. Asking for this partial reality, we are told to look

---

[z] The doctrine that nothing is good but the Good Will is clearly untenable. There are excellences for which we admire this or that man which yet cannot fairly be brought under the Good Will – health, strength, luck, and, still more, beauty. These are in various senses admirable, and, if so, desirable; and, if so, they surely must be good, though certainly not so morally. Again, when, and so far as, moral goodness becomes instinctive and natural, we do not admire it less, but often more. It tends to become good as the beautiful is good – τὸ καλόν [wood or kindling].

We cannot, as to goodness, identify the man with his morality if we take that in the strict sense. And this obviously raises the question how the morality stands to the man, how far they do not coincide, and how the man comes to have the Good Will which he has, or which (we are tempted to say) falls to his lot.

The moral judgement is here in a difficulty, and is not consistent. It mainly identifies the man with his moral goodness or badness, so far as this is willed or comes from will in the past. It tends so to judge the man, but it also tends to make *some* allowances.

In the main it does not raise the question how the man comes to will or not to will, or how in one man the will is able to be victorious, in another man not. The man *is* or is *not* so, as to his moral will, however we take that, i.e. whether as struggle only or as success.

But how such or such a moral will is allotted to such or such a man, and on what principle (if any), morality does not ask. And yet to make the allotment come from the Will would clearly be ridiculous, as the fact that the Will, or so much Will, is there must 'come first', and cannot follow from the Will *before* that is there.

Hence moral imputation in the end breaks down in principle (if you take it as ultimate and final), and we see this in the 'allowances' made morally, as we see it again in the religious point of view; i.e. the Grace of God makes all the difference between one man and another. 'There, but for the Grace of God, goes – &c.'

at that fraction of the sum of pleasures which has been reached; and we say at once, that is not actual at all; in that you have got nothing whatever. The past is past, and to have had a feeling is not to have it; so that in ordinary Hedonism I do but try to heap up what dies in the moment of its birth, and can not thus get nearer to the possession of anything.[aa] In morality on the other hand the past is present now in the will, and the will is the reality of the good. Common Hedonism can not say this.

(2) But the question remains, Does not morality pursue a fallacious object? Is it not a mere quantitative approach to zero? We answer, No it is a great deal more. On the side of the bad self the moral end is certainly to produce the nothingness of that, and mere negative morality is destroyed by our objector's question. But, as we have explained above (p. 234 of *Ethical Studies* [and p. 114 of this volume]), true morality is the positive assertion of the good will. It aims then, we may say, at the zero of morality *as such* (i. e. as struggle against the bad), but not at the zero of the positive will for good.

(3) But, let this be as it may, is not morality the approximation to an endless quantity; does it not labour in vain for the false infinite? Again we say, No. The moral end is not a sum of units: it is qualitative perfection. What I want is not mere increase of quantity; but, given a certain quantum of energy in my will, I desire the complete expenditure of that in behalf of the ideal. The object is for me to become an infinite whole by making my will one with an infinite whole. The size of the whole, as such, is not considered at all. It is true that, though mere quantity is not the end, yet the end implies quantity. Perfect good means zero of badness, and zero of neutral or un-developed energy. Hence degrees of advance to moral perfection can be measured by the lessening extent of the non-moral and the immoral. But the suppression of these negatives as such is not the end; and though the good will can legitimately be considered from one point of view as a number of units of a certain sort of energy, yet mere size is not the essence of the matter, and to say that moral perfection must rise and fall with the addition or subtraction of such units would be absolutely false.

These questions at every point have done their best to draw us beyond our depth into the abstract metaphysic which in the end

---

[aa] See note, p. 94 [of *Ethical Studies*].

they turn upon. And now we come to one which threatens to involve us more deeply, and our answer to which must remain superficial. What sense have the words 'higher' and 'lower' when applied to morality?

(1) In the strict meaning of 'moral' we have discussed this above (pp. 237–8 [of *Ethical Studies* and pp. 117–18 of this volume]). Strictly speaking, a higher stage in historical progress is not more *moral* than a lower stage. For in personal morality we consider not the relative completeness of the ideal aimed at, but the more or less identification of a given sum of energy with the particular ideal. And on this head we have dwelt as long as seemed necessary.

(2) But in the wider sense of 'moral' there is a question which we have not properly discussed. If human history is an evolution (p. 189 foll. [of *Ethical Studies*]), how is one stage of it morally higher than another? For in one sense the European certainly is morally a higher being than the savage. He is higher, because the life he has inherited and more or less realized is nearer the truth of human nature. It combines greater specification with more complete homogeneity. And he is higher *morally*, not only because the good will is better according as the type it aims at is truer, but also because that stage of the progressive realization of human nature from which the European gets his being is the historical product of a will which in the main was for good, and now at any rate is the present living embodiment of the good will. Thus if we hold that in evolution one stage is higher than another, we can say also that one stage is more moral than another. But (as before) in the strict sense general human progress is not moral, because it abstracts from the collision of good and bad in the personal self.

And here we might perhaps stop, did not a fresh question irresistibly intrude. Is there such a thing as progress? Does not progress mean the perpetual 'more', the would-be approximation to an endless sum? And, if so, is not progress the illusion of a journey in the direction of a figment? An infinite quantity we have seen to be a self-contradiction, and the advance towards it fallacious; so that 'more' does not come any nearer to 'most'. In comparison of infinity, all finite sums are equal. When you ask for the difference between each and the infinite, in order to compare these differences one with the other, you get in every case the same answer, Between the infinite and each finite alike there is a quantity, about which in no case can we say more than that it is not any finite sum. Thus against the infinite there is no difference between the finites, and we feel the full force of the objection. Progress in the sense of an advance towards the perfect seems to be a sheer illusion.

True, we can fall back on our thesis that the end is the true infinite, the complete identity of homogeneity and specification (p. 74 [of *Ethical Studies*]). This we can insist is not a quantity, and may repeat that into the definition of perfection mere size does not enter at all. But still the difficulty remains. Within the process of evolution the higher is defined as that which is *more* intensely homogeneous in a *greater* specification, and it does seem as if higher and lower were in the end reducible to quantity, extensive or intensive, since the higher man is the man who has *more* of the truth of human nature. For take an example; suppose a man to be perfectly self-contained and homogeneous, and then to get what are called higher qualities, and so become less self-contained. Is not this an advance, and an advance because a getting *more*? Is not a wider and deeper truth a higher truth? And is it not higher because you have something *beside* what you had before, or *more* of something of which before you had less? And is not, once again, the conclusion from all this that progress is an illusory quantitative advance towards a fiction?

How can we escape? Will it do to say that the higher is such because it contains the lower as an element in a larger whole; and that the lower is such because, from the point of view of the higher, it is limited and narrow, and a position in which the higher would be in contradiction with itself? But is not the question here once more, If quantity is not to be considered, *why* is the more inclusive position higher?

I know of no answer but this, that the perfect is that in which we can rest without contradiction, that the lower is such because it contradicts itself, and so is forced to advance beyond itself to another stage, which is the solution of the contradiction that existed in the lower, and so a relative perfection.[bb] If there is a whole which is not finite, and if this whole exists in the finite, the reader will see at once that the finite *must* be discrepant, not only with what is

---

[bb] On this point see [F. H. Bradley, *Essays on Truth and Reality*, Oxford, Clarendon Press, 1935] Chapter VIII.

outside itself, but also with itself. The movement towards the solution of this contradiction consists in the extension of the lower so as to take in and resolve its conflicting elements in a higher unity. And this is the reason why the advance consists in greater specification and more intense homogeneity, and therefore, to a certain extent, can be measured by quantity. On this view the higher is above the lower, not because it contains a larger number of units, but because it is the harmony of those elements which in the lower were a standing contradiction. And this conclusion I will ask the reader to take, not as positive doctrine, but as matter for his reflection.

But if any one says he must go further, and objects, Well, but in every stage the whole is realized, and in no stage is it realized free from all contradiction. It is actual and complete in the one as in the other

> As full, as perfect, in a hair as heart,
> As full, as perfect, in vile man that mourns,
> As the rapt seraph that adores and burns;
> To him no high, no low, no great, no small;
> He fills, he bounds, connects, and equals all,[4]

here I confess I can not follow, nor, if I could, would my theme allow of it. For the moral point of view holds good only *within* the process of evolution.

The question, Is evolution or progress the truth from the highest point of view? raises problems which nothing but a system of metaphysic can solve. We are forced to believe in the many, we can not help believing in the one; and, whether we desire it or not, these thoughts come together in our minds, and we say, The process of change is the truth. Is then process, still more is evolution, what we can think without contradicting ourselves? To whom in England can we go for an answer? And yet one might have thought that a part of the energy now spent in preaching the creed of evolution would well have been spent on the inquiry, What in the end *is* process in general, and, in particular, what is evolution? Is it, or is it not, a self-contradiction? And, if it is, what conclusions follow?

---

[4] Alexander Pope (1688–1744), 'An Essay on Man', *Poetical Works*, ed. Herbert Davies (London, Oxford University Press, 1966), lines 268–72.

But dogma is more pleasant than criticism, and as yet we have no English philosophy whose basis is not dogmatic.

But, whatever evolution may be, Ethics is confined within it. To ask what it is, is to rise above it, and to pass beyond the world of mere morality.

6
The Reality of the General Will

B. BOSANQUET

'There is often a great difference between the will of all and the general will; the latter looks only to the common interest; the former looks to private interest, and is nothing but a sum of individual wills; but take away from these same wills the plus, and minus, that cancel one another, and there remains, as the sum of the differences, the general will.' 'Sovereignty is only the exercise of the general will.'[a]

This celebrated antithesis, the statement of which I have translated from Rousseau's own words, has the effect of setting a problem to which Rousseau himself scarcely finds an answer. The problem is emphasised by the various reasons and indications which make it difficult to believe that the action of any community is a mere sum of the effects of wholly independent causes operating on a number of separate individual minds. No doubt, the action of a community sometimes is, and often appears to be, the sum of effects of such independent causes. One man gives a certain vote because he hates Mr. A.; another man gives the same vote because he thinks Mr. B. will do something for his trade; and a third gives the same vote because of some one out of a thousand possible social reforms which he thinks the man he is voting for will help or will hinder, as the case may be. Now, assuming these causes to be independent of one another, the direction in which they will sum up is a question of chance. Of course it is determined by causation, but it is not determined by any general cause, corresponding to a general

[a] Rousseau, *Contrat Social*, Book II., chap. i. and chap. iii.

element in the result which takes place. As related to the separate causes in operation, the general character of that result is a coincidence or matter of chance.

And this is, in fact, how Rousseau seems to regard it, and he therefore suggests what is practically, I should imagine, just the wrong method for eliminating private interest and getting at the general will. Let the citizens all vote as independent units, not organising themselves in groups or adjusting their views by private communication, and then, he thinks, as I understand him, the general interest will assert itself, as any general cause does in the elimination of chance among a great number of counteracting independent causes; that is, as he says, the independent causes, if present in sufficient numbers, may be expected to cancel, and the general cause will have a visible effect in deciding the question. If private interests are equally balanced, the public interest will affect some minds on both sides enough to turn the scale. This element of regard to the public interest is what he calls the general will, as distinct from the will of all.

I do not think that this view is false; but it is not adequate to the action of a very complex society with elaborate constructive tasks before it. It is rather adapted to a plebiscite on a single question, in which the general will is represented by a conscious though feeble inclination to what is admittedly the public interest. The discouragement of discussion and of organisation in groups, which he insists on in order to keep the chances fair, i.e. to keep all the private interests independent of one another, would make all complicated legislation impossible, and is quite incompatible with the method which I shall maintain, that necessity prescribes for the formation of the general will. He so far admits this, that the ideal legislator is for him a person outside the community, who interprets the general will into a system of laws.

What we have got then, so far, is a problem or a paradox: the idea of a will whose sole aim is the common interest, although it can exist as a will only in the minds of the human individuals who make up the community, and all of whom are for the most part occupied with their own individual interests. There is no social brain other than and separate from the brain of individuals, and because we seldom face this difficulty fairly, our great modern gospel, that society is an organism, is becoming a little stale before it has rendered us the one service which it might perhaps be able to render – that is, to make us ask ourselves in what properties or relations of individuals in society there resides anything corresponding on behalf of society to the brain or mind of each separate individual. We know that many not contemptible people speak of the individual members of any community as mostly fools, and say that the wise and those who are in the right are always in the minority, and that the ordinary man picks up his opinions out of a newspaper, and adjusts them by conversation with two or three other persons no better informed than himself. The expressions, more or less in this sense, of so eminent a writer as Mr. Bryce, in his discussion of Public Opinion in the third volume of the work on the *American Commonwealth*,[1] were what I had chiefly in my mind when I resolved to try and examine this paradox, which in that discussion Mr. Bryce fully recognises. No candid man can altogether, I think, deny the judgments to which I am referring, so far as they deal with the general capacity for intellectual processes in unfamiliar matter. Mr. Bryce indeed tries to blunt the paradox by pointing out that the so-called educated classes are *not* especially fitted, by the training which has hitherto been customary, for dealing with important practical questions; but this does not help us to see how the bulk of the community *are* able and willing to deal rightly with such questions in the common interest. If the majority of separate individuals are, on any question immediately put before them, more likely to miss the common interest than to hit it, both from blindness and from selfishness, which cannot practically be distinguished, why does not society come to grief? Aristotle says that all the citizens taken together may have more wisdom than any one.[2] Is there any meaning in this?

Is it true that the intelligent pursuit by the individual of his private interests necessarily in the system of things conduces to the preservation of the community? Not if we mean by his private interests merely certain aims which are definitely before his mind, which he might tell you are the ruling objects of his life. On the other hand, if we say that the pursuit of his private interests *as*, on the

---

[1] James Bryce, *The American Commonwealth* (London, Macmillan, 1888), vol. III, 'The Tyranny of the Majority'. Second edition, published in two volumes, 1889, vol. II, 337–44.

[2] Aristotle, *Politics*, ed. Stephen Everson (Cambridge, Cambridge University Press, 1988), Book III, chapter ix, 1281a39 ff.

whole, he pursues them, conduces to the preservation of the community, that is pretty much a tautology.

What necessity is there that this mode of action and judgment should have in it any general reference whatever? When and why is the general will a reality within individual wills?

I have taken some time to state the paradox, because I think that the facts which it indicates are of extreme importance, even if the explanation offered is inadequate. I will now attempt an explanation, borrowing in some degree the ideas of modern psychology.

By an individual will I mean a human mind considered as a machine, of which the parts are ideas or groups of ideas, all tending to pass into action, but liable to be counteracted or again to be reinforced by each other. The groups of ideas are connected with each other by associations of all degrees of intimacy, but each is, for the most part, capable of being awakened into action by the appropriate stimulus without awakening more remotely associated groups, and the will, for the time being, consists of those ideas which are guiding attention and action. The ideas are not thrown together anyhow, but are more or less organised; some being of a nature which enables them to serve as a clue or plan in which others find their places, and in a sense every group of ideas might be called a single idea, and all that there is in the mind has the character of a single idea – that is to say, all its parts are connected in various degrees, and more or less subordinated to some dominant ideas which, as a rule, dictate the place and importance of the others. We know what a ruling idea is: it is one that has got the control of the mind, and subordinates all the other ideas to itself. This mental system, with its dominant ideas in relation to external action, is the individual will.

Now, at first sight all these individual wills, or minds in action, are separate machines, locked up in separate boxes, each with its indicator outside, and the response which each of them will make to a stimulus from without is determined by its own structure, which is again determined by its own private history. If we go no further than this we seem not to get any hint of a general will, but only a sum of individual wills, which need not have any reference to each other's ideas.

But we can perhaps go behind this. The individual will is shaped by its dominant ideas. What, on the whole, determines which ideas get the upper hand? The answer seems to be that the ideas which tend to be victorious are those distinguished by logical capacity; because they are especially able to marshal the content of conscious-ness in a way suitable to themselves, checking and defeating the ideas that cannot be brought into their system, and reinforcing themselves by those that can. All practical action tends to give the victory to such ideas as these, while modifying and extending them. Any suggestion which enables you to deal with matter that you have to arrange is maintained in your mind and reinforced by the suc-cessful action to which it leads, and receives new content, which it embodies in itself, from the combinations which arise in carrying it out. Other suggestions, that 'would not do', as we say, are driven out and disappear. Still, all this is a play of ideas within the individ-ual mind locked up in its separate box.

But now, does the quality which makes certain ideas dominant in one individual mind ensure their having any relation to the ideas which are dominant in other individual minds? Under certain con-ditions, clearly this is the case. These conditions are, in brief, com-munity of life and of experience. Ideas do not spring from no-where; they are the inside which reflects the material action and real conditions that form the outside. So that the common life shared by the members of a community involves a common element in their ideas, not merely in their notions of things about them, though this is very important, but more especially in the dominant or organising ideas which rule their minds. For the matter which is before their minds to be organised consists in great measure of con-nections between persons, and life simply cannot go on unless the organising ideas in different people's minds with reference to these connections correspond definitely to one another. This is, of course, a truism, except that it is not always driven home with reference to the actual shape and content which it implies in individual minds.

It may be said this only means that different persons' minds in the same country have a good deal in common; it does not mean that they participate in any conception of a common interest, but merely that they are influenced in the same way by the same appeal, with a certain general result, which is no more *in* each of them than the waving of a field of corn before the wind is in each separate stalk of corn. Well, this comparison is just for some cases, – for the case of a mob, for instance, when they act as one man, under the influence of an identical sentiment of anger or cupidity. This is an irrational form of the general will, as a burst of feeling is of the individual will; but it is definitely general in so far as it is owing to the operation of the same sentiment in all the minds at once.

But there are stronger cases than this. Just as the material working of any industry or institution is not complete in a single person, but consists in corresponding though different actions of different persons, so it is with the dominating ideas which in different individual minds represent this working. Therefore, if we could see these minds, which are locked up in boxes tolerably like each other on the outside, we should perceive that each of them bears quite a definite reference to the others outside itself; in short, it is not really a complete machine, as the body, though to some degree marked and moulded by its habitual occupation, appears to be, but is only part of a machine, of which the other parts are the minds of other persons with whom the first is in connection. The proof of this lies in the fact that external life is organised, which organisation again consists in the fact that the dominant ideas of the persons who participate in this life constitute, when taken together, a machine whose parts play into one another.

Then we may identify the general will of any community with the whole working system of dominant ideas which determines the places and functions of its members, and of the community as a whole among other communities. The system is never quite harmonious; re-adjustment is always going on, but the direction of this readjustment is determined by the forces in collision together with the other forces of the machine. Both the more important workings of the machine, and especially the direction of its readjustment, are the most familiar *expression* of the general will. But the general will itself is the whole assemblage of individual minds, considered as a working system, with parts corresponding to one another, and producing as a result a certain life for all these parts themselves.

Such a conception seems illusory, because it is hard to define exactly where the thing which it describes begins and ends; but really in modern philosophy nothing can be parted sharply at the point of transition; it is enough if the central phenomena in each region are clear and distinguishable.

I will mark it off by three negatives.

The general will cannot be identified with the decision of a community by vote upon any single issue. Every such decision is an expression or consequence of the general will, but needs interpretation in order to say what direction of movement it really represents. In short, the general will is a system in motion, and cannot be expressed in a single proposition. And no system of voting can secure its expression, because it does not exist in a form that can be embodied in a vote.

Again, the general will is not identical with public opinion, considered as a set of judgments which form the currently expressed reflection upon the course of affairs. It may include these current notions or part of them, but it certainly includes much more, because the ideas that dominate the will do not always appear in reflection, or at least not with the importance which they have in life. The general will is more a system of wills than a system of reflections, and appears in action quite as much as in discussion.

Again, it is not merely the *de facto* tendency of all that is done by members of the community, though it is much more like this than like a vote or a set of opinions. It *is* to a great extent a *de facto* tendency, but only in so far as this tendency reveals active ideas with reference to the connection of persons or groups of persons. Other tendencies than these do not directly concern the organisation of life, and therefore do not directly form part of the active scheme of society.

Take two examples from opposite extremes in mental development. An agricultural labourer thinks, I suppose, chiefly about making his living and supporting his family. His choice of where he will work and what kind of farm work pays him best does not greatly affect the nature of his connection with other people, being all within the same general scheme. But, although he does not reflect – or even if he does not reflect – on this general scheme, yet it is represented in the shape of his mind – that is, in his customary active ideas, and in their limitations. Now, these active ideas of his in their general character – i.e. the general character and limits of what he is prepared to do and to expect with reference to other persons, – this is the factor of the general will operative in his mind. It is acted on by his daily life, and rests upon that life; but it is rather the outline or scheme of that life than the every-day details of it.

A dramatic poet, again, will exercise his conscious choice about his subjects and his form of writing, and so forth. All this makes no direct difference to other people, and they cannot directly help him in it. Society cannot write a play. But if, for example, a school of really great dramatists were to arise in England to-day, the result might be to remould the working ideas in their own and other minds. The theatre would force itself, as a matter to be taken account of, into the mental systems of individuals, and in doing so would modify their dominant notions as to the place of art in national life, and so there would be a tendency of one kind or another which would enter into the active scheme or logical machine of social relations as a factor in the general will.

After these three negatives, I will say affirmatively that we may identify the general will with public opinion in a pregnant sense; not as consisting in the things said in the newspapers, but as the *actual* tendency of the whole process in which the necessary organising ideas of all individual minds in the community are factors.

The corollary from these suggestions, which is chiefly of interest to us, concerns the process of formation of the general will, or of public opinion in this pregnant sense.

It is not essentially superficial nor sentimental. It is essentially logical.

What is the root of the whole matter? It is nothing less than the correspondence with each other of the shapes taken by separate minds, each under the stress of its particular experience giving the victory to those ideas which are able to grapple with the matter pressed upon it. If the external life of the community works as a system, then this internal life must work as a system also; the one reflects the other.

Therefore, though it seems, as we said, as though most people are wrong when they express their opinions, and as if they pick them up from hearsay or from newspapers by sheer chance, this is to a great extent a *mere* appearance. Every person who does anything which is a necessary function in the community has in virtue of this function, which is mirrored in the shape of his leading active ideas, a definite position in the logical system of the community. So far as his mind reflects the real necessities of his active life he is on solid ground, and his will is so far a factor in the general will, because his life – which is his will seen from the outside – is a factor in the general life. If we all understood our own active ideas completely and rightly in relation to those of others, then we should have the whole general will in our explicit consciousness.

But, as it is, no individual ever can have this, for two principal reasons: –

First, we are never thoroughly aware even of our own practical ideas. The will is a great mass of associated ideas guiding attention and action, of which very different portions come into play in different contexts, and our description of which in general language, however honest we are, is not infallibly true, but, just like our description of any complicated phenomenon outside us, depends on our skill, patience, and truthfulness. Nothing is commoner than to succeed in telling a man something about his own conscious action which he really did not know till you told him. Especially, the nature of practical ideas consists very much in their limitations, and of these, except by intellectual self-criticism, we are not aware. A man may honestly believe that he has no prejudice against perfect social equality, and a short cross-examination will often show him that he has a strong prejudice of the kind. We are not conscious, either of all the influences active in our will, or of its limitations.

Secondly, no one, not the greatest statesman or historical philosopher, has in his mind, even in theory, much less as a practical object, the real development in which his community is moving. In modern philosophy the contrast between man and nature is apt to be far too sharply drawn at this point, as if the whole moral world was consciously constructed by man. In very great men the relation of conscious purpose to historical result seems sometimes – as in Cavour, for example – to be considerable; but, on the whole, we are to the structure of legal, political, and economic organisation like coral insects to a coral reef. All these things, and the body of science itself, are on one side natural products – that is to say, that, although conscious purpose works in them, the effect it produces is always part of a system which is more than any particular agent intended. The process always needs the future to explain its real tendency.

Thus the general will is only in part self-conscious, and in as far as an attempt is made to formulate it in judgments it seems to become fallible. For then it ceases to be fact, and becomes interpretation of fact.

Still, it is important, in thinking of the formation of the general will with a view to its interpretation, to remember what kind of facts it consists of. The solid basis for everyone is in his own practical will determined by the real necessities of his life in discharging a function in society. The process of interpretation and rationalisation of this will is then technically a process of criticism – that is to say, of adjusting the bearings of our whole view of life to the solid data of our own necessary working ideas in relation to those of others.

Now, this process again is not entirely conscious. It has two forms – practical organisation and reflective discussion. In practical organisation, ideas adjust themselves to each other without consciousness of anything beyond an immediate daily purpose, and it is only after a long interval that people wake up and find perhaps the entire relations of classes and of industry changed as it were in their sleep. This practical organisation is probably the most important phase in the formation of the general will. Of course it includes conflict within the law. And the second phase, discussion, if it is to be of any service, ought really to be the same thing in a reflective form – that is, contrivance, organisation, ascertainment by criticism of solid data, consisting in reasonable necessities, and their adjustment in a working system, such as to satisfy them all.

Now, of course these two processes pass into one another, and will more and more do so. And the two together really make up a very great part of life, so far as the persons concerned participate in a common experience. Every person is thus always being moulded into a logical unit much more than he is aware, and the casual opinions which he expresses do not really represent the content of his will or the process by which it is formed.

We must modify the theory to admit of our belonging to more than one community. The different ideas which rule us in different relations allow easily of this. The communities to which we belong are now like a nest of boxes inside one another; but we cannot effectively share the general will of any community with which we have no common life and experience. Whether humanity can yet be said to have a general will is at least doubtful.

I do not think I am trenching on practical politics if I illustrate the importance which I attach to the unconscious or semi-conscious logic of life in contact with our neighbours by a reference to Mr. Hare's election scheme, the essence of which is that the constituency is de-localised.[3] I once spoke of this to the late Professor Green, being

---

[3] Thomas Wright first suggested a system of proportional representation with a single transferable vote in 1821. Modifications were made by C. C. G. Andrae in 1855 in order to accommodate the secret ballot. Thomas Hare put forward a

myself much fascinated by its ingenuity, and he replied, 'I rather despise all those schemes for detaching people from their locality.' Mill, on the other hand, in the *Autobiography*, speaks of it, we remember, as a real triumph of political contrivance.[4]

What I desire to point out is merely that, for good or evil, I think men would judge quite differently, acting under such a scheme, from the way in which they judge when they act in their locality. Everything depends on the context to which one's views and action have to be adjusted. If you have to fight out a set of opinions in practice and in discussion among your neighbours, that is quite a different process from letting the returning officer look out a few thousand people in Great Britain who happen to agree with you on a single point. In the one case your whole life is really an argument, both unconscious and conscious, with reference to the general working scheme of society. In the other case you simply pronounce a single casual reflective judgment. It appears to me an apt illustration of the general or organic will as contrasted with the will of all as a number of units.

I do not say that locality is a necessary condition. I only say that it is a simple case of the necessary condition, of which there may be other cases.

Well, then, how does all this apply to matters of very special information either about distant countries or about the technique of management in difficult concerns, which the community as a whole undertakes? Here, no doubt, Mr. Bryce's account becomes much more true. We know what sort of life we want for ourselves and others, but we are not generally competent to construct it *in unfamiliar relations*. In our own life, as I have tried to explain, the thing works itself out by a self-adjusting process, because, whether we *know* what is wanted or not, we ourselves *are* the want, and behave accordingly.

number of variations between 1857 and 1873. Minority representation, although a consequence of the scheme, was not its primary purpose. Hare saw the scheme as an exercise in character building. The aim was to maximise both freedom and responsibility in the choice of representatives without geographical restrictions. Voters could cast a vote for any candidate in the country. See Enid Lakeman, *How Democracies Vote* (London, Faber, 1974: 4th edn.), 287–8.

[4] Mill thought the scheme a great advance in the progress of democracy, answering as it did the problem of 'giving to a numerical majority all power, instead of only a power proportional its numbers . . .' John Stuart Mill, *Autobiography* (London, Oxford University Press, 1958), 219.

The result is, then, that the general will is a process continuously emerging from the relatively unconscious into reflective consciousness. And the reflective consciousness does its work best when it as nearly as possible carries on, in self-criticism and adjustment of purposes, the same moulding of the individual mental system, as part of a machine in which other mental systems correspond to it, as goes on unconsciously in the formation of the everyday practical will.

Is the view which I have suggested hostile to the theoretical study of social conditions? I should be very sorry if anything that I have said appeared to have such a tendency. But it is not a bad thing to bear in mind that all knowledge, whether practically or theoretically employed, is only real and vital when it is the extension of a process like that which I have been describing. Books cannot contain knowledge in a perfectly vital form; they are rather instruments or materials of knowledge than knowledge itself. In this science differs from fine art; poetry, for example, is destroyed if we destroy the particular form which it has in a book; but knowledge hardly exists for us till we have destroyed the form which it has in a book. It must be recast in the intelligence, – that is, interpreted and criticised bit by bit till we have made it all of one tissue with our own vital experience – our experience of the matter in question in its most real form, whatever that may be, whether given in observation only, or in practice as well. When this is accomplished, and not before, the knowledge is really knowledge – that is, it is present as intelligence in our view of life or nature, and not as a recollection of something printed in a book. Such intelligence, however wide-reaching, always begins at home, both in social matter and in abstract science; there is always some point where we are more especially in contact with reality, and from which we extend our ideas by analogy. In all social matters this point is furnished by our own necessarily dominant ideas prescribed by our individual life. Therefore, I say that all vital speculation is a process analogous to that which I have described as the formation of the general will, and speculation upon social matters is actually an extension of this process, ultimately radiating from the same centre. The end of the whole inquiry is to understand life, and we are not likely to understand any other life until after we have understood that which is at our doors.

7
The Rights of Minorities[a]

D. G. RITCHIE

In times past government has generally meant the rule of minorities over majorities. Even the most democratic governments of the ancient world were aristocracies of slave-owners. The free citizens of Athens were a democracy among themselves, but an aristocracy, if we think of all the human beings inhabiting Attica. And, even in cases where 'inhabitants' and 'free citizens' have been nearly convertible terms, cities and states governing themselves democratically have yet denied political rights to subject peoples. The free citizens of Uri allowed their bailiffs to rule despotically the inhabitants of the Ticino valley. Thus, the struggle for freedom has in the past generally been the struggle of the majority against a privileged minority. Where there has been no such struggle, this has been because the majority have acquiesced in their political subordination or have never yet awakened to a sense that anything else is possible except blind obedience to the one or the few. Such political torpor can continue more easily where all alike are the slaves of an absolute despot. Where the practices of free government (i.e., government by discussion, instead of government merely by force) prevail even among a limited number, an example is set, which the many in course of time will desire to imitate. It is therefore more dangerous for a republican than for a monarchical government to practise tyranny or claim exclusive privilege. The history of ancient Rome is

[a] Reprinted from the *International Journal of Ethics* (Philadelphia), January, 1891. The substance of this paper was originally given as a lecture to an Ethical Society. [For the publication details of this slightly revised version see p. xlvi].

the history of a gradual extension of citizenship to those previously excluded, – an extension won by party struggles.

Democracy, in the full modern sense, means the rule of the majority. For practical purposes the majority must be taken as, for the time being, the representative of all. If all cannot have their wishes gratified, it is the less evil to adopt the view of the greater number. This is democracy in its lowest terms; in its ideal it means a great deal more than a machine for carrying into effect the wishes of the majority. It may be urged that it is very absurd to expect the whole to yield to the decision of half *plus* one: and a democracy may limit itself by requiring that important changes can only take place with the consent of two-thirds or three-fourths of the persons voting or even of the persons entitled to vote. But no practical person will go so far as to require unanimity in large bodies. To expect unanimity, as is done in a Russian village community, belongs to a very crude stage of political thinking and is apt to mean the tyranny of the most obstinate. In judicial matters it is somewhat different; there may be good arguments for requiring unanimity in a jury, but I am not concerned to defend the English system. Yet, even with regard to that, one has heard of the Irishman who accused the other eleven of being 'obstinate'; *he* knew how to assert the rights of minorities. Obstinacy is a very good thing in its way, as I shall have occasion to point out afterwards; but, on the whole, one is likely to get a more rational expression of opinion by recognising the principle of 'counting heads'. Thus there inevitably remains a minority whose wishes are overridden. Of course this minority may be a different one on different questions; but the effect of party government is to make a great number of questions run together.

The claims of a minority to consideration may be merely a survival of claims to exclusive privilege. The dethroned rulers may not 'give way with a good grace', and may expect in a changed constitution to retain their old pre-eminence. The extent of the change, which has taken place, may be disguised from them by the way in which it has come about, as in those countries that have been fortunate enough to grow gradually out of one form into another. Birth and wealth, with the advantages of education and position which they may carry with them, give a person *prestige* in a community, however formally democratic it may be; but the person of birth or wealth may go on to demand an express recognition of his advantages. Now such a claim on the part of a minority a democracy cannot recognise without defeating its very principle; and it may be questioned how far any such recognition ultimately benefits the minority itself. An express and formal superiority awakens jealousy and dislike;[b,1] an actual superiority of any obvious kind gets in a democratic country abundant opportunities of asserting itself, – in the case of wealth only too abundant opportunities.

It is a claim of a very different and more important kind which is made in Mill's *Liberty*, – a claim for the minority, put forward, however, not so much on behalf of the interests of the minority themselves as on behalf of the future and general well-being of mankind.[2] All great movements of progress, it is pointed out, have begun with minorities; and thus, if the opinions and efforts of a minority are repressed and thwarted, progress may be hindered and future generations suffer. Others, again, go further and, echoing Carlyle's words, urge that, as the population consists mostly of fools, to allow the majority to rule is to allow the fools to rule.[3] Knowledge, except of the loosest and most meagre kind, is the possession only of the few; and so, it is argued, we must turn to the experts, and disregard the clamour of the many.

[b] E.g., the Prussian 'three-class system', according to which all primary voters are distributed into three classes according to the amount of direct taxes they pay, – classes of unequal size, but with equal voting power. The system was vigorously denounced by Lassalle.

[1] Ferdinand Johann Gottlieb Lassalle, referred to in footnote b, was a German labour leader who, like Marx, viewed liberalism as an ideological mask that disguised sinister and vested capitalist interests. In 1863 he called for an independent labour movement, and state sponsored producers' co-operatives, which in practice amounted to little. Lassalle's radicalism with regard to democratic voting rights disturbed some of the leaders of the Prussian left, as well as conservatives.

[2] Mill argues that the well being of humanity depends upon freedom of expression and opinion. He gives four grounds for his conclusion. First, an opinion condemned to silence may in fact be true. None of us are infallible in our judgement. Secondly, even erroneous opinions may contain some truth, and being exposed to to criticism, or a clash of opinions, the truth of both sides may become clearer. Thirdly, even received truth that is genuinely true needs to be periodically subjected to criticism and is strengthened in the process. And, fourthly, a doctrine that is merely accepted may be in danger becoming a 'formal expression' and of losing its meaning. J. S. Mill, *On Liberty and Other Writings*, ed. Stefan Collini (Cambridge, Cambridge University Press, 1989), 53–4.

[3] Thomas Carlyle, 'Democracy', in *Past and Present* (London, Collins, n.d.). Carlyle argues that '. . . it is a dire necessity of Nature's to bring in her ARISTOCRACIES, her BEST, even by forcible methods', p. 238.

On this subject of the authority of the few and the many respectively considerable confusion shows itself every now and then. It may be as well to try to clear it up a little. On the one hand, it is undoubtedly true that scientific truth is scientifically known only by a few experts; others must accept it on their authority. On the other hand, there has always been a tendency to believe that the mass of mankind cannot be entirely in the wrong; that there must be some truth in what is generally believed. And the actual growth of democracy and of the democratic spirit might seem to have enormously increased the force of the authority of general consent. To escape from this apparent contradiction we must carefully distinguish between the grounds on which we accept scientific truth and the grounds on which we adopt practical maxims. The vast mass of mankind have believed that the sun goes round the earth, have believed in witchcraft, in ghosts, etc. And this universality of belief is sometimes urged as an argument in favour of the truth of such opinions. It does prove that the scientific disbeliever is bound to show, not merely that such beliefs are erroneous, but also how they can have arisen and become prevalent. In the case of the relation of sun and earth, that is easy enough. The popular view, which still survives as often as the most scientifically-minded person talks of sunrise and sunset, is the first obvious interpretation of the impressions of sense. And similarly (though the matter is often much more complex) a knowledge of the mental history of the human race – a knowledge enormously increased of late by the careful study of lower races – will explain the wide acceptance of beliefs which the growth of science tends to discredit. But in all such cases the minority of trained minds has an authority that does not belong to the majority of untrained minds.

This legitimate authority of the expert is often used as an argument that government must be in the hands of a select class. It is sometimes even used as an argument for an hereditary aristocracy, – which of course it does not support at all. It might seem to support the rule of an intellectual aristocracy, if we could get together such a body, – Plato's 'philosopher kings'. On the strength of this argument the Fellows of the Royal Society might claim to teach us lessons in the art of government. But the argument rests on a confusion between what is true for the intellect and what is practically expedient. If the majority of a people have a strong, though it may seem to the educated observer a perfectly unreasonable, belief in monarchical institutions, – are ready to die for their king, – then, however superior we many think republican institutions, it would be folly to impose them from without upon an unwilling people. It is of no use to give any people the best constitution (or what we think such) unless we convince them that it is the best, so that it becomes the best *for them*. All government is based upon opinion. This is the dictum of the cautious conservative Hume as well as of the democratic prophet Rousseau. Matters of detail can indeed be best decided by experts, and cannot be properly decided at all except by them (they must, however, be experts in the art of administration, and not merely in some theoretical science). But the mass of a nation must be convinced of the value of the general principle which is being carried out; else what we might judge the most salutary changes will be ineffectual. Of course the existence of an institution is often itself an important factor in producing the opinion favourable to it; but it is the favourable opinion, and not the mere legal existence of the institution, that makes the institution of any value. If the mass of a people believe a law to be unjust, it matters not that a few highly-cultured gentlemen at the head of affairs are perfectly satisfied of its justice; to the people it is an unjust law, and has none of the binding force of law on their sentiments and conscience.[c] And laws which people generally (I do not mean a few stray persons here and there) think it right to violate are producing the very opposite moral effect from that which good laws ought to produce. That this or that law or institution is suitable for us or the reverse is not a proposition of the same kind with the proposition that such and such things do or do not happen in the course of nature or history. That the Romans lived under such and such a constitution is a proposition, with regard to whose truth or false-

---

[c] In practice the most difficult cases are those where legislation has to deal with some matter (e.g. of health) on which none but the scientific expert can in the first instance form a sound judgement. It is only too possible that democratic societies may, through popular distrust of scientific opinion, fall in some respects behind societies under enlightened despotisms. The remedy is not despotism, but popular enlightenment. The scientific specialist is bound, therefore, by patriotism as well in the interests of his own science, to end what aid he can to that popularisation of science from which he is too apt to recoil: it is the sole antidote to ignorance and pseudo-science. Those whom science neglects, fanaticism and quackery will claim for their own.

hood the opinion of the scientific historian outweighs any amount of popular belief or tradition. But that such and such a law or constitution is good for us is only true if we think it so, *after a fair trial.* (The qualification is essential.) To use a familiar illustration, it is the wearer of the shoe that knows whether the shoe pinches. The scientific shoemaker alone may know why it pinches, and how to remedy the mischief. But if the scientific shoemaker were to convince you that the shoe did not pinch, he would convince your intellect only, if the shoe continued to hurt your foot; and you would be apt to go in future to the unscientific shoemaker who could give you comfort even without science. So it is with constitutions and laws. Those who have to wear them must judge whether or not they fit; and therefore they must have the decisive voice as to the general principles, though, as already said, details had better be left to the experts. Ends must be approved by the feeling of the many; the means must be chosen by the intellect of the few. This is, in fact, the *raison d'être* of representative democracy, – the many choose the few to carry out their wishes.

The distinctions – *first*, between scientific and practical matters, *secondly*, between judgments about ends and about means – may seem almost too obvious to need statement. But obvious distinctions are apt to be overlooked; and it is worth uttering truisms, if we can get rid of the fallacious argument that because the few may be wiser than the many, therefore the few should rule the many, otherwise than as their ministers and stewards.

Those who are ready for all practical purposes to accept the will of the majority as decisive yet sometimes think it necessary to propose various expedients for securing what is called 'the representation of minorities'. The danger of the non-representation of minorities seems to me to be a good deal exaggerated by Mill and other advocates of 'proportional representation' and similar schemes.[4] It would indeed not be difficult to make out a *prima facie* case for the absurdity of the whole system of representative government, if we attended merely to the arithmetical possibilities of its mechanism. Thus, in Great Britain, the determining power lies with the majority of a Cabinet, which is supported by a majority of the

---

[4] Proposals for proportional representation had been introduced and defeated in the British Parliament in 1872 and 1888.

House of Commons, which is elected, it may be, by a bare majority of the electors; so that the representative system seems, when carried out, to defeat itself and to put power into the hands of a very small minority of the whole population, – ultimately perhaps into the hands of 'the odd man.' But this seeming absurdity results from an abstract and artificial way of looking at the matter. The will of these few persons is only effective because they do represent (or at least did, at some time, represent) something very much more than a small fraction of the population. No scheme that can be constructed by human ingenuity will make a representative chamber a quite perfect mirror of all the various sets of opinion in the community. It is only a question of more or less; and, what is very important, any arrangement that is adopted must have the merit not merely of being simple to work, but of looking simple. Even the suspicion of trickery must be avoided. This is, of course, the great advantage of the system of equal electoral districts with single members, and 'one man one vote'. Even so, it may indeed happen that a majority of the elected chamber may represent a minority of the electors, – if one party have extremely large majorities in some places and be defeated by extremely narrow majorities in others. Accidents of that sort will happen in the best regulated constitutions; but the chances are, certainly, against their happening to any very great extent. But when such arithmetical possibilities are insisted on, it is forgotten, in the first place, that each individual member has many other attributes besides being the member for so-and-so, and, in the second place, that there are elements in the living constitution of a country besides those written down by constitutional lawyers. An elected assembly is powerful indeed. It may, like the British Parliament, be legally 'omnipotent'; and yet there is a power behind it, a power that acts not merely at the time of a general election, but continuously, – the power of public opinion. The newspaper and the public meeting and the petition are real factors in a modern constitution. It is easy enough to see the defects of each of these organs of public opinion, easy enough to throw ridicule upon them. But that is to miss their true significance. The newspaper ought to represent the power of intellect applied to practical matters; it is too apt to represent largely the power of money – not merely the capital that is needed to float it, but the money that comes in through advertisements. The political and moral consequences of advertising would, however, be too long a story to begin now; to have named it may suffice. Then, as to public meetings: there are many people who scoff at them. 'Got-up agitations', 'power of the strongest lungs', and so on. Those who talk in this way seem to forget that, though you may make a 'flare-up' with a few shavings and a lucifer-match, to keep up a steady heat you need coals as well. There cannot be such a thing as an agitation that lasts, grows, and for which people sacrifice a great deal, and which is nevertheless merely 'got up'. A continuous agitation is not a cause but a symptom of discontent. Public meetings, petitions, pamphlets, newspaper articles, are, however imperfectly, organs of public opinion, and much better and more effective organs than assassination or even than epigrams, which take their place in despotically governed countries.[d]

Where there exist such organs of public opinion and a tolerably sound, even though not ideally perfect, representative system, any minority which has really got life and vigour in it can make itself felt. I do not think that, if it were possible, it would be desirable to construct any political machinery for giving a prominent place to the opinions of minorities that will not take the trouble to assert and to spread these opinions. The all-important and essential right of minorities is the right to turn themselves into majorities if they can; this means freedom of the press, freedom of association, freedom of public meeting. 'Give me', said Milton, 'the liberty to know, to utter, and to argue freely according to conscience, above all other liberties'.[5] Minorities that grumble at the whole world round them and have no desire and no hope of convincing other people are not a valuable factor in political or social life. They are, in all probability, the decaying survivals of a past type, and not the first germs of a new.

In a genuinely democratic government votes are nominally merely counted; in reality they are weighed. Not indeed in the sense that wisdom always weighs the heaviest – in what constitution, out-

---

[d] Public meetings, petitions, etc., are indeed very rudimentary 'organs' of popular sovereignty compared with the Swiss 'referendum' and 'initiative', which seem to work well – in Switzerland, at least.

[5] John Milton, 'Areopagitica: For the liberty of unlicensed printing' in *Areopagitica and Of Education*, ed. K. M. Lea (London, Oxford University Press, 1973), 38.

side Utopia, does that happen? – but in the sense that the energy and contagious enthusiasm of a few, who represent some living and growing idea, far outweigh the indifference and apathy of great numbers. Great movements begin with small minorities; but these minorities must consist of persons who wish to make others share their convictions. From this follows all that can be laid down in general terms about the rights and – what we are less apt to think of – the duties of minorities.

The right of spreading one's opinions implies two things, neither of which must be absent: first, certain legal and constitutional securities; and, secondly, a certain condition of public sentiment. Without the latter the former cannot be obtained unless exceptionally, as, for instance, under an enlightened despotism; and that is really no exception, for securities dependent on the strong will of one enlightened and big-minded man can hardly be called constitutional, and are an uncertain bulwark of liberty. On the other hand, without explicitly recognised legal safeguards public sentiment is a somewhat fickle protector of liberty. Outbursts of fear, fanaticism, and intolerance are only too possible; and a good deal may be said even for the merely moral force of a formal 'declaration of rights'. A people in its calm or its generous moments may well protect itself against its own lower moods: it is something to be able to appeal from the people drunk to the people sober. And the strong hand of the state is often needed to protect the individual against undue social pressure.

I do not think that the subject of the ethics of toleration has ever been adequately treated. Toleration is often supposed to arise solely from indifference. This is not the case. In fact, indifference makes toleration superfluous. Toleration, shown by those who 'care for none of these things', is no virtue, though it may be a public duty in a magistrate 'indifferently administering justice'. The toleration of contempt may, indeed, be very useful to those who are zealous and in earnest. The kind of toleration which is most valuable, which can only exist in a morally healthy society, and which will help to keep the society healthy and make it healthier, is toleration shown by those who have faith in the reasonableness of their own beliefs and who are, therefore, willing to face the full light of criticism. Persecution, – and by persecution I mean here not what any aggrieved individual may call such, but the forcible suppression of *opinions* (every society is obliged to use force for the suppression of certain overt actions, and the line between expedient and inexpedient compulsion will be drawn differently by different persons), – persecution arises mainly from two sources, – fear and a particular form of belief in the supernatural. If people do seriously believe that they and they alone are in possession of truth guaranteed to them by other authority than that of human reason, of course they will not accept the free use of reason as a test; and there is always a risk that, if sufficiently powerful, they will endeavour to repress the spread of what they conscientiously regard as dangerous opinions. Those who believe that Divine truth is something different from human truth will be apt to believe that the civil magistrate must defend the Deity by the power of the sword. This type of belief is really a form of fear, – it is fear of human reason; and, only as this belief becomes rarer or weaker by the secularising, or, to speak more correctly, the humanising of politics, does toleration become possible. But fear may make even those who appeal to reason persecutors in self-defence. It is difficult, if we are quite just in our historical judgments, to condemn entirely the harsh measures employed by small societies holding new beliefs, – antagonistic to those of firmly established and powerful communities, – such small societies, for instance, as the Calvinists of Geneva or the founders of the Commonwealth of Massachusetts.[e] When a society is struggling to exist at all, cohesion is so essential that it may well require uniformity of belief. A rigid bond of custom is necessary to its earlier stages. Only after cohesion has been obtained is freedom of discussion possible and advantageous. Furthermore, complete freedom of discussion is only possible and is only valuable, when there is a general diffusion of education, and when the habit of settling matters by discussion, instead of by force, has become established. In admitting this we must not, however, forget that discussion itself is one of the most important means of education. There are indeed people – 'misologists', Plato would have called them – who say: 'Controversy is of no use. Those who take part in it go away holding

---

[e] Even the most rigid sects of Protestants do in some sense professedly appeal to reason instead of ecclesiastical authority, as the interpreter of Scripture.

the same beliefs as before, only holding them more dogmatically as the result of having had to fight for them'.[6] If the fighting is physical, this is nearly always the case; it is not true of intellectual controversy fairly carried on. During the actual discussion, indeed, each may stick to his opinion: it might even be said that, unless people showed some obstinacy, a debate would always be a failure. For minds in a perfectly flabby condition discussion is impossible: it implies a certain amount of mutual resistance. But if people are really in earnest and care more for truth than for victory, it will be found that after any serious discussion both parties have probably modified their opinions, and out of the conflict of two opposing principles may spring a new one, victorious over both. It is by the conflict of ideas that intellectual progress is made.

Professor Bryce in his great work on *The American Commonwealth* has made clear a very important distinction between 'the tyranny of the majority' and 'the fatalism of the multitude', which is often confused with it. 'A majority is tyrannical', he says (vol. iii. p. 133),[7] 'when it decides without hearing the minority, when it suppresses fair and temperate criticism on its own acts, when it insists on restraining men in matters where restraint is not required by the common interest, when it forces men to contribute money to objects which they disapprove and which the common interest does not demand.[f] The element of tyranny lies in the wantonness of the act, – a wantonness

---

[f] I assume that the 'and' is emphatic, and that this clause must be taken as qualifying the previous clause. If a tax is legally imposed by the majority for a purpose which the common interest (in their judgement) demands, a minority may disapprove this purpose, but they have no *moral* right to refuse payment of the tax, unless they are conscientiously convinced that such an act of rebellion is their *duty*, as the best means of bringing about what they regard as a better state of affairs.

[6] Plato, *Phaedo*, 89c in *The Last Days of Socrates* (Harmondsworth, Penguin 1993) 150–1; and *Republic* translated by Desmond Lee (Harmondsworth, Penguin, revised edition, 1987), 411d. A misologist is a hater of arguments, discussion or knowledge. The relevant passage in *Republic* reads: 'And so he becomes an intelligent philistine, with no use for reasoned discussion, and an animal addiction to settle everything by brute force.'

[7] James Bryce, *The American Commonwealth* (London, Macmillan, 1888): the second edition was published in two volumes in 1889. The quotation appears on page 332 of the second edition. He defines the 'Fatalism of the Multitude' as: 'This tendency to acquiescence and submission, this belief that the affairs of men are swayed by large forces whose movement may be studied but cannot be turned . . .'

springing from the sense of overwhelming power, or in the fact that it is a misuse for one purpose of power granted for another.'

Simply because the minority disapprove of the enactments of the majority, they cannot rightly describe the rule of the majority as 'tyrannical'. In a democratic constitution, with elections recurring sufficiently often, and proper safeguards for liberty of expressing and spreading opinions, the right of the minority is, as I have said, to turn themselves into a majority if they can; and it must be added, it is their duty also, if they continue to believe in themselves. But here comes in that 'fatalism', which is so often wrongly described as the tyranny of the majority; the apathy of minorities is one of the frequent weaknesses in democratic communities. As Professor Bryce has put it, 'the belief in the rights of the majority lies very near to the belief that the majority must be right' (ib., p. 124).[8] To give way for the time to the legally expressed will of the majority is a necessary and salutary consequence of popular government; but to lose heart and give up effort is an illegitimate and evil consequence of it. It is the duty of a minority to obey, unless conscience absolutely forbids; in which extreme case it may become a duty to resist. If we are using language strictly, there never can be a *right* of resistance. Rights are the creation of society, and there can be no right of the individual or of any number of individuals *against* the society of which they are members. When we speak of 'natural rights', we really mean those rights which we think to be the very least that a well-organised society should secure to its members. In the American 'Declaration of Independence' the time-honoured phrase about the right of resistance is wisely supplemented by the addition of the better and truer word, 'duty'.[9]

[8] In the second edition Bryce talks of dominant beliefs and feelings, one of which 'is that the majority must prevail . . . To deny the majority is therefore both a necessity and a duty, a duty because the alternative would be ruin and the breaking-up of laws . . . the majority is right', vol II, 329.

[9] The Declaration expresses a theory of natural rights at variance with Ritchie's view. The Declation asserts the natural equality of men and their God-given possession of inalienable rights. The purpose of government is to sustain these rights. A government that is destructive of them can and must be resisted: 'But when a long train of abuses and usurpations, pursuing invariably the same object evinces a design to reduce them under absolute Despotism, it is their right, it is their duty, to throw off such Government . . .' 'Declaration of Independence, 4 July, 1776'. See *American Historical Documents: The Presidency*, ed. M. J. C. Vile (London, Harrap, 1974), 18.

Resistance may, in extreme cases, be the only way of protesting against what we hold to be an unjust and mischievous law and the only way of getting it altered. But the problems of practical ethics involved in this question are not easy. The limits of justifiable compromise cannot be laid down in any hard and fast *a priori* rules. If it really goes against a man's conscience to obey a *law* (I am not speaking of arbitrary, illegal commands, where the right and duty of disobedience are clear enough), he can, if we use language strictly, claim no right to disobey, but it is his duty to disobey, at whatever cost; if he obeys against his conscience, he loses his own self-respect and lowers his character. Only let him be perfectly sure that it is his conscience that urges him and not some merely selfish motive of personal dislike or offended pride. To justify this state-ment and this distinction, it would of course be necessary to explain what is meant by 'conscience'. Suffice it to say for the present – and I think the supporters of most ethical systems would agree with this statement – that the dictates of a man's conscience will on the whole correspond to the better spirit of the community round him, or at least to what he regards as such; and therefore the man, who disobeys a law *'for conscience' sake'*, is acting in the interests of what he conceives to be the future well-being of society. Of course a man's conscience may correspond to a superseded social type, but it will not be a superseded type in his own judgment. Posterity may come to disapprove many actions, and yet bestow admiration on the motives of those who did them. Even where an individual has no conscientious objection to render obedience himself, it may occasionally be his duty, in the interests of the future well-being of society, to join others in resisting and even in rebelling, provided that there is no reasonable hope of getting a bad law or a bad consti-tution altered by peaceable means, and provided also that there is a reasonable hope that the resistance or rebellion will be so successful as to lead to an alteration in the right direction.[g] Such is the terrible duty that occasionally falls on the shoulders of a minority, to bear the brand of the criminal now that others in time to come may render a willing obedience to better laws. Society is apt to make mistakes, to number the patriot or the saint among transgressors, to crucify a prophet between two thieves. But the individual is apt

[g] On the Ethics of Resistance, see T. H. Green, *Philosophical Works*, II. p. 455, *seq.*

to make mistakes also, and there have been honest martyrs for bad causes.

If, however, democracies prove at all true to their ideal, if they live according to the ethics of the age of discussion and not according to those of the earlier ages of force, this duty of resistance should become less and less needed. If majorities, while requiring obedience to laws constitutionally passed, after full and free deliberation, in what they sincerely believe to be the interest of the whole community, sacredly preserve the liberty of thought and discussion both by express legal securities and by a general sentiment of toleration, it is the duty of a minority, while yielding a loyal obedience to the opinion that has prevailed for the time (except in those rare cases to which I have referred), if not convinced of its excellence, to continue a peaceable agitation till their own opinion prevails. If we are really in earnest about our opinions, it is a duty to endeavour to get others to accept them by means of the appeal to reason; it is also a duty, and often a very hard one, to give them up candidly, if we are genuinely convinced that we have been in the wrong. It is a duty to assert our opinions, wisely of course, and with toleration for others, *even if those others be in the majority*; but it is a prior duty to use all the care we can to make sure that our opinions are right, that what we assert eagerly and persistently is really worth asserting. It is utterly untrue to say that we are not responsible for our opinions. That was a bad argument used for a good purpose, – the attack upon religious persecution. Opinions are not trivial matters. What is quietly thought and talked about now will affect what is done very soon. The opinions of a few in one generation may, in the next generation, become the sentiments or the prejudices of the many. Ethical legislation is constantly going on in our every-day conversation, wherever two or three are gathered together – to discuss the conduct of their neighbours. And we cannot escape our responsibility for our share in this ethical legislation, however insignificant we may feel ourselves in presence of the great multitudes of our fellow-mortals. To these great multitudes each of us is responsible; and we owe it to them to oppose them, then and then only, when reason and conscience urge us to do so.

8

The Dangers of Democracy[a]

J. S. MACKENZIE

It is hardly open to doubt, I suppose, that the general tendency expressed by the term 'Democracy' is increasingly prevalent at the present time. Some may think that what is called 'Imperialism' is a strong counteracting force; but even this is at least ostensibly based upon the general will, and in any case can hardly be regarded as more than a slight and temporary check upon the democratic movement. In these circumstances it is surely important that we should try to understand the significance of this general movement and to take note of any special dangers that are incident to it. This is what I propose in the present lecture to attempt, though of course I do not aim at anything like an exhaustive treatment.

Within such limits as are here at my disposal, it will probably be wise not to attempt any precise definition of the term 'Democracy'. It has been used in various senses, wider and narrower, looser and more exact; but for our present purpose it is perhaps enough to connect it with its common popular description, and to regard it as covering any movement that tends to secure 'Government, of the people, by the people, for the people.'[1] This is what our modern Democracy is generally understood to be aiming at; and what we have here to inquire is whether there are any special dangers that

---

[a] A lecture to Ethical and similar societies delivered at various places in South Wales.

[1] Theodore Parker, *Discourses on Slavery* (1863), i. He says that the American idea demands a government 'of all the people, for all the people; of course, a governement after the principles of eternal justice, the unchanging law of God; for short-ness' sake, I will call it the idea of freedom'.

are inseparable from this aim. Before we refer to its dangers, however, we ought, I think, to endeavour to be clear about its attrac-
tions. The first question to be asked, accordingly is – What are the
special advantages that are claimed for Democracy, and that lead to
its increasing prevalence?

Now there are some who would at once demur to the form in
which this question is expressed. It is not, they would say, properly
a question of use or advantage at all, but rather of an essential and
imperious demand of human nature. It is in this spirit, for instance,
that a bright journalist has recently claimed that Democracy is an
end in itself – that, even if all its results could be shown to be
prejudicial, we must still value it infinitely on its own account. A
writer in the INTERNATIONAL JOURNAL OF ETHICS, a few years
ago, went even further than this, by inditing an eloquent article on
'American Democracy as a Religion'.[2] And of course the utterances
of Walt Whitman on this subject are even more remarkable and
memorable.[3] Such claims may seem to others to be extravagantly
overstrained; and yet I believe we can never hope to understand the
power that modern Democracy has wielded if we do not bear in
mind that for some – perhaps I might even say for many – it has
been far more than a mere political expedient, and might almost be
characterized as a religion, a passion, an end of inestimable worth.
It may of course be urged that, when Democracy is spoken of in
this fashion, it is not simply a particular form of government that
men have in their minds. What they are thinking of is rather the
autonomy of the individual man, the 'glorious privilege of being
independent'[4] in the general conduct of his life and management of
his affairs. And it may be urged that this independence of the individual life has no particular connection with any form of political

---

[2] I was unable to find any title resembling this in the index for the journal.

[3] After a youthful enthusiasm for democracy Whitman deplored the influence upon
society of what he regarded as the rabble. He says: 'By the unprecedented open-
ing-up of humanity en-masse in the United States, the last hundred years, under
our institutions, not only the good qualities of the race, but just as much the bad
ones, are prominently brought forward. Man is about the same, in the main,
whether with despotism, or whether with freedom'. Walt Whitman, 'Democracy
in the New World', *Complete Prose* (New York, Appleton, 1909), 325–6. Cf.
Democratic Vistas, 197–250.

[4] Edward Gibbon says something similar to this in his *Autobiography*, ed. Lord
Sheffield (London, World Classics edition, 1901), 176 'The first of earthly bless-
ings, independence'.

rule – that it might be secured by a Marcus Aurelius in the imperial purple or by a Tolstoy under the Russian autocracy, as well as by a Socrates or a Thoreau under systems avowedly more democratic. But it seems clear that this would only be to some extent true. Inner freedom cannot be wholly divorced from external freedom. The autonomy of the individual must at least be harder to achieve and more exceptional in its realization when the right of self government is not in any degree recognized in public affairs. If a Tolstoy can grow in Russia, he must at least be something of a revolutionist there. If, then, we recognize the supreme importance of inner freedom in human life, we can hardly fail to be opposed to all forms of slavery, at least as permanent institutions in human society; and it is but a step from this to maintain that no government which is not in its essence democratic can in the end be regarded as tolerable. In this sense, then, it scarcely seems an exaggeration to say that Democracy may really be regarded as an end in itself, and something to be valued with an almost religious fervour. It is on this high ground that Democracy has been defended by such men as Mazzini, and, indeed, I suppose no one could really be described as a thorough democrat who did not, in some degree, feel the truth of this contention.

In comparison with this transcendent claim, any other advantages that can be ascribed to Democracy must appear trivial and scarcely worthy of enumeration. But I believe its supporters generally value it also on some subordinate grounds. It is believed to be more truly educative for the citizen than any other form of government, to give a more complete guarantee of justice and general welfare, and to be less subject to the vagaries of individual caprice. On the other hand, it is sometimes admitted to be a little lacking in unity and inner coherence, to be distracted by party spirit, and to be somewhat inefficient in great emergencies. I do not intend to make any effort to deal exhaustively with these various advantages and defects, but will rather try to direct your attention to what appear to me to be the main points. We may perhaps be led most directly to these by considering some of the most remarkable criticisms to which the principle of Democracy has been subjected. And here we are at once confronted by a circumstance that can hardly fail to strike us, at least on a first view, as somewhat astonishing. For, if Democracy can justly put forward those high claims that have just been indicated, we should naturally expect to find among its most ardent supporters those who have felt most deeply the importance of man's moral development. It comes, therefore, as something of a surprise to find among the severest critics of Democracy the two writers in ancient Greece who did most to establish a systematic theory of the moral life, and the two writers in modern England who have probably impressed men most by their moral enthusiasm, the two whom one can hardly help characterizing as 'prophets'. I mean of course Plato, Aristotle, Carlyle and Ruskin. All of these may be said broadly to regard an aristocracy of talent as the ideal form of government; and all would appear to regard Democracy as one of the least desirable forms.[5] It is noteworthy also, in this connection, that the first two write on the assumption of the existence of a society in which slavery has a place; while one at least of the other two has explicitly defended slavery. Yet they were all face to face with governments that were to a large extent democratic; and, in most cases, it is not easy to point to any circumstances that might be supposed to have given them a personal bias against it. Hence it can hardly fail to be a profitable inquiry to ask ourselves what were the chief grounds that led these writers to distrust Democracy. This inquiry cannot here be attempted in any exhaustive form; but I may sum up what appear to me to be the main points.

I think the main dangers that are in the minds of these writers may be conveniently considered in connection with the general popular description of Democracy to which I referred at the outset. What they maintain is, in effect, that in practice Democracy fails to be what it purports to aim at being, that it is not really a government of the people, by the people, and for the people. If I am right in thinking that this is the gist of what they have to say, then I believe it will appear, upon reflection, that their criticisms are not so much

<hr/>

[5] Plato, *The Republic* (Harmondsworth, Penguin, 1987), part nine, book eight, §6 and §7 (555b–62a); Aristotle, *Politics*, ed. Stephen Everson (Cambridge, Cambridge University Press, 1988). See, for example, 1279b–1280a, and 1317b–21; Thomas Carlyle, 'Democracy' in *Past and Present* (London, Collins, n.d.), 233–44; John Ruskin distrusted Democracy and thought majority rule would bring about mediocrity and banality in social affairs. Work should be distributed and organised according to abilities. See *Munera Pulveris* in *The Works of John Ruskin*, eds. E. T. Cook and A. Edderburn (London, George Allen, 1903–12), vol. xvii.

attacks on *Democracy* as on *Democracies*, and that they attack these by trying to show that they fail to realize the essential principles of Democracy itself. Perhaps we may hope that some consideration of these attacks may help us to realize more fully what Democracy really is and aims at, and how it may best succeed in realizing its aims.

The first danger, then, that is apprehended in Democracy is that it may fail to be a 'Government of the people' – in other words that it may only be a kind of Anarchy. This is the danger that is specially emphasized by Plato in the *Republic*. 'First of all', he says, 'Are they not free, and does not liberty of act and speech abound in the city, and has not a man license therein to do what he will?' Again – 'It will be, in all likelihood, an agreeable, lawless, particoloured commonwealth, dealing with all alike on a footing of equality, whether they be really equal or not.' Again, speaking of the type of man who tends to be bred in a Democracy, he goes on – 'He lives from day to day to the end, in the gratification of the casual appetite – now drinking himself drunk to the sound of music, and presently putting himself under training; – sometimes idling and neglecting everything, and then living like a student of philosophy . . . And there is no order or constraining rule in his life; but he calls this life of his pleasant, and liberal, and happy, and follows it out to the end.' Such, he says, is the life of 'a man whose motto is liberty and equality.' ('Republic', Book VIII, Davies and Vaughan's translation.) And he goes on to add further characteristics of the same sort. Now, it is to a large extent the same dangers that are constantly emphasized by Carlyle and Ruskin. They consider that, if you disregard the qualitative differences among men, and treat all as having a right to share in the rule of the State, you are destroying the very basis of the State. This is what Ruskin means when he says that he is 'a Tory of the old school – the school of Homer and Scott',[6] the school that believes in qualitative differences and the

---

[6] Ruskin first described himself as a 'Communist of the old school – reddest also of the red'. *Fors Clavigera*, letter for July, 1871, *The Works*, vol. XXVII, 116. Shortly afterwards in the *Fors* letter for October 1871, he declares himself to be, as his father had been before him, 'a vilent Tory of the old school (Walter Scott's school, that is to say, and Homer's)', *Works*, XXVII, 167. The same quotation appears without the parentheses and with minor changes of punctuation in Ruskin's unfinished autobiography, *Praeterita*, *Works*, vol. XXXV, 13.

rule of the best, or, in Shakespeare's language, in the importance of 'degree'.[b]

The experience of modern Democracies, however, does not seem altogether to bear out this view of their anarchical tendencies. The evidence of Professor Bryce is worth noticing on this point. 'Plato', says Bryce, 'indulges his fancy so far as to describe the very mules and asses of a Democracy as prancing along the roads, scarcely deigning to bear their burdens. The passion for unrestrained license, for novelty, for variety, is to him the note of Democracy, whereas monotony and ever obstinate conservatism are the faults which the latest European critics bid us expect.' ('American Commonwealth', Part VI, ch. cvii.) Again – 'Of the uniformity of political institutions over the whole United States I have spoken already. Every where the same system of State governments, everywhere the same municipal governments, and almost uniformly bad or good in proportion to the greater or smaller population of the city . . . The schools are practically identical in organization, in the subjects taught, in the methods of teaching, though the administration of them is as completely decentralized as can be imagined, even the State commissioner having no right to do more than suggest or report. So it is with the charitable institutions, with the libraries, the lecture courses, the public amusements . . . It is the same with social habits and usages. Travel where you will, you feel that what you have found in one place that you will find in another. The thing which hath been, will be; you can no more escape from it than you can quit the land to live in the sea.' (Chap. cxiii.).[7]

b   The heavens themselves, the planets, and this centre,
Observe degree, priority and place.
* * * * * * * *
Take but degree away, Untune that string,
And, hark, What discord follows!
* * * * * * * *
Force should be right; or rather, right and wrong –
Between whose endless jar justice resides –
Should lose their names, and so should justice too.
Then everything includes itself in power,
Power into will, will into appetite;
And appetite, an universal wolf,
So doubly seconded with will and power,
Must make perforce an universal prey,
And last eat up himself.

[Shakespeare, *Troilus and Cressida*, Act One, Scene Three.]

7 James Bryce, *The American Commonwealth* (London, Macmillan, 1888).

Are we then to conclude that Plato was completely at fault in his estimate of the tendencies of Democracy? Not, I think, entirely. Bryce himself doubts whether the uniformity which he noted in America has much connection with Democracy. 'Democracy', he says, 'has in reality not much to do with it, except in so far as such a government helps to induce that deference of individuals to the mass which strengthens a dominant type, whether of ideas, of institutions, or of manners.'[8] Still, this does, at any rate, throw doubt on Plato's view of the general tendency of democratic institutions. But what we must remember is that the Democracy of which Plato was thinking was in reality something widely different from that which Bryce was observing in America, or indeed from any kind of Democracy that can be observed at the present time. He was thinking of a Democracy in which every one is actually ruler as well as subject – taking his turn of office, perhaps, by lot – whereas we practically always understand by Democracy in modern times some form of representative government. Sometimes this is thought of only as a matter of practical convenience, it being impossible for everyone to take an active part in public affairs, while yet the method of representation is more truly Democratic than election by lot would be. But it seems clear that representative government involves a considerable modification in the idea of pure Democracy. It involves the recognition that the rule is not directly that of all, but rather that of typical members; and, further, it practically always involves the tacit, if not explicit, recognition that some are better fitted than others to rule. There is thus an element of aristocracy in all modern Democracies; and even a Democratic leader like Gladstone was able to gratify Ruskin (he would not, I suppose, have gratified Tolstoy) by describing himself as an 'inequalitarian'. (Morley's 'Life of Gladstone', Book VIII, chap. v.)[9] And an aristocracy that represents the 'general will' can hardly fail to have a more pervading influence than one that rests upon a more arbitrary basis. What we may say, then, is that modern Democracy has to a large extent succeeded in avoiding this particular danger that Plato had in mind, by the device of representative government, whereby it is

---

[8] Bryce, *American Commonwealth*, second edition (London, Macmillan, 1889), vol. II, p. 695.
[9] Morley, *The Life of William Ewart Gladstone*, 3 vols. (London, Macmillan, 1903).

able to incorporate in itself an element of aristocracy, i.e of what Shakespeare calls 'Degree'.

Here, indeed, I cannot but think that Democracy has 'builded better than it knew'.[10] Often we find that those who represent modern Democracy have very little consciousness of the value of the element of aristocracy which it thus contains. They think of it simply as the rule of the majority, and regard it as little more than an accident, or a merely mechanical device, that the will of this majority expresses itself through selected representatives. Probably it would be quite as true to regard the selection of representatives as the essential point, and the fact that they are chosen by majorities as the mere mechanical device; though this also would be a one-sided view. It can hardly be doubted that there has been a tendency to pay an exaggerated deference to majorities, and sometimes almost to think of the expression of their will as if it were in truth 'the voice of God'. I think Carlyle was to a large extent right in connecting this tendency with those mechanical views of the world that have been fostered by modern physical science. The natural sciences, especially in their more exact and abstract forms, tend to eliminate the qualitative aspects of experience, and to concentrate attention on those things that can be weighed, measured, and counted. The growth of the biological sciences in recent years has once more brought the qualitative aspect of experience into prominence; and we begin to see the results of this, not only in such fantastic conceptions as those of Nietzsche, but also in more rational attempts to determine what is meant by superiority of type, and so once more to give 'quality' or 'degree' a real place in human life. This, however, is a very large subject – perhaps the most important of all subjects for thinking men, or at least for thinking politicians, at the present time – and here I can only hint at it. All that it is necessary to note at present is that modern Democracy seems to have partly escaped

---

[10] Ralph Waldo Emerson (1803–1882),

> The hand that rounded Peter's dome,
> and groined the aisles of Christian Rome,
> Wrought in a sad sincerity:
> Himself from God he could not free;
> He builded better than he knew; –
> The conscious stone to beauty grew.

'The Problem', *Poems* in *Complete Works* (London, Routledge, 1903).

from the main danger that was feared by Plato, through declining to take its stand upon equality, and leaving open a place for the recognition of qualitative difference.

But this leads us to notice the second great danger of Democracy – viz.: that it may fail to realize the second element in its ideal, that of being a government 'by the people'. It may be said that modern Democracy is not really government by the people, but rather government by the representatives of an organized majority, who may not give by any means a true expression of the general will. Even the majority itself may not be properly represented. The organization of it may really have been in the hands of some skilful demagogue or influential plutocrat.ᶜ And the minority, at any rate, may be hopelessly ineffective. Yet the minority also is part of the people; and, from the point of view of quality, to which we have just referred, it may even be the most important part. On this point, reference may again be made to Professor Bryce. 'Where a majority has erred', he says, 'the only remedy against the prolongation or repetition of its error is in the continued protests and agitation of the majority, an agitation which ought to be peaceably conducted, carried on by voice and pen, but which must be vehement enough to rouse the people and deliver them from the consequences of their blunders. But the more complete the sway majorities is, so much the less disposed is a minority to maintain the contest. It loses faith in its cause and in itself, and allows its voice to be silenced by the triumphant cries of its opponents.' (Part IV, chap. 1 xxvii.) Again 'The belief in the rights of the majority lies very near to the belief that the majority must be right. As self-government is based on the idea that each man is more likely to be right than to be wrong, and that one man's opinion must be treated as equally good with another's, there is a presumption that when twenty thousand vote one way and twenty-one thousand another, the view of the greater number is the better view ... A conscientious citizen feels that he ought to obey the determination of the majority, and naturally prefers to think that which he obeys to be right. A citizen languidly interested in the question at issue finds it easier to comply with and adopt the view of the majority than to hold out against it.'

ᶜ Sir Henry Maine even urges (in his 'Essay on Popular Government') that government by the people inevitably comes to mean government by wire-pullers [*Popular Government*, fifth edition (London, John Murray, 1909)].

(Chap. 1 xxxiv.) Thus the minority tends gradually to be silenced altogether, a tendency which Bryce describes as 'the Fatalism of the Multitude'.

It is perhaps this, more than anything else, that Carlyle has in view in his denunciations of Democracy. He has confidence in nothing but his Heroes, or supremely wise men; and they of course are very few. Hence he is horrified by the tendency to a constant silencing of their voices by the shouts of the majority, and is inclined to believe that Democracy, even in its most modern form, provides no machinery at all for securing that what is worthiest in the people shall have any chance of ruling. 'The notion', as he scornfully puts it, 'that a man's liberty consists in giving his vote at election-hustings, and saying, "Behold, now I too have my twenty-thousandth part of a Talker in our National Palaver; will not all the gods be good to me", is one of the pleasantest!' ('Past and Present', Book III, chap. xiii.)[11] Obviously Democracy, in this sense, does not go far to secure the ideal of self-government for its citizens. And, indeed, this way of looking at it almost forces us to ask, What do we really mean by the self-government of a people? If we mean that every individual among the people is to exercise the right of government, then it seems clear that to secure (or, it may even be, to fail to secure) the twenty-thousandth part of a representative in what is, after all, only one part of the machinery of government, is not a very satisfactory way of realizing this ideal. But perhaps this is not what we really mean.

When we speak of the self-government of a people, we are, I fancy, thinking of the people as a whole, as if it had almost an individual life. And I think we are to a large extent justified in doing this. Any people, worthy of the name, is a real unity, capable of acting, thinking, and feeling together. And what is meant by the self-government of such a people is that the ruling principle lies within itself, that it is, somehow, contained within the life of the whole. This does not mean that each individual rules, nor even that each individual has any considerable share in ruling. What it means is rather, on the one hand, that there is no sovereign who controls the system in a purely external way; and, on the other hand, that there is no subject who is controlled by it in a purely external way.

[11] Thomas Carlyle, *Past and Present* (London, Collins, n.d.), 242.

All are real members in a living whole.[d] But if that is what we properly mean by self-government or Democracy, we may accept it as an end in itself, a thing of supreme worth, and yet regard representative systems and the reckoning of majorities as little better than mechanical devices, whose only value lies in their contributing to the possibility that each one may share, to some extent, in the life of the whole. If this is what Democracy means, it really involves in itself a considerable element of what is commonly called Aristocracy. Perhaps the ideal Republic of Plato would, in this sense, be more truly Democratic than many modern states that lay claim to the designation. For what could be more truly Democratic – in the sense of the real self-government of the whole – than Plato's principle of ideal justice, that every one is to fill the place and perform the work for which he is best qualified? If his Republic falls short of the true Democratic spirit, it is only in so far as the rulers are conceived as dealing with those whom they govern too purely from above, while no adequate provision is made for the cultivation of the spirit of citizenship in the lowest class of the people. This no doubt is foreign to Democracy; and, as Aristotle was well aware, it was also this, more than anything else, that made Plato's ideal unworkable. A real Democracy, in short, must be aristocratic – it must aim at government by the best; and there can be no practical realization of aristocracy except through the cultivation of the Democratic spirit – the spirit that is ready to recognize that to be governed by its best is to be governed by itself.

We are often told that what stands in the way of our advancement in Great Britain is our suspicion of the expert; and it is sometimes thought that this is largely due to the growth of the spirit of Democracy among us. I doubt whether it has much connection with Democracy. The Americans appear to have largely outgrown it. Nor is it entirely my meaning that we should learn to trust to the expert. The expert is often narrow-minded and conservative. What I mean is rather that we must learn to put our confidence in those who are interested in particular things, in those who know about them and care about them; and must recognize that it is an essential part of

---

[d] I should like to refer, in connection with this point, to Bosanquet's treatment of the 'General Will' in his 'Philosophical Theory of the State', [Bernard Bosanquet, *The Philosophical Theory of the State* (London, Macmillan, 1899: fourth edition, 1923)].

the true Democratic spirit to be ready to follow where such men lead. Democracy does not mean trusting important matters to the care of 'the man in the street'; it rather means finding for everything the man who is best fitted to take care of it, and leaving him to manage it. This, however, is probably the lesson that Democracies are in general most slow to learn. Louis XIV has been much laughed at for saying, 'The State, I am the State'; but each of us is rather apt in practice to say, 'Self-government of the people: that means that I govern.' Yet in small matters we all learn that it is not so. If we want to go to America, we do not consider how we are to navigate ourselves across: we choose a suitable steamer, and trust to the captain and crew. If we are sick, we do not collect the votes of our acquaintances as to the most suitable treatment: we rather take the advice, as a rule, of some expert physician. And this is surely a quite democratic method of procedure. We rule over the captain and the physician. We tell the one to take us to America, and the other to make us well. But they rule over us in the process. We choose the end that we think desirable: there we are very probably the best judges. But we trust to men of special skill to show us how we are to get what we want. If this principle were carried all through life, every one would be ruling in that which he knows about, and submitting to rule in that about which he is ignorant; and I cannot but think that a people in which this was the practice would be most truly a self-governing people, a people in which the true principle of Democracy was realized.

On the whole, then, I admit that a Democracy is often liable to this particular danger; that it may fail to be, in any true sense, a government 'by the people'. Democracy is not, in Carlyle's phrase a 'Morrison's Pill'.[12] It is not something that is sure to put us right, whether we think about it or not. If Democracy is to mean anything really great and desirable for us, we must see to it that it is what we intend it to be. Self-government, in fact, means mainly this, that every one of us is trying to co-operate in securing that the rule is the best possible. But we are not really co-operating if we are interfering with some one who knows better than we do. Sometimes we may even co-operate best by standing aside: – 'They also serve who

---

[12] Carlyle, *Past and Present*, 29: 'Brothers, I am sorry I have got no Morrison's Pill for curing the maladies of Society.'

only stand and wait.'[13] But generally our best service will lie in finding something that we can do – something, if possible, that we can do better, at the moment, than anyone else. If we succeed in doing this, we are, I think, in that act realizing the best meaning of Democracy and Aristocracy in one. It is the rule of the people, and it is the rule of the best. But this, you may say, is a mere ideal. Yes, and everything that is worth anything in human life is or contains an ideal. The important thing is that the ideal we have before us should be something that has real value. Now, if we mean by Democracy only ballot-boxes and majorities, there cannot be much value in that, whether we realize it or not. But if we mean by Democracy a real self-government of the people, each one being allowed to do, and trusted to do, that for which he is best fitted, then I believe we mean something which has a considerable value for us, even if we do not wholly succeed in achieving it. Even only to aim at it, is to realize its spirit; and to realize its spirit is to go a long way towards its complete achievement.

And this leads me naturally to notice the third great danger of Democracy – that it may fail to be a government 'for the people'. It was chiefly, I think, on this account that Democracy was condemned by Aristotle. Aristotle divided forms of government into bad and good, according as they existed for their own sakes or for the sake of those who are governed; and he placed Democracy among the bad ones. To most modern readers this is a paradox, because they naturally think of Democracy as being government 'for the people'. But it is intelligible enough when we bear in mind the distinction between the people as a whole and the people as a mere collection of units. If each one is fighting for himself, you may

---

[13] Milton:

> 'Doth God exact day-labour, light deny'd'
> I fondly ask; But patience to prevent
> That murmur, soon replies, 'God doth not need
> Either man's work of his own gifts. Who best
> Bear his mild yoke, they serve him best, his State
> Is Kingly: thousands at his bidding speed
> And post o'er Land and Ocean without rest;
> They also serve who only stand and wait.

'On His Blindness', *The Works of John Milton* (Ware; Hertfordshire, Wordsworth, 1994), 80.

say, in a sense, that all are fighting for all; but, if so, you are using the word 'all' in a rather peculiar and sophistical fashion. At any rate, there can be no true harmony unless each is fighting for all. Now, a Democracy is too often conceived as meaning simply a state in which one has an eye to his own interest; and it is sometimes supposed that in this way the interests of all will be served. I think Aristotle was right in regarding a Democracy of this sort as intrinsically bad. The mere struggle of competing interests cannot reasonably be expected to lead to the good of the whole. In economics this is now, I believe, pretty generally recognized: pure *laisser faire* is a discredited principle. But is it any more reliable in general politics? Few, I fancy, would seriously, on calm reflection, maintain that it is. But if not, then we must recognize that this is a real danger confronting our modern democratic states; and it is one of the dangers that was much in the minds of Carlyle and Ruskin, as well as in that of Aristotle. Can we hope that our modern Democracies will guard against it?

So far as I can see, the only real way of guarding against it is by the cultivation of the spirit of citizenship. The citizen must be taught it to think of himself, not as an isolated individual with private interests of his own, but as a member of a great system, in which he has a definite place and function. This is perhaps most readily learned through the gradual discipline of smaller unities. The man who has learned to be loyal to his family, his school, or his club, is at least on the way to learn loyalty to the larger social unity, of which these are parts; and I believe it would be difficult to overestimate the value of this element in education. The Americans are, I believe, much in advance of Great Britain in the application of this idea; and so probably are the French, and certainly the Japanese. The essential principles of self-government may easily be acquired in schools. Interesting – and apparently successful – experiments have been made, especially in America, in the way of conducting schools on purely self-governing principles; but, without even going so far as this, it is easy to see that much may be done to make the spirit of citizenship a reality; and I am convinced that, if Democracy is ever to be a real success among us, it can only be through the cultivation of such a spirit. No one can be a genuine democrat unless he is also an enthusiast for the welfare of the society to which he belongs. We must learn, as Mazzini so constantly insisted, to concentrate our attention upon our duties as citizens, rather than upon our rights as individuals.[14]

There are no doubt other dangers of Democracy besides those to which I have now alluded. A Democracy is commonly said to be somewhat inefficient, especially in great emergencies that call for our united action: but this is extremely doubtful; it seems to depend entirely upon the extent to which the society has become a real unity. The American government is probably as efficient as that of Russia. Again, it is sometimes said that in a Democracy there is apt to be a certain lack of an adequate sense of responsibility on the part of public officials. There seems to be some truth in this. Bryce, for instance, notes that in America 'the tone of public life is lower than one expects to find it in so great a nation . . . In Europe, where the traditions of aristocracy survive, everybody condemns as mean and unworthy acts done or language held by a great official which would pass unnoticed in a private citizen. It is the principle of *noblesse oblige*. . . . Such a sentiment is comparatively weak in America. A cabinet minister, or senator, or governor of a state, sometimes even a President, hardly feels himself more bound by it than the director of a railway company or the mayor of a town does in Europe. Not assuming himself to be individually wiser, stronger, or better than his fellow-citizens, he acts and speaks as if he were still simply one of them, and so far from magnifying his office and making it honorable, seems anxious to show that he is the mere creature of the popular vote, so filled by the sense that it is the people and not he who governs as to fear that he should be deemed to have forgotten his personal insignificance.' (Chap. xcv.) I am afraid there are some signs of such a lowering of the tone of public

---

[14] Mazzini says, for example:

> Declaration of principles and not of rights. The distinction alone, if properly understood and developed, will suffice to secure the Italian initiative in Europe. Our national pact will asssume a religious character, and become the expression of an epoch, the *aim* of which is *association*.
>
> The declaration of right, which all constitutions persist in servilely copying from the French, expressed an epoch which was summed up and exhausted, to her eternal glory, by France. The aim of that epoch was the assertion of the rights of the *individual* and it only expressed one half of the problem.
>
> *Life and Writings of Joseph Mazzini*, vol. I, *Autobiographical and Political* (London, Smith Elder, 1891), 297–8fn.

life in this country, as well as in America; and it appears to be a real danger of Democracy. But I need not emphasize it further, as it appears to be simply one illustration of the danger to which I have already alluded, of a misinterpretation of what is meant by government 'by the people'. It can only be remedied by the gradual recognition that in a true Democracy, no less than in an aristocracy each one has his own definite place and function, his own work to do, his own responsibility to bear; that democratic rule does not mean the rule of 'the man in the street', but the rule of those who know and are prepared to do. Let the man who knows control the thing that he knows about – that is the essence of good government: provided always that he is subject to the criticism of others upon the results of his work.

There may be still other dangers in Democracy. It may be apt to be fickle and commonplace and deficient in length of view.

But I have not thought it desirable to dwell upon such subordinate dangers. What I have sought to emphasize in this paper, and what I believe to be true, is that the one great danger of Democracy – the only danger that it need ultimately fear – is that it may fail to be true to itself, that it may forget its own ideals.

I may sum up the results of the view to which I am led, and which I have been trying to bring before you, in this way. Democracy, in the best sense of the word, means the self-government of a people; and this is the highest possible conception of government. But there is a constant danger that it may be misinterpreted in practice, and become only the rule of the majority, which is certainly not in itself a high conception of government. I do not mean that we can set aside the method of estimating majorities. What I mean is that that is not the essence of Democracy, in the best meaning of the term. Democracy, in the best sense, means the rule of the people as a living whole, by the people as living whole, and for the sake of the people as a living whole; and this ought to mean, in practice, that everything is done by him who is best fitted to do it, and under the guidance of those who know most about it. I do not believe in Plato's philosopher-king. If a real philosopher were made king, his first act would probably be to abdicate his office, or at least to secure, as rapidly as possible, that the real work of government was distributed among the competent citizens of the State. Human capacity is practically always departmental: there is no one who is fitted to be a ruler in everything; and there is hardly anyone who is not fitted to be in charge of something, and to be responsible for seeing that it is done. The truest Democracy – and the truest aristocracy as well – is a state in which everyone exercises rule, just so far as he is fitted to do so. If we constantly remember that this is what Democracy aims at, and that ballot-boxes and other instruments of government are only the machinery by which we seek to bring this about,[c] then I think there is some chance that our modern Democracy may gradually come to live in its own proper spirit, and to realize, through constant effort, that form of a well ordered state, at once truly democratic and truly aristocratic, of which Plato and Carlyle could only vaguely dream.

---

[c] I may refer, in connection with this, to the excellent discussion of popular government contained in MacCunn's 'Ethics of Citizenship'. [John MacCunn, *Ethics of Citizenship* (Glasgow, Maclehose, 1894: fifth edition, 1911).]

9
The Present State of the Controversy Between Individualism and Socialism

EDWARD CAIRD

As an old citizen of Glasgow, whose life was for many years bound up with its great University, I count it no little honour to give the opening address to its new Civic Society. Glasgow as any one may know who will turn over the pages of the magnificent record of civic progress published by Sir James Bell,[a] is undoubtedly one of the cities which stand in the front rank of municipal achievement, one of those cities which have realized most clearly what municipal organization can do to improve the external conditions of life for its citizens. Owing to its situation, its climate, the extent of its trade and manufactures, and the consequent great influx and increase of population within its boundaries, it has had early to face many of the most serious difficulties as to the safety, the health, the economic and the social welfare of the people, which beset modern communities. It has had to consider, not as a matter of theory but as a pressing practical necessity, the great problem how the community can interfere with the life of individuals so as to strengthen and develop their energies, and not to weaken or pauperize them. And if it has not discovered any general solution of this problem – as who has discovered such a solution? – yet I think it is not doubted by many that the steps it has so far taken have been judicious, and that none of them will need to be retracted or reversed. There are some for whose impatience progress has seemed far too slow, and many who think that we have as yet dealt only with the first and

---

[a] *Glasgow, its Municipal Organization and Administration.* By Sir James Bell, Bart., and James Paton, F.L.S. Glasgow: James MacLehose & Sons.

173

more obvious phases of the difficulty. But no one who really appreciates the difficulty would wish that the gradual tentative and experimental methods which have hitherto guided the advance of the city in these matters should be changed for a bolder spirit of innovation. On the contrary, men are coming to see more and more clearly that there is no royal road to social welfare, no simple 'open sesame' which will enable us to unlock all the complex and intricate problems of modern life. Man is after all the most puzzling of beings to himself, and the question what effect any institution or any measure to relieve his wants or draw forth his powers, any plan for helping, educating, or giving even amusement to him, will have upon a class or community of men, whether it will really aid or hinder them in the long run, is not to be settled except by the most careful watching of experience and the most thorough analysis of it and reflexion upon its bearings.

Every one who has given himself to any kind of scientific investigation knows how difficult it is to grasp the full meaning of a body of facts, to see all their aspects and to combine them in one view. Scientific men are constantly tempted to theorize on insufficient data, to make things simpler than they are. They have, therefore, to train themselves to doubt and question every explanation that suggests itself to them, and to accept none, till they have tried their utmost to find objections to it. In the far more complex problems of human life, this necessity is still more pressing, for the temptations to one-sidedness are much greater. Every one of us in the great division of labour in modern life has been learning – one might almost say, has been carefully teaching himself – to be *one-sided* to look at the facts of experience under one light, and to turn away his eyes from their other aspects. Even a Shakspeare could complain that his nature was 'subdued to what it worked in like the dyer's hand'.[1] And how is it with ordinary men? Every one knows that the

---

[1] Shakespeare,

> O, for my sake do you with Fortune chide,
> The guilty goddess of my harmful deeds,
> That did not better for my life provide
> Than public means which public manners breeds,
>   And almost thence my nature is subdued
>   To what it works in, like the dyer's hand

Sonnet III.

class to which he belongs has a strong bias in one direction, or if he has not imagination enough to see this, and thinks the views of his own class quite just and unprejudiced, he can at any rate see very clearly that every other class has such a bias. And if we chance to find ourselves in a society quite different from our own, we are ready to wonder how narrow and prejudiced it is. Take an assemblage of the average men of any profession or trade, of average clergymen, average lawyers, average schoolmasters or academic teachers, average employers of labour, or average artizans; take any class you like, and you will find they persistently repeat to each other certain views of life till it becomes difficult for them to conceive that other views could honestly be held by any one.

Now, it is not altogether a misfortune that we should have our class feelings, our class points of view, that we should see certain aspects of things very vividly and emphasize them strongly. A certain division of labour seems to be inevitable in thought as well as in action. But there is great danger lest these different points of view should harden into exclusive dogmas that make it impossible for us to understand each other. And it is of the highest importance that those who maintain them should be brought together so as to have a close and intimate perception of each other's feelings and thoughts. This is the best, perhaps the only adequate, prescription for enabling us to escape from ourselves, to get away from the idols of our own dens, and to correct our personal or class bias. It might even be maintained that we never thoroughly appreciate an opinion, especially if it is opposed to our usual way of thinking, and never thoroughly realize its force and meaning, till we meet with one who honestly maintains it.

A Civic Society may therefore do a great deal to help the development of sound and comprehensive ideas on social subjects, if it brings together men whose points of view are essentially different and enables them to understand each other. The first effect may indeed be only to show them how much they are opposed. But if they persist, each of them resolving fully and frankly to speak his own mind, and at the same time to tolerate and encourage the expression of opinions and arguments opposed to his own, however unsound he may think them, the gain may be great. Such discussion may prepare the way for a more comprehensive view of the questions discussed than previously existed in the mind of any of the disputants. For those who can discuss their opposition fairly are inevitably forced to recognize that there are reasons which might lead honest men to an opposite view from their own and to consider how far their own view is comprehensive enough to make room for them. They can no longer hold that all the sheep are on the one side, and all the goats, on the other. They are forced in some points to make admissions to their opponents, and, if they do not convince each other, yet they make it possible for themselves, or at least for more impartial minds, to see the questions on all sides and to seek for a solution that does justice to them all.

By way of illustration of what I mean, I should like shortly to refer to a great controversy in regard to social and economical subjects of which we have heard much in recent years and are likely to hear more in the future, the controversy between Individualism and Socialism, and to point out what progress has been made towards an understanding between the opposite parties. Before, however, entering upon the special question, I should like to make one general remark. It has been said that the present age is an age of criticism and reconciliation, as contrasted with previous ages which were given up to the war of opposing dogmatisms. And undoubtedly it is a marked characteristic of our time that in many departments of thought it has broken through lines of division which were formerly supposed to be absolute. If we look back to the seventeenth, or even to the eighteenth century, we find that controversies as to religion or philosophy or politics were apt to take the form of a sharp and decisive collision of opposites between which no middle term was allowed to exist. Men were supposed to live mentally between the horns of a dilemma. Thus in religion they were called upon to choose between authority and reason, between a fixed dogmatic system hallowed by all the sacred memories of the past, and the dictates of an individual understanding which emancipated itself from all control of tradition and regarded any reverence for it as superstitious. In philosophy they were asked to choose between a pure empiricism that recognized no power in the mind of man to do aught but accept what was given it from without through the senses, and a pure intuitionalism which made that mind, at least as to its most fundamental ideas, entirely independent of experience. In like manner, in dealing with the history of religions, it was assumed that if Christianity was true, it must contain all religious

truth without any alloy, and that if other religions were in comparison false, they must contain nothing but lying and imposture.

Now, the same way of thinking prevailed also in the sphere of
politics and social philosophy, and determined the course of the
controversy between individualism and Socialism. On the one side
many voices asserted the doctrine of unfettered freedom for the
individual, the doctrine that the one way to good economical and
social results was to remove all restrictions, all social pressure, all
limits upon individual opinion or action. Godwin even tried to demonstrate that nature of itself would bring men to goodness and happiness, if only the unnatural restraints of law were removed; and
Shelley, in melodious verse, proclaimed the absolute purity of natural impulse, and echoed the dogma that the one source of all evil is
the policeman.[2] Even those who did not take such an optimistic
view of the results of freedom, held that restraint upon competition
between individuals is always an evil, or that if it brings disasters
with it, yet these are never so bad as the effects of any restriction
of it or interference with it. On the other side, in opposition to this
glorification of *Laissez faire*, there arose an equally abstract Socialism which regarded competition as essentially evil, as the exploitation of the weak by the strong; which declared private property
to be theft, and even denounced the exclusive personal relations of
the family as unsocial; which therefore maintained that the only
safety for society must lie in establishing a fixed order, in which all
private initiative was suppressed; and that the individual must be
reduced into an instrument of the community which should compel
him to work according to his capacity, and reward him according
to his wants. Thus the one system seemed to deny that society could
do anything for the individual, except to refuse to interfere with
him, and allow him to compete or co-operate with his fellows as he
pleased; while the other viewed him as a creature of society, who is
only what society makes him, and can never be allowed safely to
escape from its despotic beneficence. Such was the frank dogmatic
Socialism which writers like Fourier and Owen opposed to the

---

[2] Percy B. Shelley married the the daughter of Godwin and Mary Wollstonecraft.
The sentiments to which Caird refers are to be found in Shelley, 'Queen Mab' in
The Complete Poetical Works of Shelley (Oxford, Clarendon Press, 1904), pp. 853–
92. In the notes to this poem Shelley quotes Godwin at length in support of his
own views.

equally dogmatic enthusiasts of *Laissez faire* even up to the beginning of this century.[3]

Now, I think I may venture to say that no such Socialism and no such Individualism exists in the mind of any tolerably educated man at the present day. There are many who cling to the names of Individualism or Socialism, but there are none, or almost none, who maintain the simple abstract doctrines once associated with them. And there is much of what I can only describe as an unconscious tendency to *hedge* among the partizans of either side. Thus there are many writers who will tell you that a *true* Individualism is one which allows much room for the action of society, especially through the State and the Municipality; and not merely *negative* action in the way of protecting person and property, but also positive action in measures to further the health, the comfort, the moral and intellectual education, and even the recreation of the people. And on the other side, there are not a few who call themselves socialists who altogether repudiate communism and tell us that for a *true* or scientific Socialism 'the criterion of economic machinery is simply, Does it or does it not make for a greater amount and quality of life and character' in the individuals of which the society is composed? These are the words of Mr. Sidney Ball in a tract recently published as an expression of the views of the Fabian Society. Mr. Ball goes on to say,

> The older Socialism rested upon such ideas as 'the right to live', 'the right to work', 'payment according to needs', the denial of 'the rent of ability', 'expropriation without compensation', 'minimizing' or 'materializing' of wants – all ideas of retrogressive rather than of progressive 'selection'. But it would not be too much to say that all these ideas are either silently ignored or expressly repudiated by the modern Socialism: the 'idealogy' of the older socialists has given way to a deliberately, and in some ways rigidly, scientific treatment of life. Modern Socialism recognizes the laws of social growth and development in setting itself against 'catastrophic

[3] Charles Fourier (1772–1837) was branded a 'utopian socialist' by Marx and Engels. His ideas were put into practice in Romania, Swiss Jura and California. See *Fourier: The Utopian Vision of Charles Fourier*, ed. J. Beecher and R. Bienvenu (London, Cape, 1972). Robert Owen (1771–1858) was a Welsh socialist and philanthropist, famous for his socialist experiments in New Lanark, England and New Harmony, USA. Robert Owen, *A New View of Society*, ed. G. D. H. Cole, (London, Dent, 1927).

impossibilism' and the manufacture of mechanical Utopias; it recognizes the moral continuity of society in its consideration for 'vested interests'; it does not base industrial organization on the 'right to work' so much as on the 'right of the worker', not on 'payment according to needs' so much as on 'payment according to services'; it recognizes the remuneration of ability, provided that the ability does not merely represent a monopoly of privileged and non-competitive advantage; it is aware of the utility of capital, without making the individualist's confusion between the employment of capital and the ownership of it; it is not concerned about the inequality of property, except so far as it conflicts with sound national economy; it does not desire so much to minimize as to rationalize wants, and attaches the utmost importance to the qualitative development of consumption; and finally, not to enumerate more distinctly economic developments, it recognizes 'the abiding necessity for contest, competition, and selection', as means of development, when it presses for such an organization of industry as shall make selection according to ability and character the determining factor in the remuneration of labour.[b]

Now, while I appreciate highly these attempts on each side to correct the one-sided dogmas of an earlier time, and while I am quite prepared to admit and to maintain that in a sense a true Socialism and a true Individualism must be one, I would urge, in the interest of fair discussion and clear thinking, that neither of them can be permitted to appropriate without acknowledgment whatever elements it thinks good from the adversary, while still insisting on the purity of its own doctrine and keeping up all the severity of its former censures upon that adversary. If we oppose Socialism and Individualism as abstract principles, we must take the latter as the assertion of the unlimited freedom of the individual to compete or co-operate with his fellow as he pleases, and we must take the former as the absolute negation of such freedom and the reduction of the individual under the control of society, to the exclusion of individual initiative. Logically carried out, the one can be nothing less than anarchism and the other social despotism. Neither of these systems, indeed, has ever been actually realized, though there have been approximations to the system of Individual-

---

[b] [Sidney Ball,] 'The Moral Basis of Socialism', *International Journal of Ethics*, [vi] (1896), [294]. Reprinted as *Fabian Tract*, No. 72, p. 4.

ism in communities where the State was very weak or very limited in the sphere of its action; and there have been approximations to the system of Socialism in some communities of a primitive kind in which the idea of individual right had not yet arisen, as well as in some smaller societies (which were not States but special organizations within the State), such as the monasteries, or the various socialistic experiments which are now being tried in the United States. To realize the full working out of socialistic or individualistic principles, therefore, we must go, on the one side, to the ideal Commonwealth of Plato or the various Utopias which have been constructed by More and his successors down to Morris with his *News from Nowhere*;[4] and, on the other hand, to the descriptions of the state of nature in Rousseau and Diderot and Godwin.

Setting aside pure Individualism and pure Socialism as abstractions, we find many halting places between the two modifications of socialistic or individualistic systems, which rest really, though not confessedly, on the plan of borrowing whatever elements seemed desirable from the opposite system. Thus the earliest and best known of the compromises of Individualism is that which has been epigrammatically characterized as 'anarchy plus a street constable', the theory which would give to the State the duty of protecting the rights of person and property, and then leave everything else to the action of individuals. But there are hardly any individualists who hold to this limitation of State action now. Almost every one who has a right to be heard would admit that, as a nation, we must deal with pauperism, though there are of course many views as to the best kind of Poor Law. Almost every one admits that there are some general services, such as the Post Office, which it is expedient that the State should perform for the community, and that there are a number of natural monopolies which the State, the Municipality, or some public authority must either take into its own hands, or at least regulate and control. And almost every one admits that the State must concern itself with the great business of education, either directly and continually, or by occasional interferences with the independent authorities in whose hands the management of it is left. And though the limits of municipal action are still a matter

---

[4] William Morris, *News From Nowhere* (Boston: Mass., Robert Brothers, 1890: London, Reeves and Turner, 1891).

of controversy, I should be surprised if there are many Glasgow individualists who do not approve of a considerable part of that which the Municipality has done for its citizens. On the other hand, we find that the simple communistic principle, which rests on the annihilation of all rights of person and property and also on the suppression of the family, has been very greatly modified in modern Socialism. Almost all modern systems have introduced the principle that the reward of the individual's labour must have respect to the service done by him to the community, and not merely to his wants; almost all have admitted within certain limits the necessity of allowing him to acquire private property, even when they refuse to let him use it as capital. And, although the language of socialists in relation to the family is still very uncertain, there are among those who call themselves by that name many who recognize that a pure domestic life and the sanctity of the home are the indispensable basis of the moral as well as the economical organization of society. And if we can take Mr. Sidney Ball, who speaks for the Fabian Society, as our authority, the modification of the socialistic system has gone much farther. Mr. Ball indeed cautiously says that the 'Fabian Society has for *the most part* sown its wild oats',[c] so that perhaps we may expect farther developments when the whole crop of wild oats has been sown. But already his Socialism is one which fully recognizes the remuneration of ability and the inequality of property, 'except so far as it conflicts with equality of opportunity and equality of consideration for all social workers', and it admits also the 'abiding necessity for conflict, competition, and the natural selection' which arises out of such competition – regarding these as essential means to development of individuals who shall be true members of the social organism, and not a pauperized proletariat who must be a continual hindrance to its progress. His Socialism, therefore, consists almost entirely in his holding that all capital, i.e. all the funds employed in carrying on the various industries of the

---

[c] *International Journal of Ethics*, 1896. [Ball says: 'The older Socialism rested upon such ideas as "the right to live", "the right to work", "payment according to needs", the denial of "the rent of ability", "expropriation without compensation", "minimumizing" or "materializing" of wants – all ideas of retrogressive rather than progressive "selection". But it would not be too much to say that all these ideas are either silently ignored or expressly repudiated by the "Scientific" Socialism, of which "Fabianism", now that it has for the most part sown its wild oats, is the most thoughtful expression.' p. 293.]

country, should be administered by some public authority, which should supersede the employer or 'undertaker'. Furthermore he, with many of the most thoughtful of the Socialists, has entirely renounced the purpose of realizing this ideal by any sudden revolution, and has acknowledged that the State, and public authorities generally, are at present entirely unfitted to take upon themselves the general administration of capital, and that they can only become so by a long process of social education. In short, such socialists look upon their own scheme, not as a project for immediate realization, but as a goal towards which modern society is tending – a goal we may add, which it cannot reach until the character and capacity necessary for its realization have been developed. And they are content in the meanwhile to work, through County Councils, School Boards, and Poor Law Authorities, as well as through Parliament, for such partial improvements of the condition of the people as from time to time seem to become possible.

After this review I think I may venture to say that it is altogether a mistake to think that at the present time individualists and socialists generally stand to each other as absolutely opposed sects, holding reciprocally exclusive dogmas, and unable to make any concessions to each other. There are, of course, now as always, men on both sides who are incapable of seeing that a question has more than one aspect, and who ride their favourite abstraction to death, or perhaps, we should rather say, are ridden to death by it. And there are many who think abstractly, simply because of want of education, or of that practical knowledge of the problems of social life and the difficulties of solving them, which can be acquired only in direct contact with affairs. But with the exception of these prophets or victims of one idea, there are no such beings as pure socialists or pure individualists. 'We are all socialists now', an eminent person [George Bernard Shaw] is reported to have said. And I think that with equal approximation to truth it might be said that 'we are all individualists now'. There are few men who think seriously upon such topics, who do not realize in some degree that we can help individuals effectively only by enabling them to help themselves, by drawing out their individual energy and resolution. And there are few who do not see that it is impossible to do this without giving to the individual a control over his own earnings, without opening to him a career in which he can be useful to himself and to society, and, on the other hand, without allowing him to suffer by his own idleness or improvidence. Nor are there many now who think that society would be benefited if the individual was deprived of the right of having a home of his own, in which he may enjoy the highest blessing of life, the blessing of the household union of husband and wife and children; or if he were relieved from the responsibilities of maintaining those he has brought into the world, and to the best of his power preparing them for the duties of life. That is the *essential truth of Individualism*, which Aristotle long ago maintained against the socialistic proposals of Plato.[5] On the other hand, it is as true now as it was for Aristotle and Plato, that man is essentially a social and political animal, that the individual apart from the community is like a hand cut off from the living body; that the savage 'war of all against all'[6] is ruin, and that unlimited competition is little better: that the State, comprehending in itself all municipal and other partial organs of its activity, is the great organization upon which the welfare of all is dependent, and that it is its duty, not only to protect the private rights of individuals, but to control and modify the action of all individuals and classes, so that, so far as may be, they may work together for the good of the whole community; and further, to take upon itself every public service which can be more effectively discharged by itself than by the independent action of individuals. This is the *essential truth of Socialism*, which has been too much forgotten, but which no community can forget without danger.

If we look upon this picture and upon that, we see that the opposition of individualists and socialists is now becoming confined within narrow limits, and that there is no such difference of principle between them that they should find it difficult to discuss any practical question. They agree very closely in their ideal. For what socialists, or the most thoughtful of them, now profess to want is that the State should protect individuals from that hurtful and destructive competition which means the crushing of the weak by the strong; that it should do its utmost to promote the growth of

---

[5] Aristotle, *Politics*, ed. Stephen Everson (Cambridge, Cambridge University Press, 1988), 1260b27–1266a30.

[6] This, of course, is an allusion to Hobbes, 'such a warre as is of everyman against everyman', ed. Richard Tuck, *Leviathan* (Cambridge, Cambridge University Press, 1991), 88 [62].

individual energy and character, and to give every one a fair chance of living a healthful and useful life; but that it should do nothing to pauperize men by charity, to weaken their personal responsibility for their own lives, or to stop that healthful competition which draws out capacity and character, and determines in what position the individual can best serve the community. On the other side, individualists, if they watch narrowly and anxiously the encroachments of the State or the Municipality upon any sphere of the public service hitherto left to individual enterprise, base their opposition on the admitted dangers of any attempt to do for individuals what they ought to do, and can effectually do, only for themselves, and they no longer deny that there are many services – how many is the question – in which it is expedient that public should supersede private action.

Now, I do not say that it is indifferent from which side of the question we take it up, or that we can expect to escape great controversy and conflict between the two parties. But I do say that there is no antagonism of principle between them such as was formerly supposed to exist, and such as should prevent an ultimate agreement being arrived at by discussion and the careful questioning of experience. Their difference as to the form which society is likely to assume in the future, when the changes now going on have borne their last fruit, and especially the question as to the extent which society will undertake the regulation or conduct of industry, is, no doubt, theoretically very important. But it is not an irreconcilable difference. For it is admitted on the one hand that the public authority *ought* to take into its hand such services as it can discharge more efficiently and economically than private individuals; and, again, that it *must* do all it can to help the poor and strengthen the weak, and to give every one born in the community opportunities for the education and the development of his powers, and to open a free career to his talents when they have been developed; and it is admitted, on the other hand, that in securing such ends it must be careful above all not to lay too heavy burdens on the community, such burdens as might check the growth of its resources and break down the independence of its poorer members; and finally, it is confessed, at least by the most reasonable men on both sides, that no attempt to change the economic conditions of life by a sudden revolution can be effectual; nay, that any such attempt would be certain to bring economic and social ruin by throwing upon the State and the subordinate public authorities functions which they are not prepared to discharge. Starting from these admissions on each side, we may fairly say that the opposition between them reduces itself to a difference as to the ultimate result of the gradual evolution through which society is now passing – a point upon which no one has a right to speak very dogmatically; and what is really more important, both parties are able to discuss with each other on common grounds the expediency of each particular measure which is proposed. For though they may look upon it from opposite points of view, yet each must confess to a certain extent the legitimacy of the point of view of the other, and there is no practical consideration which one can allege which the other is precluded by his principles from considering with judicial fairness.

Now, it may be said, that in the preceding remarks I have exaggerated the actual approximation of the two parties, that I have made too much of the concessions of a few of their most reasonable or conciliatory members on each side, and that I have not paid sufficient regard to the violent utterances that come from Conferences of Socialists on the one side, and to the uncompromising assertions of the representatives of Leagues for the defence of Liberty and Property on the other. But I venture to think that the real drift of opinion is not permanently affected by partizan vehemencies, and that there is a great and growing force of thought and experience which is steadily beating down the noise of faction, and gaining ground for wider and more comprehensive views. 'The mills of God grind slowly, but they grind exceeding small.'[7] Ideas win their way by inches and very silently, but what ground they win is never lost. And the great idea which rules the mind of this age, the idea of organic evolution, is surely leading us away from the 'falsehood of extremes'. The power of this idea is unquestionable. It

---

[7] This saying comes from Henry W. Longfellow's (1807–82) translation of Friedrich von Logau (1604–1655), *Sinngedichte*.

> THOUGH the mills of God grind
> slowly, yet they grind exceeding small;
> Tough with patience he stands waiting, with exactness grinds
> he all.

'Retribution' in *Poetic Aphorisms* (1654). See *The Works of Henry Wadsworth Longfellow* (Ware; Hertfordshire, Wordsworth, 1994), 141.

has already transformed, or is transforming, all our scientific conceptions. In particular, it has already revolutionized the biological sciences: it has given a new meaning to History, and it is rapidly remoulding our Economics and creating a new kind of ethical and political and social science. Now, the idea of evolution is a *reconciling idea*, which enables us to do justice to both the aspects of social life which have been opposed in the past, and to rise above their opposition. Thus, let us take the formula of evolution which Mr. Herbert Spencer has given, that it is a *progress at once in differentiation and integration*, or less technically, a progress towards the division of labour and the independence of the parts, and at the same time towards their co-operation and the unity of the whole.[8] Apply this idea to society, and what does it mean? It means something which we hope the future of society may one day realize, it means the utmost development of individual capacity, the utmost strengthening of individual independence, and at the same time a close interdependence and connection of all the individuals with each other, such that the common good of society shall evoke the greatest devotion on the part of all the members of it. And it means that these two ends are not opposed, but essentially one, so that it is impossible for a society to be strong, if its members are weak, or for the members to be strong, except through the same means which secure the greatest material and moral unity of the society. The division of labour is in order to the co-operation of labour, and that co-operation cannot be complete, unless the life of the whole is present in every part, unless each individual feels and realizes in all his work that he is the organ of the community. And, on the other hand, a truly organic society cannot be made except out of independent, self-respecting, self-governing individuals. Division without such union is on the way to death by disintegration; unity without such independence is on the way to death by paralysis. To pursue the one end in opposition to the other is to sacrifice both.

It is true that a different interpretation has sometimes been given to the idea of evolution. In his great work on the *Origin of Species*,

[8] For a brief example of Spencer's conception of this process see his 'The Social Organism'. First published in *The Westminster Review*, January, 1860. It has more recently been reprinted in *The Man Versus the State: With Six Essays on Government, Society and Freedom* (Indianapolis, Liberty, 1982), 383–434. Also see Herbert Spencer, *Principles of Sociology* (London, Williams and Norgate, 1876–96), vols. 6–8 of *A System of Synthetic Philosophy*.

Darwin, following Malthus, pointed to the struggle for existence and the survival of the fittest as essential to the development of vegetable and animal life; and there have been many ready to draw the inference that in human life the only security for progress is unrestricted competition. But already, in his earliest book, Darwin had pointed out, though he did not emphasize the fact, that this competition of individuals is limited and controlled by powerful sexual and parental instincts, which bind individuals together so that they do *not* compete; and in a later book he directly put forward the principle of sexual selection as almost co-ordinate with his original principle.[9] In fact, it might be said that if the animals carry out the principle of competition in its extremest form, yet, on the other hand, there are no such rigid socialists as they, none who carry out the sacrifice of individuals to the common good with such remorseless thoroughness as, e.g., the bees and the ants. And when we turn to mankind, Darwin himself showed that it is the very condition of human existence that competition should be not between individuals, but between societies, and that within each society competition between individuals should be subordinated to the common good. And if we were to trace out the evolution of man in history, we should find that if, on the one hand, it has tended to the emancipation of individuals from direct social pressure – tended to make them more and more independent, and so to enable them to compete more freely – yet, at the same time, every step in civilization has been a step toward the limitation of the worst form of competition, which is war and also of the next worst form of competition, which is fraud and the exploitation of the weak by the strong; and a step towards the introduction of a form of competition which is only the natural process whereby the individual is pressed up or down, till he finds his proper place – the place in which he can best serve the community. We are, indeed, far from the realization of a community in which these ends are even approximately attained. We have much of the wrong kind of competition – that which determines the position of individuals by the simple law of battle; and, side by side with it, as the necessary correlative of it, we have much of the bad kind of Socialism, in which charity and help are given

---

[9] Charles Darwin, *The Origin of Species*, sixth edition (Harmondsworth, Penguin, 1985), 136–8; Charles Darwin, *The Descent of Man and Selection in Relation to Sex*, second edition (London, Murray, 1888), 133–45.

to individuals by society or by other individuals in a partial and unjust way – in a way that weakens rather than strengthens those to whom it is given: and also much industrial co-operation which degrades the individual. And we have to allow for the fact that the advance is not made in a direct line towards the ideal, but rather with much swaying from side to side, action and reaction being distributed over considerable periods of time. Thus the excess of the movement of the last century towards the emancipation of the individual, which resulted in breaking the semi-feudal bonds of society, has been compensated in this century by a movement towards the restoration of social unity and the re-assertion of the claims of society upon the individual. But what I am interested here to show is, that the idea of the organic evolution of society is equally opposed to both, and that it is gradually teaching all who think seriously and who try by its means to interpret the lessons of experience, to repudiate both, and to accept – as the ideal towards which we are inevitably, if with such painful slowness, tending – the ideal of a society which shall neither enslave men in order to unite them, nor break the bonds of humanity that knit them to each other in order to set them free.

Before concluding these remarks I should like to refer to one other point in which the idea of organic evolution is gradually but irresistibly lifting us above abstract and one-sided ways of thinking. It may safely be said that before this century the conditions of historical progress were very imperfectly understood. Those who wished for a better state of things generally hoped and expected it to be brought about, if it was brought about at all, by some sudden and revolutionary change of the fundamental institutions of society. Plato, the first great political idealist, met the question how his ideal was to be realized with the answer, that it would be realized only by the advent of some great philosopher-king, i.e. by the coming of some legislative leader of men, who should destroy at a stroke the imperfect institutions of the past, and lay the foundations of a new society on scientific principles. And it is easy to see that similar expectations were entertained by many at the time of the Puritan revolution in this country, and still more at the beginning of the French revolution. Men believed that, if they could remove those evils which they had inherited, a far better order of things could without much difficulty be established. But in both cases it was found that the work of destroying was easy, but the work of rebuilding supremely hard. This is the more remarkable in the case of the English revolution, because the immediate result of it was, in a sense, to set up a philosopher king – to raise to the highest position a man of great political genius, whose ideas on religious freedom, on the education of the people, and on the constitution of parliament as a representative assembly, anticipated many reforms which have only been realized in the present century. But Cromwell, great as were his achievements, found himself quite unable to raise the nation to the level of such institutions; and the immediate consequence of his premature attempts was a reaction of despair and a recurrence to the government of the Stuarts, which was the beginning of what we may call the most un-ideal period of English history. The seed of the future had been planted, but it took two centuries to grow to maturity. For it was impossible to make men free by setting up the institutions of freedom. What was needed was to create in the whole nation the spirit that could work such institutions, and that could not be done by any direct action of the law. Hence so often revolution is followed by reaction. 'Raw haste is half-sister to delay,'[10] and the eagerness that would not wait for the process of growth is compensated by a far longer period of despondency and waiting than would otherwise have been necessary.

I remember that in this city I once had the opportunity of listening to a very eminent socialist lecturer giving his description of what he conceived to be the ideal of social and economical organization, giving us in short 'Good news from Nowhere',[11] and I remember that, after the lecture, a working man – who must have been a good Scottish Calvinist – asked the lecturer whether he thought that, *if* the new ideal order of things was introduced to-morrow, the depravity of human nature would not begin soon to undermine it. The lecturer's answer I cannot exactly recall, but it

[10] Alfred, Lord Tennyson (1802–1892),

> To-morrow yet would reap to-day,
> As we bear blossom of the dead:
> Earn will the thrifty months, nor wed
> Raw Haste, half-sister to Delay

'Love they thou land, with love far brought' in *The Works of Tennyson: The Eversley Edition*, edited by Lord Hallam (London, Macmillan, 1907–8), lines 93–6.
[11] The allusion is, of course, to William Morris.

practically amounted to this, that the depravity of human nature was in the main due to bad institutions, and that in the new order of things every one would be so well satisfied with his lot that no such recoil need be feared. Alas! if one's hope for the future depended on the possibility of satisfying the insatiable desires of man, it would be the hope of filling the sieve of the Danaides.[12] That hope must lie in a progressive amelioration of institutions going along with the development of a higher social morality, and of a willingness and capacity in individuals to undertake the higher civic duties and responsibilities which such institutions bring. Improvement of institutions is useful only when it is due to the effort to make channels for new energies of individuals, who are at the same time becoming morally and intellectually fitted for the discharge of the new functions. Sometimes, indeed, the very energy called out in the struggle to establish such institutions goes far to produce the habitual cast of mind which is necessary to work them. But the possibilities on either side are strictly limited by the conditions of human life, and it is as absurd to suppose that we can make men suddenly virtuous and happy by a fundamental change in the outward conditions of their existence as to suppose that we can improve men permanently without ameliorating the outward conditions of their existence. The application of the idea of evolution to human life is teaching us to avoid two opposite errors. On the one hand, it is teaching us to avoid the error, in which even great writers of the last century like Adam Smith were entangled, the error of treating human nature as a fixed quantity, and supposing that what was practicable and expedient for the men of their own time was in some peculiar sense natural, and had been, and always would be, practicable and expedient for mankind in all past and future ages. It is teaching us that human nature is extraordinarily flexible, that it is even capable of the most fundamental changes by the growth of new habits and ways of life, that it has a wonderful power of adapting itself to new circumstances, and that

---

[12] The fifty daughters of Danaus, King of Argos, were known as the Danaides. They married the fifty sons of Aegyptus. On their wedding night, commanded by their father, they murdered their husbands and presented their father with their husbands' heads. They were condemned to eternal punishment in Hades, with the exception of Hypermnestra who disobeyed the order, by having infinitely to draw water in sieves from a deep well.

it is absurd, therefore, to argue from the effect of any measure on the modern Englishman or Scotsman what would have been its effect upon his medieval predecessors, still more to its effect upon the ancient Romans or Greeks. And it is as uncertain to argue from the present to the future as to the past. The idea of evolution, therefore, suggests to us a lesson of hope. It enables us to believe that human life and character may be, to a degree not easily calculable, remoulded by the new ideas that are now pouring in upon us from so many sources; and that more perfect relations of men with men may be established in the future society than have ever yet been imagined. On the other hand, it teaches us that such changes cannot be the creation of a day or a year, but only of the slow working of man's new circumstances upon his thoughts, and of the continuous reaction of his thoughts upon his circumstances. It teaches us that the ultimate result of such action and reaction, the form into which the future life of man will eventually be cast, is not capable of being anticipated by the wisest of men, except in dim and distant outline. The future, no doubt, will grow out of the present, but the process of growth is too complex to be definitely forecast. Yet, on the other hand, it must be admitted that growth in man's life is increasingly the result of conscious and deliberate action. We cannot draw the plan of the future commonwealth which will be the result of the combined working of all human minds upon each other, and upon their circumstances. But each one can co-operate with the progressive forces that are working around him, can give his best thought and consideration to the particular improvements in the condition of men that are possible in the field in which his lot is cast, and which therefore he understands.

The problem of human life, it has been said, is to 'turn necessity into freedom'. In other words, man cannot determine the primary conditions of his life, or prevent them from continually being changed by a process which neither the individual, nor even, beyond a small extent, the nation, can control. But he can react upon these conditions and make them the means of developing a better kind of life in himself. Within our own time circumstances have altered more rapidly than in any precious generation. The world, so to speak, has been drawing close together and becoming one instead of many worlds. Not many years ago nations carried on their lives almost in separation, or were connected only at one or two points of contact. But now every strong influence passes rapidly from one nation to another. The discovery of the laws of nature and the invention of ways in which such discoveries may be turned to the uses of man, are carried on by the continuous co-operation of men of science throughout the world, and every movement of artistic or scientific thought spreads unhindered by any difficulties of communication. The movements of trade and commerce have become cosmopolitan, so that waves of elevation and depression pass over the globe, involving the success or ruin to the thousands who had nothing to do with their origination. The horizon of politics has widened, so that the ebb and flow of reforming or conservative influences in every nation become part of one great movement. And we can see that these causes will go on operating in still more decisive ways in the future, till it shall become impossible to avoid a kind of co-operation and even union of all nations, of which we now see only the beginnings.

Now, I mention these obvious facts, because, as I have already said, the problem of the modern world *is to turn these necessities into freedom*. It is, in other words, to make them the means of improving our lives, instead of allowing them to crush us. We cannot, e.g, prevent the enormous growth and concentration of trade, the enormous development of great cities, with all the dangers that they bring, especially the danger of the formation of a pauperized and lawless class of men who either by accident or by their own fault, or by a mixture of the two, have been thrown out of their place in the social organism, and must therefore seek to prey upon it. But we can set ourselves to think how these new and increasing dangers are to be met, and the bonds of society to be reknit under the new conditions. It cannot be done by any simple and mechanical prescription. It is folly to suppose that any abstract principle of Socialism or Individualism will be adequate to the task of elevating the whole character of a nation and remoulding its institutions into the fit organ and support of such a renewed character. What is wanted is no such quack medicine for all the diseases of the social body, but a patient study of all the new circumstances of the people's life, and an equally patient effort to find the ways of turning them to a good issue.

One of the most encouraging symptoms of the present state of things is the way in which the municipal authorities of the great cities of this country have been trying to do their duty. The first experiments of the union of freedom and order, which were made by mankind, were made in municipalities, in the civic communities of Greece; and it is a good sign of the times that there is such a reawaking of civic life and such a renewed effort to face the diffi- culties which have arisen in our crowded modern city populations. I do not need to tell you that what success they have had is due in great measure to the fact that so many experienced men of business have been willing to devote to the service of the city the same energy and ability which have gained them success in their own private affairs. And every step in advance in the future must be gained by the same means. Two at least of our prominent political leaders have learned their first lessons of administration in municipal work, and it is perhaps to this source as much as to any other that we can look for the training of statesmen, who will combine wide views of policy and devotion to the people's good with practical experience of affairs, states men who believe in progress without being led away by revolutionary and impracticable ideals.[13] And perhaps this Civic Society may do something to help in the development of such powers.[14] I have no great belief in mere theory to produce any good result, even when such theory is the result of a genuine sympathy with suffering and a genuine desire to promote the common good. But I have a great belief in the theories of those who have such sympathy, when they are developed in close and patient contact

---

[13] He is obviously alluding to Joseph Chamberlain (1836–1914) who was three times Mayor of Birmingham and became MP for Birmingham West. He was President of the Board of Trade (1880–5) and President of the Local Government Board (1886). At the time of this address he was Secretary of State for Colonies (1895–1903). A number of other prominent politicians at this time rose through the ranks of local government and on to prominence at Westminster, including John Burns (1858–1943) and John Poyntz Spencer (1835–1910).

[14] Henry Jones established the Glasgow Civic Society in 1897. In a letter to Mary Talbot, Caird summarised the aim of his lecture:

'My object is to show that in several matters we are getting beyond the abstractness of socialism and individualism – that we are all really, whatever we call ourselves, both Socialists and Individualists and that the idea of the organic nature of society and of its development affords a common basis on which the members of a Civic Society may discuss each particular measure for the welfare of the community'.

Sir Henry Jones and J. H. Muirhead, *The Life and Philosophy of Edward Caird* (Glasgow, Maclehose, Jackson and Co., 1921) 217–18.

with facts, and when they are tested by thorough discussion with those who possess an equally valuable, though somewhat dissimilar, experience, and who therefore look upon the subject from different points of view. I believe that, if they are carried on under such conditions, the discussions of this Society may at least do something to develop in its members that temper of mind which combines practical energy and hopefulness with the impartiality and security of science.

10
The Coming of Socialism

HENRY JONES

The progress of social reform must be slow and uncertain, so long as the nature of society is not understood; and society can not be understood till the methods of science are substituted for the empiricism which distinguishes the right way from the wrong only by trying both.

This was the subject of our first Article.[1]

Even science must fail to interpret society unless it adopts as its regulative hypothesis the principle which has produced society. It must, therefore, cease to employ the mechanical metaphors derived from 'Nature', and seek in the conception of rational spirit its only clue.

This was the theme of our second Article.[2]

But spirit itself has been mechanically understood, even by many Idealists; for they have opposed the activities by which spirit unites its objects with itself to those by which it asserts and establishes facts against itself. They have proved that the real world is ideal, but not that the ideal world is real. They have shown that spirit makes all things into elements in its own life, but not that in doing so it deepens and enriches their independent objective significance.

This was shown in our third Article.[3]

In the present Article I shall first test the truth of this view of the concurrent realisation of the self and the not-self by reference

---

[1] First essay in *The Working Faith of the Social Reformer and Other Essays* (London, Macmillan, 1910).
[2] Second essay in *WFSR*.
[3] Third essay in *WFSR*.

to Private Property, and then illustrate the significance of it by applying it to the general relations of Individualism and Socialism.

Private property manifestly provides a crucial instance for testing the truth of our principle. Here, if anywhere, the concurrent realisation of the self and the not-self is impossible; for the very essence of private property appears to be an unmitigated assertion of exclusive rights. Surely, it will be said, what is mine is not another's, and what is another's is not mine. The privacy of property disappears when it is made common; its community when it is made private.

The only exception, the only property which can be both mine and another's is 'spiritual' property, if the term can be allowed. Men may share the *same* opinions, seek and secure the *same* moral or social ends, and each grow richer thereby. The share of each in spiritual spoils grows with their distribution. No individual becomes ignorant by teaching others; nor do the wills which unite in the pursuit of a common good lose either their privacy or their spontaneity.

But *material* property seems to have nothing of this character. Gold or land cannot be mine unless it is not another's, nor another's unless it is not mine. It can become another's only if I relinquish it or am deprived of it. Nor does it matter whether that 'other' be another individual, or a civic community, or a State.

In this contrast between material property, such as land or gold, and spiritual property, such as knowledge or virtue, we come once more upon the essential distinction between spirit and nature. Physical nature is always self-resistant; its parts are held together as a whole by the mechanical strain of mutual exclusion, and by the dependence which is necessity. But spirit can have no genuine 'other'. It must be universal, un–divided or individual, penetrate its object, and therefore be *itself* in its opposite.

Hence, if self-exclusion, the mutual repulsion of parts and elements, be the last word about material things, and if property be purely a material thing, then the assertion of one economic will against another, the 'struggle for existence', the brute force of competition, in which the individual not only strengthens himself but weakens his neighbour, are ultimate facts of social life. The individual will, so far as it asserts itself in material property, must therefore be expelled, if social ends are to be harmoniously sought.

But Idealism, in asserting the relation of the object to the subject, has denied the utter or complete materiality of any object whatsoever. And it is precisely this assumption – that 'property', is at any time, or in any object, a *merely* material fact – which I desire to question. I must question it the more closely because it is the source of some of the most stubborn obstacles to practical progress in social matters and of some of the most difficult social problems. I refer, in particular, to such problems as the extension and limits of communal or State enterprise in manufacturing and trading, the rights of the State to prohibit or regulate trusts, combinations and unions, and, in general, the apparent antagonism of socialistic and individualistic ends, of private and social rights.

Let us first make the assumption clear. If we take public opinion as it stands to-day, we shall find it well-nigh unanimous on one point. Both those who advocate and those who resist the extension of the business functions of a municipality or State consider that such extension can be effected only by limiting the range of individual enterprise. It seems too obvious for discussion that the more the organised community undertakes to possess, or control, or do, the narrower the sphere of individual activity, enterprise, and owner-ship. But, while Socialists and Individualists agree as to the effects of the extension of the communal powers, they differ as to their practical value. The former welcome the extension on the ground that it would limit the individual's opportunity for doing wrong; the latter oppose it on the ground that it must limit the individual's opportunity for doing right.

Public ownership of the means of production is advocated, not merely or primarily because the community would show greater enterprise, or be economically a more efficient producer than the private person, but because it seems to be the only means within our power of avoiding the manifold evils which spring from the cupidity that comes of irresponsible private ownership. The word 'State', we are told, has taken to itself new connotations – 'the State idea has changed its content. Whatever State control may have meant fifty years ago, it never meant hostility to private property as such. Now, for us, and for as far ahead as we can see, it means this and little else.'[a,4]

[a] *Fabian Essays*, p. 208.

[4] Hubert Bland, 'The Outlook', in *Fabian Essays*, ed. G. Bernard Shaw (London, Allen, 1920: first edition 1889), 208.

Public ownership is resisted on the same ground. The individualist insists, sometimes wrongly and sometimes rightly, that communal production is wasteful and economically inefficient. But his real objection to it does not spring from that cause. On the contrary, he objects to it whether it be wasteful or not, and objects to it more vigorously even if it is *not* wasteful, for in that case it invades the province of individual rights more successfully, commits a wrong without bringing immediate retribution, and therefore, in the long run, brings the greater social danger. For he, too, sees in communal appropriation 'hostility to private property', and in State and municipal trading the competition of the whole with its own members.

Full agreement as to the *exclusive* relation of the private and the public will, and the direct antagonism of private and public rights of ownership – such is the attitude of both Individualists and Socialists.

It follows that this social problem is material or economical only on the surface. In its deeper bearings it is ethical: it is the question of the rights of personality. And questions of right are always fundamental; for rights are ultimate, and involve the person. A nation or individual which is fighting for its rights is fighting for its life. It is as a right that the Individualist would limit the enterprises of the State or municipality ; it is as a right that the Socialist would extend them. And to do them justice we must admit that 'rights' are sacred to both alike. No Socialist would advocate the violation of a citizen's *rights*: but he does not admit that the citizen has rights of property against the State. All property, he believes, belongs to the State; it is held by the individual as a loan or trust; and the State can resume its borrowed property whenever, in peace or war, it sees occasion. The Individualist, on the other hand, believes that the rights of the individual are final. Even if they did emanate originally from social relations, and the State has given them as well as helped to maintain them, still the gift is a veritable gift, made once for all. If the State in national straits has to resume them, its resumption is only a borrowing from the individual, to be repaid with interest when once the crisis is over.

The collision of views between the Individualist and Socialist is thus direct. The opponents stand on the same ground: for both assume that individual *and* social rights in the *same* objects are incompatible, and that the rights in each case are fundamental. Hence any compromise necessitated by the exigencies of social life is deplored as a wrong; and it is effected only after a severe struggle between the parties. The equilibrium thus secured is essentially unstable, and it is disturbed whenever a new exigency arises.

This is one of the main causes both of the present social unrest and of the helpless empiricism of our social methods. Nor is there any hope of better ways except in examining the ground from which the antagonism springs. And this can be done with the better prospect of success inasmuch as the assumption made by both sides has been examined by neither, nor has either side realised the significance of its own negation. The controversy persists, in fact, just because both the defence and the attack have lacked uncompromising thoroughness.

The Individualist can prove that the utter denial of all rights of private property will destroy the State, on whose behalf it is made, by destroying the individuality of its members. Let the individual own nothing but himself, and he will not have a self to own. Having no foothold whatsoever in the outer world, he would live only on sufferance; having no right to impress his own will on any object he would not be able to express himself in any act: he would have no sphere for his activities, no trust or responsibilities, no duties, and, therefore, no opportunity of realising his personality or learning virtue.

The State – if, indeed, such a community of mere dependants could be called a State – might be benevolent to him, feeding, clothing, and housing him, satisfying every want as it arose, or forestalling them like a mother with her babe. But as man reaches manhood he develops other wants than these. He wants to rule his own life, to exercise his own powers, to pursue his own ends. The State might engage him; but it would be in labour not his 'own', upon objects not his own, and in the service of purposes not his own; for the State has said of all things, 'Not Thine, but Mine.' In short, if Socialism is verily the extinction of all individual property, men would be reduced into things. This result is concealed from the advocate of such extinction by the fact that he unconsciously retains the sense and rights of individual ownership. Indeed, he makes every citizen heir to the good of the whole State. But this is either to reinstate Individualism in an aggravated form, or it is to rise above the distinction of 'Mine and Thine' from which the whole controversy has originated. Private property may, as is alleged, give occasion for cupidity, competition, aggression, the untold miseries of extreme poverty, and the no less tragedy of unjust, profligate, and irresponsible wealth. Nevertheless it is the condition of the opposite virtues – of loyal service, of justice, of generosity, of manhood itself. The means of doing what is right are the same as the means of doing wrong. There must be choice between them, and the choice must be real; and that is not possible unless personality has its own sphere and inalienable station in the outer world. The remedy does not lie, as the Socialist believes, in removing the *occasion* of cupidity and the other evils, but in putting the occasion to a better use. The Individualist is right in insisting upon private property as unconditionally necessary both for the individual and the State.

But to acknowledge this exclusive side of property and even of self-hood, and to acknowledge it in a full and unqualified way, is, after all, to admit only one half of the truth.

If we examine the conception of private property more closely, we shall find that it means more than mere possession by one person to the exclusion of others. Mere possession and exclusion does not exhaust the significance or express the sacredness of private property. It does not account for the *right*, which is the essential element. A man may possess a thing which he does not own; he may hold it against others, like a robber his booty. To convert it into *property* requires more than his private will to own it himself and to exclude others. In the first place, property must be regarded as an instrument of utility. A claim to a thing which a man can never use, either directly or by exchange, is a claim to an encumbrance. In owning such a thing he owns less than nothing. Property incapable of use is really not property but dead matter, and matter out of place. To make it property is to make it the possible instrument of a will ; and anything which doubles or halves its use, doubles or halves the property. It is relation to man's desires and will, that is, it is the spiritual aspect of a thing which makes it property.

In the next place, property implies not only utility to the owner, but the *recognition of the ownership* by the society in which he lives. It is true that I must be able to say of an object that it is mine, and mine as means of possible personal ends; but I must also be able to add that it is mine *by right*. And in order that I may say this, society must be a partner in my act of appropriation. The purely individual or isolated will cannot constitute a right, for a right is an essentially social matter. To my statement, 'It is Mine', Society must add, 'It is Thine, and Thine by my enactment.'

An important principle lies here, which it will be well to illustrate. When I say that a thing is mine by right, I mean that my possession of it *ought* to be recognised by others. My possession implies a social obligation on my fellows. I consider that they must refrain of their own accord from appropriating or injuring my property. Their recognition of my ownership is not an act of grace on their part, but a claim I have upon them. I consider myself wronged if I must protect my property by force, as if I were a robber. The most individualistic of private owners, the most strenuous in asserting that he can do as he likes with his own and that his property is the mere instrument and creation of his own private will, is usually the first to call upon the State to assert and make good his rights. But he is not aware that, in doing so, he is acknowledging that his property is an expression of the social will; that his ownership, whenever it becomes a right, is due not alone nor primarily to his having said *Mine*, but to the State having said *Thine*. He is calling the State to ratify not his will, but its own.

Hence we can condemn the mere Individualist from his own mouth. In his claim for the acknowledgment and defence of his property as a right, he is admitting that his property is an institution of the State. His demand that the State shall throw its aegis over his property means that the State, in protecting him, is only making good its own decrees.

Hence, further, the property of an individual is a symbol of renunciation on the part of society. Property is an ethical fact, implying, on the part of society, the recognition of a restraining and binding though self-imposed law. Indeed, the essence of private property is that it is the result of an act whereby society endows its individual members with rights against itself. Merely private self-assertion can never of itself create property; that can be done only by the affirmation of the social will. The individual's rights are therefore not individual in the isolating sense, but social. They are rights because they are *not* merely private. The more private they are the more they tend to vanish as rights, and the more the property becomes a mere possession held by force. On the other hand, the more full and sacred the rights the more they embody the mind of society, and are endowed and endorsed by the social will.

We arrive thus at a conclusion which is as important as it is interesting. We took up the conception of private property for analysis because it seemed *prima facie* to contradict our main thesis, namely, that spirit, in breaking down all final antagonism to itself and abolishing every exclusive 'other', nevertheless did not absorb that other or nullify its opposition to itself, but rather fortified its opposite against itself by putting *itself* into it. But instead of contradicting, it illustrates our main principle, exhibiting the same phenomena as we have already observed in knowledge and in morals. If, in knowing, reason does away with the dualism of spirit and nature, it at the same time establishes the order of nature as a reality (though no longer an unspiritual reality), which gives the rule to reason and stands as the ideal of the whole process of knowing. If, in action, spirit negates the rights of the passions to war against reason, it at the same time gives them new rights and a new freedom and range of utterance as the instruments of reason, and even as its elements and self-expression.

In a similar way, as private property is really property only when it is an instrument which the individual can use, or when it is means of his self-realisation through action, it implies, and indeed is, a social fact. Property is a sphere of activities, a 'station and its duties',[5] a system of obligations set up by the individual against himself. On the other hand, as private property is more than individual appropriation, as it is rightful ownership, it means the recognition by society of a law which imposes restraints on its own caprice, and a system of obligations which it must observe, and observe the more scrupulously, regard as the more binding, because they are expressions of its own will. Private property, in a word, is an institution wherein the individual finds a rule of action in society and society a rule of action in the individual.

With the progress of civilisation the rights which the individual on the one side or the State on the other establishes within its

---

[5] This, of course is an allusion to Bradley's doctrine of my station and its duties articulated in *Ethical Studies* (Oxford, Clarendon Press, 1872).

'other' become at once more wide and various and more sacred. The more highly developed an individual's morality, that is, the more his will is socialised, the more his property and person find their use and function in social activities. And, on the other hand, a developed society accords more independence to its members than any other. It recognizes more of their rights, and it is more strenuous in their defence. So complete is the self-alienation of the State, that it will maintain the rights of its citizen against itself. He can confront its actions with its laws by help of the laws; and, by constitutional means, he can arraign the State-that-is before the State-that-ought-to-be. In short, in the right that it accords its citizens, the State gives a convincing example of the evolution of spiritual subjects by fortifying their opposites against themselves; for it plants *itself* in its own members. Even 'private property' illustrates the concurrent growth of both the subjective and objective aspects of spirit.

I must now endeavour to apply our principle to one of the gravest social problems of our time.

Amongst the social changes most desired and most feared in our times is that interference with individual rights, or that extension of communal activity, implied in the word 'Socialism'. Both those who desire and those who fear this change are prone to regard it as inevitable, and as taking place with an accelerating velocity. The new economic conditions arising from industrial combinations, the vastness and compactness of the organisations both of capital and labour, and the shock of their impact when they collide, seem to many reflective people to threaten both the freedom of the individual and the stability of the State. It is concluded, and often unwillingly concluded, that the State must put forth more powers; must control, or buy out, or appropriate, or socialise by some method or other the means of production. If it does not, it will either become the victim of the will of the Capitalist, or fall into the hands of United Labour, which is hindered from seizing the reins of the State only because, as yet, it is not fully awake to its own powers.

Nay, we are told that Socialism is already come.

> Step by step the political power and political organisation of the country have been used for individual ends, until to-day the largest employer of labour is one of the ministers of the Crown (the Postmaster-General), and almost every conceivable trade is, some-

where or other, carried on by parish, municipality, or the National Government itself, without the intervention of any middleman or capitalist ... Besides our international relations, and the army, navy, police, and the courts of justice, the community now carries on for itself, in some part or other of these islands, the post-office, telegraphs, carriage of small commodities, coinage, surveys, the regulation of the currency and note issue, the provision of weights and measures, the making, sweeping, lighting, and repairing of streets, roads, and bridges, life insurance, the grant of annuities, shipbuilding, stockbroking, banking, farming, and money-lending. It provides for many thousands of us from birth to burial – midwifery, nursery, education, board and lodging, vaccination, medical attendance, medicine, public worship, amusements, and interment. It furnishes and maintains its own museums, parks, art-galleries, libraries, concert-halls ... markets, slaughter-houses, fire-engines, lighthouses, pilots, ferries, surf-boats ... public baths, wash-houses ... cow meadows, etc., etc.

Besides its direct supersession of private enterprise, the State now registers, inspects, and controls nearly all the industrial functions which it has not yet absorbed.[b]

Then follows another significant list, concluding with the words:

Even the kind of package in which some articles shall be sold is duly prescribed, so that the individual capitalist shall take no advantage of his position. On every side he is being registered, inspected, controlled, and eventually superseded by the community; and in the meantime he is compelled to cede for public purposes an ever-increasing share of his rent and interest. Even in the fields still abandoned to private enterprise, its operations are thus every day more closely limited, in order that the anarchic competition of private greed ... may not utterly destroy the State. All this has been done by 'practical' men, ignorant, that is to say, of any scientific sociology, believing Socialism to be the most foolish of dreams.[c]

Now what are we to say of this picture? That it is partly the effect of rhetorical grouping? And that where operations are so various and so extensive in scale as they are in a great State, skilful grouping may bring out almost any result? Not merely so, I believe. The facts are in the main accurately set forth, and the general tend-

---

[b] See *Fabian Essays*, pp. 47–8. [The quotation is from Sidney Webb, 'The Basis of Socialism: Historic'.]

[c] *Ibid.*, pp. 49, 50. [Sidney Webb.]

ency of the times is not in the least doubtful. The manifold industries now conducted by public bodies were all 'at one time left to private individuals, and were a source of legitimate investment and capital'. Social industrial functions have enormously increased, and they have all been assumed through the dispossession of individuals.

But before we take the side of the Socialist in rejoicing at this fact, or with the Individualist in bewailing it – before we take sides, if take sides we must – it will be well to ask a question which both have practically overlooked. There is no doubt that State and civic enterprise have increased, but has private enterprise contracted? Can the former increase only at the expense of the latter? Are the two spheres mutually exclusive, or is it possible that the general law of the growth of spiritual subjects, whether individual or social, holds here too, and that each in developing may strengthen its opposite?

Let us look once more at the facts of the case – the facts cited by the Socialist to prove that 'every day they limit private enterprise more closely, and by eliminating private ownership remove the anarchic competition of private greed'. What do we see when we look abroad at the commercial and industrial community of to-day? Is it a mammoth State, a Leviathan, gradually absorbing its citizens into itself, annihilating their private wills and all the good and evil which spring therefrom, and reducing them first into mere employees and then into mere tools? Or is it a country whose people are more free, whose private wealth is greater, whose individual enterprises are more far-reaching, whose persons are more effective in their command of the material conditions of life than at any other period in its history? And is competition less keen, and the race for wealth no longer run, except by the few? We are told by those who are engaged in business, whether its scale be great or small, that competition is daily becoming more sharp, and that the weak and incompetent are being eliminated with more and more automatic certainty and less and less mercy. And is private greed disappearing under the new régime? What does the moralist fear more, or with better reasons to-day, than that the new industrial conditions will absorb the mind of the nation to a degree that imperils the deeper foundations of its welfare?

The contention that 'Socialism is already upon us' is true, if by that is meant that the method of organised communal enterprise is more in use; but it is not true if it means that the individual's sphere of action, or his power to extract utilities, that is, wealth, out of his material environment has been limited. It is being overlooked that the displacement of the individual is but the first step in his re-instalment; and that what is represented as the 'Coming of Social-ism' may, with equal truth, be called the 'Coming of Individualism'. *The functions of the State and City on the one side and those of the individual on the other, have grown together.* Both private and communal enterprise have enormously increased during the last century, and, account for it as we may, they are both still increasing. Hence it is possible that here, once more, the principle is illustrated according to which the realisation of the self, whether on the part of the individual or of the State, is at the same time the realisation of the self's opposite. It is possible that the State as a single organ-ism grows in power, even as its citizens acquire freedom; and that the more free and enterprising the citizens, the more sure the order and the more extensive the operations of the State. The antagonism of the State and the citizen is one of those things, taken for granted without being examined, which have done most mischief in social matters. It is possible, at least, that by its regulation of industries the State while limiting caprice has enlarged freedom; that in appro-priating industrial enterprises it has liberated the economic power of its citizens – nay, that it has multiplied owners, and increased for them the utilities of wealth, which is to increase wealth itself.

If we judged things solely by their first appearances, the con-clusion is inevitable that appropriation by the State means the expropriation of the citizen, and nothing further. Did the State not carry our letters, it is certain that private enterprise would do so, and reap the profits. And yet I can conceive no one, from the king to the beggar, who would take the carrying of letters from the hands of the State. Everyone recognises that by the present method his private purposes are being realised better than they could by any other. And the publicity of the means in nowise militates against the privacy of the communications. Nor does the use of that means by all diminish their value for each. On the contrary, through the combined desires of the many the desires of each are met with greater facility and efficiency.

We must, therefore, take into account not only the displacement of the individual capitalist who might have run the penny post, but also the productive use of the capital of the vast multitude who employ the penny post. The actual result of this State invention is to make us all shareholders in a vast enterprise whose services and utilities are greater to each because they are open to all – or to all who can buy stamps. The State in this undertaking has indeed prevented the individual from saying '*Not Thine*' to his neighbours; but it has also enabled its citizens to say '*Mine*', with new significance over a wider range of utilities. And the essence and value of property do not lie in exclusion, in saying '*Not Thine*', as the unsocialised and unmoralised agent believes, but in its inclusion, in widening and deepening the meaning of '*Mine*'.

But this aspect of the truth is ignored by the Socialist. He sees in this instance only the supersession of the one private capitalist, and he ignores the creation of the millions of active shareholders. He sees the displacement, but overlooks the re-instalment. He overlooks the fact that the State only holds the capital for its members, that it gives back the profits in utilities, and that it makes itself the instrument of the individual will, and thereby indefinitely enlarges its powers. For the State, after all, acts for the individual, and by means of the individual in this matter; it organises the powers of its citizens, but it does not annul them.

We should reach the same results, on the whole, if we examined other State and Civic undertakings. And although I am by no means prepared to say that there is no limit or rule to State and Civic enterprises, I may claim that both the abstract opposition to, and the abstract advocacy of, State or municipal action, on the ground that it is an encroachment on individual enterprise and nothing else, are radically unintelligent and false. They rest on categories of mere exclusion, which in the sphere of rational activities are never true.

All legitimate State or Civic enterprise means the organisation rather than the elimination of individual wills; and this, in turn, means not only more united action on the part of the whole, but more efficient action and a deeper individuality on the part of the members.

Organisation no doubt carries with it limitation. When we become members of a club, or church, or a body of college fellows, or a business concern, we give up something of our own will. In this respect all social usages, traditions, institutions, and laws, are what Rousseau thought them – bonds and chains; and the free man would be the man who ran wild in woods, enjoyed the liberty of the consistent Individualist, and of the wild ass. But, precisely in the degree to which the purposes of the society are rational and it attains these purposes, what is limited for the individual is not his freedom but his caprice, not his power to do right but his inclination to do wrong.

And such, on the whole, are the so-called 'interferences with the individual', which are implied in the restrictions, the control, the activities of the State and the city. Either by explicit ordinances, or by a recognised code of usages, customs and manners, we are limited in a thousand ways. We cannot ramble whither we will over meadow and through forest as our blue-painted ancestors could; we must keep to the paths and roads. We cannot be judges in our own cause, nor right our own wrongs. We cannot even make any bargains we please, nor do quite as we like with our own. We cannot employ women in pits though they be willing, nor little children in factories, nor men in foul air and unwholesome premises.

But the good citizen and the intelligent capitalist does not desire to do these things. What the legislature has done, on the whole, is to limit the will to do what is wrong and stupid. It is only the pseudo-freedom of irrational caprice which has been limited. Nor has the State invaded any rights in such action; for the liberty to do wrong is not a right, but the perversion of a right and its negation; and the elimination of caprice is no loss to any one: it is one of the ends of all moral and social development.

But there is much more than this negation and limitation of the individual's caprice involved in his organisation into society. A good law, or social institution, is, at bottom, not negative but positive. It apportions rights, and gives the individual a more effective personality. In taking from the individual the right to be judge of his own cause, and avenger of his own wrongs, it re-instates it on a better basis. Though at the moment of contention we might desire to take the law into our own hands, we recognise that our neighbour would also desire it, and that on the whole the State can do this business better for both. The State does not annul the will for justice of either party, but puts an instrument in their hands for the better realisation of that will.

Now I believe this reinstatement of the individual will on a more effective basis takes place in nearly all of the matters which the State and the city undertake to perform. At least, it is a striking fact that, in this country at least, in spite of its purely empirical and unscientific social methods, there has been very little disposition to withdraw from the city or the State any industrial or other undertakings which have been once committed to them. It is not merely that it is difficult to do so, that private enterprise cannot enter into the arena or hold its own against a trading municipality or State, but that, except in the rarest instances, the reversion to private enterprise is not desired.

The reason is that, in spite of displacement, the individual has received from State and Civic organisation a vast accession of strength. The organisation of modern activities, of which the State is only the supreme instance, has placed in the hands of private persons the means of conceiving and carrying out enterprises that were beyond the dreams of the richest of capitalists in the past. The merchant in his office, the employer in his yard, can command far wider and more varied services, and make their will felt to the ends of the earth. The imperial post, the telegraphic system, the civic lighting and cleansing of the streets – what are they except most powerful instruments of the individual will? The State and the city have appropriated these undertakings and many more, but it makes over their utilities to the citizen, liberates his will for other purposes, and multiplies its power a thousandfold. More men can now say 'Mine' of more things. Citizens have been drawn into the activities of the State, for their good has been identified with it in new ways; and enterprises which in previous times were outside the range of their lives are now within it. We can say '*Ours*' of parks, tramways, bridges, art-galleries, public libraries and museums; and if we are worthy of membership in this organism of many functions, we would as soon impair or destroy these common goods as squander our 'private' wealth. No doubt in all these cases we must say '*Thine*' as well as 'Mine', for the utilities are common. The negative aspect of property is becoming more contracted, but that is no loss to anyone, not even to the jealous and unsocialised unit, if he would only believe it.

Once it is clearly seen that the essence of property is the ownership of utilities, the exclusion of others becomes a secondary matter. It is quite true that common ownership and common enterprises turn us into limited proprietors; but they make us limited proprietors of indefinitely large utilities. Through the common use of public means to meet individual wants, the real possessions and power of every one are enlarged. Break up the common use, and the use for each by himself will be less. Take the individual out of the organised state, disentangle his life from that of his neighbours, give him 'the freedom of the wild ass', make him king of an empire of savages, and he will be as naked and poor and powerless as the lowest of his subjects – except, perhaps, for some extra plumes and shells.

Thus we return once more to our main principle; in the mechanical sphere equilibrium implies exclusion and resistance; in the sphere of life, and especially of rational life, mutual exclusion gives way to mutual inclusion. State and citizen live and develop only in and through each other. It is the unmoralised community and the unsocialised individual which follow methods of resistance and mutual exclusion. As they grow in strength – that is, in the power to conceive wider ends and to carry them out – State and citizen enter more deeply the one into the other. If the State owns the citizen the citizen also owns the State; each finds in the other the means of its power and the defence of its rights. So that the Individualist might well desire more 'State interference' and the socialist more 'private rights'; for the best means of producing strong men is a highly organised State, and the only way of producing a strong State is to make the citizens own so much, care for so much, be responsible for so much, that each can say, without injury to his neighbour, 'The State is mine'.

This concurrent evolution of social and individual rights, duties, and powers is inconceivable on the ordinary view. But history teaches it. I am not sure that the growth of civilisation teaches anything else of equal importance. The civic States of Greece, first experiments as they were in corporate freedom, both gave more freedom to their citizens and performed more functions themselves than the earlier despotisms. But if we contrast the Greek with modern States and municipalities we shall find that their service to their citizens was as much less varied and effective as the recognition of their private rights was more limited. Life was not so safe on the streets of Athens as it is in London, nor were the conditions of public health or the means of satisfying so many wants so fully or securely provided. Athens did far less for its citizens. On the other hand, it is not necessary to add that it respected their rights much less.

It is the inspiring spectacle of all men caring better for each, and each caring more for all, that the evolution of human society presents. That this is the conscious purpose and set aim of either men or States in general may be impossible to maintain. But the principles of life operate when they are not observed: men reason without knowing logic, and social motives operate when they are not watched. Indeed, the human spirit is never completely conscious of itself, and the ends attained both by men and States are often greater than their aims. Men set forth to realise private ends, to seek their private welfare, and they find that in doing so they have helped to realise the social order. And the same truth holds of States: in seeking the well-being of the citizens, which is becoming more and more their ruling purpose, they not only enlarge their own functions, but strengthen and secure themselves. So that, taking both sides together, and viewing both aspects of the truth, the process shows itself to be both a more intense integration and a more diverse articulation of the moral cosmos. It is synthesis and analysis at one stroke; it is the growth of society as an active unity with an ever-increasing number of obligations and variety of services to the individual, and also the deepening of the individuality of the citizens as free and efficient personalities.

If this be true, we are entitled to look to the future not without confidence. No doubt the creation of ever new and more powerful combinations within the State brings difficulties. They can neither be let alone nor 'regulated' or 'annulled' rashly. And in our dealings with them we cannot lean on the experience of the race, for in this respect our times are untried. Nevertheless these combinations, whether of labour or capital, and the regulation or assumption of their functions by the State, are not things to be in themselves deplored. Organisation is economy and power, and never the *mere* negation and displacement of the private will. It is not, therefore, to be resisted and retarded as a matter of course. It is possible for order and liberty to grow together: it is certain that they cannot grow apart.

But, it will be asked, does this mean that we are to welcome any and every municipal or State activity? Is all increase of corporate enterprise a liberation of the individual's force? By no means, I would answer. There are many reasons why every new departure should be carefully scrutinised, and tried by every test. The dislocation of private enterprises is not to be lightly entered upon: probably never, if the good results which accrue terminate in a class and do not raise the State as a whole, or if private combination can serve the purpose with equal efficiency. The entrance of a municipality or State into the competitive field is not in all respects on a par with the entrance of a private competitor. And, above all, the range of the activities of the State or municipality varies with its intellectual capacity and moral strength. There is hardly too narrow a limit to the functions of a weak State or a corrupt city, or too wide a limit for the intelligent and strong.

The essential point, however, is this – that the limits are not to be fixed by any conception of the abstract antagonism of society and the individual: for each of these is true to itself precisely in the degree to which it is faithful to its opposite. The criterion of the action of the State is the effective freedom of its citizens. There remains in the moral life of the citizens an intensely individual element which the State must never over-ride. The rights of personality can be wisely sacrificed to nothing, nor its good postponed to either city or State or humanity. But, on the other hand, the sovereignty of the individual's will and all its sacredness come from its identification with a wider will. His rights are rooted in the rights of others; and all the rights alike draw their life-sap from the moral law, the universal good, the *objective* rightness, of which no jot or tittle can pass away. Hence, the individual can resist the will of the community or the extension of the functions of his city or State only when he has identified his own will with a will that is more universal, more concrete, and the source of higher imperatives than either. And this means that he can resist the State only for the good of the State, and never *merely* for his own profit. The content of the authoritative will must always be the common good, and the common good must always assume a personal form.

In a word, the essence of society is moral. It is only on moral grounds that we can determine the nature and limits of its functions. And the social reformer who comprehends this fact, so far from either welcoming or resisting the increase of social enterprises as a matter of course, will seek for only one supreme innovation, namely, that of *moralising our social relations as they stand.* And the need for this is paramount. We have been teaching rights: henceforth we have by practice and precept to teach duties; and of all these duties, most of all the duty of sanctifying our daily sphere of ordinary labour. We have been teaching Charity; but charity must become justice yet – not in the way of partitioning goods, but of rightly appraising services. To both master and man the social reformer must teach that every industry in the land is meant to be a school of virtue.

We must come back to ourselves, or rather reach forward to ourselves; for we ourselves are the roots of all our problems, and in ourselves alone is their solution to be found. *We must moralise our social relations as they stand,* and every other reform will come as a thing of course.

The State and International Relations

11
The Right of the State over the
Individual in War

T. H. GREEN

157. (1) It may be admitted that to describe war as 'multitudinous murder' is a figure of speech. The essence of murder does not lie in the fact that one man takes away the life of another, but that he does this to 'gain his private ends' and with 'malice' against the person killed. I am not here speaking of the legal definition of murder, but of murder as a term of moral reprobation, in which sense it must be used by those who speak of war as 'multitudinous murder'. They cannot mean murder in the legal sense, because in that sense only 'unlawful killing', which killing in war is not, is murder. When I speak of 'malice', therefore, I am not using 'malice' in the legal sense. In that sense 'malice' is understood to be the attribute of every sense 'wrongful act done intentionally without just or lawful excuse',[a] and is ascribed to acts (such as killing an officer of justice, knowing him to be such, while resisting him in a riot) in which there is no ill-will of the kind which we suppose in murder, when we apply the term in its natural sense as one of moral disapprobation. Of murder in the moral sense the characteristics are those stated, and these are not present in the case of a soldier who kills one on the other side in battle. He has no ill-will to that particular person or to any particular person. He incurs an equal risk with the person whom he kills, and incurs that risk not for the sake of killing him. His object in undergoing it is not private to himself but a service (or what he supposes to be a service) to his country,

---

[a] Markby, *Elements of Law*, sec. 226. [Sir William Markby, *Elements of Law Considered with Reference to the Principles of General Jurisprudence* (Oxford, Clarendon Press, 1871: sixth edition 1905).]

a good which is his own no doubt (that is implied in his desiring it), but which he presents to himself as common to him with others. Indeed, those who might speak of war as 'multitudinous murder' would not look upon the soldier as a murderer. If reminded that there cannot be a murder without a murderer, and pressed to say who, when a bloody battle takes place, the murderer or murderers are, they would probably point to the authors of the war. It may be questioned, by the way, whether there has ever been a war of which the origination could be truly said to rest with a definite person or persons, in the same way in which the origination of an act which would be called murder in the ordinary sense rests with a particular person. No doubt there have been wars for which certain assignable individuals were specially blameable, wars which they specially helped to bring about or had special means of preventing (and the more the wickedness of such persons is kept in mind the better); but even in these cases the cause of the war can scarcely be held to be gathered up within the will of any individual, or the combined will of certain individuals, in the same way as is the cause of murder or other punishable acts. When A. B. is murdered, the sole cause lies in some definite volition of C. D. or others, however that volition may have been caused. But when a war 'breaks out', though it is not to be considered, as we are too apt to consider it, a natural calamity which could not be prevented, it would be hard to maintain that the sole cause lies in some definite volition on the part of some assignable person or persons, even of those who are most to blame. Passing over this point, however, if the acts of killing in war are not murders (in the *moral* sense, the *legal* being out of the question) because they lack those characteristics on the part of the agent's state of mind which are necessary to constitute a murder, the persons who cause those acts to be committed, if such persons can be pointed out, are not the authors of murder, multitudinous or other. They would only be so if the characteristic of 'malice', which is absent on the part of the immediate agent of the act, were present on their part as its ultimate agents. But this is not the case. However selfish their motives, they cannot fairly be construed into ill-will towards the persons who happened to be killed in the war; and therefore, whatever wickedness the persons responsible for the war are guilty of, they are not guilty of 'murder' in any natural sense of the term, nor is there any murder in the case at all.

158. It does not follow from this, however, that war is ever other than a great wrong, as a violation on a multitudinous scale of the individual's right to life. Whether it is so or not must be discussed on other grounds. If there is such a thing as a right to life on the part of the individual man as such, is there any reason to doubt that this right is violated in the case of every man killed in war? It is not to the purpose to allege that in order to a violation of right there must be not only a suffering of some kind on the part of the subject of a right, but an intentional act causing it on the part of a human agent. There is of course no violation of right when a man is killed by a wild beast or a stroke of lightning, because there is no right as between a man and a beast or between a man and a natural force. But the deaths in a battle are caused distinctly by human agency and intentional agency. The individual soldier may not have any very distinct intention when he fires his rifle except to obey orders, but the commanders of the army and the statesmen who send it into the field intend the death of as many men as may be necessary for their purpose. It is true they do not intend the death of this or that particular person, but no more did the Irishman who fired into a body of police guarding the Fenian prisoners. It might fairly be held that this circumstance exempted the Irishman from the special moral guilt of murder, though according to our law it did not exempt him from the legal guilt expressed by that term; but no one would argue that it made the act other than a violation of the right to life on the part of the policeman killed.[1] No more can the absence of an intention to kill this or that specific person on the part of those who cause men to be killed in battle save their act from being a violation of the right to life.

159. Is there then any condition on the part of the persons killed that saves the act from having this character? It may be urged that when the war is conducted according to usages that obtain between civilised nations, (not when it is a village-burning war like that between the English and Afghans), the persons killed are voluntary

---

[1] Colonel Kelly, the 'Chief Organiser', and a Fenian colleague were apprehended in Manchester in September 1867. On their way to prison their comrades pulled off a dramatic rescue, in the course of which a police-guard was accidentally killed. On the basis of dubious evidence, and a trial that did not inspire confidence, the 'Manchester Martyrs', Allen, Larkin and O'Brien, were found guilty and executed. See F. S. L. Lyons, *Ireland Since the Famine* (London, Fontana Collins, 1973), 137.

combatants, and οὐδεὶς ἀδικεῖται ἑκών[2] Soldiers, it may be said, are in the position of men who voluntarily undertake a dangerous employment. If some of them are killed, this is not more a violation of the human right to life than is the death of men who have engaged to work in a dangerous coal-pit. To this it must be answered that if soldiers did in fact voluntarily incur the special risk of death incidental to their calling, it would not follow that the right to life was not violated in their being killed. It is not a right which it rests with a man to retain or give up at his pleasure. It is not the less a wrong that a man should be a slave because he has sold himself into slavery. The individual's right to live is but the other side of the right which society has in his living. The individual can no more voluntarily rid himself of it than he can of the social capacity, the human nature, on which it is founded. Thus, however ready men may be for high wages to work in a dangerous pit, a wrong is held to be done if they are killed in it. If provisions which might have made it safe have been neglected, someone is held responsible. If nothing could make it safe, the working of the pit would not be allowed. The reason for not more generally applying the power of the state to prevent voluntary noxious employments, is not that there is no wrong in the death of the individual through the incidents of an employment which he has voluntarily undertaken, but that the wrong is more effectually prevented by training and trusting individuals to protect themselves than by the state protecting them. Thus the waste of life in war would not be the less a wrong, – not the less a violation of the right, which subsists between all members of society, and which none can alienate, that each should have his life respected by society, – if it were the fact that those whose lives are wasted voluntarily incurred the risk of losing them. But it can scarcely be held to be the fact. Not only is it

---

[2] In the context this means that no one is voluntarily treated unjustly. It probably derives from Aristotle. See *Nicomachean Ethics*, trans. Terence Irwin (Indianapolis, Hackett, 1985), 1138a, lines 10–15:

Now if someone murders himself because of anger, he does this willingly, in violation of correct reason, when the law forbids it; hence he does injustice. But injustice to whom? Surely to the city, not to himself, since he suffers injustice. That is why the city both penalizes him and inflicts further dishonour on him for destroying himself, on the assumption that he is doing injustice to the city.

impossible, even when war is conducted on the most civilised methods, to prevent great incidental loss of life (to say nothing of other injury) among non-combatants; the waste of the life of the combatants is one which the power of the state compels. This is equally true whether the army is raised by voluntary enlistment or by conscription. It is obviously so in the case of conscription; but under a system of voluntary enlistment, though the individual soldier cannot say that he in particular has been compelled by the government to risk his life, it is still the case that the state compels the risk of a certain number of lives. It decrees that an army of such a size shall be raised, though if it can get the men by voluntary hiring it does not exercise compulsion on the men of a particular age, and it sends the army into the field. Its compulsive agency causes the death of the soldiers killed, not any voluntary action on the part of the soldiers themselves. The action of the soldiers no doubt contributes to the result, for if they all refused to fight there would be no killing, but it is an action put in motion and directed by the power of the state, which is compulsive in the sense that it operates on the individual in the last resort through fear of death.

160. We have then in war a destruction of human life inflicted on the sufferers intentionally by voluntary human agency. It is true, as we saw, that it is not easy to say in any case by whose agency in particular. We may say indeed that it is by the agency of the state, but what exactly does that mean? The state here must = the sovereign power in the state; but it is always difficult to say by whom that power is wielded, and if we could in any case specify its present holders, the further question will arise whether their course of action has not been shaped for them by previous holders of power. But however widely distributed the agency may be which causes the destruction of life in war, it is still intentional human agency. The destruction is not the work of accident or of nature. If then it is to be other than a wrong, because a violation of the right to mutual protection of life involved in the membership of human society, it can only be because there is exercised in war some right that is paramount to this. It may be argued that this is the case; that there is no right to the preservation of life at the cost of losing the necessary conditions of 'living well'; that war is in some cases the only means of maintaining these conditions, and that where this

is so, the wrong of causing the destruction of physical life disappears in the paramount right of preserving the conditions under which alone moral life is possible.

161. This argument, however, seems to be only available for shifting the quarter in which we might be at first disposed to lay the blame of the wrong involved in war, not for changing the character of that wrong. It goes to show that the wrong involved in the death of certain soldiers does not necessarily lie with the government which sends those soldiers into the field, because this may be the only means by which the government can prevent more serious wrong; it does not show that there is no wrong in their death. If the integrity of any state can only be maintained at the cost of war, and if that state is more than what many so-called states have been, – more than an aggregation of individuals or communities under one ruling power, – if it so far fulfils the idea of a state, that its maintenance is necessary to the free development of the people belonging to it; then by the authorities or people of that state no wrong is done by the destruction of life which war involves, except so far as they are responsible for the state of things which renders the maintenance of the integrity of the state impossible by other means. But how does it come about that the integrity of such a state is endangered? Not by accident or by the forces of nature, but by intentional human agency in some form or other, however complicated; and with that agency lies the wrong-doing. To determine it (as we might be able to do if a horde of barbarians broke in on a civilised state, compelling it to resort to war for its defence) is a matter of small importance: what *is* important to bear in mind (being one of those obvious truths out of which we may allow ourselves to be sophisticated), is that the destruction of life in war is always wrong-doing, whoever be the wrong-doer, and that in the wars most strictly defensive of political freedom the wrong-doing is only removed from the defenders of political freedom to be transferred elsewhere. If it is difficult in any case to say precisely where, that is only a reason for more general self-reproach, for a more humbling sense[3] (as the preachers would say) of complicity in that radical (but conquerable, because moral) evil of mankind which ren-

---

[3] 'What does the Lord require of thee, but to do justly, and to love mercy, and to walk humbly with thy God?' King James *Bible*, Micah, 6:8.

ders such a means of maintaining political freedom necessary. The language, indeed, which we hear from the pulpit about war being a punishment for the sins of mankind, is perfectly true, but it needs to be accompanied by the reminder that this punishment of sin is simply a consequence of the sin and itself a further sin, brought about by the action of the sinner, not, an external infliction brought about by agencies to which man is not a party.

162. In fact, however, if most wars had been wars for the maintenance or acquisition of political freedom, the difficulty of fixing the blame of them, or at any rate of freeing one of the parties in each case from blame, would be much less than it really is. Of the European wars of the last four hundred years, how many could be fairly said to have been wars in which either or any of the parties were fighting for this end? Perhaps the wars in which the Dutch Republics defended themselves against Spain and against Louis XIV, and that in which Germany shook off the dominion of Napoleon. Perhaps the more recent struggles of Italy and Hungary against the Austrian Government. Perhaps in the first outset of the war of 1792 the French may be fairly held to have been defending institutions necessary for the development of social freedom and equality. In this war, however, the issue very soon ceased to be one between the defenders of such institutions on the one side, and their assailants on the other, and in most modern wars the issue has not been of this kind at all. The wars have arisen primarily out of the rival ambition of kings and dynasties for territorial aggrandisement, with national antipathies and ecclesiastical ambitions, and the passions arising out of religious partisanship, as complicating influences. As nations have come more and more to distinguish and solidify themselves, and a national consciousness has come definitely to be formed in each, the rival ambitions of nations have tended more and more first to support, then perhaps to supersede, the ambitions of dynasties as causes of war. The delusion has been practically dominant that the gain of one nation must mean the loss of another. Hence national jealousies in regard to colonial extension, hostile tariffs and the effort of each nation to exclude others from its markets. The explosion of this idea in the region of political economy has had little effect in weakening its hold on men's minds. The people of one nation still hear with jealousy of another nation's advance in commerce, as if it meant some decay of their own. And

if the commercial jealousy of nations is very slow in disappearing, their vanity, their desire apart from trade each to become or to seem stronger than the other, has very much increased. A hundred and fifty years ago national vanity could scarcely be said to be an influence in politics. The people under one ruler were not homogeneous enough, had not enough of a corporate consciousness, to develop a national vanity. Now (under the name of patriotism) it has become, a more serious disturber of peace than dynastic ambition. Where the latter is dangerous, it is because it has national vanity to work upon.

163. Our conclusion then is that the destruction of life in war (to say nothing of other evils incidental to it with which we are not here concerned) is always wrong-doing, with whomsoever the guilt of the wrong-doing may lie; that only those parties to a war are exempt from a share in the guilt who can truly plead that to them war is the only means of maintaining the social conditions of the moral development of man, and that there have been very few cases in which this plea could be truly made. In saying this it is not forgotten, either that many virtues are called into exercise by war, or that wars have been a means by which the movement of mankind, which there is reason for considering a progress to higher good, has been carried on. These facts do not make the wrong-doing involved in war any less so. If nothing is to be accounted wrong-doing through which final good is wrought, we must give up either the idea of there being such a thing as wrong-doing, or the idea of there being such a thing as final good. If final good results from the world of our experience, it results from processes in which wrong-doing is an inseparable element. Wrong-doing is voluntary action, either (in the deeper moral sense) proceeding from a will uninfluenced by the desire to be good on the part of the agent (which may be taken to include action tending to produce such action), or (in the sense contemplated by the '*jus naturae*') it is action that interferes with the conditions necessary to the free-play and development of a good-will on the part of others. It may be that, according to the divine scheme of the world, such wrong-doing is an element in a process by which men gradually approximate more nearly to good (in the sense of a good will). We cannot think of God as a moral being without supposing this to be the case. But this makes no difference to wrong-doing in those relations in which it *is* wrong-doing, and with which alone we are concerned, viz. in relation to

the will of human agents and to the results which those agents can foresee and intend to produce. If an action, so far as any results go which the agent can have in view or over which he has control, interferes with conditions necessary to the free-play and development of a good-will on the part of others, it is not the less wrong-doing because, through some agency which is not his, the effects which he intended, and which rendered it wrong-doing, come to contribute to an ulterior good. Nor, if it issues from bad will (in the sense explained), is it less wrong (in the moral sense) because this will is itself, in the view of Some higher being, contributory to a moral good which is not, in whole or part, within the view of the agent. If then war is wrong-doing in both the above senses (as it is always, at any rate on the part of those with whom the ultimate responsibility for it lies), it does not cease to be so on account of any good resulting from it in a scheme of providence.

164. 'But', it may be asked, 'are we justified in saying that it is always wrong-doing on the part of those with whom the ultimate responsibility lies? It is admitted that certain virtues may be evoked by war; that it may have results contributory to the moral progress of mankind; may not the eliciting of these virtues, the production of these results, be contemplated by the originators of war, and does not the origination of war, so far as influenced by such motives, cease to be wrong-doing? It must be admitted that Caesar's wars in Gaul were unprovoked wars of conquest, but their effect was the establishment of Roman civilisation with its equal law over a great part of western Europe, in such a way that it was never wholly swept away, and that a permanent influence in the progress of the European polity can be traced to it. May he not be credited with having had, however indefinitely, such an effect as this in view? Even if his wish to extend Roman civilisation was secondary to a plan for raising an army by which he might master the Republic, is he to have no credit for the beneficent results which are admitted to have ensued from the success of that plan? May not a similar justification be urged for English wars in India? If again, the establishment of the civil unity of Germany and the liberation of Christian populations in Turkey are admitted to have been gains to mankind, is not that a justification of the persons concerned in the origination of the wars that brought about those results, so far as they can be supposed to have been influenced by a desire for them?'

165. These objections might be to the purpose if we were attempting the task (generally, if not always, an impossible one) of determining the moral desert, good or ill, of those who have been concerned in bringing this or that war about. Their tendency merely is to distribute the blame of the wrong-doing involved in war, to show how widely ramified is the agency in that wrong-doing, not to affect its character as wrong-doing. If the only way of civilising Gaul was to kill all the people whom Caesar's wars caused to be killed, and if the desire for civilising it was a prevailing motive in Caesar's mind, so much the better for Caesar, but so much the worse for the other unassignable and innumerable human agents who brought it about that such an object could only be attained in such a way. We are not, indeed, entitled to say that it could have been brought about in any other way. It is true to say (if we know what we are about in saying it) that nothing which happens in the world could have happened otherwise than it has. The question for us is, whether that condition of things which rendered e.g. Caesar's Gallic wars, with the violation of human rights which they involved, the interference in the case of innumerable persons with the conditions under which man can be helpful to man (physical life being the first of these), the *sine qua non* in the promotion of ulterior human welfare, was or was not the work of human agency. If it was (and there is no doubt that it was, for to what merely natural agency could the necessity be ascribed?), then in that ordinary sense of the word 'could' in which it expresses our responsibility for our actions, men *could* have brought about the good result without the evil means. They could have done so if they had been better. It was owing to human wickedness – if less on Caesar's part, then so much the more on the part of innumerable others – that the wrong-doing of those wars was the appropriate means to this ulterior good. So in regard to the other cases instanced. It is idle to speculate on other means by which the permanent pacification of India, or the unification of Germany, or the liberation of Christians in European Turkey might have been brought about; but it is important to bear in mind that the innumerable wrong acts involved in achieving them – acts wrong, because violations of the rights of those directly affected by them -- did not cease to be wrong acts because under the given condition of things the results specified would not have been obtained without them. This given condition of things was not

like that (e.g.) which compels the castaways from a shipwreck, so many days from shore, and with only so much provision in their boat, to draw lots which shall be thrown overboard. It was a condition of things which human wickedness, through traceable and untraceable channels, brought about. If the individual promoters of wars, which through the medium of multitudinous wrong-doing have yielded good to mankind, have been really influenced by a desire for any such good, – and much scepticism is justified in regard to such a supposition, – then so much less of the guilt of the wrong-doing has been theirs. No nation, at any rate, that has taken part in such wars can fairly take credit for having been governed by such a motive. It has been either a passive instrument in the hands of its rulers, or has been animated by less worthy motives, very mixed, but of which perhaps a diffused desire for excitement has been the most innocent. On what reasonable ground can Englishmen or Germans or Russians claim that their several nations took part in the wars by which India was pacified, Germany unified, Bulgaria liberated, under the dominant influence of a desire for human good? Rather, if the action of a national conscience in such matters is possible at all, they should take shame for their share in that general human selfishness which rendered certain conditions of human development only attainable by such means.

166. (2) Reverting then to the questions which arose[b] out of the assertion of a right to free life on the part of the individual man as such, it appears that the first must be answered in the negative. No state of war can make the destruction of man's life by man other than a wrong, though the wrong is not always chargeable upon all the parties to a war. The second question is virtually answered by what has been said about the first. In regard to the state according to its idea the question could not arise, for according to its idea the state is an institution in which all rights are harmoniously maintained, in which all the capacities that give rise to rights have free-play given to them. No action in its own interest of a state that fulfilled this idea could conflict with any true interest or right of general society, of the men not subject to its law taken as a whole. There is no such thing as an inevitable conflict between states. There is nothing in the nature of the state that, given a multiplicity

[b] Above, sec. 156.

of states, should make the gain of the one the loss of the other. The more perfectly each one of them attains its proper object of giving free scope to the capacities of all persons living on a certain range of territory, the easier it is for others to do so; and in proportion as they all do so the danger of conflict disappears.

167. On the other hand, the imperfect realisation of civil equality in the full sense of the term in certain states, is in greater or less degree a source of danger to all. The presence in states either of a prerogatived class or of a body of people who, whether by open denial of civil rights or by restrictive laws, are thwarted in the free development of their capacities, or of an ecclesiastical organisation which disputes the authority of the state on matters of right and thus prevents the perfect civil fusion of its members with other citizens, always breeds an imagination of there being some competition of interests between states. The privileged class involuntarily believes and spreads the belief that the interest of the state lies in some extension without, not in an improvement of organisation within. A suffering class attracts sympathy from without and invites interference with the state which contains it; and that state responds, not by healing the sore, but by defending against aggression what it conceives to be its special interests, but which are only special on account of its bad organisation. Or perhaps the suffering population overflows into another state, as the Irish into America, and there becomes a source not only of internal difficulty but of hostile feeling between it and the state where the suffering population still survives. People, again, who in matters which the state treats as belonging to itself, take their direction from an ecclesiastical power external to the state under which they live, are necessarily in certain relations alien to that state, and may at any time prove a source of apparently conflicting interests between it and some other state, which under the influence of the hostile ecclesiastical power espouses their cause. Remove from European states, as they are and have been during the last hundred years, the occasions of conflict, the sources of apparently competing interests, which arise in one or other of the ways mentioned, – either from the mistaken view of state-interests which a privileged class inevitably takes, or from the presence in them of oppressed populations, or from what we improperly call the antagonism of religious confessions, – and there would not be or have been anything to disturb

the peace between them. And this is to say that the source of war between states lies in their incomplete fulfilment of their function; in the fact that there is some defect in the maintenance or reconciliation of rights among their subjects.

168. This is equally true in regard to those causes of conflict which are loosely called 'religious'. These do not arise out of any differences between the convictions of different people in regard to the nature of God or their relations to Him, or the right way of worshipping Him. They arise either out of some aggression upon the religious freedom of certain people, made or allowed by the powers of the state, which thus puts these people in the position of an alien or unenfranchised class, or else out of an aggression on the rights of the state by some corporation calling itself spiritual but really claiming sovereignty over men's actions in the same relations in which the state claims to determine them. There would be nothing tending to international disturbance in the fact that bodies of people who worship God in the Catholic manner live in a state where the majority worship in the Greek or Protestant manner, and alongside of another state where the majority is Catholic, but for one or other or both of these circumstances, viz. that the Catholic worship and teaching is interfered with by the Protestant or Greek state, and that Catholics are liable to a direction by a power which claims to regulate men's transactions with each other by a law of its own, and which may see fit (e.g.) to prohibit the Catholic subjects in the Greek or Protestant state from being married, or having their parents buried, or their children taught the necessary arts, in the manner which the state directs. This reciprocal invasion of right, the invasion of the rights of the state by the church on the one side, and on the other the restriction placed by the sovereign upon the subject's freedom, not of conscience, (for that is impossible), but of expressing his conscience in word and act, has sometimes caused a state of things in which certain of the subjects of a state have been better affected to another state than to their own, and in such a case there is an element of natural hostility between the states. An obvious instance to give of this relation between states would have been that between Russia and Turkey, if Turkey could be considered to have been constituted as a state at all. Perhaps a better instance would be the position of Ireland in the past; its disaffection to England and gravitation, first to France, then to the United States,

caused chiefly by Protestant penal laws which in turn were at least
provoked by the aggressive attitude of the church towards the
English state. Whenever a like invasion of rights still takes place,
e.g. in the treatment of the Catholic subjects of Russia in Poland,
in the ultramontane movement of resistance to certain requirements
of the state among the Catholic subjects of Germany, it tends to
international conflict. And what is now a somewhat remote tendency
has in the past been a formidable stimulant to war.

169. It is nothing then in the necessary organisation of the state,
but rather some defect of that organisation in relation to its proper
function of maintaining and reconciling rights, of giving scope to
capacities, that leads to a conflict of apparent interests between one
state and another. The wrong, therefore, which results to human
society from conflicts between states cannot be condoned on the
ground that it is a necessary incident of the existence of states. The
wrong cannot be held to be lost in a higher right, which attaches to
the maintenance of the state as the institution through which alone
the freedom of man is realised. It is not the state, as such, but this
or that particular state, which by no means fulfils its purpose, and
might perhaps be swept away and superseded by another with
advantage to the ends for which the true state exists, that needs to
defend its interests by action injurious to those outside it. Hence
there is no ground for holding that a state is justified in doing
whatever its interests seem to require, irrespectively of effects on
other men. If those effects are bad, as involving either a direct violation of personal rights or obstruction to the moral development of
society anywhere in the world, then there is no ultimate justification
for the political action that gives rise to them. The question can
only be (as we have seen generally in regard to the wrong-doing
of war), where in particular the blame lies. Whether there is any
justification for a particular state, which in defence of its interests
inflicts an injury on some portion of mankind; whether, e.g., the
Germans are justified in holding Metz, on the supposition that their
tenure of such a thoroughly French town necessarily thwarts in
many ways the healthy activity of the inhabitants, or the English in
carrying fire and sword into Afghanistan for the sake of acquiring a
scientific frontier; this must depend (1) on the nature of the interests
thus defended, (2) on the impossibility of otherwise defending
them, (3) on the question how they came to be endangered. If they

are interests of which the maintenance is essential to those ends as a means to which the state has its value, if the state which defends them has not itself been a joint cause of their being endangered, and if they cannot be defended except at the cost of injury to some portion of mankind, then the state which defends them is clear of the guilt of that injury. But the guilt is removed from it only to be somewhere else, however wide its distribution may be. It may be doubted, however, whether the second question could ever be answered altogether in favour of a state which finds it necessary to protect its interests at the cost of inflicting an injury on mankind.

170. It will be said, perhaps, that these formal arguments in proof of the wrong-doing involved in war, and of the unjustifiability of the policy which nations constantly adopt in defence of their apparent interests, carry very little conviction; that a state is not an abstract complex of institutions for the maintenance of rights, but a nation, a people, possessing such institutions; that the nation has its passions which inevitably lead it to judge all questions of international right from its own point of view, and to consider its apparent national interests as justifying anything; that if it were otherwise, if the cosmopolitan point of view could be adopted by nations, patriotism would be at an end; that whether this be desirable or no, such an extinction of national passions is impossible; that while they continue, wars are as inevitable between nations as they would be between individuals, if individuals were living in what philosophers have imagined to be the state of nature, without recognition of a common superior; that nations in short are in the position of men judging their own causes, which it is admitted that no one can do impartially; and that this state of things cannot be altered without the establishment of a common constraining power, which would mean the extinction of the life of independent states, – a result as undesirable as it is unattainable. Projects of perpetual peace, to be logical, must be projects of all-embracing empire.

171. There is some cogency in language of this kind. It is true that when we speak of a state as a living agency, we mean, not an institution or complex of institutions, but a nation organised in a certain way; and that members of the nation in their corporate or associated action are animated by certain passions, arising out of their association, which, though not egoistic relatively to the individual subjects of them (for they are motives to self-sacrifice), may,

in their influence on the dealings of one nation with another, have an effect analogous to that which egoistic passions, properly so called, have upon the dealings of individuals with each other. On the other hand, it must be remembered that the national passion, which in any good sense is simply the public spirit of the good citizen, may take, and every day is taking, directions which lead to no collision between one nation and another; (or, to say the same thing negatively, that it is utterly false to speak as if the desire for one's own nation to show more military strength than others were the only or the right form of patriotism); and that though a nation, with national feeling of its own, must everywhere underlie a state, properly so called, yet still, just so far as the perfect organisation of rights within each nation, which entitles it to be called a state, is attained, the occasions of conflict between nations disappear; and again, that by the same process, just so far as it is satisfactorily carried out, an organ of expression and action is established for each nation in dealing with other nations, which is not really liable to be influenced by the same egoistic passions in dealing with the government of another nation as embroil individuals with each other. The love of mankind, no doubt, needs to be particularised in order to have any power over life and action. Just as there can be no true friendship except towards this or that individual, so there can be no true public spirit which is not localised in some way. The man whose desire to serve his kind is not centred primarily in some home, radiating from it to a commune, a municipality, and a nation, presumably has no effectual desire to serve his kind at all. But there is no reason why this localised or nationalised philanthropy should take the form of a jealousy of other nations or a desire to fight them, personally or by proxy. Those in whom it is strongest are every day expressing it in good works which benefit their fellow-citizens without interfering with the men of other nations. Those who from time to time talk of the need of a great war to bring unselfish impulses into play, give us reason to suspect that they are too selfish themselves to recognise the unselfish activity that is going on all round them. Till all the methods have been exhausted by which nature can be brought into the service of man, till society is so organised that everyone's capacities have free scope for their development, there is no need to resort to war for a field in which patriotism may display itself.

172. In fact, just so far as states are thoroughly formed, the diversion of patriotism into the military channel tends to come to an end. It is a survival from a condition of things in which, as yet, the state, in the full sense, was not; in the sense, namely, that in each territory controlled by a single independent government, the rights of all persons, as founded on their capacities for contributing to a common good, are equally established by one system of law. If each separately governed territory were inhabited by a people so organised within itself, there would be nothing to lead to the association of the public spirit of the good citizen with military aggressiveness, – an association which belongs properly not to the πολιτεία [a constitutional state], but to the δυναστεία [an Oligarchy].[4] The Greek states, however complete might be the equality of their citizens among themselves, were all δυναστεῖαι in relation to some subject populations, and, as such, jealous of each other. The Peloponnesian war was eminently a war of rival δυναστεῖαι. And those habits and institutions and modes of feeling in Europe of the present day, which tend to international conflict, are either survivals from the δυναστεῖαι of the past, or arise out of the very incomplete manner in which, as yet, over most of Europe the πολιτεία has superseded the δυναστεία. Patriotism, in that special military sense in which it is distinguished from public spirit, is not the temper of the citizen dealing with fellow-citizens, or with men who are themselves citizens of their several states, but that of the follower of the feudal chief, or of the member of a privileged class conscious of a power, resting ultimately on force, over an inferior population, or of a nation holding empire over other nations.

173. Standing armies, again, though existing on a larger scale now than ever before, are not products of the civilisation of Europe, but of the predominance over that civilisation of the old δυναστεῖαι. The influences which have given rise to and keep up those armies essentially belong to a state of things in which mankind – even European mankind – is not yet thoroughly organised into political life. Roughly summarised, they are these: (1). The temporary confiscation by Napoleon to his own account of the

---

[4] The distinction comes from Aristotle's *Politics*, edited by Stephen Everson (Cambridge, Cambridge University Press, 1988), 1272b, lines 10–12: 'This shows that the Cretan Government, although possessing some of the characteristics of a constitutional state, is really a dynasty.'

products of the French Revolution, which thus, though founded on a true idea of a citizenship in which not the few only, but all men, should partake, for the time issued in a δυναστεία over the countries which most directly felt the effects of the revolution. (2). The consequent revival in dynastic forms, under the influence of antagonism to France, of national life in Germany. (3). The aspiration after national unity elsewhere in Europe, – a movement which must precede the organisation of states on a sound basis, and for the time readily yields itself to direction by a δυναστεία. (4). The existence, over all the Slavonic side of Europe, of populations which are only just beginning to make any approach to political life – the life of the πολιτεία, or 'civitas' – and still offer a tempting field to the ambition of rival δυναστείαι, Austrian, Russian, and Turkish (which, indeed, are by no means to be put on a level, but are alike as not resting on a basis of citizenship). (5). The tenure of a great Indian empire by England, which not only gives it a military character which would not belong to it simply as a state, but brings it into outward relations with the δυναστείαι just spoken of. This is no doubt a very incomplete account of the influences which have combined to 'turn Europe into a great camp' (a very exaggerated expression); but it may serve to show what a fuller account would show more clearly, that the military system of Europe is no necessary incident of the relations between independent states, but arises from the fact that the organisation of state-life, even with those peoples that have been brought under its influence at all, is still so incomplete.

174. The more complete that organisation becomes, the more the motives and occasions of international conflict tend to disappear, while the bonds of unity become stronger. The latter is the case, if for no other reason, yet for this; that the better organisation of the state means freer scope to the individual (not necessarily to do as he likes, e.g. in the buying and selling of alcohol, but in such development of activity as is good on the whole). This again means intercourse between members of one state and those of another, and in particular more freedom of trade. All restrictions on freedom of wholesome trade are really based on special class-interests, and must disappear with the realisation of that idea of individual right, founded on the capacity of every man for free contribution to social good, which is the true idea of the state. And as trade between

members of different states becomes freer and more full, the sense of common interests between them, which war would infringe, becomes stronger. The bond of peace thus established is sometimes depreciated as a selfish one, but it need be no more selfish than that which keeps the peace between members of the same state, who have no acquaintance with each other. In one case as in the other it may be said that the individual tries to prevent a breach of the peace because he knows that he has more to gain than to lose by it. In the latter case, however, this account of the matter would be, to say the least, insufficient. The good citizen observes the law in letter and in spirit, not from any fear of consequences to himself if he did not, but from an idea of the mutual respect by men for each other's rights as that which should be an idea which has become habitual with him, and regulates his conduct without his asking any questions about it. There was a time, however, when this idea only thus acted spontaneously in regulating a man's action towards his family or immediate neighbours or friends. Considerations of interest were the medium through which a wider range of persons came to be brought within its range. And thus, although considerations of an identity of interests, arising out of trade, may be the occasion of men's recognising in men of other nations those rights which war violates, there is no reason why, upon that occasion and through the familiarity which trade brings about, an idea of justice, as a relation which should subsist between all mankind as well as between members of the same state, may not come to act on men's minds as independently of all calculation of their several interests as does the idea which regulates the conduct of the good citizen.

175. If the necessary or impelling power of the idea of what is due from members of different nations to each other is weak, it must be observed on the other hand that the individual members of a nation have no such apparent interest in their government's dealing unfairly with another nation as one individual may have in getting the advantage of another. Thus, so far as this idea comes to form part of the habit of men's minds, there ceases to be anything in the passions of the people which a government represents to stimulate the government to that unfairness in dealing with another government, to which an individual might be moved by self-seeking passions in dealing with another individual, in the absence of an impartial authority having power over both. If at the same time the

several governments are purely representative of the several peoples, as they should become with the due organisation of the state, and thus have no dynastic interests of their own in embroiling one nation with another, there seems to be no reason why they should not arrive at a passionless impartiality in dealing with each other, which would be beyond the reach of the individual in defending his own cause against another. At any rate, if no government can ever get rid of some bias in its own favour, there remains the possibility of mediation in cases of dispute by disinterested governments. With the abatement of national jealousies and the removal of those deeply-seated causes of war which, as we have seen, are connected with the deficient organisation of states, the dream of an international court with authority resting on the consent of independent states may come to be realised. Such a result may be very remote, but it is important to bear in mind that there is nothing in the intrinsic nature of a system of independent states incompatible with it, but that on the contrary every advance in the organisation of man kind into states in the sense explained is a step towards it.

12
What Imperialism Means
J. H. MUIRHEAD

More than any event in the memory of the present generation –
more than the American War of the sixties, more even than the
Home Rule proposals of the eighties – the present war has come
with a sword into our midst.[1] It has searched the hearts and tried
the reins not only of the great political parties of the State, but of
more homogeneous groups of politicians, which we have hitherto
been accustomed to think of as bound together in 'solid simplicity'.
At first the controversy was chiefly confined to the circumstances
out of which the war arose, but as it has gone on it has come more
and more to turn upon the meaning and justification of the whole
policy that goes by the name of Imperialism. This is as it should
be. No question can be conceived which more vitally concerns the
future well-being of the nation, and we might say of the world. The
sooner, therefore, we can get away from the heated atmosphere of
current controversy, and turn to the wider issues that have been
brought to the front by it with the sincere desire to understand
them, the better for us as a nation. The present article is an attempt
to consider, without reference to South African politics, or party
politics of any kind, two questions which everyone will admit are
fundamental. First, what is the meaning of the thing we call
Imperialism? and second, what ought to be our attitude towards it?

In trying to find an answer to the former of these questions, the
first thing that strikes us is, that Imperialism is not new, but may

---

[1] Muirhead is here referring to the second Boer War of 1899–1902 which caused a
considerable split in the Liberal Party. For a contemporary opposition account of

be said to have come into existence with our Empire itself. Sir John Seeley has shown that if we would understand the meaning of English History in the eighteenth and early nineteenth century, we must see it in the light of the great struggle that was going on between the nations of Europe, and especially of the great duel between England and France for the possession of the New World, and with it for a place among the great Powers of the future. The world-wide character of the wars of the period is seen in the places of their battles – Arcot, the Heights of Abraham, the Nile, the Ohio. Even the Continental war that goes by the name was not really for the 'Spanish Succession', but for succession to the new Empire across the seas. Seeley adds, indeed, that during that period we conquered and peopled half the world in a fit of absence of mind.[2] But this is only partly true. The leading men of the time were well aware of what they had done, and of its importance for the English nation.[3] Tory politicians had their own ideas as to the way the new acquisitions should be governed, but they had no doubt at all as to their value. Even Radicals like Dr. Priestley assumed the retention of the Colonies as an axiom of their political creed.[4] But in order to understand how the wider outlook had taken possession of the higher mind of the nation in the third quarter of the eighteenth century, we must go to the speeches of the great Whig politician, Edmund Burke. It has never, I think, been sufficiently recognised (partly, perhaps, because Burke's most popular biographer is also the biographer of Richard Cobden)[5] that all the greatest of these speeches, that on *Present Discontents*, on *Conciliation with America*,

the war see J. A. Hobson, *The War in Southern Africa: Its Causes and Effects* (London, Nisbet, 1900).

[2] Sir John Seeley, *The Expansion of England* (London, Macmillan, 1883), 8. For Seeley on the Spanish Succession, see 32–3.

[3] For a detailed study of the different meanings of the term imperialism in the nineteenth century see Richard Koebner and Helmut Dan Schmidt, *Imperialism: The Story of a Political Word, 1840–1960* (Cambridge, Cambridge University Press, 1964).

[4] See, for example, Joseph Priestley, *The Present State of Liberty in Great Britain and Her Colonies* (1769) in *Political Writings*, ed. Peter Miller (Cambridge, Cambridge University Press, 1993). Priestley argues that: 'The most equitable maxims, as well as the best policy, in our conduct to the Americans, is to lay aside all jealousy of them, not to indulge the idea of superiority, and to consult the good of the whole, as one united empire . . .', 144.

[5] John Morley, *Burke* (London, Macmillan, 1879); *The Life of Richard Cobden* (London, Chapman and Hall, 1881).

and the whole series upon our conduct in India, were inspired by this larger outlook. Through all, Burke has his eye on the new position we occupied among the nations and the new duties it imposed. To him, at least, if to no one else, our dependencies appeared as 'the first, the dearest, the most delicate objects of the internal policy of this Empire'.[6]

While the Imperial sentiment is thus a creation of the eighteenth century, the form it has assumed to-day can only be understood in the light of the phases through which it has passed in the interval – the remarkable eclipse which it underwent in the early part of the present century, and the equally remarkable development that has taken place in our own time. How are we to explain these changes – enthusiasm passing into indifference, and finally into hostility, to the very idea of an Empire, and then again developing into a consuming passion?

The first is comparatively easy to understand. Though the leading political authors and writers were perfectly conscious of the new destiny of England as a nation, the people at large remained absent minded, and still thought of England as an island power, 'in a great pond, a swan's nest'.[7] This view was further confirmed both by the actual distance that divided her from her colonists, and by the prevailing sentiment with which they were regarded. To Burke, as we have seen, they were the 'dearest, the most delicate objects of our policy'; but to the great mass of the people of England they were dissenters and refugees who had forsaken home and country in quest of a liberty it had denied to them. In final confirmation of this view there came the logic of fact, 'the only kind of reasoning', as Jowett used to say, 'that points to the true tendencies of things';[8] and the separation of the American Colonies seemed to set its seal

---

[6] I have been unable to identify the source of this quotation.
[7] Shakespeare,

> Our Britain seems as of it, but not in't;
> In a great pool a swan's nest: prithee, think
> There's livers out of Britain.

Cymbeline, Act Three, Scene Four. Seeley says in this respect: 'Nor have we even now ceased to think of ourselves as simply a race inhabiting an island off the northern coast of the Continent of Europe.' *Expansion of England*, 8. Seeley cites the quotation from Shakespeare on p. 165.

[8] Muirhead was a student at Balliol College, Oxford, when Jowett was Master.

to the well-known epigram of Turgot, that 'colonies are like fruits that drop off when they are ripe'.[9]

But the significance of the change in the succeeding generation can only be fully understood when taken in connection with the utilitarianism, practical and philosophical, that was its leading characteristic. To the utilitarian in every period colonies have appeared in the light of 'commercial assets', whose value to the mother country has consisted in the command they give her of their markets. When, therefore, it was proved by Adam Smith that the monopoly our colonies promised us was no real advantage, there seemed no longer any valid reason why we should trouble ourselves further on their behalf, and Bentham could bring the whole force of powerful rhetoric to prove that a nation had no interest as it had no right, and indeed no power, to retain them. Let people cease to regard them with 'the greedy eye of fiscality',[10] and they would soon cease to regret the loss of them; a view which received a sort of sacramental authority for succeeding Radicals by being embalmed in James Mill's celebrated article upon Colonies, in the *Encyclopedia Britannica* of the time.[11] It is true that John Stuart Mill took a wider view in the next generation, advocating the retention of our colonial

[9] Seeley cites this epigram: 'It is an old saying, to which Turgot gave utterance a quarter of a century before the Declaration of Independence, "Colonies are like fruits which cling to the tree only till they ripen." He added, "As soon as America can take care of herself, she will do what Carthage did." ' *Expansion of England*, 15.

[10] Smith is particularly concerned with colonial measures that restricted free trade. He says, for example: 'The exclusive trade of the mother countries tends to diminish, or, at least to keep down below what they would otherwise rise to, both the enjoyments and industry of all those nations in general, and of the American colonies in particular ... By rendering the colony produce dearer in all other countries, it lessens its consumption, and thereby cramps the industry of the colonies, and both the enjoyments and the industry of all other countries, which both enjoy less when they pay more for what they enjoy, and produce less when they get less for what they produce.' Adam Smith, *An Inquiry into the Nature and Causes of the Wealth of Nations*, ed. R. H. Campbell, A. S. Skinner and W. B. Todd (Indianapolis, Liberty, 1976), IV, vii, c. 9. Bentham frequently voiced his concerns about the European and colonial wars. He was not always consistent, but in many instances he argues that the loss from such ventures was far greater than the gain. He argued, for instance, that the acquisition of colonies led, not to increased trade, but to the expansion of the executive power of goverment in the form of the military and civil service. *The Works of Jeremy Bentham*, ed. John Bowring (Edinburgh, William Tait, 1843), vol. II, 558–60.

[11] 'Colony', Supplement to the third edition of *Encyclopædia Britannica* (Edinburgh, Thomas Bonar, 1803). It was printed separately by J. Innes in London (n.d., circ. 1820), 33.

empire as a guarantee of peace and free trade, and as likely to strengthen the moral influence in the counsels of Europe of 'the power which, of all in existence, best understands liberty; and whatever may have been its errors in the past, has attained to more of conscience and moral principle in its dealings with foreigners than any other great nation seems either to conceive as possible or recognise as desirable'.[12] But this 'imperialist' view was powerless against the rising tide of Manchesterism, which took up and carried to its logical issue the earlier form of the utilitarian doctrine. According to the view that had come to be prevalent in the middle classes in these years, the destiny of England was to become the workshop of the world, its dense city populations compensated for the loss of the beauties of nature and freer forms of life by the cheapness of coal and calico. In such a 'calico millennium' there was clearly no place for the luxury of colonies, much less of an Indian Empire. And though the opinions of John Bright, the greatest of this school, have been much misrepresented there can be no doubt that on the whole he exercised in this respect a narrowing influence on the national imagination, and carried on into our own time, with a growing weight of authority, the ideas accepted as axiomatic by the early radicals.[13] It would be a mistake, however, to suppose that this indifference was confined to any one school or party. There is a story told of Lord Palmerston, the least provincial of Ministers, that having on one occasion at a Cabinet meeting a difficulty in finding anyone who would take the post of Colonial Secretary, he finally remarked that he supposed he must take it himself, and, turning to Sir Arthur Helps,[14] who was present, asked him to come upstairs after the meeting was over and 'show him where these places were'. The contrast between this and the present day is sufficiently obvious, and brings us to the question of the causes of so remarkable a change.

---

[12] Mill was of the view that civilised nations owed each other sacred duties which were not owed to the lower races. This was, in his view, the position of England in relation to India: 'The sacred duties which civilized nations owe to the independence and nationality of each other, are not binding towards those to whom nationality and independence are a certain evil, or at best a questionable good.' J. S. Mill, 'A Few Words on Non-Intervention', in *Dissertations and Discussions* (London, J. W. Parker, 1875), vol. III, 167–71.

[13] See George Macauley Trevelyan, *The Life of John Bright* (London, Constable, 1913).

[14] Sir Aurthur Helps (1813–1875) was clerk of the Privy Council.

Many explanations have been offered by speakers and writers in the last few months. A common opinion is, that it was the work of Disraeli; Lord Salisbury attributes it to the Primrose League; Mr. Bernard Shaw to the Fabian Society. But influences such as these, so far as they are connected with it at all, are only flies upon the wheel. They have not made the dust, far less the wheel itself. They are all part of a wider movement which, when we closely regard it, we shall find, I think, to be nothing less than the Spirit of the Century itself now taking bodily shape and meeting us in a new form of national consciousness at the end of it. And if we ask what the burden of this spirit is, and where we are to look for its growing expression, we can best reply by pointing to the great writers who, as the 'soul of their age',[15] have best understood it. I can only here indicate one or two great names and passages.

For the first clear note of its meaning we must go, I believe (as for so much that is needful for the true understanding of ourselves), to Goethe. In two well-known passages he strikes it with startling clearness. The first is at the end of *Faust*, the second at the end of *Wilhelm Meister*. In both of these he indicates the spirit of industry, organisation, civilisation, as the hope of mankind. In both he suggests the mission of Europe to carry this beyond the seas and make the world into a home. 'Let us hasten', cries Lenardo in the latter, 'to the shore of the ocean and convince ourselves what boundless spaces are still lying open to activity. It has been said, and over again said, where I am well is my country! But this consolatory saw were better worded, where I am useful is my country.'[16]

But the Germany to which Goethe spoke was as yet unprepared for his message. It had a nation to create at home before looking for an empire abroad. England, however, was in a different position, and it was Carlyle's merit to have first caught the note that Goethe had sounded and to have applied it to ourselves. If there is any

---

[15] Ben Jonson:

>   Soul of the Age!
>   The Applause! delight! the wonder of our stage!

'42. To the Memory of My Beloved, the Author, Mr. William Shakespeare and What He Hath Left Us' in *Uncollected Poetry* reprinted in *The Complete Poetry of Ben Jonson*, ed. William B. Hunter (New York, University Press, 1963), 372.

[16] J. W. Goethe, *Faust*, ed. Cyrus Hamilton, trans. Walter Arndt Jr. (New York, Norton, 1976); and J. W. Goethe, *Wilhelm Meister*, trans. Thomas Carlyle (London, Chapman, 1899), two vols.

single name more than another that represents the ideas for which our new imperialism stands, it is Carlyle's. It was the great Empire builders of the past, the Cromwells and the Fredericks, that attracted his attention as an historian. It is the call of our own lands across the seas to which he gives voice in his political writings.

> This poor nation, painfully dark about said tasks and the way of doing them, means to keep its colonies, nevertheless, as things which somehow or other must have a value, were it better seen into. They are portions of the general earth where the children of Britain now dwell; where the gods have so far sanctioned our endeavour as to say that they have a right to dwell. England will not readily admit that her own children are worth nothing but to be flung out of doors? England, looking on her Colonies, can say, 'Here are lands and seas, spice-lands, corn-lands, timber-lands, overarched by Zodiacs and stars, clasped by many sounding seas; wide spaces of the Maker's building, fit for the cradle yet of mighty Nations and their Sciences and Heroisms. Unspeakable deliverance and new destiny of thousandfold expanded manfulness for all men dawns out of the future here, to me has fallen the godlike task of initiative all that: of me and of my Colonies, the abstruse future asks: Are you wise enough for so sublime a destiny? Are you too foolish?[a]

But even Carlyle, in England, was as yet a voice crying in the wilderness. Two things were still wanting to give wings to his words – means of communication and a true political connection. But at the very time that Carlyle was writing, the first of these wants was on the point of being supplied; the 'organic filaments' of the dispersed English race were beginning to come together. New arteries and nerve systems were beginning to be formed. The first steamer to Australia ran in 1852, the first cable was opened in 1872, and by 1879, the date of the cable to South Africa, connection had been established over the whole group. It is perhaps Kipling's happiest stroke to have fixed on 'Deep Sea Cables' as the symbol of the unity of the English race.[17]

---

[a] 'The New Downing Street', 1850. [Thomas Carlyle, *Latter Day Pamphlets* (London, Chapman, 1858), 124–57.]

[17] Rudyard Kipling,

> There is no sound, no echo of sound, in the deserts of the deep
> Or the great grey level plains of ooze where the Shell-burred cables creep
> Here in the womb of the world – here on the tie-ribs of the earth

Political connection has been of slower growth. But already in the thirties the foundation had been laid in Canada of a new form of Federal union, and when, by the British North American Act of 1867, the Dominion of Canada was created on a plan that has since proved completely successful, the problem here also may be said, in principle at least, to have been solved.[18]

It is difficult and, indeed, fallacious to attempt to fix a particular date for the birth of a movement such as that we are discussing, but it cannot be said to have attained any great depth or cohesion till the early eighties. This was the date of the great awakening that followed the death of Gordon. This was also the date of the publication of two books which, more than anything else, brought home to the reading public the new outlook of our country. Seeley's *Expansion of England* was published in 1883, and Froude's *Oceana* in 1885.[19] Two things are interesting to the reader of these books in connection with the present sketch. The Colonies are no longer fruits that drop off when they are ripe. Both writers consciously alter the metaphor, preferring that of leaves and branches that nourish while they spread the influence of the tree; or, better still, of the banana tree, whose branches root themselves in the ground and add support to the parent stem. In the second place the argument from America is turned. America is no longer an argument for separation, but for retention. It has shown how political union may be maintained over an immense territory. It has proved, further, that it may be worth while going to war to maintain it. During the last decade the ideas of these historians have been carried far and wide by the foundation of Imperial Federation and kindred leagues, and by the spread of a new form of literature to which poets, journalists, novelists, civil servants, anthropologists, have contributed, making us more familiar with India, Egypt, Africa, and Burmah than with the West of Ireland or the Highlands of Scotland.

Words, and the words of men, flutter and flutter and beat.

'Deep-Sea Cables', *Rudyard Kipling's Verse: Inclusive Edition 1885–1918*, vol. I (London, Hodder and Stoughton, 1919).

[18] The Act addressed public concern about defence in the light of the American Civil War. Religious and racial differences, as well as difficulties in integrating an inter-provincial railway, led to the union of New Brunswick, Nova Scotia, Ontario and Quebec in the Dominion of Canada.

[19] James Anthony Froude, *Oceana, or England and her Colonies* (London, Longman, 1886).

I have connected the great movement in the midst of which we find ourselves with the spirit to which Goethe appeals when he summoned Europe to the work of peopling and organising the world and which Carlyle saw had its readiest instrument in the British nation. The question may still be raised, whether this is not a lying spirit, and whether we are wise in following its guidance. Wisdom is justified of its children. It is justified, too, of its parents. 'Our Imperialism', it may be argued, 'does not derive much justification from either. It has been begotten in greed and treachery, and in endless, unrecorded slaughter. It has produced, and is likely to produce, an endless progeny of similar horrors. Its opponents have included not only the supporters of a pinchbeck utilitarianism, but the greatest men of the century, those who have stood for peace and good-will among men, freedom and justice among peoples. All that has been said makes Imperialism more comprehensible; it does not justify it. Granted that our material and political discoveries have proved to us how our colonies can be held together. They tell us nothing – are quite irrelevant to the problem – of the government of four hundred million human beings of every race by a handful of Europeans. We had no right to undertake this duty. We have no means of performing it. The attempt only plunges us deeper in the crimes of the past; distracts attention from needed home reforms, and presses on the masses of the people with an ever-growing burden of taxation.'

Although this view is probably not widely held at the present moment, it seems so reasonable in itself, and has the support of so great names, that it deserves every consideration. I shall state, as shortly as I can, wherein I think it is in error not only from a practical but from an ethical point of view. In the ethics of human affairs there are two questions that require always to be clearly distinguished: How did the circumstances in which we find ourselves arise? What do these circumstances require of us? With regard to the former, it is irrelevant to ask what with our present knowledge and present standards we should have done. Only to a very limited extent, even in private life, have we chosen the responsibilities of our situation in the light of present standards. They have grown out of actions often thoughtlessly, perhaps imprudently or even wickedly, undertaken. The good man does not think of repudiating them on that account. He is, on the contrary, the readier to accept them in all their fullness. *A fortiori* is a nation tied to its past. To repudiate its responsibilities, to retire from tasks it has undertaken, however thoughtlessly at the time, is the poorest sort of corporate repentance. In the case of an empire like ours this would be a crime outweighing all we have committed in creating it. The question is not whether we were right in undertaking all it involves, but how best we shall perform it.

In order to answer this question with any profit, the first thing is to have a clear understanding of what the task precisely is. Mistake on this point will be fatal. Yet our ideas on the subject are commonly of the vaguest. We think, indeed, of our Empire as an amalgam of self-governing colonies and dependent or protected States, but we seldom realise the difference in the kind and extent of the responsibility entailed by these different elements. In respect to the first, the problem is mainly political, the discovery, namely, of a system of government which, while extending the Anglo-Saxon form of liberty, will keep the members of the Empire in organic connection with one another. In spite of our recent success in Canada and Australia, it would be rash to suggest that this problem has been finally solved. Ireland at home, and South Africa abroad, are sufficient evidence to the contrary. Yet it is a problem of comparatively limited extent; it is one, moreover, of essentially the same nature as that to the successful solution of which England, from the days of the Heptarchy,[20] has been progressively approximating. The other task is of an entirely different kind and of immensely wider extent. It is not political, but mainly social and educational. It is concerned not with the government of a few million Europeans in accordance with European traditions, but the reconstruction of the moral, industrial, and political ideas of some four or five hundred millions of souls of every race and religion and at every stage of civilisation except our own. The thought of it might well stagger us, so unprecedented is it in size, so unprecedented in character, so unlike any for which we have as yet shown any national aptitude. I lay stress on all this, not by way of discouragement from the attempt to grapple with it, but to indicate the necessity of bringing the best qualities of our race to bear upon the problem that is before us.

[20] The Heptarchy is the period from the sixth to the eighth century in England when the kingdoms of Kent, Sussex, Wessex, Essex, East Anglia, Mercia and Northumbria co-existed under the overlordship of Bretwalda.

The chief requisites are Courage to face and Wisdom to execute our self imposed task. The importance of realising what these severally involve must be my excuse for dwelling upon them.

1. Let us be quite clear, in the first place, as to what the courage is of which we are speaking. It is as different as may be from current jingoism. It differs from it not only in the motive that inspires it, but in the temper to which it is allied. Genuine courage, as Aristotle pointed out long ago, differs from counterfeit in the nobility of its object. The courage of which I am now speaking must draw its inspiration from no less an object than the development of human faculty in something like a quarter of the inhabitants of the globe. *Rule* of some kind, it may be admitted, is a condition of the attainment of this object, *trade* may be its effect, but neither can be the leading motive of the nation that is courageous in the sense described. It differs from jingoism, further, in its temper. It must be as remote from a rash expansionism as from a craven timidity. We can never too often remind ourselves that there is nothing inherently permanent about an Empire such as ours. Its very growth brings its own lesson with it, teaching us that the Empire we have gained Portugal, Holland, Spain, France, have lost; none of them, if we are to believe the historians, from any inherent lack of the spirit of enterprise, but the first two because their empires were founded on too narrow a basis – the last two (to quote Sir John Seeley) for no other reason than that 'they had too many irons in the fire'.[21] The wealth of England is, of course, incomparably greater than any which these States had at command, but it is not inexhaustible. She also has a narrow basis. She also has many irons in the fire. Recent events have shown how her resources in men, in administrative organisation, even in money, may be strained. One element in the Imperial caution which all this suggests, is the spirit of conciliation. The word has fallen into disrepute in these days by reason of its special application, but the thing itself is as necessary as in the days of Burke's great speech. The arguments in favour of it and the objections to the spirit of violence, which is its opposite, are the same as they were then, and can never be too often recalled. Force is a temporary expedient: 'A nation is not governed which is

---

[21] This is certainly the import of Seeley's argument, but I have been unable to find the exact words.

perpetually to be conquered.' It is uncertain in its operation: 'terror is not always the effect of force.' It impairs the object it endeavours to preserve: 'the thing you fought for is not the thing you recover, but depreciated, sunk, wasted, consumed in the contest.'[22] And the spirit of conciliation that is necessary in dealing with dependent peoples is not less necessary in our relations with our neighbours in Europe. I do not admit that we hold our Empire by the indulgence of our neighbours, but I am perfectly sure we can never make it a success without their friendship. Here, too, we have much to learn; and there has been nothing more statesmanlike in the recent utterances of politicians than Lord Rosebery's emphasis on the necessity of securing the acquiescence, if not the co-operation, of other nations.[23]

2. The second of the two conditions I have mentioned is, that we should be prepared to bring our best intelligence to bear on the real problem as above defined, in order to arrive at some clear idea as to the principles on which we ought to proceed. In the history of our past dealings with subject races two phases of policy are clearly distinguishable. There was the long period during which we did nothing as a nation either for negro or Indian. Writing of India in 1783, Burke could say, 'England has erected no churches, no hospitals, no schools, has built no bridges, made no roads, cut no navigations, dug out no reservoirs. Should we be driven out this day nothing would remain to tell that it had been possessed by anything better than the ourang-outang or the tiger.'[24] But in the early part of this century all this was changed. We began to think of the negro as a fellow Christian; we deliberately adopted the policy of Europeanising India. Much, however, has happened since then, and grave doubts have begun to beset us, not only as to the adequacy (about this there can be no two opinions), but as to the principle of the means we have hitherto employed. As to one part of this mission

---

[22] Edmund Burke, 'Speech on Moving the Resolutions for Conciliation with the Colonies, March 22, 1775', *Works* (London, Oxford University Press, 1915), vol. II, 184.
[23] See Gordon Martel, *Imperial Diplomacy: Rosebery and the Failure of Foreign Policy* (London, Mansell, 1986).
[24] Edmund Burke, 'Speech on Fox's East India Bill, December 1, 1783', *Works*, III, 79. The sentence which precedes the one quoted reads: 'Every other conqueror of every other description has left some monument, either of state or beneficence, behind him.'

of civilisation there need, of course, be no hesitation – viz., the spread of European ideas of truth and justice, and again of European science. Justice is justice, and science is science, all the world over. The one is the basis of the moral, as the other of the material, well-being of any people. But to apply European ideas in these departments is one thing, to make European ideas the basis of all that is taught in schools and colleges is another, and it is here that the doubt arises. Are these nations fit for the education we are giving them? Have they capacity enough to make it worth our while to give it? Granting that they have the capacity, are we setting about the task of developing it in the right way? The results of recent study of native life go a long way in providing an answer to these two questions, as favourable to our hopes in the one case as it is unfavourable in the other. They go to show, on the one hand, the wealth of human capacity that underlies the most unpromising material, and on the other the almost complete failure of the efforts hitherto employed, whether by missions or Governments, to develop it. To take only one passage in the former subject, from one who was a pioneer in scientific methods of study. Speaking of the Gold Coast negro, not (one would have thought) hopeful subject, Miss Kingsley wrote: –

> The true negro is, I believe, by far the better man than the Asiatic; he is physically superior, and he is more like an Englishman than the Asiatic; he is a logical, practical man, with feelings that are a credit to him and are particularly strong in the direction of property; he has a way of thinking he has rights, whether he likes to use them or no, and will fight for them when he is driven to it. His make of mind is exceedingly like the make of mind of thousands of Englishmen of the stand-no-nonsense, Englishman's-house-is-his-castle type. Yet withal a law-abiding man, loving a live lord, holding loudly that women should be kept in their place, yet often grievously henpecked by his wives and little better than a slave to his mother, whom he loves with a love he gives to none other.[25]

But while the best evidence thus goes to show that the children of our Empire have all the necessary stuff, it also goes to prove that

---

[25] See Mary Kingsley, *Travels in West Africa, Congo Francais and Cameroons* (London, Macmillan, 1897). Also see Mary Kingsley, *The Scent of the Cameroons Peak and Travels in French Congo* (Liverpool, Liverpool Geographical Society, 1896), vol. 123, 491.

we have hitherto failed to work it to much profit. Travellers like Mary Kingsley, journalists like G. W. Steevens, students like Sir Alfred Lyall, all give the same account.[26] The more intelligent of the natives divide themselves into two classes – those who are sullenly hostile to European ideas as portending dissolution to their cherished customs, and those who take to them with avidity as likely to pay. Education in the case of the latter class consists of a thin veneer of European ideas sufficient to destroy the beliefs and sentiments that gave the mind a hold on the realities of life, but wholly insufficient to provide it with anything that can take their place. Like the young lady from the Cameroons[b] Miss Kingsley tells of, they learn everything, but it amounts to nothing. Deep-rooted customs and superstitions as in Africa, ancient philosophical faiths as in India, are being replaced by the cast-off clothing of orthodox European sects, or a superficial acquaintance with European science and its too frequent accompaniment, European materialism.

The mistake, of course, is that in setting about the education of these people we have taken no trouble to understand the people we are educating. We have not yet taken to heart and applied abroad what we have known for the last half-century at home, that there can be no true education where the ideas we aim at imparting stand in no organic connection with the ideas already there. We have Child Study Associations, based upon this conception of education, and a whole literature of child psychology in England. What is wanted is a Child Study Association on a large scale, of which every civil servant and teacher in India and Africa shall be members, for the sympathetic study of the children of our Empire. For of all the

---

[b] Asked what they had taught at the Mission School where she had been educated, she replied 'Everything.' Asked what she had *learned*, she gave the same answer. 'Then, of course, you know the answer to a question that has long puzzled me, why you are black', said Miss K. 'Oh yaas!' was the answer; 'it is because one of my pa's pas saw dem Patriarch Noah wivout his clothes.'

[26] Mary Henrietta Kingsley (1862–1900) was a writer and extensive traveller. She was in Cape Town during the Boer War and died of enteric fever. Sir Alfred Comyn Lyall (1835–1911), son of the philosopher Alfred Lyall (1795–1865), was a writer, Indian Civil servant and later a distinguished lecturer on colonial matters. George Warrington Steevens (1869–1900) was a Fellow of Pembroke College, Oxford, and later an editor and journalist on various newspapers. He joined the staff of the *Daily Mail* in 1896 and reported from many foreign places including Egypt, Greece and South Africa.

prophecies to which we can commit ourselves this surely is the least uncertain, that we shall make no headway, nor accomplish anything of any value to our-subjects, to ourselves, or to the world, without it.

It is here that our main problem lies, for it is just here, as already suggested, that the natural advantages we have hitherto possessed are likely to fail us. So long as it is a question of order, discipline, administration, the Anglo-Saxon combination of patience and pluck, energy and adaptability to circumstances, give us probably an advantage over any other nation. It is when we come to more delicate tasks, such as education and social reconstruction, requiring higher refinements of insight, tact, and sympathy, that our national genius is apt to forsake us. This is, of course, no reason why we should despair of them. It is a reason, however, why we should bring all our intelligence to bear upon the problem of discovering the best that is known as to the right method of proceeding about them, and the most fitting instruments for their accomplishment.

Is all this (end and means alike as so conceived) a wicked and vainglorious dream? Ten or twenty years ago it might well have seemed so. We had then no solid accomplishment to which to point. But this can no longer be said. There is one corner of the world in which results have been achieved, the significance of which can hardly be over-estimated. The case of Egypt has shown what British administration can achieve when it takes its stand on the principle that in foreign as in home policy the good of the subject is the first object of government, when it has the courage to grasp and under-take all that the situation requires for this object, when it is prepared to bring the best intelligence of the nation to bear on the task it has undertaken, and when, without flinching from the policy the circumstances dictate, it uses every opportunity to conciliate the better elements of European opinion. The details of this masterly piece of work are to be found, as everyone knows, in Sir Alfred Milner's *England in Egypt*[27] a book which illustrates from every

---

[27] London, Edward Arnold, 1892. Milner (1806–73) was a pro-imperialist Liberal who became a Viscount in 1902. He had been a journalist and civil servant in Britain and Egypt, and in 1897 he became High Commissioner in South Africa and Governor of Cape Colony. Before returning to Britain to take his place in The House of Lords he was Governor of the Transvaal and Orange River Colony from 1902–6.

department of administration what Imperialism can be at its best, and what it must be if it would be anything at all. It has, perhaps, least to tell us on what I have ventured to indicate as the central problem of the future, the reconciliation of Western science and culture with Eastern modes of thought. Yet here, also, there is much that is instructive and much that is hopeful in the methods adopted in Egypt. Even in respect to that most difficult of all problems, the reconciliation of science and religion, the narrative is not without a hint as to one, at least, of the directions in which a solution may be sought. A story is told of an English engineer who, in a particularly dry year, saved the crops of thousands of the people of Upper Egypt by his prompt energy and unremitting labour. Their joy was unbounded, and nothing would content them, at the great Thanksgiving that was held in consequence in the chief Mosque of the district, but that the Englishman should be present. This was an unheard-of thing, but such was the gratitude of the people that the most deep-rooted superstition was overcome, and the stranger not only was permitted, but compelled, to share in their worship. Religion and science were for once reconciled. And after all, one may ask, why not? For is not the essence both of science and religion, whether in the East or West the same? The aim and essence of science, both moral and material, is to secure that justice shall be done, and that the forces of nature from the enemy shall become the friend of man. What else than this is the essence also of religion? If we are to believe the Eastern prophet, this too is 'to do justice and love mercy.'[28]

---

[28] From one of the twelve minor prophetic books of the Old Testament. It is attributed to Micah of Moresheth who was active in the late eighth century BC. It champions the poor against social injustices. Micah says: 'What does the Lord Require of thee, but to do justly, and to love mercy, and to walk humbly with thy God.' 6:8.

13
German Philosophy and the War

JOHN WATSON

I fear it will be very hard for me in a short paper to give more than a general idea of the relations of German philosophy and the dreadful war into which her rulers, either purposely or by their wretched diplomacy, have plunged Europe and the overseas dominions of Great Britain. Philosophy, just because of its comprehensive character, and because by its nature it eschews prophecy when it is true to itself, never acts immediately and directly upon life; but while this is true, it would be a great mistake to imagine that it has no influence whatever. The forces that in the long run are most powerful are those which work quietly and unostentatiously; and of these not the least important are those speculative ideas that, since the time of Plato, philosophers have believed to exercise a profound influence on human character and human action. If this seems a hard saying, it will perhaps appear more intelligible if we remember that in our complex modern civilization such ideas are not confined to those whose special function it is to build up or to defend philosophical systems, but include all who reflect in a large and comprehensive way upon the world in which we live, the foundations of human conduct, and the principles that lie at the basis of the universe. It is, I am convinced, only apparently paradoxical to say, that the fierce conflict which even now convulses the world is at bottom the clash of opposing ideals of life rather than the shock of armed hosts. Ideas, as Luther said, are living things with hands and feet.[1]

---

[1] Caird cites this expression in his introduction to Plato's *Cratylus* in *The Dialogues of Plato*, vol. III (Oxford, Clarendon Press, 1871).

It is therefore no mere curious enquiry, but one that deserves and demands the most careful investigation, what is the responsibility for the present war of the speculative minds of Germany, whether their special walk in life has led them to devote attention mainly to politics, history, or philosophy proper.

When in the year 1790 word was brought to Konigsberg that the French people had set up a Republic, Kant (born 1724: died 1804) turned to his friends, and with tears in his eyes exclaimed: 'Now I can say with Simeon, "Lord let Thy servant depart in peace, for mine eyes have seen Thy salvation".'[2] The venerable philosopher fondly believed that his dream of a perpetual peace on the basis of a republican constitution of humanity had begun to be realized in European countries as well as on the continent of the New World; and the fact seemed to him to be a good omen for its final realization in every state in the whole world. Whether, like Wordsworth, he might not later have been disillusioned, when he learned of the excesses and the intolerance of the French Republicans,[3] one can only conjecture; but his enthusiasm of humanity in the presence of the declaration of freedom by the French is unmistakable, and indeed was shared in by his immediate followers, Schelling and Hegel, who in their undergraduate days, as we are told, went out one day with a number of their fellow-students and planted a Tree of Liberty in the market-place of Tübingen.[4] It is true that Hegel in his later days constructed a political philosophy which his

[2] G. P. Gooch points out that this quotation was attributed to Kant in 1817 by Stägeman who knew Kant well. Gooch adds that its authenticity is not widely accepted. *Germany and the French Revolution* (London, Longmans Green, 1920), 264.

[3] There are three poems that bear testimony to this view. 'xxviii. French Revolution as it Appeared to Enthusiasts At Its Commencement', *Wordsworth's Poetical Works*, ed. E. De Selincourt, 2nd edn (Oxford, Clarendon Press, 1954), vol. II, 264–5; 'Feelings Of A French Royalist, On The Disinternment Of The Remains Of The Duke D'Enghieu', *Poetical Works* (1954), vol. 3, 149; 'In Allusion to Various Recent Histories And Notices Of The French Revolution: Concluded', *Poetical Works* (1947), vol. III, 130. In the last he warns the English not to be blind to the bloody consequences of the French Revolution.

[4] Caird says of this alleged incident: 'There was even a tradition – which has now been proved to refer to another time – that he and Schelling went out one fine spring morning to plant a tree of Liberty in the market-place of Tübingen. At any rate, it is certain that Hegel fully shared in the wonderful hopes which at the time stirred all that was generous and imaginative in Europe.' Edward Caird, *Hegel* (Edinburgh, Blackwood, 1893), 10–11.

opponents claimed to have been modelled after the Prussian constitution; into that controversy I cannot at present enter, but it is at least certain that he not only did not endorse, but expressly attacked, the doctrine that the State rests upon force: 'its binding cord', as he expressly says, being 'not force but the deep-seated feeling of order which is possessed by us all'. And in criticizing Haller, the von Treitschke of his day, he says: 'It is not the power of the right that Haller means, but the power of the vulture which tears in pieces the innocent lamb' (*Philosophy of Right*, p. 245 n.).[5] When we further remember that Fichte, in his noble and impassioned *Addresses to the German People*,[6] was seeking to lift his countrymen above their narrow and selfish point of view, and to unite them in the faith of a common patriotism, it will be evident that these philosophers of Germany's heroic age, so far from being distinguished by the arrogance and boastfulness of some of their present successors, were rather in the position of men who were trying to persuade their countrymen that only by banding together and sacrificing their selfish and personal interests was it possible to have a country at all. But, when we pass from these philosophers of the early nineteenth century to our own day, we find an entire change in temper, and spirit and outlook. Here is the venerable Herr Doctor Adolf Lasson, one of the editors of Hegel's works, and indeed a successor to his chair in Berlin, giving utterance to a boastful self-satisfaction that one could hardly excuse in a youth of eighteen. In Russia, he tells us, 'everything is dishonourable and depraved'. It is painful to a cultured German to think that the German army, 'with qualities such as no other nation can produce', should be faced by 'raw barbarian hordes on the East, and in the West by the military bagmen who drag their bones to market at a salary and commission in the service of a nation of shopkeepers'.

---

[5] For Hegel the basis of the state 'is the power of reason actualising itself as will' (Philosophy of Right, §258A). In other words it is the power of Spirit whose essence is freedom with which Hegel wishes to associate the State, and not with the physical force of Nature. This distinction is in fact the basis of his criticism of Carl Ludwig von Haller, who although Swiss by birth was very influential among the Prussian nobility. See Robert M. Berdahl, *The Politics of the Prussian Nobility: The Development of a Conservative Ideology* (Princeton, Princeton University Press, 1988), 236.

[6] Fichte, *Addresses to the German People*, trans. R. F. Jones and G. H. Turnbull (London, Open Court, 1922). The lectures were delivered in 1808.

(Alas, poor England!) The French, he proceeds, unlike the Russians and the English, are an intelligent people, but they 'live on crazes and illusions and allow their imaginations to run away with them'. 'With such a rabble must our splendid men and dear lads draw swords.' 'In truth', he complacently adds, 'we Germans are the foremost people of the new age. The whole of European culture, which is in effect universal human culture, is focussed as by a lens on this German soil and in the heart of the German people . . .We Germans represent the latest and highest product of European culture in general, and European culture is universal culture' (QED).[7]

Obviously something remarkable must have happened between the first decade of the nineteenth century and the first decade of the twentieth, to account for the conversion of a simple and, on the whole, a modest people into this portentous exhibition of national arrogance verging upon stupidity. What is that something?

For one thing, as we all know, Prussia has got the upper hand, and Prussia, since the days of the great elector, has always been distinguished for its arrogance and its brutal disregard of the rights of other nationalities. There are differences in the temper and character and ability of the Great Elector, Frederick the Great, and William the Second; but in one thing they are agreed, namely, in their thorough conviction that the world has been made for the aggrandizement of the great German people. When armed with the highest products of modern science a man so ill-balanced and erratic as William the Second is necessarily a menace to all other nations. Having absolutely no capacity for self-criticism, and being filled with a colossal and superstitious self-admiration, it is little wonder that, urged on by a military *entourage* even blinder than himself, he has been led to plunge the world into the horrors of the present war. The foolish old man, whose words I have already quoted, is unfortunately representative of much of the articulate voice of professorial Germany; and what one is interested to learn is whether there is anything in the history of Germany and German philosophy to account for the phenomena that we are now witnessing; and, if so, whether there is a reasonable hope that the German people, when they have recovered from their bad dream, may regain that

---

[7] Watson's reference is loose and misleading. The famous Hegel editor is Georg Lasson (1862–1932).

large outlook on life and that sanity which are characteristic of an earlier period and of their great philosophers. To give some answer to these questions will be the main object of this paper.

'It is a melancholy thing', says Hegel, 'when a people has no longer a political philosophy, and not less melancholy when it has lost its metaphysic and no longer seeks to comprehend its own inner nature.'[8] In view of the actual history of philosophy in Germany, these words sound like a solemn warning. That the countrymen of Hegel have put the world under obligation in many respects no unbiased person will deny, but in the construction of a philosophy, in the large sense of the word, the successors of Hegel, in spite of brilliant sallies by individual thinkers, have been singularly unsuccessful. Nor have they been any more successful in the construction of a Philosophy of Religion. True, they have taken up the task begun by Spinoza, and carried forward so far by the English Deists, the task of subjecting the Scriptures to the cold and severe test of historical criticism; but their labours have only resulted in supplying materials for a revision of traditional theology, and cannot for a moment be taken as a substitute for a philosophy of religion. Historical criticism, valuable as it is, is no more a philosophy of religion than researches in biology on the basis of the new ideas supplied by Charles Darwin and Alfred Russel Wallace are a metaphysic. A proof of the incapacity of the German philosopher to construct a philosophy of religion may be found in the vogue of Schopenhauer and Nietzsche. A theology without a God is impossible, and there is no God in the system of these thinkers. The Absolute of Schopenhauer is an abstract Force, while the God of Nietzsche is his Superman. I do not deny the value of these thinkers as supplying incentives to others, but they have no philosophy of religion themselves. In making these charges against the philosophers of Germany, I am not unmindful of the fact that there are German thinkers who have not bowed the knee to Baal. Lotze, Fechner, Pfleiderer and Paulsen must always command our respect; but none of these

---

[8] This comes from the preface to the first edition of Hegel's *Science of Logic*. A. V. Millar translates the passage as follows: 'If it is remarkable when a nation has become indifferent to its constitutional theory, to its national sentiments, its ethical customs and virtues, it is certainly no less remarkable when a nation loses its metaphysics, when the spirit which contemplates its own pure essence is no longer a present reality in the life of the nation.' *Hegel's Science of Logic* (London, Allen and Unwin, 1969), 25.

thinkers has really appealed to the minds of their blinded country-men.[9] While Lotze has been neglected, except by a few cultured students, the young men, yes, and the young women, of Germany have been intoxicated and bewildered by the dangerous half-truths of Nietzsche. Fechner no doubt has appealed on the one hand to minds of a mystical type, and on the other hand by his scientific psychology to the prevalent type of German scholar: Pfleiderer has had more influence in England than in his own country; but neither of them has had any permanent effect on the main current of German thought. Treitschke, again, was pouring forth his impassioned glorification of Germany and perverting the minds of his youthful hearers by a false reading of political history, punctu-ated by unmeasured scorn of other nations, especially of England, while the moderate and reasonable Paulsen was listened to respect-fully but without enthusiasm. These things require explanation; and the explanation lies to a large extent in the political and economic history of Germany.

The history of Germany during the last one hundred and twenty years may be divided into three great periods: from 1794 to 1870, from 1870 to 1888, and from 1888 to the present day; and it will be found that in a general way the movements in philosophy, in politics, and in political economy correspond. The political unity of Germany was secured comparatively late, partly because of the strong individuality, not to say the selfishness, of the two hundred states into which the Teutonic people were divided. At the begin-ning of our first period the economic condition of Germany was as poor as possible. Systems of common cultivation and of partial vil-leinage prevailed; and industrial development could hardly be expected from a people split up into separate states, and almost hermetically sealed against one another, not only by tariff barriers,

---

[9] Rudolph Herman Lotze (1817–81) was a German idealist who made considerable concessions to empiricism for which he was taken to task by Henry Jones in his *A Critical Account of the Philosophy of Lotze* (Glasgow, Maclehose, 1895). Bernard Bosanquet translated Lotze's principal works as *Lotze's System of Philosophy* in 1884. Gustav Theodor Fechner (1801–87) was a German scientist and philosopher who wrote on a wide range of subjects, including ethics. Pfleiderer (1839–1908) delivered the Gifford Lectures at Edinburgh in 1894, published as *Philosophy and the Development of Religion* (Edinburgh, Blackwood, 1894). Friedrich Paulsen (1846–1908) was a German philosopher and educational theorist who described himself as an idealist monist. He was part of the broader mid-nineteenth century trend to revive the philosophies of Aristotle and Kant.

but by differences in measures and money, in customs and laws. From 1850 to 1860, however, the foundations of Germany as an industrial state were laid, although its rate of progress was retarded by the rivalry of other countries, especially in iron and steel and other mineral industries. A new order of things was initiated by the reforms of Stein and Hardenberg and several others, and it is significant that these reformers were none of them Prussians.[10] Stein was aided in awakening Germany to self-consciousness by the addresses of Fichte already referred to; but the mass of the people were kept out of even moderate rights for many years by the pedantic Frederick William the Third and his pedantic statesmen; so that in Germany, almost alone of the great European powers, the democratic and national movements towards unity and liberty were stifled in their birth.

In the second period of her history Germany entered upon a new career under the guidance of Bismarck, the final result of which was the unification of Germany and the contemporary organization of the Prussian army by Roon, while the military strategy of Moltke resulted in the triumph of Prussia, first over Austria and later over France. The effect of the war on the German people was to stimulate their consciousness of unity, and, under Bismarck's guidance, to develop the rich mineral resources of the country, thus emancipating Germany from its dependence on foreign countries.

The third period of the political history of Germany begins with the accession of the present Emperor in 1888. There immediately followed a great increase in numbers of the regular army and the development of an ambitious naval policy. The country has been during his reign commercially prosperous in the highest degree, and so far as trade and industry are concerned there was no need to long for 'a place in the sun', which Germany already possessed. But, contrary to the policy of Bismarck, the rulers of Germany have

---

[10] Karl Freiherr von Stein rose to ministerial status in Prussia before 1806, and although he fought vehemently against Napoleon, was like most 'German patriots' willing to collaborate after the German defeats of 1806. He then put forward proposals for reform and was dismissed from office in January 1807. In his enforced retirement he wrote the famous 'Nassau Denkschrift' which focused on civic participation and cuts in government expenditure. In October 1807 he was appointed chief minister and almost a year later was dismissed from office on Napoleon's insistence. Karl August von Hardenburg was Prussian Chancellor and government reformer.

acted on the principle that an extension of territory is indispensable in a great power. As a matter of fact, Germany's best customers, as one of themselves has pointed out,[a] have been found in foreign countries, their colonies having been so far only a source of expense. It is not necessary to discuss the question of where the responsibility of the present war should be placed. What is certain is that till the eleventh hour Sir Edward Grey[11] worked with all his might to prevent the present disastrous conflagration, and was balked at every turn by the apparent determination of the German Government to provoke hostilities, for which Germany alone was adequately prepared. On that topic nothing more need be said, and I gladly turn to my main subject, the relation of German philosophy to the present war.

One cannot but be struck by the enormous influence on the whole development of German philosophy exercised by Immanuel Kant. Not only is it true that a vast amount of industry has been devoted by philosophical writers to the elucidation of the letter of Kant, but even writers who belong to an entirely different school of thought have been unable to escape from his all-pervasive influence. This fact is not at all difficult to explain, when we remember the genius of this 'epoch making philosopher', as his countrymen call him, and reflect that the Critical Philosophy is itself the result of a sort of compromise between discrepant conceptions of life, and covers with its three Critiques the whole realm of philosophy: epistemological, ethical, aesthetic and religious. The philosophy of Kant sought to effect a synthesis of empiricism and rationalism; but the attempt, while in spirit it was on the whole successful, achieved its end by a method which in its literal acceptation was bound to lead to divergence and dissension. The 'rift in the lute'[12] indeed appeared during the lifetime of Kant himself. Nor had the immediate successors of Kant – Fichte, Schelling, and Hegel – all triumphant as they were in the first instance, everything their own way. Even in the lifetime

---

[a] The anonymous author of *J'Accuse*.

[11] Sir Edward Grey (1862–1933) was Foreign Secretary 1905–16.
[12] Alfred Lord Tennyson,

> It is the little rift within the lute,
> That by and by will make the music mute,
> And ever widening slowly silence all.

Works (Ware, Hertfordshire, Wordsworth, 1994), 480.

of Hegel, Schopenhauer, with the peculiar arrogance that we have come to associate with the Prussian character, dissented violently from the teaching of Hegel, and, as a Privat-docent in Berlin University, openly displayed his hostility by fixing his lectures at the same hour. The result was hardly what, in his self-confidence, he had anticipated; for Hegel's lecture-room continued to be crowded, while in Schopenhauer's there was no difficulty in getting an empty bench to oneself. Nevertheless, in a sense the immediate future was with Schopenhauer; for, although the large and comprehensive philosophy of Hegel, whatever may be said of its specific doctrines, has undoubtedly in it this fundamental truth, that the universe is a rational system and that in the great process of humanity goodness is bound in the long run to prevail; yet, in the first reaction against his triumphant idealism, the theoretical one-sidedness and the pessimism of Schopenhauer caught the public ear, and the history of the former *Maestro di coloro che sanno* [teacher of those who know][13] was temporarily obscured. Only temporarily, for Hegel can no more be ignored than Plato or Aristotle. He belongs to the apostolic succession of the great heroes of philosophy; while Schopenhauer, with all his literary gifts and his immediate success, was the author of an untenable metaphysic and an impossible theory of ethics, which can only be compared to one of those discords in music that help to enrich the general harmony. Even Nietzsche once declared, in a flash of inspiration, that Schopenhauer, 'by his unintelligent rage against Hegel, succeeded in severing a whole generation from its connection with German culture' (*Beyond Good and Evil*, sec. 204.)[14]

The bone of dispute concerned the nature of the ultimate principle of the universe and the organ by which it may be reached. Kant's view was that the circle of knowledge does not extend, roughly speaking, beyond the realm of the natural sciences, and that the realities, which in his view undoubtedly exist, fall outside of

---

[13] Dante,

> Higher I raised my brows and further scanned,
> and saw the Master of the men who know,
> Seated amid the philosophic band;

Inferno (Harmondsworth, Penguin, 1949), Canto IV, line 131.

[14] For a more recent translation see Friedrich Nietzsche, *Beyond Good and Evil: Prelude to a Philosophy of the Future*, trans. R. J. Hollingdale (Harmondsworth, Penguin, 1975) sec. 204.

this circle, and are a matter of rational faith, not of knowledge. The contention of his idealistic followers, brought to a point in Hegel, was, that the Absolute or God not only exists, but is the source of all knowledge, and indeed is in the strict sense the only object really knowable. To deny knowledge of this principle, or to ignore it, is to commit intellectual suicide. What these thinkers were contending for is expressed in more ordinary language in the words of Scripture, that God is 'not far from any one of us, being in our mouths and in our hearts'.[15] Schopenhauer, on the other hand, maintained that the ultimate principle is not Intelligence, but Will; and by Will, as we soon find, he meant something that only differs from Force by its indefiniteness and unknowability. This blind unconscious principle, lying beyond the sphere of the human intellect, is for Schopenhauer the true principle of the universe; the popular idea of a self-conscious deity being to his mind merely the survival of an obsolete superstition.

Here then we have the issue fairly stated. Shall we accept the idealistic doctrine of a self-conscious Principle as the true source and explanation of reality, or must we fall back upon some unknowable Power, figured to ourselves after the analogy of the forces of nature? The tragedy of German philosophy seems to me to be this: that, for reasons hard to disentangle and impossible to set forth at present in detail, the idealists have lost ground, while the positivists have captured the popular ear. No doubt Nietzsche, the one man of genius whom Germany has produced in the lifetime of men now living, had a horror of the direction in which his countrymen were blindly drifting; but the romantic and immaterial principle for which he was contending was later materialized, and employed in support of a bureaucratic system that was the special object of his detestation.

Leaving aside the names of Nietzsche, Lotze, von Hartmann, Sigwart, Wundt, Paulsen and Windelband – all of whom belong more or less to the idealistic tradition – let us turn our attention to

---

[15] Deuteronomy 30: 11–15. 'Now what I am commanding you today is not too difficult for you or beyond your reach. It is not up in heaven, so that you have to ask, "Who will ascend in heaven to get it and proclaim it to us so we may obey it?" Nor is it beyond the sea, so that you have to ask, "Who will cross the sea to get it and proclaim it to us so we may obey it." No, the word is very near you; it is in your mouth and in your heart so you may obey it.'

the undercurrent of German philosophy in its second period, beginning with the publication of Liebmann's *Kant und die Epigonen* in 1865.[16] Liebmann indeed was not by any means the first to reject the larger idealistic view of the world; for, as we have seen, Schopenhauer had already done so, proclaiming himself to be the true follower of Kant. The strong meat of Schopenhauer, however, was too rich for the digestion of the ordinary German professor of philosophy; and the cry of Liebmann, 'Back to Kant' (which really meant, 'Back to the Letter of Kant'), comforted their Philistine souls. The charge brought by Liebmann against the idealists was that they had forsaken the realm of verifiable experience and presumptuously attempted to define and comprehend the ultimate nature of reality. It does not seem to have occurred to him that the limitation of knowledge to that which presents itself within human consciousness is the *fons et origo* [the source and origin] of that very 'thing-in-itself' which he assails with his spluttering and noisy battery. The illusion which besets those who claim that while we are able to determine the character of the objects that fall within our experience, we can never emerge from this kingdom of shadows, exercises upon Liebmann its usual fascination, and he never seems to be aware that a theory of the insuperable limitations of our knowledge assumes that very 'thing-in-itself' which he falsely attributes to the genuine idealist. If true reality is behind and beyond knowledge, it must be unknown and even unknowable. It matters not that ostensibly Liebmann confines himself within the narrow bounds of human experience; for back of all this experience lies the empty Absolute, which nothing but a fiction of abstraction prevents from vanishing into nothingness. Thus the real dualist is not the idealist who claims that we live in a rational and intelligible universe, but the realistic epistemologist with his express or tacit opposition of the knowable and the real.

Besides the general denial of any knowledge beyond that of the ordinary world of our experience, German philosophy in this second period of its history upheld an ethical doctrine, wrongly attributed to Kant, which maintained that the function of knowl-

---

[16] Otto Liebmann (1840–1912) was a neo-Kantian who rejected contemporary German philosophy and advocated a return to Kant. He believed that Kant's real contribution was the discovery of the transcendental, but nevertheless thought that it had to be dissociated from the idea of things in themselves.

edge is practical rather than theoretical, being simply the method by which, living within the world, the inner nature of which is to us unintelligible, we set up practical rules that enable us to make progress in morality without ever coming in contact with the universe in its ultimate nature. Vaihinger,[17] the expositor of Kant, departs so far from the ordered world of experience maintained by Kant as to deny that the conceptions by which we organize our world have any other value than as convenient fictions enabling us to find our way in a world too vast and too mysterious to be understood. It will hardly be denied that doctrines like these afford only too good an excuse for those whose interest it is to maintain that 'Might is Right'. If we cannot know the inner nature of things, what can our morality be but the prudential rules of finite beings who have to live somehow with one another, and who in the absence of fixed principles are engaged in the process of each trying to raise his head above the others? For the same reason, religion can have no absolute value, and what is put in its place must be some overmastering impulse, in itself ultimately indefensible. Accepting these premises we can partly understand how the German people have gradually been converted to the belief that the old sophistical doctrine, 'Might is Right' and 'Justice the interest of the stronger', is the true principle of philosophy. In this way one can also understand how Nietzsche's gospel of the Superman should be transformed into Treitschke's confident belief in the omnipotence of the Prussian state, or rather the Prussian Government; and we can even discern how a still lower deep than the lowest deep to which Treitschke had sunk should be reached by General von Bernhardi,[18] with his crude soldier's theory that the world was made for the glory of Kaiser Wilhelm der Zweite and the great Hohenzollern family. The pity of it all is that German philosophy in its popular form has lost all rational belief in Love and Righteousness, and has enthroned in its stead the fetish of Force and Fraud and Frightfulness. Are there any symptoms that this debasing creed will be out-

---

[17] Hans Vaihinger (1852–1933) is the founder of the 'as if approach' to philosophy. He was also a distinguished Kant scholar and founded the journal *Kant Studien*.

[18] Heinrich von Trietschke (1834–1896) was an influential German historian and General Friedrich von Bernhardi was a career soldier who became Commanding General of the VIIth Army Corps in 1907. He advocated war as the answer to Germany's economic problems. Both were extensively cited during the inter-war period as archetypal German militarists.

grown? Are there no philosophers of recent times who have got at least a glimpse of a truer way? I think there are, as a consideration of the third phase of German philosophy seems to indicate, a phase which extends from the year 1888 down to the present day.

The philosophers of the Second Period, as we have seen, are all convinced epistemologists, that is, they are agreed in denying that we can ever comprehend the inner nature of the universe, and must therefore content ourselves with a working theory of life, leaving the attempted solution of ultimate problems to the weak and muddled heads who waste their energies on unpractical and idle problems. We of the English tradition find nothing especially new in this attitude. Some fifty years ago, George Henry Lewes wrote a History of Philosophy,[19] to prove that it presented the melancholy spectacle of the best minds engaged for centuries on a task similar to that of squaring the circle; and the burden of the philosophy of Herbert Spencer is that the Absolute is by its very nature unknowable. Like much of the supposed advances of the last fifty years of the nineteenth century, the successes claimed by their countrymen for the German epistemologists are largely due to thinkers of the despised 'nation of shop-keepers' whom cultivated Englishmen believe themselves to have out-grown. Be that as it may, it is certain that with the third period, beginning with the publication of Avenarius' *Critique of Pure Experience*,[20] we seem to see the dawn of a better day for German philosophy. For, though this careful writer cannot be placed alongside of men like Lotze or Fechner or Nietzsche, he is a sober and careful thinker not devoid of a certain degree of metaphysical insight. Our ideas, he says, are no doubt determined by our experience or environment; and yet he will venture to affirm that knowledge is something more than an instrument of action, being by its very nature an orderly system, existing no doubt only for us as conscious and intelligent beings, but in no

---

[19] *A Biographical History of Philosophy*. Series I, *Ancient Philosophers*, and Series II, *From Bacon to the Present Day*. Published in London in 1845 and 1836. It was enlarged and revised in 1857. There were new editions in 1867, 1871, 1880 and 1891.

[20] Richard Avenarius (1843–1896) independently developed ideas similar to those of Ernst Mach. Avenarius was the initiator of empirio criticism. It was a radical epistemological doctrine that tried to jettison metaphysics and derive from pure experience a concept of the world that was essentially natural. He published his two-volume work *Kritik der reinen Erfahrung*, 1888–1890.

sense arbitrarily made by us. This idea, true as it is, is expressed by Avenarius in a somewhat halting and ambiguous way, when he tells us that we must abolish the opposition of physical and psychical, since mind differs from matter, not in fundamental nature, but only as containing more in it. Still more decisively Cassirer, who belongs to the Marburg school of philosophy, approximates to the main doctrine of the early idealists, in so far as he holds that we are capable of rising above a purely individual point of view and discovering the actual connections of things.[21] No doubt it is in the conceptions of mathematics that he finds the categories by which this truer view of the world may be obtained; but, though the idealists would regard this limitation to mathematical conceptions as itself a limitation, they would entirely agree with Cassirer and the Marburg school generally in their view that really fruitful conceptions are never the product of an arbitrary process of classification by abstraction or elimination. To the same effect it is argued by Husserl, that in our experience there are necessary distinctions and relations, by the proper comprehension of which we are not only enabled to see the relative truth of our ordinary view of the world, but to see beyond it. Thus Husserl seems to intimate, 'as by a side-gesture', that we are not entirely deprived of a true grasp of the world. It may be admitted that the empirical tradition is still too strong for these thinkers to seek for a reconstruction of philosophy on a rational or idealistic basis; but I think it can hardly be denied that, after wandering for many years in the wilderness, with eyes obstinately fixed on the earth, the better class of German minds have begun, almost shamefacedly, to glance upwards to the heavens; and one is disposed to believe that the very thoroughness of the German intellect may, in its slow and laboured way, yet come to work out in a reasoned system that which thinkers of other nations obtain in a flash of inspiration. Nor must we forget that in the more positive departments of philosophy we owe the plodding German a debt of gratitude. Fechner and Wundt, assisted by a host of philo-

---

[21] The Marburg School comprised a group of neo-Kantians, including Hermann Cohen (1842–1918) and Paul Natorp (1854–1924), committed to take account of the presuppositions or 'the fact of science'. It launched a journal in 1906 entitled *Philosophische Arbeiten*. Ernst Cassirer (1874–1945) was the last of the important representatives of the School who sought to develop a general theory of culture on Kantian principles.

sophical hod-carriers, have done much to advance the cause of a precise and accurate psychology; and the contributions of these and other thinkers to the theory of art and the history of religion and of political institutions cannot be overlooked. Nor have all professors of philosophy, or even all Berlin professors, subscribed to the crude theory of the state expressed by Treitschke. Here, for example, are a few sentences from Paulsen, which show that he saw the danger of an autocratic government, especially when its policy is dictated by a military oligarchy. In a lecture on *Party Politics and Morals*, delivered in Dresden in 1900, he says:

> The most perfect type of organization from above is the army, in which combination and division of labour are carried to the minutest point, to the entire exclusion of all combination from below. Of the same type is an absolute monarchy ... Strict unity of will gives to this form of government great weight in attack. But a danger confronts the advantage – the danger that it may concentrate intellect and will on a single point, and cause a general decay in the peripheral members, because of the absence in them of independent activity. Losing all initiation and spontaneity, they come to present the phenomena of a palsied intelligence, will and conscience: the body as a whole loses its sensibility; internal disease may develop without being felt, and may have far advanced before there is in the members any consciousness of a failure of sensibility and responsibility. The rule of the Bourbons and that of Frederick the Great are historical examples of the fact that in an autocracy the citizens submit to the Government with an indifference verging on stupidity.

To this indictment of a despotic form of government may be added Paulsen's warning against the claim of Germany to rule the world.

> Since the sixties, [he says], a new faith has sprung up, at first timidly and- shamefacedly – belief in power and the will to power. This gave to the close of the nineteenth century its special significance ... Political questions are questions of power! So said Bismarck with incisive and offensive bluntness, and because history is on his side the German people now think what he has taught them to think, and often in a much more one-sided way. The doctrine is held to apply not only to questions of foreign policy, but to domestic politics as well. He who has the strongest will and power to enforce it, is claimed to have right on his side. Compared

with this, what is the value, it is asked, of the old parchments? *Sic volo sic jubeo, sit pro ratione voluntas*,[b] has no doubt always been the point of view of men in authority, but only in our day has it been openly expressed as a maxim of policy.

Let me cite one more voice of warning. Speaking of the achievements of the German State, Windelband only five years ago gave utterance to his uneasiness in these words:

> Nowadays, (he says), we find ourselves irresistibly drawn into a whirl of practical work, which claims and absorbs every power, every interest and every activity in the highest degree ... There is scant time for inward meditation, for theoretical reflection: the national energy is so dispersed outwardly that it is unable to gather itself together within ... The zenith of our political life has produced no great poem, and no adequate philosophy, to express in terms of reflection the mind and life of the nation.

These words may well suggest the pertinent comment of Professor A. S. Ferguson[c]: 'Perhaps the din about German culture which troubles one's ears today owes some of its loudness to faint stirrings of uneasiness.' Many more sayings similar to those of Paulsen and Windelband might be quoted, but I must hurry to a close. One may at least derive from them the hope that, in spite of the appalling ferocity and barbarity with which the present war has been conducted by Germany; notwithstanding the wild and whirling words of an Emperor devoid of self-knowledge; beneath the vapourings of a press which reflects the inflated notions of a people giddy with unforeseen success; one may hope that in the breasts of many sensible Germans, at present forced to be silent, there beats a more equable pulse; and that, at the close of the war there will emerge a chastened and subdued Germany, which has learned the 'open secret', that no nation can respect itself that does not respect others. It cannot be necessary to point out the distinction between brute force and the just power of a State which can appeal to reason in defence of its acts. It is lamentable that a nation of thinkers should be misled by the sophistry which opines that, because each State has power to enforce its decrees on its own citizens, therefore one State may coerce all other nations in its own interest. No State

[b] 'My will is my only reason.'
[c] University Magazine. [Queen's University, Ontario, Canada] April 1915, p. 224.

may enforce a single law, even on its own citizens, much less make or break a single treaty, in defiance of universal principles of reason. The true foundation of the State is not force and fraud, but humanity and sympathy. We who are subjects of the British Empire do not claim that England has in all cases been free from blame; but we may fairly say that, with all her stumblings and mistakes, she has on the whole acted honourably and justly. Three hundred years ago England learned in her Civil War this great truth, that the real strength of a nation lies in the free and self-conscious development of the whole people – the aim of Government being to educate every citizen to an appreciation of the grounds on which it acts, and to condemn all unjust legislation and partisan administration. Nothing less can sanctify the employment, of force; which, divorced from reason, becomes unjust and pernicious. Of stark Power we may surely say what Tennyson says of knowledge:

> What is she, cut from love and faith,
> But some wild Pallas from the brain
> Of Demons? fiery hot to burst
> All barriers in her onward race
> For Power. Let her know her place:
> She is the Second – not the first.[22]

---

[22] Alfred Lord Tennyson, 'In Memoriam A. H. H. OBITT MDCCCXXXIII', lines 2443–8, in *Enoch and In Memoriam, The Works of Tennyson: The Eversley Edition* (London, Macmillan, 1907–8), 9 vols.

14
The Function of the State in Promoting the Unity of Mankind[a]

BERNARD BOSANQUET

I wish to present a brief positive account of the theory of the state as I understand it, more particularly with reference to the state in its external relations, and the conditions essential to federations or a world-state.

It seems to me that much misconception is prevalent as to the views which in fact great philosophers have held upon this problem. But I do not wish to raise mere questions in the history of philosophy, but to meet the issue as it seems to me to stand to-day. The ideas which I express are therefore my own, in the sense that no

[a] Cf. the lectures by Professor A. C. Bradley on 'International Morality: the United States of Europe', and Mr. B. Bosanquet on 'Patriotism in the Perfect State', in *The International Crisis*, Oxford University Press, 1915; and Lord Haldane's Montreal address, 'Higher Nationality'. In speaking of the critics, I have had in mind, besides the writers in the Aristotelian *Proceedings* for 1915–16. Mr. A. D. Lindsay's lecture in the Bedford College volume, *Theory of the State*, and some remarks of Professor Jacks in *From the Human End, together with the general reaction against what is supposed to be the 'German' theory of the state.*[1]

[1] The full references are: A. C. Bradley, 'International Morality: the United States of Europe' and Bernard Bosanquet, 'Patriotism in the Perfect State', in *The International Crisis in its Ethical and Psychological Aspects* (London, Oxford University Press, 1915); Viscount Haldane, 'The Higher Nationality', in *The Conduct of Life and Other Addresses* (London, John Murray, 1914); *Proceedings of the Aristotelian Society*, xvi (1915–16); A. D. Lindsay, 'The State and Society', *The International Crisis: The Theory of the State* (London, Oxford University Press, 1916); Lawrence Pearsall Jacks, *From the Human End* (London, Williams and Norgate, 1916). The principle texts alluded to in the 'general reaction' are: L. T. Hobhouse, *The Metaphysical Theory of the State* (London, Allen and Unwin, 1917); G. Santayana, *Egotism in German Philosophy* (London, Dent, 1914); and John Dewey, *German Philosophy and Politics* (New York, Holt, 1915)).

one else is responsible for the form I give them. But, to the best of my judgment, they represent the Greek tradition as renewed by Hegel and by English thought.

In considering any problem affecting the state I take the primary question to be how self-government is possible. For anything which interferes with the possibility of self-government destroys altogether the conditions of true government. The answer is drawn, I take it, from the conception of the general will, which involves the existence of an actual community, of such a nature as to share an identical mind and feeling. There is no other way of explaining how a free man can put up with compulsion and even welcome it.

Here then we have the universal condition of legitimate outward authority. City-state, Nation-state, Commonwealth, Federation, World-state, it makes no difference. Behind all force there must be a general will, and the general will must represent a communal-mind.[b] All other contrivances for government are external and tyr-annical.

1. This is the reason of the unique relation between the state and the individual which is caricatured by critics as state absolutism. Of course the state is not the ultimate end of life. The ultimate end, if we avoid religious phraseology, which would probably furnish the truest expression of it, is surely the best life. I understand by the state the power which, as the organ of a community, has the func-tion of maintaining the external conditions necessary to the best life. These conditions are called rights. They are the claims recog-nised by the will of a community as the *sine qua non* of the highest obtainable fulfilment of the capacities for the best life possessed by its members.

Now the relation between the state and the individual is the external equivalent of that between the community and the individ-ual. And it is a unique relation, because there is no other body that bears the same relation to the individual's will as that community which is represented by a state in the external world.

This can be said with as much precision as human affairs admit, because there is reason to expect that the community which organ-ises itself as a state will be for every group the largest body which possesses the unity of experience necessary for constituting a gen-

[b] See Lord Haldane's address referred to above.

eral will. There is, as we shall see, no other body at all comparable with it in intensity of unity. 'A national purpose is the most unconquerable and victorious of all things on earth.'ᶜ And the individual's private will, we must bear in mind, is certainly and literally a part of the communal will. There is no other material of which his will can be made. If he rejects the communal will in part, he rejects it on the basis of what it is in him, not from any will of his own which has a different source. This is the ground of the duty of rebellion.

This unique relation between the individual and the community which the state represents – it may be a nation or any other community – is what seems to me to dominate the whole problem. It is further determined when we add the consideration that the state is an organ of action in the external world. In this sphere, which is its special sphere as an organ exercising force, it may really be called absolute, that is, if power extending to life and death and complete disposal of property can be called absolute. This does not mean that it is the whole end of life,ᵈ nor that it is the only object of loyalty.ᵉ It means, as I understand it, that, being the special organ of arrangement in the external world, corresponding to that particular community whose will *is* our own will when most highly organised, it has the distinctive function of dictating the final adjustment in matters of external action. This is the only sense in which I have called it absolute,ᶠ and the ground is obvious and simple. It lies in the

ᶜ A. E., *Imaginations*, etc., p. 107.²
ᵈ Hegel in one place calls the state an end-in-itself, when he is contrasting his view of it with the reduction of its purpose to the protection of property or the right of the stronger. He regards it as having in it some of the end of life, viz., the embodiment of liberty; of course, not the whole end. It is for him the basis of the further more specialised achievements (art, philosophy, and the like), – *Rechtsphilosophie*, Sect. 258.³
ᵉ See below, p. 283. [p. 281 in this vol.].
ᶠ *Philosophy of the State*, ch. viii. 3, and Introduction to 2nd edn [Bernard Bosanquet, *Philosophical Theory of the State* (London, Macmillan, 1899: 2nd edn, 1910; 3rd edn, 1920; 4th edn, 1923].

² George William Russell (1867–1935), (A.E.), *Imaginations and Reveries* (Dublin and London, Mounsel, 1915), 107. He was an Irish journalist, economist, poet, painter and friend of W. B. Yeats.
³ Hegel, *Elements of the Philosophy of Right*, ed. Allen W. Wood and trans., H. B. Nisbet (Cambridge, Cambridge University Press, 1991), /258, Addition (G):

The state in and for itself is the ethical whole, the actualisation of freedom, and it is the absolute end of reason that freedom should be actual. The state is the spirit which is present in the world and which *consciously* realises itself therein . . .

tendency of the world of action to bring into collision factors which, apart from action, might never conflict. However purely non-political two associations may be, and however cosmopolitan, if they claim the same funds or the same building they must come before a power which can adjust the difference without appeal. And if such a power were not single in respect of them, obviously there could be no certainty of adjustment without a conflict between the two or more powers which might claim jurisdiction. Cases like that supposed are frequent, of course, with churches.

Thus there are two connected points, which, I think, the critics confuse under the name of absolutism. One is the power of the state as sustainer of all adjustments in the world of external action, on the ground which has just been explained. The other is the unique relation to the individual of such a community as is at present exemplified by his nation-state, because it represents, as nothing else in the world does, that special system of rights and sentiments, the complement of his own being, which the general will of his group has formed a state to maintain.

It is the result, I take it, of these two grounds of unity co-operating, that in times of stress the state, as the organ of the community, will suspend or subject to conditions any form of intercourse between its members and persons or associations within or without its territory, and will require any service that it thinks fit from any of its members. It does, in Mr. Bradley's words, 'with the moral approval of all what the explicit theory of scarcely one will morally justify'.[g] That it does not exercise such powers to anything like the same degree in ordinary times, and that it recognises the rights of conscience even in times of stress, flows from the fact that its primary end is the maintenance of rights, and it will override no right by force where an adjustment is possible compatibly with the good life of the whole. And of this possibility it is the sole judge. What it permits, it permits by reason of its end, and no theory can stand which will not justify in principle its habitual action in time of stress.

2. 'The state', as I understand the words, is a phrase framed in the normal way, to express that one is dealing with the members of a class strictly according to the connotation of the class-name. If a

[g] [F. H. Bradley] *Ethical Studies* [Oxford, Clarendon Press, 1876], p. 166.

plural noun is used, there can be no certainty whether we are speaking of characteristics which belong to the class-members as such, or of circumstances which may occur in each of them for independent reasons. 'The state', in a word, is a brief expression for 'states *qua* states'. I confess that I am a good deal surprised that nearly all recent critics have stumbled, as it seems to me, in this simple matter of interpretation.[h,4] Would they find the same difficulty in the title of a book on 'the heart' or 'the steam-engine'? It would be urged, perhaps, that a heart does not imply other hearts, but that a state does imply other states; but if the thing implies other things its name implies the reference to them.

And, indeed, the whole *raison d'etre* of our theory is to show why, and in what sense, there must be states wherever there are groups of human beings, and to explain for what reasons men are distinguished into separate adjacent political bodies instead of forming a single system over the whole earth's surface.

Our theory has told us, for example, that states represent differentiations of the single human spirit (Hegel), whose extent and intensity determine and are determined by territorial limits. They are members, we are told by Plato and Hegel, of an ethical family of nations, so far, at least, as the European world is concerned; they are characterised – it is Mazzini's well-known doctrine – by

---

[h] Hegel pointed out this ambiguity, *Th. des REchts*, Set. 258; cf. also A. C. Bradley, *International Crisis*, p. 47. With the phrase 'philosophy of men', which is offered as a counter-example as against 'philosophy of *the State*', we may compare the two expressions 'knowledger of man' and 'knowledge of men'. The former means something like philosophy; the latter means the knowledge of individual peculiarities and defects, gathered by the experience of a worldling. The former belongs to Plato or Shakespeare, the latter to Major [Arthur] Pendennis. ['If there was any question about etiquette, society, who was married to whom, of what age such and such a duke was, Pendennis was the man to whom everyone appealed'. W. M. Thackeray, *The History of Pendennis* (London, Bradbury and Evans, 1849), vol. I, p. 2.]

[4] 'In considering the Idea of the State, we must not have any particular states or particular institutions in mind; instead, we should consider the Idea, this actual God, in its own right.' Hegel, *Elements of the Philosophy of Right*, 258. The A. C. Bradley article referred to is, 'International Morality: The United States of Europe', in Eleanor M. Sidgwick *et. al.*, *The International Crisis in its Ethical and Psychological Aspects* (London, Oxford University Press, 1915).

individual missions[i,5] or functions which furnish for every state its distinctive contribution to human life. They have a similar task to achieve, each within its territory allotted by history, so Green argues, and the more perfectly each of them attains its proper object of giving free scope to the capacities of all persons living on a certain range of territory, the easier it is for others to do so.[j] Obviously they are co-operating units. This is throughout the essence of the theory.

Now it is not, I think, unfair to point out that my critics, dealing unguardedly with 'states' and not with 'the state' or with 'states *qua* states', have on the whole founded their account of states not upon what they are, so far as states, but just upon what, *qua* states, they are not; upon defects which appear unequally in the several communities, consisting in those evils which the organisation of the state exists in order to remove, and does progressively remove in so far as true self-government is attained. Such evils are war, exploitation within or without, class privilege, arbitrary authority, discontent directing ambitions to foreign conquest and to jealousy of other states, the doctrine that one state's gain is *ipso facto* another's loss.

3. Space and time do not permit me to discuss, what I should be interested in discussing at some length, the continuous relations which extend beyond the frontiers of individual states, their importance compared with that of other continuities which are co-extensive with the area of the states and constituent of them, and why it is necessary to recognise, in spite of the former, separate sovereign political units which undoubtedly, while imperfect, tend to break down at the frontier, in a regrettable way, the continuities

---

[i] The term I have myself selected to describe the ethical unity of a nation-state (*Phil. of state*, p. 321).

[j] [T. H.] Green, [*Lectures on*] *Principles of Political Obligation* edited by Bernard Bosanquet (London, Longman Green, 1917), p. 170. [See this volume p. 227.]

[5] Greek city-states, for Plato, were naturally friends, and comprised a community. Citizens of Plato's state 'will love their fellow-Greeks, and think of Greece as their own land, in whose common religion they share'. Plato, *The Republic*, trans. Desmond Lee (Harmondsworth, Penguin, 1987), 471a. Hegel argues that: 'The European nations form a family with respect to the universal principle of their legislations, customs, and culture, so that their conduct in terms of international law is modified accordingly in a situation which is otherwise dominated by mutual infliction of evils'. *Elements of the Philosophy of Right*, §339 Addition.

which pass beyond it.[k] Broadly speaking, the reason lies, I take it, in the exceptionally intense unity and concreteness of certain group-minds,[l] in which innumerable continuities coincide, while other continuities, which extend beyond the group, nevertheless do not coincide with any marked rival unity.

4. It follows from our theory, as we saw, that the normal relation of states is co-operative.[m] Their influence on each other's structure and culture is mainly a question of wants and materials. The characteristic dealing with them depends after all upon the national mind, as we see in the contrast of Athens and Sparta, the two leading

---

[k] This problem is suggested by the opening sentences of [Rufus Quintus] Curtius' *History of Greece*, with reference to the unity of continental Greece and Ionia, or by the natural unity of the basin of the North Sea (in the Hanseatic League). The case of England and Scotland, compared with that of England and Ireland, repays study.

[l] See above, p. 272. I do not say 'national' minds, because I observe that the phrase is used with various unduly restricted meanings; cp. Lord Acton, who considers nationality a mere physical kinship. Plato shows the right line, surely. The group must have the same myth, i.e. the same consciousness of unity. It does not matter how they got it.[6]

[m] Hobbes, it must be remembered, with kindred theorists, is far removed from the philosophy of which we are speaking.[7]

---

[6] This is not an altogether accurate reading of the sense of Acton's remarks. Acton argues that civilised life depends upon the combination of different nations within the state. Nationality is an inferior form of attachment to patriotism.

The difference between nationality and the state is exhibited in the nature of patriotic attachment. Our connection with the race is merely natural or physical, whilst our duties to the political nation are ethical. One is a community of affections and instincts infinitely important and powerful in savage life, but pertaining more to the animal than to the civilised man; the other is an authority governing by laws, imposing obligations, and giving a moral sanction and character to the natural relations of society . . . But in the political order moral purposes are realised and public ends are pursued to which private interests and even existence must be sacrificed.'

Lord Acton, 'Nationality', in *The History of Freedom and Other Essays* (London, Macmillan, 1919), 292–3.

The reference to Plato relates to the so-called 'noble lie', or now more accurately referred to as the 'magnificent myth', laying the foundation for the class structure in society. Rulers are born with gold in their souls, Guardians with silver, and farmers and other workers iron and bronze. He does insist that the barriers are permeable. *Republic*, 415a–d.

[7] International relations for Hobbes is the nearest analogue we have to the state of nature. Thomas Hobbes, *Leviathan*, ed. Richard Tuck (Cambridge, Cambridge University Press, 1991), 90 [63].

states of one and the same civilisation. It is a curious fallacy in the disparagement of the state that the recognition of a debt to foreign culture has been pushed so far as to suggest that nothing great originates in any state because everything is imported from some other.[n]

Further, it follows that the maintenance of this normal relation, or its attainment where unattained, depends on the right discharge by states of their internal function – the maintenance of rights as the conditions of good life. War, as Plato showed, is not of the essence of states, but has its causes in their internal disease and distraction, leading to policies of 'expansion'.[9] Therefore, in this sense, to begin with, we want more of the state and not less. In order to reinforce the organisation of rights by other states, the main thing it has to do is to complete its own. This fundamental truth none of the critics seem to have observed, and to have emphasised it appears to me a very great merit in our philosophy.[o] The fundamental principle is that states *qua* states are – 'the state' is – the human mind doing the same work in different localities with different materials. Obviously, in as far as it succeeds, its efforts assist each other.

5. Thus every state as such – that is, 'the state' – is 'the guardian of a whole moral world', maintaining the peculiar contribution of its community to the total of human life and of human mind. We shall see why this double expression is necessary. And it is very important to observe that this moral world includes a whole distinctive attitude to life and humanity. It is an attitude *of* the community, but *to* the world. Thus you cannot get away from it. All individuals

---

[n] Compare the malevolent gossips in *Middlemarch*, who referred the husband's book to the wife's special knowledge, and *vice versa*, so that they did not need to give credit to either for the books they wrote.[8]

[o] Cf. especially Green, *Principles of Political Obligation*, Sect. 167 ff. The root of venom in the present conflict lies surely in two things: (α) In the medieval condition of the Prussian franchise, which the Monistic League of several hundred thousand members, with Ostwald at its head, was pledged to see reformed, and (β) the false political economy of 'your gain is my loss', which such an internal situation promotes.

---

[8] George Eliot, *Middlemarch* (Oxford, Oxford University Press, 1988).

[9] 'When Greek fights Greek we shall say that they are naturally friends, but that Greece is sick and torn by faction, and that the quarrel should be called "civil strife".' *Republic*, 470c–d.

share it, more or less, and every relation of the group, external or internal, is brought to a meeting point within their consciousness, and elicits a response from it.

It is easy to discern how such guardianship on the part of bodies so highly individualised, so deeply conscious of a function and as yet so imperfectly organised, may lead, from time to time, to differences which can only be resolved by force. It is a profound mistake, I am convinced, to direct the moral of the present calamity against the communal sense of a function and a mission; against, in a word, the belief that a community has a conscience. Yet this belief is the root of the doctrine caricatured under the name of state absolutism. It seems to me foolish to take a hostile attitude to a general truth because it displays the root of serious evils. For, indeed, what displays their root is the only indication of the remedy. The true moral is, surely, not that a community should have no overmastering purpose, no consciousness of a mission and no conscience, but simply that its conscience should as far as possible be enlightened. Enlightened consciences, I venture to assume, cannot bring actions into conflict. But, being internally ill organised, and correspondingly biassed and unenlightened, communities enter into conflicts from time to time with their whole heart and soul, just because they *have* consciences and *have* moral worlds to guard. It happens naturally to them as to private persons that they throw their whole sense of right into what is wrong. In order to produce a disastrous collision, we must bear in mind, the aspirations of two communities need not be in conflict at every point. It is like two trains running side by side, where an encroachment of an inch is enough to produce a calamity. Aspirations may be irreconcilable in practice which have a very large factor of agreement. This factor is the ground for hope, which consists in their being, after all, aspirations of communities which possess reason and conscience. Reconciliation of them by harmonious adjustment, though impracticable at certain moments, is never inconceivable.

Now it is surely plain that no power on earth can deal with such a cause of conflict, except something that enables the biassed and erroneous factors of the conflicting claims to be eliminated. And this can never be done by external force, but must mainly depend on a better organisation of rights by every state at home, with a consequent correction of its ambitions and outlook on the world. A healthy state is not militant.

But the mischief is, that the popular mind, observing that the present trouble has arisen through aspirations in others which we pronounce perverse, is inclined to attribute to a false philosophy the whole conception of national aspirations as representing the conscience of a people and its overmastering sense of duty. Men do not reflect that precisely such aspirations are determining their own group-action at every step. They say, as our critics are saying, that the theory of the unity of a people in the moral consciousness of a pre-eminent duty, and the principle of its expression through an organ supreme in practical life, are absolutism, and ought to be weakened or abandoned. The unique obligation of the private person to the community as incomparably the fullest representative of himself is to be put on a level with isolated abstract obligations arising in the course of this or that special relation, although it is on the communal mind that the task of harmonising them must ultimately fall. In short, the whole moral status and moral being of the community is to be indefinitely but considerably lowered.

All this seems to me to point exactly the wrong way. We all know, in modern society more especially, that we pay for the existence of great organising agencies by the possibility of their conflicting. But that does not make us desire to weaken them; it makes us desire to amplify their members' faith in them, and to get them to do their work more completely. The remedy for disorganisation is not less organisation, but more. All organisation, of course, brings a concurrent risk of conflict. You bring claims together, and you find points which for the moment cannot be adjusted. It is a flat contradiction to maintain that the state is morally responsible, and also that it must not face an actual conflict where its conscience is concerned. Even within the community, where obligations to the common will are so high and so determinate, the conscientious objector will follow his conscience to the end, and if we believe him to be sincere we all respect him for it. Why should the community, an individual in a far deeper sense than the citizen, being the nearest approach to a true individual that exists upon the earth, be expected not to follow its conscience? The clause on which I have just insisted is, as Rousseau pointed out,[p] the fundamental issue. The point to be remembered is that the individual only has his individuality through the social consciousness. The nearer he approaches to being himself

[p] Rousseau, *Contrat Social*, I, vii.

the more he approaches identification with the communal mind.[q] This mind can only be expressed as what the individual would be if he possessed in completeness all that his actual consciousness implies regarding the group-life. If he sees reason to rebel, it is still as a social duty. It cannot be in virtue of some right of his own, as he would be, *per impossible*, apart.

No doubt, when there is strife between communities, a wrong is being committed somewhere. But the way to right it is not for the conscientious group to make a rule of yielding on points which it holds fundamental to its function.

Now I think that the critics of our theory speak uncertainly here. Is our fault in saying that the community which asserts itself through the state *is a* moral being, and *has* a conscience, or is not a moral being and has not a conscience? They seem to me in effect to say both at once. But only one can be true.

It is clear, I think, that we are accused of denying the moral responsibility of the community which has the state for its organ. But it can hardly be doubted that we are also accused of putting this moral responsibility much too high. Thus the critics find themselves driven to treat the community which is a state as a mere association of individuals, which cannot possess an organic moral conscience nor general will. Though in one passage disclaiming individualism,[r] the argument breathes its spirit. If you call the state an association, you speak the language of individualism, and still more so, if you speak of individual rights which can be asserted against it, and of the individual judgment as ultimate. To call it an 'association' is

---

[q] Cf. Bradley's *Ethical Studies*, Essays II. and V.

[r] In Mr. Cole's paper, Mr. Russell, I think, does not disclaim it, seeing, if I understand him, no common mind in men capable of a common will. I am prepared to receive what comes from him with great respect, and I agree with his disbelief in the likelihood of an international authority being established after this war; and I take it that he agrees with me that *Si vis pacem, para bellum*, is self-contradictory. But his view of the state and its aim seems to me just introspective in the bad sense. It represents the conscious reflections of minds unappreciative of the actual work done in legislation and administration. It is quite extraordinarily akin to Horace Walpole's attitude, e.g. letter to Sir H. Mann, November 2, 1765.[10]

[10] C. Delisle Burns, Bertrand Russell, and G. D. H. Cole, 'Symposium: The Nature of the State in View of its External Relations', in *Proceedings of the Aristotelian Society*, xvi (1915–16). Horrace Walpole letter to H. Mann, 2 November 1765. *Horace Walpole's Correspondence With Sir Horace Mann*, ed. W. S. Lewis (Yale, University of Yale Press, 1971).

contrary, I think, both to usage and to truth. The word is, I presume, employed intentionally as paradoxical and aggressive.

It is really, then, the moral being and moral responsibility of the
state which we affirm, and which the main attack desires to undermine. The opposite suggestion, that we do not recognise the moral
responsibility of the members of a group for its action, is, as we shall
see, a mere misconception, derived from the fact that we observe the
moral action of a community not to be capable of being criticised
by the method of comparison with that of an individual.

The unique position of the state springs, as I said at starting,
from the fact that it is moulded, as no mere association is, by and
for the special task of maintaining in a certain territory the external
conditions of good life as a whole. Its territorial area adjusts itself
to that unity of communal experience which is most favourable to
the maintenance of an organised will, so that it tends to cover the
largest area within which, for a certain group, the conditions of such
an experience exist.

It is an error, I think, resting on a confusion regarding the sphere
of the state, to suggest that obedience to it can conflict with the
existence of loyalty to associations – I refuse to say *other* associations – at home or abroad. The state's peculiar function is in the
world of external action, and it does not inquire into the sentiments
of men and women further than to establish the *bona fide* intention
which the law includes in the meaning of an act. But whatever
loyalties may exist in the mind, the state will undoubtedly, when
need arises, of which it through constitutional methods is the sole
judge, prohibit and prevent the expression, in external acts, of any
loyalty but that to the community which it represents. Absoluteness
in this sense is inherent in the state, for the reason which we have
noted.[s]

But even for loyalties which we inwardly cherish, and which appear
to us irreconcilable with the concrete communal will, we pay a severe
penalty in a felt contradiction which is a constant sore in our mind. It
forms a continual demand for reconciliation by adjustment, and so for
a new response and an enlarged and not restricted operation of the
social consciousness, which if it passes into action will reflect itself in

---

[s] Pp. 272–3, [and 272–3 in this volume] above. Even the duty of rebellion is not in
principle a limit upon this power; for it does not rest on a non-social right, but on
a recognition that the state is divided against itself.

a new and ampler initiative on the part of the state. Every conflict as a matter of course is a stimulus to fresh reaction.

6. So much for the *rationale* of the so-called absolutism of the state, which is in the main a caricature of its position as sole organiser of rights and as guardian of moral values.

I believe that the principal difficulty which is felt about the view which I am trying to explain arises from its denial that the moral obligations of a state can be deduced from the consideration of those which attach to a private person under what are taken to be analogous circumstances.[1] This difficulty seems to depend on the crude belief that morality consists in the observance of abstract absolute rules, unmodified by relations and situations, such that you can paint the world of outward actions, as it were, with two colours only, right and wrong, which will stand fast for all moral beings under all conditions. I do not think it could possibly be felt by any mind which had once grasped the point that duty is a systematic structure, such as to bring home its universal demand in a particular and appropriate form to every moral being according to its conditions, and that the best brief summary of it is 'to be equal to the situation.'

When this is grasped, I think that the moral criticism of our view is easily seen to rest on mere misunderstanding. We assume *ab initio* that the state has a mission or a function, a contribution to make to the life of the world such as no other body or person can pretend to. The question is whether comparison with the moral task of a private person can throw light on our judgment of what it does or of what it ought to do.

A word on the case of the private person himself will, perhaps, make the matter plainer. Even his morality is ultimately a very different thing, not from what common sense recognises, but from what popular theory assumes. There is no such thing in ethics as an absolute rule or an absolute obligation, unless it were that of so far as possible realising the best life. In every action the moral agent confronts a conflict of duties, and has in some degree to steer an uncharted course. Every situation is in some degree, however slightly, new; and his moral duty is to be equal to it, to deal with it, to mould it, in accordance with the moral spirit which is in him, into a contribution to the realisation of the best life. There is perhaps no act that we can think of which, if we do not set it down by

[1] See Professor A. C. Bradley's lecture, above referred to, pp. 62 ff.

definition as an act of the bad will, could not conceivably be a duty. The room for immoral casuistry is infinite, and there is no security but to grasp so far as possible the actual obligations, which in accordance with the ethical spirit acquired from social discipline and applying itself anew in a similar sense, are plainly incumbent upon the particular moral agent. With all the aids of moral convention, of a life organised in extreme detail within a framework of social and legal obligations, of the communal sentiment engrained and embodied in his habitual will, the private individual has still in principle a new morality constantly to create, though in practice, assuming *bona fides*, he has in general little difficulty in discerning his duty at the moment. A strictly moral judgment of others is scarcely open to him at all.

Now turn to the community organised as a state. In quiet times, and over a great part of its conduct, its course, like that of the individual, may be considered as plainly marked.[u] But at any moment some huge new problem may crop up, involving, one might say, a whole philosophy or prophecy of the future history of the world.[v] Suppose the British Empire confronted by an opponent or by an international Peace League or Tribunal with some proposed regulation which it (the Empire) judged fatal to sea power.[w,11] Is it not plain what we mean by saying that there is no organised moral world within which a course of duty under such conditions is prescribed to the state? Even assuming a disinterested tribunal – which at present would be quite impossible – who could determine with authority the effect on the world's future of any such regulation? Of course such a question is not justiciable. But when you get beyond justiciable questions you are in the ocean of speculation as to elements of future welfare. As to the really effective type of worldwide authority, I will say more below.

But at present the point is this. In the case supposed the unit in question has one great certainty. It has the moral world of which,

---

[u] I am quite aware of the immense amount of international co-operation, for desirable ends, which goes on in normal times.

[v] Conflicting philosophies of history are ultimately, one might say, the root of bitterness between the Germans and ourselves. They sincerely think one course of things best for the world, and we sincerely think another. We are fighting for our faiths.

[w] The hypothesis is taken from *The War and Democracy*, p. 376.

11 See Alfred E. Zimmern, 'German Culture and the British Commonwealth' in R. W. Seton-Watson, J, Dover Wilson, Alfred E. Zimmern and Arthur Greenwood, *The War and Democracy* (London, Macmillan, 1915).

so far, it has been the guardian, which is the source of the mission or function which its conscience and general will recognise as its own, and of the view of humanity and the world at large which it holds to be the highest. *If* it believes itself to see clearly that the proposed regulation must destroy or gravely endanger that form of good life and that attitude to humanity with which it has so far identified itself, it will possess in this conviction the only definite element in this moral problem. I do not mean that it must be so in the case of every innovation; but it very well may be so. In as far as it is so, the consideration of this certainty would probably present itself as an overwhelming ground of action.[x] There is nothing here analogous to the tissue of obligation within which the individual lives. It is not the mere absence of a sanction that makes the difference; an external sanction cannot affect your own moral obligation. It is partly, no doubt, the absence of an external order on the maintenance of which you can rely; but it is still more, and more intimately, the absence of a recognised moral order such as to guide the conscience itself.

In the case suggested it is proposed to reshape the world; and it may well happen that in dealing with the proposal the unit has no guide but to defend the best thing it knows. This is what we mean by saying that it is the guardian of a whole moral world, but does not itself act within a moral world. Say, if you like, that it is within the society of states. But the life of this society, as a whole, has up to the present no moral tradition, imposing adapted and appropriate obligations on all units, comparable with the social consciousness which constitutes the whole basis and material of the normal individual will. In any case analogous to that just supposed, it is not likely to afford any help whatever. There is no middle term, so to speak, between the unit which has to act, and the general obligation of realising what is best – none, that is, except the form of good life with which the unit is already identified. And we have seen that its special form of good life, being a moral consciousness, is not merely a self-contained habit of conduct in the members of a group, but is an attitude and moral outlook which, though existing in them, has for its object the whole world, and is determined by the view and spirit which the group has evolved for itself, implying its conception of the best thing for the

[x] See Professor Bradley, ['International Morality'] comparing the right of a state and of an individual to sacrifice themselves or risk their own suppression.

world. Devotion to humanity as a best, as a supreme quality, is, unless and until the organism of mankind becomes actual, better represented by the moral world of the highest communities than by anything common to the whole multitude of mankind.[y]

7. After these explanations, I hope it may be hardly necessary to refute the charge of immorality brought against the thesis that a state simply cannot do all immoral acts which a single human being can. We have seen that morality is relative to the special obligation of the particular moral being, and it is obviously also relative to his capacity for action. Now a community simply cannot express its will directly, as a man or woman can, in a bodily act. To act is to make a will pass into fact, and how a community can do this is an old question and not an easy one. Rousseau held that nothing but a law, a decision dealing with something of general interest, could be an act of the sovereign power, and, in the main, I believe he was right. It is plain surely that even a mere aggregate of men cannot commit a single bodily act as one man can. It may be answered, 'They may be accomplices before or after the fact.' But we should consider what would have to be proved to bring in a nation as accomplices in a breach of the Decalogue. An act of attainder is, I should think, the nearest thing to murder by a state, and such an act, like all privilegia, is, I believe, now considered abhorrent to the spirit of law.[z] Surely it is better and even more impressive to recognise obvious distinctions and call things by their right names.

[y] See p. 291 [p. 287 this vol.].
[z] Cf. the decision of the Athenian Assembly to put the Mityleneans to death, and its recall.[12]

[12] After the revolt at Mytilene (428–7 BC) the Athenians decided to put the whole population to death. The following day after the trireme was despatched to give the order, the matter was reconsidered by the Athenian Assembly. Cleon reminds the Athenians of the responsibilities and dangers of holding an empire. The Mytilenians should be made an example of, 'for it is a general rule of human nature that people despise those who make concessions. Let them now therefore have the punishment which their crime deserves.' Such action would deter other cities from revolting. The Assembly was swayed, however, by Diototus who maintained that whatever the injustice of the revolt, it was not in the interest of Athens to put both the innocent and guilty Mytilenians to death: 'For those who make wise decisions are more formidable to their enemies than those who rush madly into strong action.' The second trireme reached Mytilene in time to prevent the first order being carried out. Thucydides, *The Peloponnesian War*, trans. Rex Warner (Harmondsworth, Penguin, 1972), III, 36–50.

The fundamental point is in the defective individuality of human beings. If a man could be inspired by the whole living system of the communal mind, then the community as active – the state – might be fully responsible for what he does. And in practice we make a great distinction, which nothing else can account for, between the degrees of its responsibility for the sayings and doings of its different agents. A Cabinet minister acts for the state in a different degree from a police constable. For, as any man or woman's mind is always but a fragment of the general mind and will, it is plain that the community which acts through them can only answer for as much of their act as represents the degree of its will which it can fairly be said to have succeeded in communicating to them; that is, in practice, for their appointment and dismissal, their instructions, and the general system under which they work. And the recognition of this is enough, and more effective in practice than an attempt to impute something more, which would always fail. 'Power can be delegated, but not will.' You may order special acts to be done by another, but you cannot transfer to him the general exercise of your will.

I admit that recent events have done something to show that the responsibility of a community for single wicked actions of men may be more intimate than I had thought possible. But I still think that all this will look very different when the conditions of such action come to be criticised in cold blood. And in any case I have rightly stated the hypothetical conditions of such responsibility.[aa] If agents thought of their duty more in terms of a community's obligations and less in terms of private conscience, much evil would be avoided. It has been the private conscience that has been responsible, very largely at least, for religious persecution and active intolerance of all kinds, which have been not an advantage, but a distinct obstruction to the community in its function.

8. I will pass on to the question of a wider loyalty, or a larger political unit than those which centre in the nation-state.

It is natural to infer from the social organism to an organism of humanity, and to look for the supreme authority or object of devotion in this as the inclusive unit. But here, again, is a difficulty

---

[aa] *Phil. Theory of State*, p. 324.

in the facts – a double difficulty, which our theory is framed to meet, and which its critics seem not to have heeded.

The first thing that strikes us is that, in fact, at present there *is* no organism of humanity. For such an organism, consciousness of connection is necessary. Mere causal connection exists in the mere physical world. And putting aside the question of past and future human beings, will any one say that even the existing multitude of humanity possesses any connected communal consciousness whatever? But if not, there is at present no community outside those which speak through the state, which can at all pretend to be a moral purpose or to be endowed with a conscience.

And secondly, considering as an aggregate all the human beings on the earth's surface, we can find in them no common character in which the values to which we are devoted as the qualitative essence of humanity are adequately represented. I do not say that something of humanity in the highest sense is not present wherever there are human beings. But it is plain that neither the main values which govern our aspirations to the best life, nor the valuation of them, are possessions common to mankind. It is not to the multitudes of all mankind that we go for 'love and beauty and delight'. At their best they are possessions of particular communities, and form elements in the diverse moral worlds which states exist to guard. Thus, to put it bluntly, a duty to realise the best life cannot be shown to coincide with a duty to the multitude of mankind. Our primary loyalty is to a quality, not to a crowd. If you see the two as one, it is by faith only, and at any given moment they may conflict. This makes the moral alternative between, say, the self-defence of a highly civilised state and submission in the interests of the whole world's peace, a really tragic crisis, and entitles us to say that there is nothing in the interstate world to guide its units in moral choices.

It is not unnecessary to guard ourselves, as we are doing, against the assumption that humanity is a real corporate being, an object of devotion and a guide to moral duty. This formed the central doctrine of Comtism, and, seeming to correspond to a natural expansion of our interest, tends to make us fancy that we apprehend an ultimate visible community to which our devotion is due, and with which we can have a will in common. It is conceivable, of course, that such a community may one day come into being. But there are suggestions which point elsewhere. M. Romain Rolland has spoken of our only dwelling-places being our earthly fatherland and the City of God.[bb] I do not know whether by the second phrase he understands a visible community. The antithesis seems to suggest a different idea, and the truly complete community, which religion, for instance, assumes as ultimate, cannot possibly be that with which the Comtist confused it, the multitude of human beings either alive at any given moment, or including all that have been and that will be.

However this may be, whatever may prove to be the extent of the effective unity which at any time may be realised among mankind, the condition of its realisation, if our theory is sound, admits of no dispute. The body which is to be in sole or supreme command of force for the common good must possess a true general will, and for that reason must be a genuine community sharing a common sentiment and animated by a common tradition. With less than this the supreme authority must become an administration of general rules, external to the needs and consciences of the communities which it is meant to unite, and incapable therefore of appreciating the more serious problems which will confront them, or those needs of their lives which demand a certain social structure. This is why I view with apprehension the tendency to minimise the function of the state which is current to-day, owing, as I believe, to a too special explanation of causes which led to the present conflict. The first thing needed is the better adjustment and maintenance of rights within the communities which form states at the present moment. That is to say, the more complete discharge of their functions by existing states, and, if need be, the formation of new ones, adapted to similar tasks. More of the state, that is, and not less, is required within communities. And so, too, without. If larger units are needed and can be realised, they too must fulfil the conditions of states. Here, also, more of the state is needed, and not less. Leagues, alliances, united states, which have not the spirit of true communi-

[bb] See *The War and Democracy*, p. 13.[13]

[13] The reference appears in A. E. Zimmern's introduction to *War and Democracy*. Rolland's article first appeared in the *Journal de Genève*. It was translated for the *Cambridge Magazine* and was reprinted in *Public Opinion*, 27 November 1914.

ties, carry the germs of disruption within them, and the probability, as Hegel explained, of antagonism without. External antagonism, and not a deep-seated general will, is, as a rule, their binding force. Here I am thoroughly at one with Mr. Russell as to the improbability of an international authority being created as an outcome of the present war. I confess that I see something of the same danger in the unit which has been spoken of as the commonwealth – say, the British Empire in its present stage of development.[14] For it is its essence, as I understand the doctrine, that its constituent members are to be on an unequal footing, unified only by a reign of external law which leaves their national consciousness untouched and unreconciled.[cc,15] I cannot believe that this is satisfactory. If the members remain heterogeneous and unequal, there is no general will. If the point is that they are to be trained to freedom and equality, then it seems to me to matter little whether in the end they go their own way in peace, or choose to form an effective unity with the other members, which shall be a true state. But the 'commonwealth' as described is neither one thing nor the other, and is justified, I should have said, only by its possible future.

9. Thus it seems clear to me that the organisation of rights can only be complete in a community which satisfies the conditions necessary to the possession of a general will; that is to say, a very high degree of common experience, tradition, and aspiration. Such communities are not now to be found except in the nation-state. The commonwealth of nations alluded to above does not, I believe, fulfil the condition in respect of the dependencies included in it. But I do not suggest that larger units than nation-states can never

---

cc Lord Acton, ['Nationality' in] *Freedom and other Essays*, p. 290 [Cf. 291–3]; see [A. E. Zimmern] *The War and Democracy*, p. 370. Lord Acton does not use the term Commonwealth in the sense referred to by the latter writer. It is discussed, of course, in Mr. Curtis' works.

14 Russell argues that: 'It is this universal acquiescence in the authority of each partial state over its own citizens that makes it hard to find a way by which each state could yield up a portion of its sovereignty to some international authority.' 'Symposium', *Proceedings of the Aristotelian Society*, xvi (1915–16), 306.

15 A. E. Zimmern, 'German Culture and the British Commonwealth', 370. He quotes Acton approvingly . He nevertheless gives a different emphasis rather than a different meaning to the idea of a commonwealth. Instead of the metaphor of a cauldron Zimmern talks of the state as 'a body whose perfection consists in the very variety of the functions of its several members', 371.

come to fulfil these conditions; only that, if they do, they must have achieved a unity comparable to that which we now experience in nationality alone. I do not say this is impossible to be realised at some remote period even in a world-state. But in so far as it is not realised, any unitary authority which it may be attempted to set up will be superficial, external, arbitrary, and liable to disruption.

And this contemplation of remote possibilities is making people neglect the plain facts and the nearer remedies. Whatever may happen in the future, there is nothing in the world to-day that can compare for a moment in power and intimacy and concreteness with the type of corporate being which we call the nation-state. The organism of humanity, though conceivable, is at present as we saw a mere possibility, and the idea of it contains a serious contradiction between quality and totality.

A system of nation-states or of commonwealths (I have said why I cannot recognise the distinction as one of principle) each internally well organised, would not perhaps give us all that a world-state might give us, but it would place the world in a wholly different ethical position from that which it occupies to-day. It would involve, I assume, universal freedom of trade and intercourse. Interference with this I take to be the result of internal distraction, giving rise to the doctrine of 'your gain my loss', which is the principal source of war.

There is no reason that I can see for considering it a defective arrangement that world-wide relations or associations shall pass under the dominion of different sovereign powers in different regions of the earth. It seems to me that a very doubtful assumption is made when we are told that economic relations have outstripped political relations. This is actually to assume that there cannot be friendly and efficient co-operation between different political bodies in respect of world-wide relations. It is a pessimistic view, for which our theory recognises no ground whatever. Each local power, we consider, has expressly evolved itself from the need and demand for an organisation of rights in a certain territory. And it is quite arguable that every world-wide relation or association – say, for example, the Roman Catholic Church – is better protected and developed by co-operation with such a local power in every region, than it would be by a world-wide political unit. The fear that this will not be so is itself a relic of that barbarous suspicion directed against foreign communities which belongs to the identification of states with agencies for war and exploitation.

The case of relations to units outside a state makes no difference of principle. It is quite plain that if our mind and will are to be at one with themselves, our loyalty and co-operation with, say, an international labour movement or an association in a foreign country, must be reconciled with that system of our mind which is our national[dd] consciousness and conscience. If not, there must be a constant sore in our moral being, and, of course, there are many such sores, and while we live in this world they are not likely altogether to cease.

But there is no reason in principle why a system of states, each doing with fair completeness its local work of organisation, and recognising, with or without active modification, the world-wide relations which pass through them, should not result in a world as peaceful as one under a more unitary system, and much richer in quality.[ee] Those who think it cannot be so, must believe that states are naturally at war, and do not, so far as I can see, understand what the nature of the state is, nor how a group-mind (like every mind) is an attitude to the world at large, nor for what reasons it is that communities are apt to be hostile.

I do not think it necessary that such a system of states should form an explicit federation. Federations are apt to be unsuccessful unless they possess, like the United States of America, an obvious

---

[dd] I take the term 'national' as adjective of any sovereign community which has a general will.

[ee] I cannot see the least relevance in the suggestion that our theory requires relations which pass beyond the frontier to be suppressed (Lindsay, *Theory of State*, p. 101).[16] The group-mind, we saw, is a species of world-mind, and has not the group for its sole object. All external relations, therefore, are focussed in it along with the group-relations proper, and constitute, of course, a demand for unification by a response.

---

[16] Lindsay is critical of what he calls the German theory of the state which identifies the state and society. He argues that such a theory of the state *qua* state implies that 'what separates one community from another is the possession of an independent political organisation, and therefore that men's social relations are to conform to their political relations, that States should be, though they are not, entirely comprehensive of the social relations within them, and that they should not be, though they are, interpenetrated by relations from without.' A. D. Lindsay, 'The State and Society' in Louise Creighton *et al.*, *The International Crisis: The Theory of the State* (London, Oxford University Press, 1916) p. 99.

and increasing tendency to assume the national type. Those who think federation necessary for the sake of a central force, obviously believe in force rather than in friendship. But without friendship the force is dangerous, and with it, perhaps, hardly necessary. I am assuming that the experience and tradition of states remain as they are to-day, too highly individual to permit of a thoroughly common mind and of a true general will, but that they remain peaceful neighbours with their full national differences, because they have every reason for friendship and none for enmity, and are united in all sorts of common enterprises.

It seems to me an advantage of this conception that it leaves room for the widest diversity in the contributions of the several communities to the life of the world, and it confronts the difficulty which arises as we saw from the fact that the higher gifts of humanity have hitherto, at any rate, sprung from localised minds, and have not been characteristic of mankind at large nor acceptable to it. It might be that this is the law of life; and that reciprocal good will, with understanding and appreciation, even intensified by the sense of foreignness and mystery, are all that the different types of mankind are ever to have in common; that the great gifts are still to be, as they have been, achievements of diversely intensified life-centres, which seem to leave the rest behind.

The opposite ideal, that of a world-state, is, of course, conceivable. The point of interest is, I think, whether the identification of spirit and experience necessary as the basis of a general will could be achieved without the sacrifice of the valuable individual qualities of national minds.

Is our love of local peculiarities – of local dialects, for example – purely an obscurantist superstition; and how far do local styles and traditions of beauty depend upon conditions like those of local dialects? Certainly it appears as if anything ought to go which keeps people barbarous and makes mutual understanding impossible.

This analogy of language, I think, is helpful.[ff] We should desire, I suppose, to preserve the languages of the world in all their glory and individuality, but that they should become for mankind a means of entrance into each other's minds and not a bar to it. If we compare this ideal with that of a universal artificial language, we shall

---

[ff] Cf. *Philosophical Theory of the State*, p. 330.

see perhaps the true distinction between what we desire and what we should reject.

But the problem still returns upon us. Will the high civilisation of the future be a single thing, fusing into one the individualities of all regions and of all former nations? Or will national and local genius develop new internal resources, and even diverge into fresh and several types of greatness, instead of merging in a homogeneous character?

I do not think that the future of political organisation can be treated apart from the consideration of questions like these. And there is a homely remark which occurs to me as very relevant. Many people are very good friends apart who would quarrel if they kept house together. Is not this likely to be true of nations?

And, in conclusion, I wish to draw attention to an assumption of popular philosophy which I suspect of having a serious bearing upon current ideas of the international future. I mean the popular belief in a progress of the species which is to end in a condition of the world that shall compensate for the wrongs and sufferings of the past; in a word, in the evanescence of evil. We have had it explicitly argued by Herbert Spencer;[17] and there is hardly any popular writing about the future which does not assume it. Now I am inclined to think that the notion of a necessary advance towards the inclusion of mankind in a single political body is an offshoot of this naive form of optimism. The nature of consciousness in retaining the past as a basis for the future, together with its imperative demand for improvement, does make it fairly certain that man must tend on the whole to add to his moral and social achievements. But it is clear, I think, that any progress of future generations towards happiness could not compensate for the wrong and suffering of the past, and therefore this widely operating motive for assuming its likelihood must be dismissed, while in itself the evanescence of evil seems altogether self-contradictory. Therefore, while I believe in a nobler future, I do not believe in any simple advance towards comfort and tranquillity.

Another ancient superstition comes to my mind which illustrates the same popular tendency. The idea of a Millennium – of the

---

[17] Progress could of course be perverted by government 'interference' which he tried to show was both unnatural and impractical. See David Wiltshire, *The Social and Political Thought of Herbert Spencer* (Oxford, Oxford University Press, 1978).

reign of Christ on earth – passed gradually into the more modern conviction that at least the whole world was one day to be brought under the sway of Christianity, or perhaps of Western enlightenment as typified by nineteenth century science.[gg] All this, I take it, is gone by. The development of opinion has been in the contrary direction. The best Churchmen will admit, I believe, that to a great extent at least the peoples of the world have already the religions that suit them best. And we all see that the gospel of Western science, valuable as it is, has no exclusive claim to be the doctrine even of civilised man. A number of great systems, very profoundly differing in life, mind, and institutions, existing side by side in peace and co-operation, and each contributing to the world an individual best, irreducible to terms of the others – this might be, I do not say must be, a finer and higher thing[hh] than a single body with a homogeneous civilisation and a single communal will.

And what about war? It is certain, to my mind, that evil and suffering must be permanent in the world, because man is a self-contradictory being, in an environment to which he can never be adapted, seeing that at least his own activity is always transforming it. And in principle there can be no reason for treating war as an exceptional case, as if presided over by a special devil apart from every other form of wrong. Neither the possibility of eradicating war, nor the incidental good that comes of it, can reasonably be discussed, as they commonly are, apart from the general problem of evil in the world. While man has a conscience, and things he values above life, and yet his conscience is liable to err, the root of war exists. Issues may arise between group and group which cannot be compromised. Within the state itself, which is cited as the convincing analogy for a universal reign of law, both civil war and individual rebellion remain possible.

But man is bound, with this evil as with any other, to do what he can for its removal. And I do not doubt that its occasions may be immensely diminished by the reform of states, and their reconstruction in certain cases, and by, what this will promote, a truer economic creed.

[gg] E.g. of Positivism, as Comte held.

[hh] Cf. the sentence from A. E. quoted above, p. 272 [p. 272 this vol.]. I do not mean that the nation-unit is final. But I think any change would be a grave loss which did not, if it had to go, give us something as rich in qualities in its place.

The critics' confusion of the character of the state with the vices of states has led them into hopeless dilemmas. They argue from these vices that it should be weakened, while admitting a character which implies that it can hardly be too strong. It is quite impossible to unite a demonstration of growing demands on the state for organising activity, with a demonstration that its rank and authority already demand diminution.

It is quite impossible to unite a demonstration that the state has a conscience and moral responsibility with a demonstration that it shows itself non-moral when it throws itself heart and soul into its individual duty.

Ultimately, it seems to me, the critics' error is just that which they believe themselves to be attacking. Having misconceived the real spring of organisation and enlightenment, they are driven to put their faith in external force.

Index

Abraham, 3n
absolute, x, xiii, 257, 262, 263, 265
absolute idealism, xii, xiii
Acton, Lord 276n, 289n
Acts, 118n
Address to the German People, 255
administrative nihilism, 62
Afghans, 219, 230
Africa, 245, 250, 251
Agnosticism, 46, 47
Ahab, 4
altruism, 25, 26
American Civil War, xxxvi, xxxvii, 237,
    244
American Commonwealth, 132, 152
anarchy, xxvi, 70, 84, 91, 92, 93, 160,
    179, 180, 204
Anderson, Francis, 53n
Andrae, C. C. G., 139n
Arcot, 238
Aristeides, 58
aristocracy, xxvi, 84, 85, 87, 88, 90, 132,
    142, 145, 159, 162, 163, 166, 168,
    170, 171, 172
Aristotelian Society, xxxiv, xlii
Aristotle, xix, xxviii, 78, 91, 110, 159,
    166, 168, 169, 183, 220n, 233, 247,
    258n, 261
Arnold, Mathew, xxv, xxvii, 35, 47–8
Asiatic, 249
Asquith, A. A. , xxiii, xxix, xxxvii
Athenaeum, 30, 33
Athens, 86, 142, 210, 276, 285
atomism, 3, 11, 13

Australia, 246
Austria, 223, 234
Avenarius, Richard, 265, 266

Baal, 257
Bagehot, Walter, xv, xxvi, xxix
Baillie, J. B., xlii
Ball, Sidney, 178, 181
Bell, Sir James 173
Bellamy, R., 67
Bangor Normal College, xxxviii
Bentham, xxv, 81, 240
Berkeley, xii
Bernhardi, General Friedrich von, 264
biology, 4, 68, 69, 70, 73, 74, 75, 76, 77,
    78, 80, 86, 87, 186
Birkin, xxxvii
Bismarck, 259
Bland, Hubert, 197
Blatchford, Robert, 67
Boer War, xxix, xxxvi, xl, 237, 250
Bosanquet, Bernard, viii, xiii, xv, xviii,
    xxi, xxii, xxiii, xxv, xxviii, xxix,
    xxxi, xxxiv–v, xxxvi, 270n
Bosanquet, Helen, xxxiv
Bourbons, 267
Bradley, A. C., xxiv, 270n, 274n, 282n,
    284
Bradley, F. H., vii, viii, ix, xiii, xx, xxi,
    xxxi, xxxiv, xxxv, xlv, 273, 280
Bright, John, 241
British Academy, xxxv, xxxvi, xxxviii,
    xxxix, xl, xli
British Government, xxx

296

Index

Index

Index

self-sacrice, 107
Sell, A. P. F., xxxvii
sensation, 11, 12, 18
Seth, Andrew, see Pringle Pattison
Shakespeare, William, 5, 14, 111n, 161,
    163, 174, 239n, 242n
Shaw, G. B., 67, 242
Shelley, Percy Bysshe, 45n, 177
Skinner, Quentin, vii
slavery, 24, 85, 91, 142, 158, 159, 220
Slavonic, 234
Smith, Adam, 190, 240
social contract, 69
social evolution, 52, 68–93
social organism, ix, xxi, xxxi, 3–29, 68,
    69, 78, 79, 80, 82, 112, 113n, 131,
    181, 192, 206, 286
social reform, xxviii, 195
social reformer, 57, 69, 212, 213
social welfare, 174
social work, xi, 181
Socialism, xxiv, xxv, xxxvi, 50n, 53, 66,
    70, 173–194, 195–213
Socialists, xi, xlii, 67, 197
Sociology, 68, 75, 86, 204
Socrates, 158
Sorley, W. R., viii, xxxii, xl, xli
South Africa, xxix, 237, 246, 250n
Spain, 223, 247
Spanish Succession, 238
Sparta, 276
Speculum Mentis, viii
Spencer, Herbert, xv, xvi, xix, xx, xxiv,
    xxix, xxxix, 329, 30, 37, 38, 42, 43,
    44, 51n, 52, 55, 57, 59, 64n, 68, 74,
    186, 265, 293
Spencer, John Poyntz, 193n
Spinoza, 257
spirit, xiv, xv, xvii, xviii, xx, 21, 38, 47,
    103, 195, 235, 242, 280
spiritual, 13, 17, 74, 196
spiritual unity, x, 3, 38
State, viii, ix, x, xxi, xxii, xxiii, xxiv,
    xxvii, xxx, xxxiii, xxxiv, 16, 17, 23,
    24, 27, 52, 53n, 60, 61, 160, 161,
    168n, 169, 171, 172, 178, 180, 182,
    183, 185, 196, 197, 198, 200, 201,
    217–36, 248n, 255, 268, 270–295
    intervention, xxiii, xxiv, xxxiii, 63, 92,
    195–213
station and my duties, xxi, xiv, 10, 102,
    103, 104, 110, 112, 115, 200, 202

Steevans, G. W., 250
Stein, Karl Freiherr, 259
Stephen, James Fitzjames, xxvi
Stephen, Leslie, xx, xxi, xxix, 30, 38, 40,
    41, 434
Stoic, 31, 46, 47
struggle for existence, xvi, xxviii, xxix,
    31, 32, 33, 41, 43, 44, 52, 53, 54,
    55, 56, 578, 59, 62, 66, 67, 70, 79,
    80, 91, 187, 196
Stuarts, 189
Sturt, Henry, xiii
subjective, 20, 21, 22, 23, 25, 45n, 111
survival of the fittest, xv, xvii, xviii, 412,
    43, 58
Switzerland, 86

Talbot, Mary, 193
Taylor, A. E., xxxv
Taylor, C., ix
Taylor, M. V., xxivn
temperance, xxvii, xxxvii, 234
Tennyson, Alfred Lord, 49, 189n, 260n,
    269
Tess of the D'Urbervilles, 35, 36
theatre, 137
Thompson, Janna, ix
Thoreau, P., 158
Thucydides, 285n
Tocqueville, A., xxv
toleration, 150, 155
Tolstoy, 158
Tory, 160, 238
Toynbee, Arnold, xlii
Toynbee Hall, xxxvi
Treitschke, H. Von., xxxii, 255, 258,
    264, 267
Trevelyan, G. M., 241n
Truth, 142, 146, 151, 177, 195, 196
Truth, coherence theory of, ix, xiii
Turgot, 240
Turkey, 225, 226, 229, 234

United States of America, xxxi, 81, 93n,
    157, 161, 162, 166, 167, 169, 170,
    171, 228, 229, 238n, 239, 240n, 244,
    291
unity, xi, xii, xiii, xv, xvi, xviii, xix, xxvi,
    8, 9, 11, 12, 13, 24, 27, 28, 37, 44,
    47, 48, 69, 113, 128, 158, 165, 169,
    170, 186, 188, 211, 234, 258, 259,
    272, 273, 275, 276, 279, 281

303

Cambridge Texts in the History of Political Thought

Titles published in the series thus far

Gramsci *Pre-Prison Writings* (edited by Richard Bellamy)
Guicciardini *Dialogue on the Government of Florence* (edited by Alison Brown)
Harrington *A Commonwealth of Oceana* and *A System of Politics* (edited by J. G. A. Pocock)
Hegel *Elements of the Philosophy of Right* (edited by Allen W. Wood and H. B. Nisbet)
Hobbes *Leviathan* (edited by Richard Tuck)
Hobhouse *Liberalism and other Writings* (edited by James Meadowcroft)
Hooker *Of the Laws of Ecclesiastical Polity* (edited by A. S. McGrade)
Hume *Political Essays* (edited by Knud Haakonssen)
King James VI and I *Political Writings* (edited by Johann P. Sommerville)
John of Salisbury *Policraticus* (edited by Cary Nederman)
Kant *Political Writings* (edited by H. S. Reiss and H. B. Nisbet)
Knox *On Rebellion* (edited by Roger A. Mason)
Kropotkin *The Conquest of Bread and other Writings* (edited by Marshall Shatz)
Lawson *Politica sacra et civilis* (edited by Conal Condren)
Leibniz *Political Writings* (edited by Patrick Riley)
Locke *Political Essays* (edited by Mark Goldie)
Locke *Two Treatises of Government* (edited by Peter Laslett)
Loyseau *A Treatise of Orders and Plain Dignities* (edited by Howell A. Lloyd)
Luther and Calvin on Secular Authority (edited by Harro Höpfl)
Machiavelli *The Prince* (edited by Quentin Skinner and Russell Price)
de Maistre *Considerations on France* (edited by Isaiah Berlin and Richard Lebrun)
Malthus *An Essay on the Principle of Population* (edited by Donald Winch)
Marsiglio of Padua *Defensor minor* and *De translatione Imperii* (edited by Cary Nederman)
Marx *Early Political Writings* (edited by Joseph O'Malley)
Marx *Later Political Writings* (edited by Terell Carver)
James Mill *Political Writings* (edited by Terence Ball)
J. S. Mill *On Liberty*, with *The Subjection of Women* and *Chapters on Socialism* (edited by Stefan Collini)
Milton *Political Writings* (edited by Martin Dzelzainis)

Montesquieu *The Spirit of the Laws* (edited by Anne M. Cohler, Basia Carolyn Miller and Harold Samuel Stone)

More *Utopia* (edited by George M. Logan and Robert M. Adams)

Morris *News from Nowhere* (edited by Krishan Kumar)

Nicholas of Cusa *The Catholic Concordance* (edited by Paul E. Sigmund)

Nietzsche *On the Genealogy of Morality* (edited by Keith Ansell-Pearson)

Paine *Political Writings* (edited by Bruce Kuklick)

Plato *Statesman* (edited by Julia Annas and Robin Waterfield)

Price *Political Writings* (edited by D. O. Thomas)

Priestley *Political Writings* (edited by Peter Miller)

Proudhon *What is Property?* (edited by Donald R. Kelley and Bonnie G. Smith)

Pufendorf *On the Duty of Man and Citizen According to Natural Law* (edited by James Tully)

The Radical Reformation (edited by Michael G. Baylor)

Rousseau *The Discourses and other early political writings* (edited by Victor Gourevitch)

Rousseau *The Social Contract and other later political writings* (edited by Victor Gourevitch)

Seneca *Moral and Political Essays* (edited by John Cooper and John Procope)

Sidney *Court Maxims* (edited by Hans W. Blom, Eco Haitsma Mulier and Ronald Janse)

Spencer *Man versus the State* and *The Proper Sphere of Government* (edited by John Offer)

Stirner *The Ego and its Own* (edited by David Leopold)

Thoreau *Political Writings* (edited by Nancy Rosenblum)

Utopias of the British Enlightenment (edited by Gregory Claeys)

Vitoria *Political Writings* (edited by Anthony Pagden and Jeremy Lawrance)

Voltaire *Political Writings* (edited by David Williams)

Weber *Political Writings* (edited by Peter Lassman and Ronald Speirs)

William of Ockham *A Short Discourse on Tyrannical Government* (edited by A. S. McGrade and John Kilcullen)

William of Ockham *A Letter to the Friars Minor and other Writings* (edited by A. S. McGrade and John Kilcullen)

Wollstonecraft *A Vindication of the Rights of Men* and *A Vindication of the Rights of Woman* (edited by Sylvana Tomaselli)